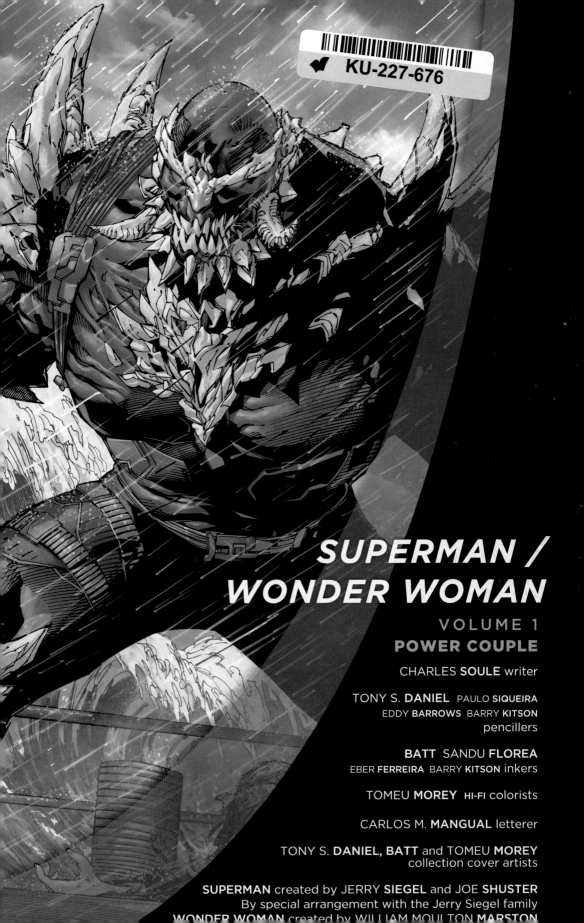

SUPERMAN / WONDER WOMAN

VOLUME 1
POWER COUPLE

CHARLES **SOULE** writer

TONY S. **DANIEL** PAULO **SIQUEIRA**
EDDY **BARROWS** BARRY **KITSON**
pencillers

BATT SANDU **FLOREA**
EBER **FERREIRA** BARRY **KITSON** inkers

TOMEU **MOREY** **HI-FI** colorists

CARLOS M. **MANGUAL** letterer

TONY S. **DANIEL, BATT** and TOMEU **MOREY**
collection cover artists

SUPERMAN created by JERRY **SIEGEL** and JOE **SHUSTER**
By special arrangement with the Jerry Siegel family
WONDER WOMAN created by WILLIAM MOULTON MARSTON

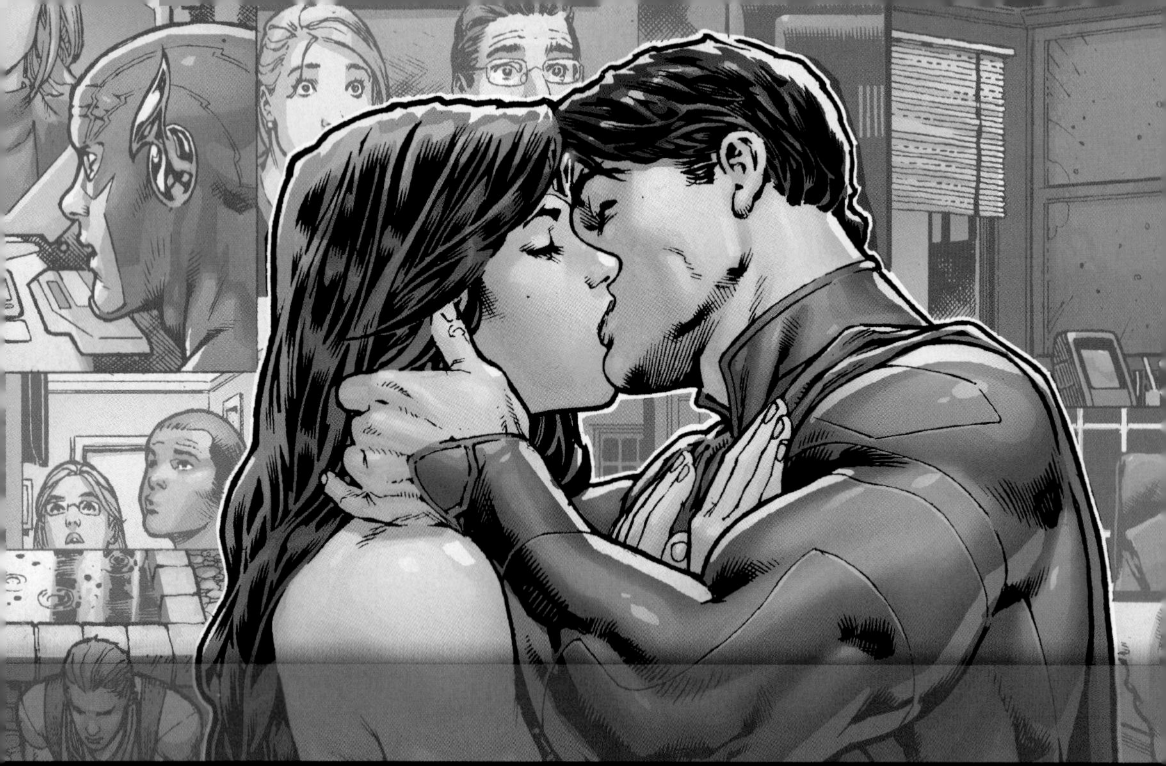

EDDIE BERGANZA Editor – Original Series RICKEY PURDIN Associate Editor – Original Series
ANTHONY MARQUES Assistant Editor – Original Series PETER HAMBOUSSI Editor
ROBBIN BROSTERMAN Design Director – Books

BOB HARRAS Senior VP – Editor-in-Chief, DC Comics

DIANE NELSON President DAN DIDIO and JIM LEE Co-Publishers GEOFF JOHNS Chief Creative Officer
AMIT DESAI Senior VP – Marketing and Franchise Management
AMY GENKINS Senior VP – Business and Legal Affairs NAIRI GARDINER Senior VP – Finance
JEFF BOISON VP – Publishing Planning MARK CHIARELLO VP – Art Direction and Design
JOHN CUNNINGHAM VP – Marketing TERRI CUNNINGHAM VP – Editorial Administration
LARRY GANEM VP – Talent Relations and Services ALISON GILL Senior VP – Manufacturing and Operations
HANK KANALZ Senior VP – Vertigo and Integrated Publishing JAY KOGAN VP – Business and Legal Affairs, Publishing
JACK MAHAN VP – Business Affairs, Talent NICK NAPOLITANO VP – Manufacturing Administration SUE POHJA VP – Book Sales
FRED RUIZ VP – Manufacturing Operations COURTNEY SIMMONS Senior VP – Publicity BOB WAYNE Senior VP – Sales

SUPERMAN/WONDER WOMAN VOLUME 1: POWER COUPLE

DC Comics, 1700 Broadway, New York, NY 10019
A Warner Bros. Entertainment Company.
Printed by RR Donnelley, Salem, VA, USA. 2/13/15. First Printing.

ISBN: 978-1-4012-5346-2

Library of Congress Cataloging-in-Publication Data

Soule, Charles.
Superman/Wonder Woman. Volume 1, Power Couple / Charles Soule, Tony Daniel.
pages cm. — (The New 52!)
ISBN 978-1-4012-5346-2
1. Graphic novels. I. Daniel, Tony S. (Antonio Salvador) II. Title. III. Title: Power Couple.
PN6728.S9S65 2014
741.5'973—dc23
2014018207

SUSTAINABLE FORESTRY INITIATIVE
Certified Chain of Custody
20% Certified Forest Content,
80% Certified Sourcing
www.sfiprogram.org
SFI-01042

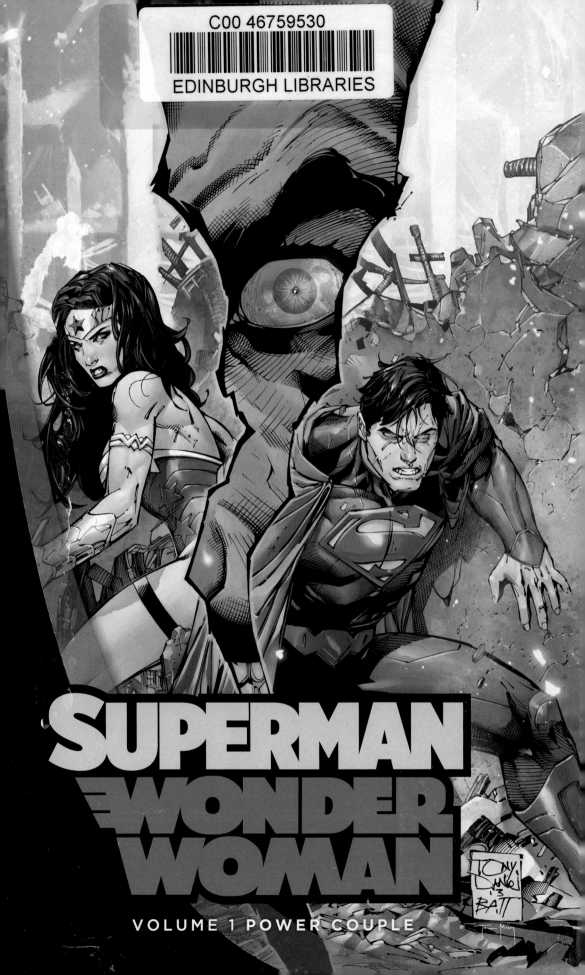

SUPERMAN

WONDER WOMAN

VOLUME 1 POWER COUPLE

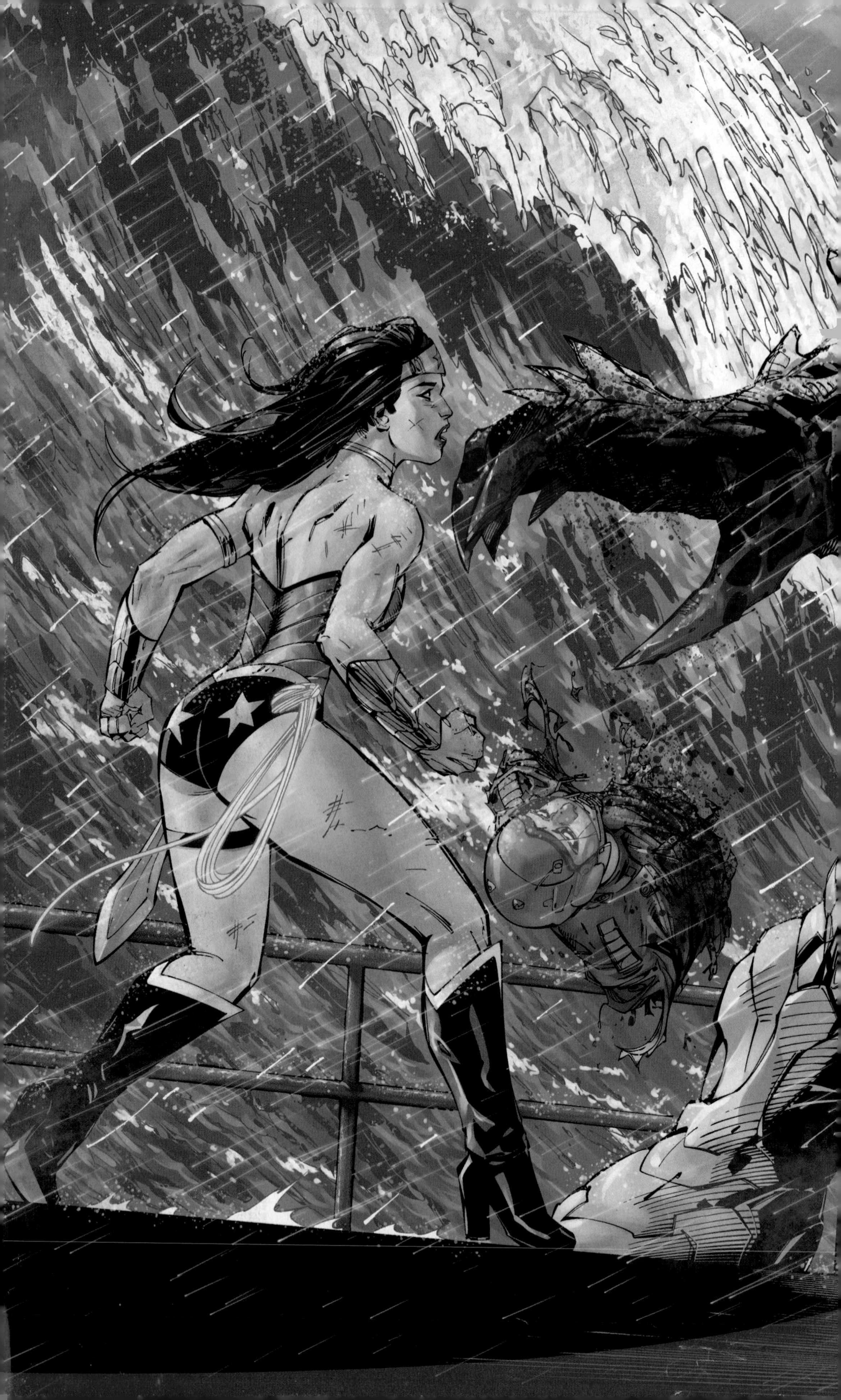

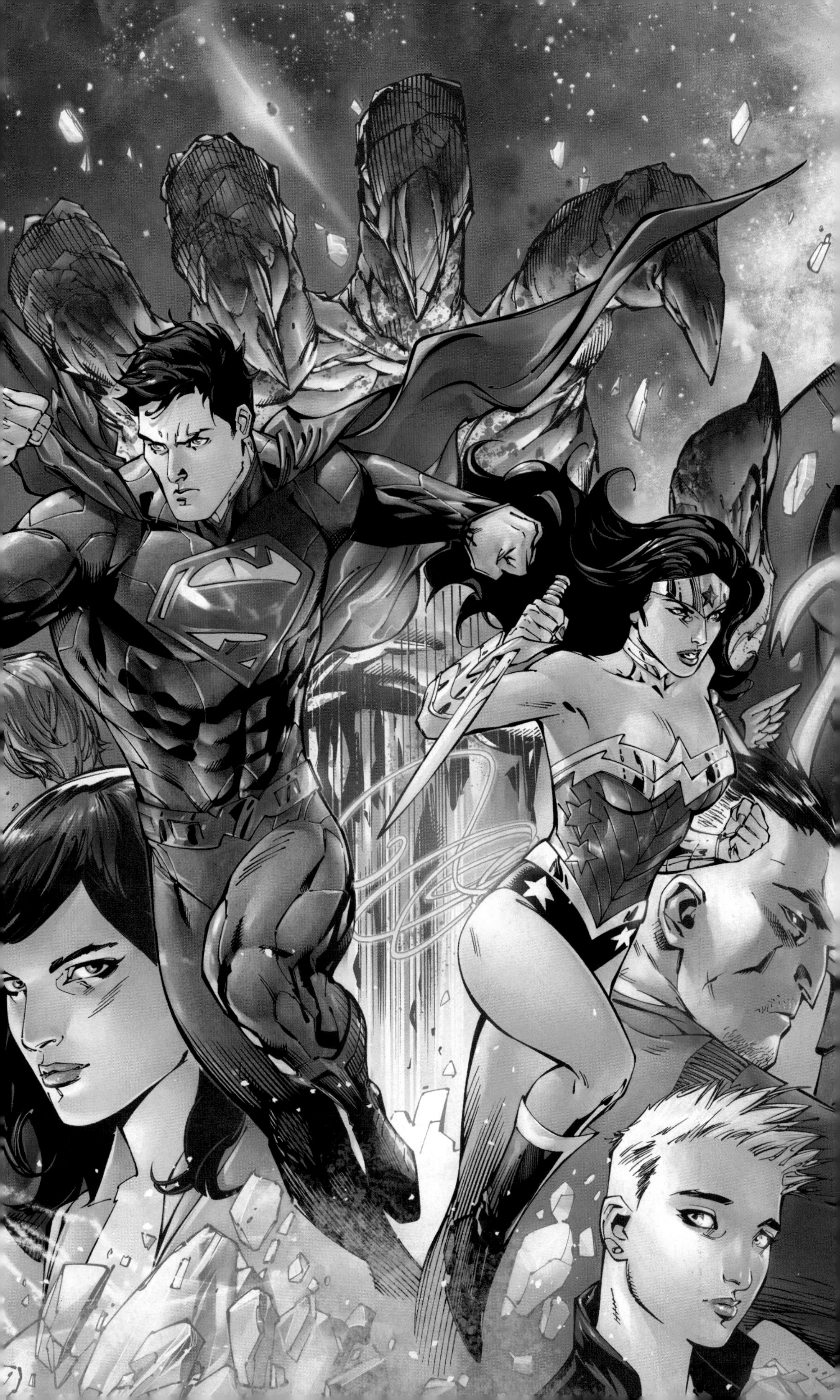

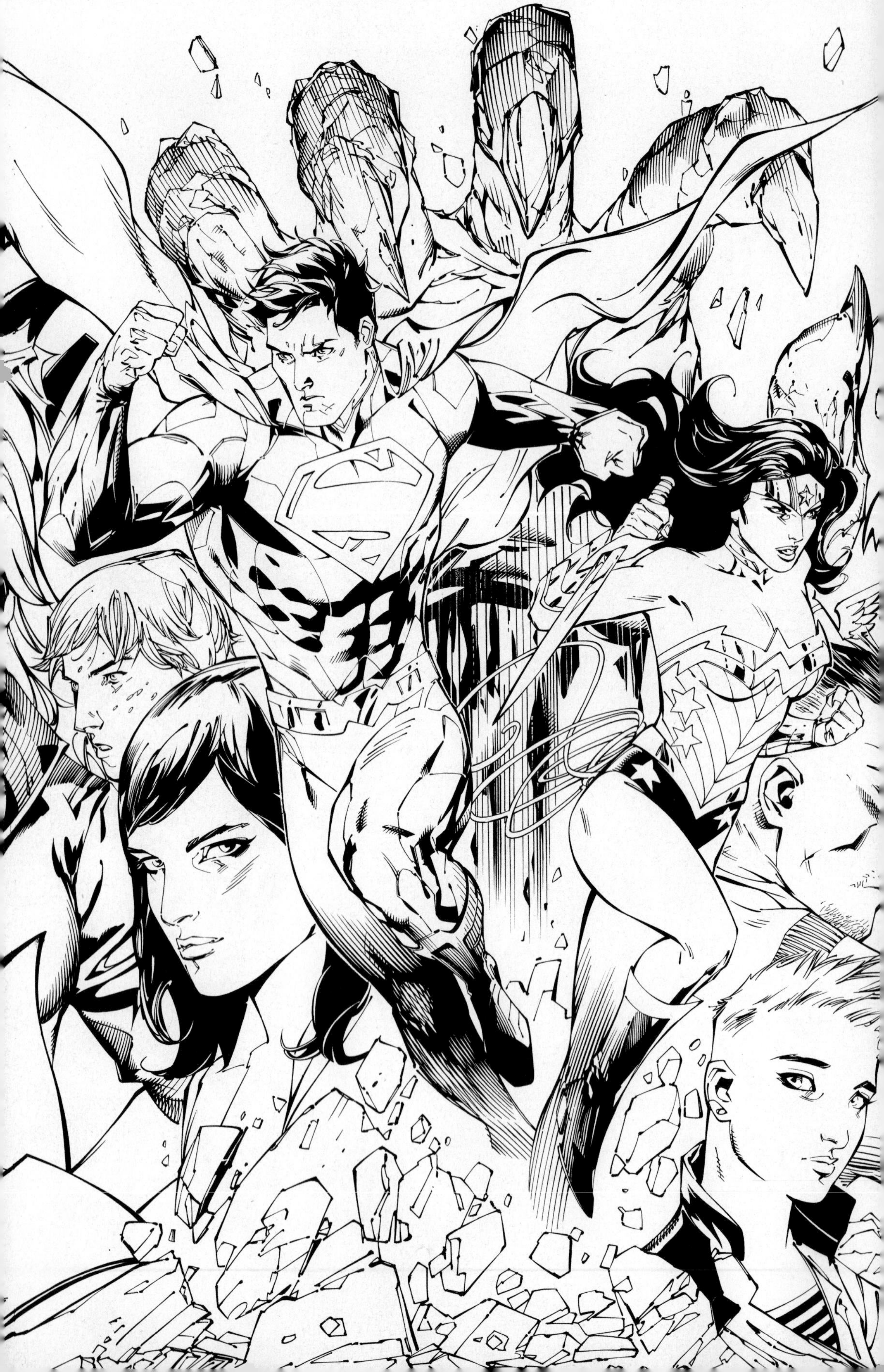

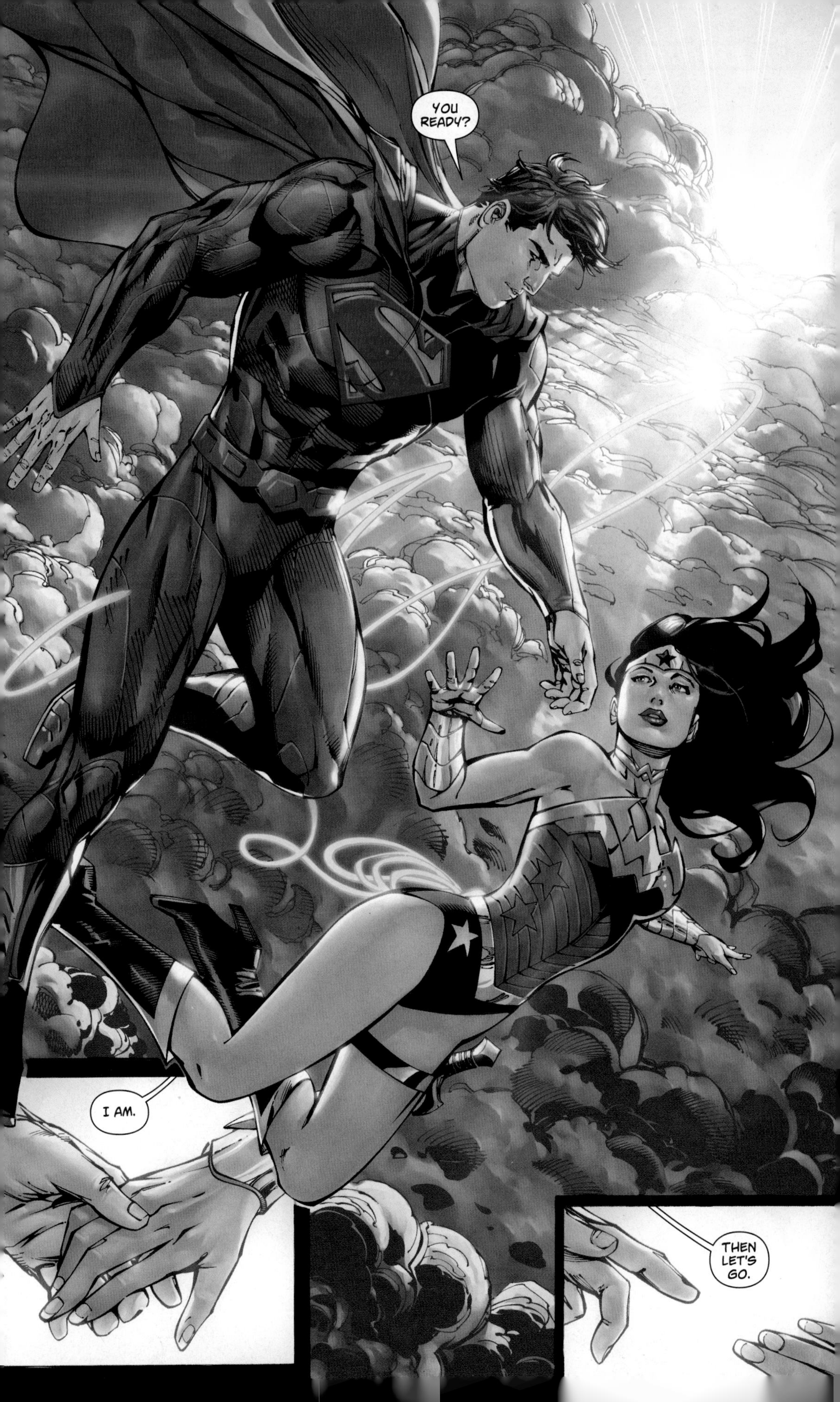
YOU READY?
I AM.
THEN LET'S GO.

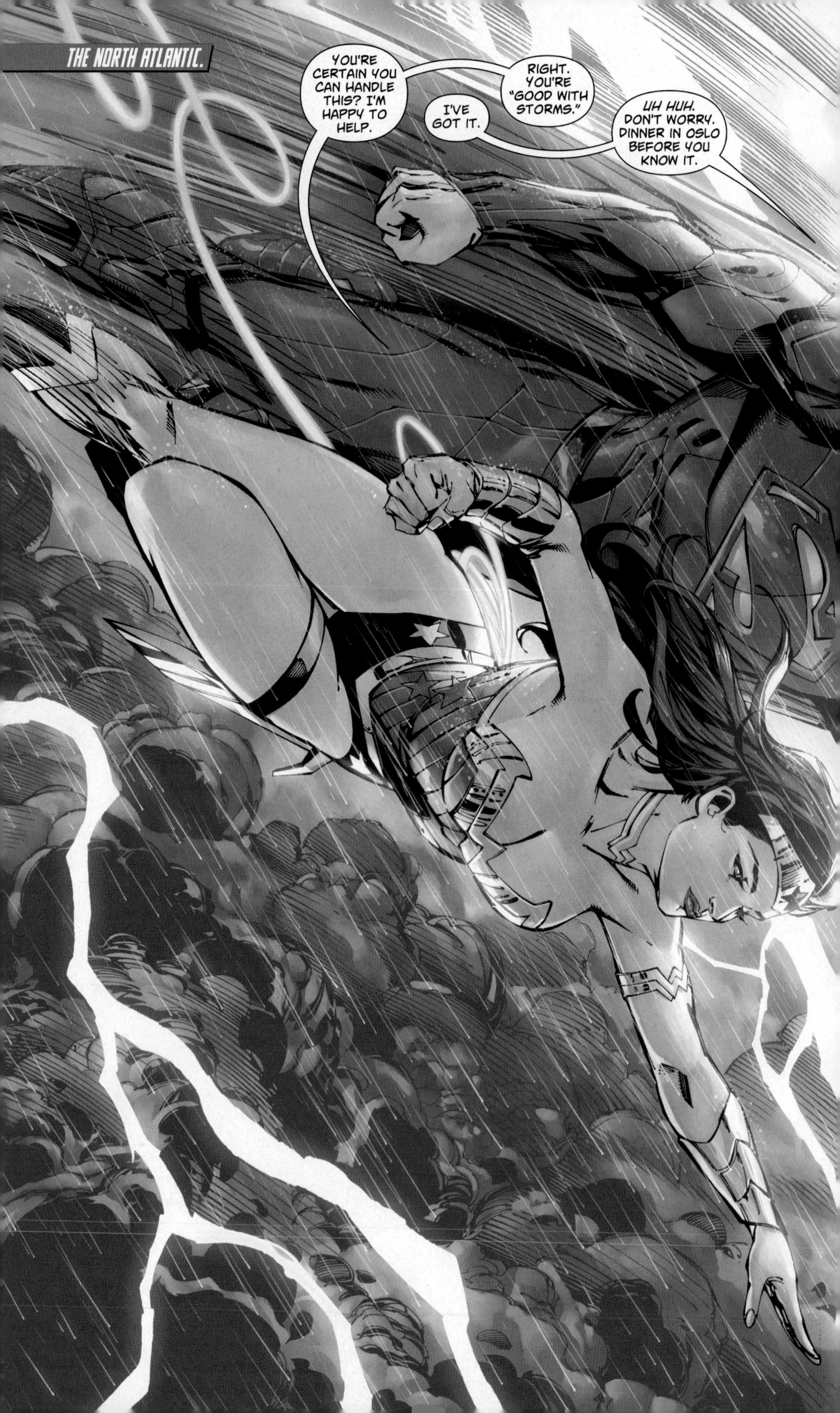
THE NORTH ATLANTIC.
YOU'RE CERTAIN YOU CAN HANDLE THIS? I'M HAPPY TO HELP.
I'VE GOT IT.
RIGHT. YOU'RE "GOOD WITH STORMS."
UH HUH. DON'T WORRY. DINNER IN OSLO BEFORE YOU KNOW IT.

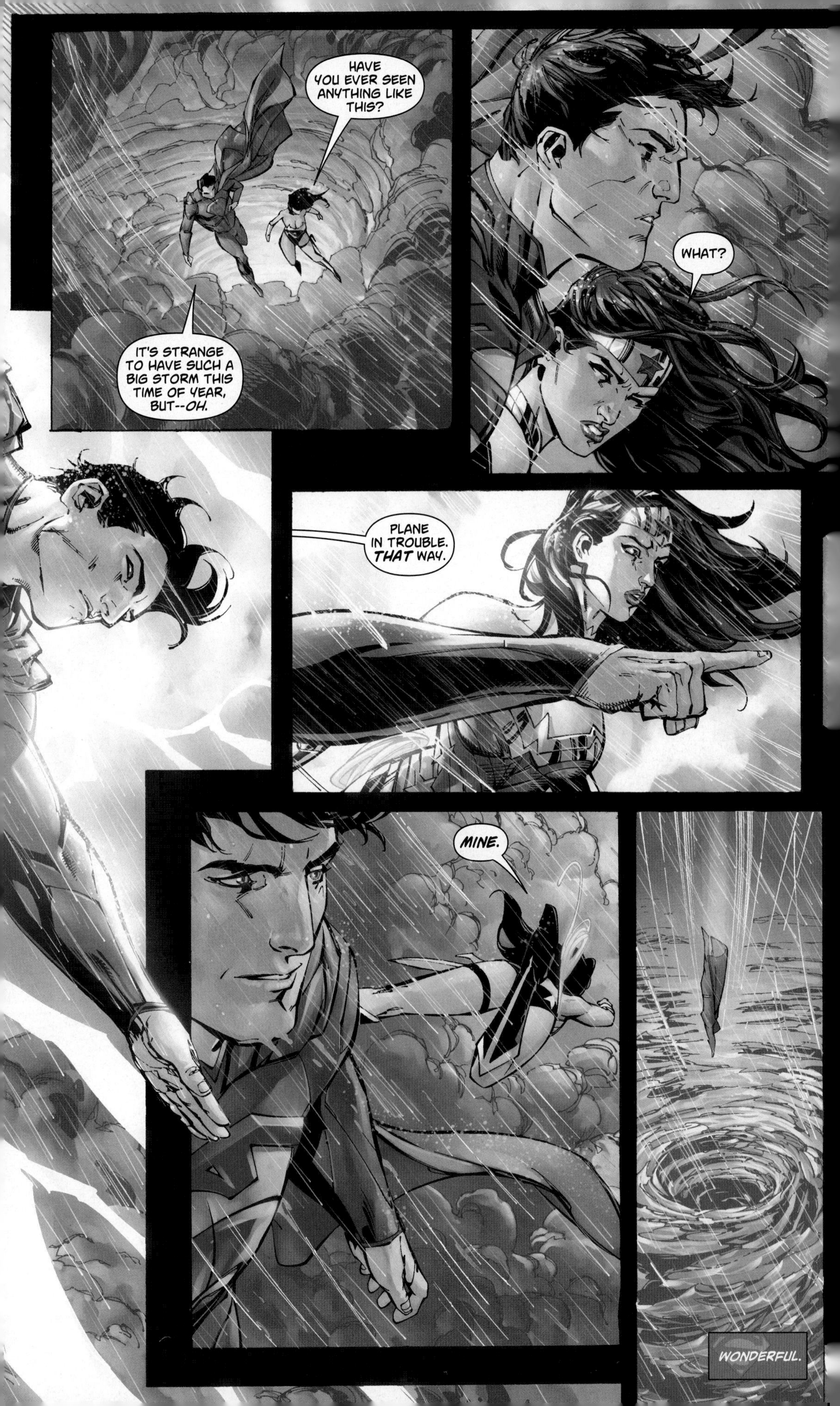
HAVE YOU EVER SEEN ANYTHING LIKE THIS?
IT'S STRANGE TO HAVE SUCH A BIG STORM THIS TIME OF YEAR, BUT--*OH.*
WHAT?
PLANE IN TROUBLE. ***THAT*** WAY.
MINE.
WONDERFUL.

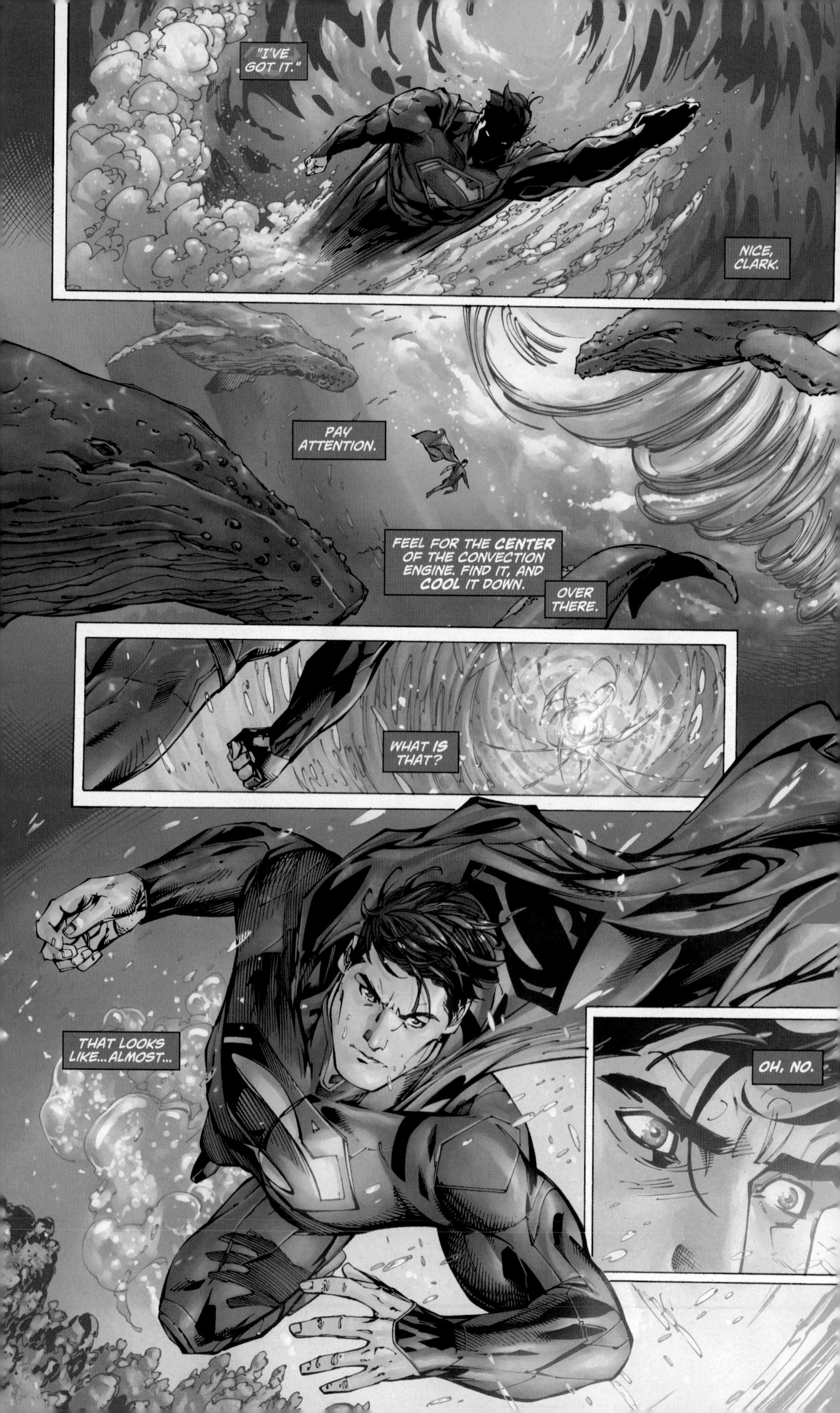
"I'VE GOT IT."
NICE, CLARK.
PAY ATTENTION.
FEEL FOR THE CENTER OF THE CONVECTION ENGINE. FIND IT, AND COOL IT DOWN.
OVER THERE.
WHAT IS THAT?
THAT LOOKS LIKE...ALMOST...
OH, NO.

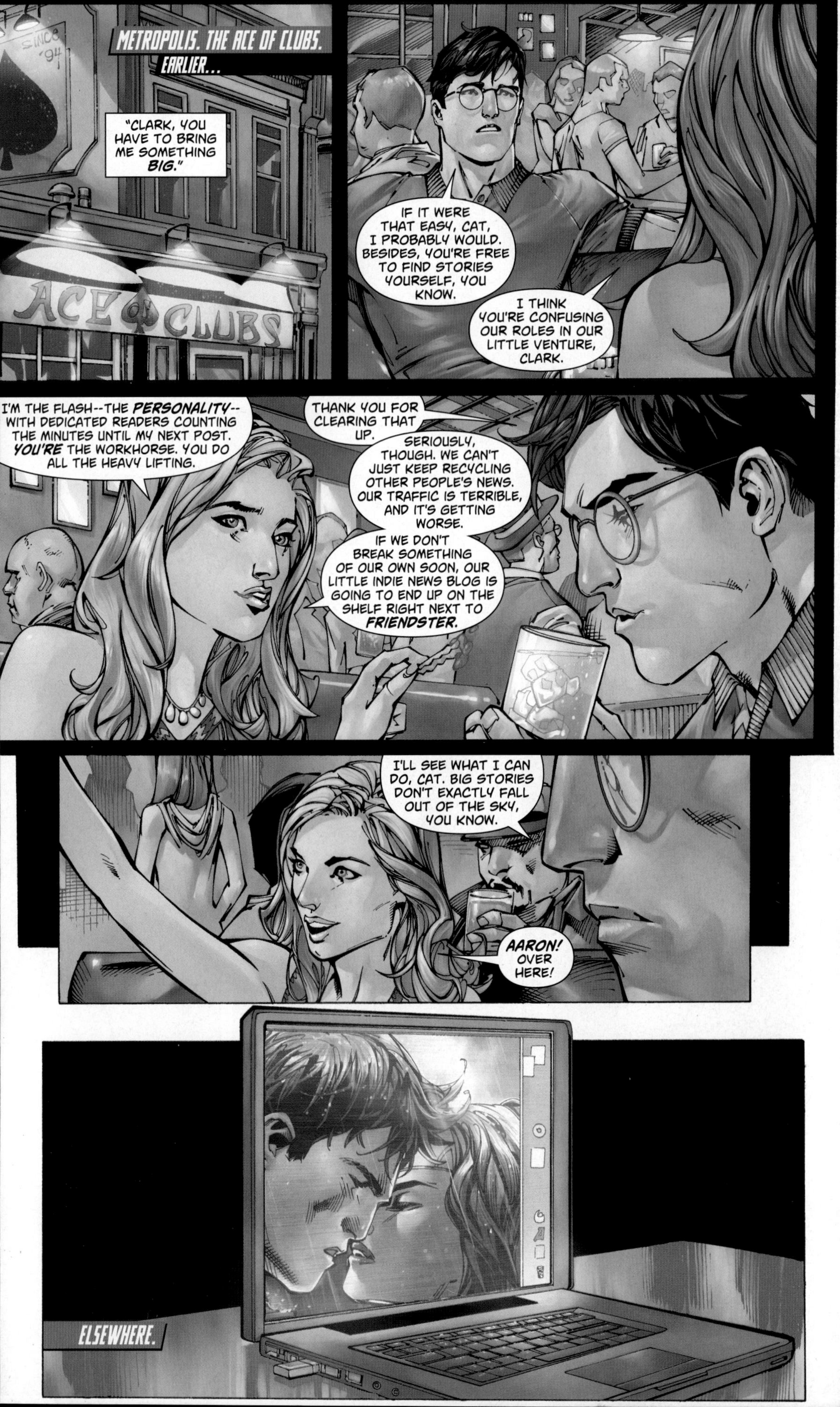
METROPOLIS. THE ACE OF CLUBS.
EARLIER...
"CLARK, YOU HAVE TO BRING ME SOMETHING BIG."
SINCE '94
ACE CLUBS
IF IT WERE THAT EASY, CAT, I PROBABLY WOULD. BESIDES, YOU'RE FREE TO FIND STORIES YOURSELF, YOU KNOW.
I THINK YOU'RE CONFUSING OUR ROLES IN OUR LITTLE VENTURE, CLARK.
I'M THE FLASH--THE PERSONALITY--WITH DEDICATED READERS COUNTING THE MINUTES UNTIL MY NEXT POST. YOU'RE THE WORKHORSE. YOU DO ALL THE HEAVY LIFTING.
THANK YOU FOR CLEARING THAT UP.
SERIOUSLY, THOUGH. WE CAN'T JUST KEEP RECYCLING OTHER PEOPLE'S NEWS. OUR TRAFFIC IS TERRIBLE, AND IT'S GETTING WORSE.
IF WE DON'T BREAK SOMETHING OF OUR OWN SOON, OUR LITTLE INDIE NEWS BLOG IS GOING TO END UP ON THE SHELF RIGHT NEXT TO FRIENDSTER.
I'LL SEE WHAT I CAN DO, CAT. BIG STORIES DON'T EXACTLY FALL OUT OF THE SKY, YOU KNOW.
AARON! OVER HERE!
ELSEWHERE.

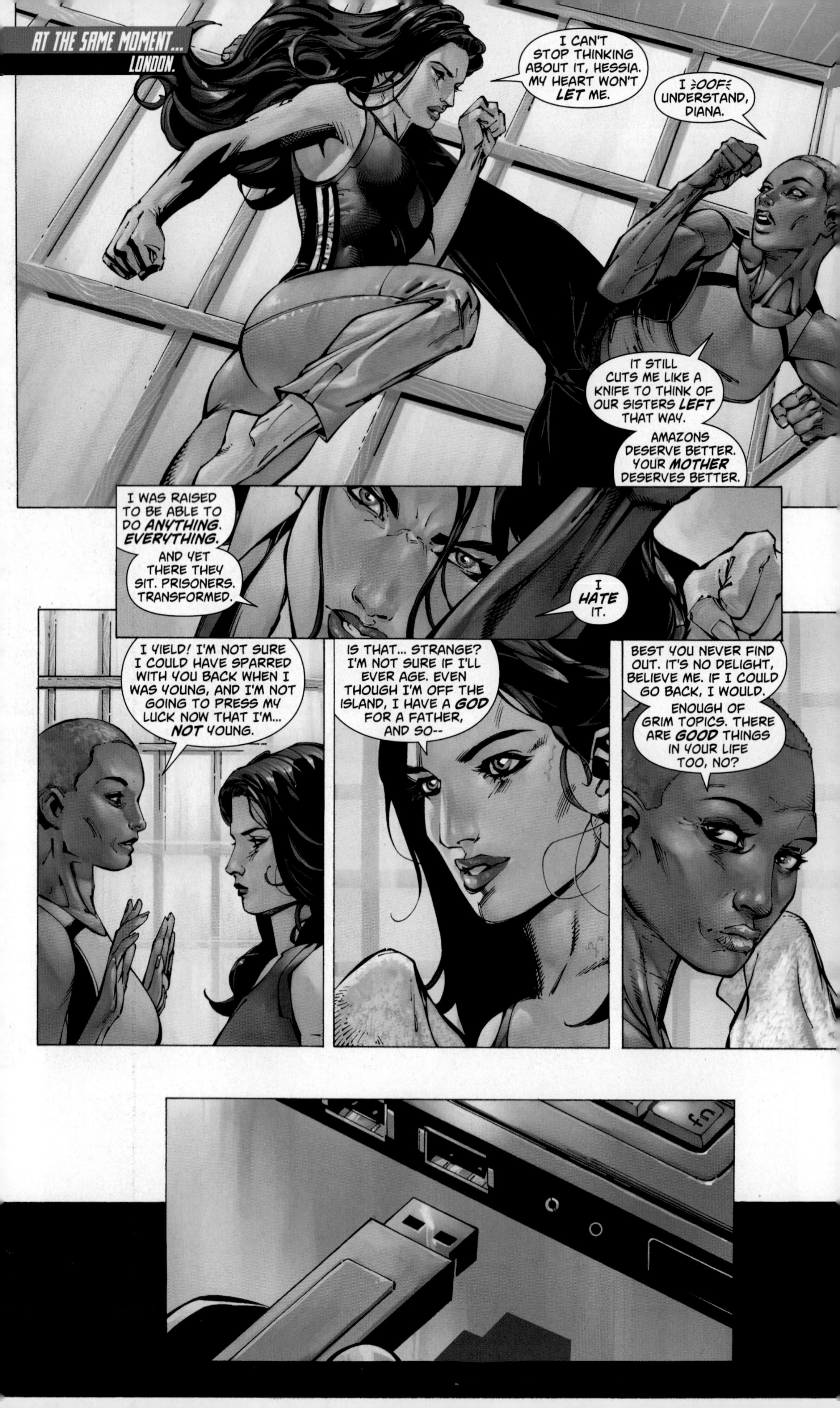
AT THE SAME MOMENT... LONDON.
I CAN'T STOP THINKING ABOUT IT, HESSIA. MY HEART WON'T LET ME.
I *OOF* UNDERSTAND, DIANA.
IT STILL CUTS ME LIKE A KNIFE TO THINK OF OUR SISTERS LEFT THAT WAY.
AMAZONS DESERVE BETTER. YOUR MOTHER DESERVES BETTER.
I WAS RAISED TO BE ABLE TO DO ANYTHING. EVERYTHING.
AND YET THERE THEY SIT. PRISONERS. TRANSFORMED.
I HATE IT.
I YIELD! I'M NOT SURE I COULD HAVE SPARRED WITH YOU BACK WHEN I WAS YOUNG, AND I'M NOT GOING TO PRESS MY LUCK NOW THAT I'M... NOT YOUNG.
IS THAT... STRANGE? I'M NOT SURE IF I'LL EVER AGE. EVEN THOUGH I'M OFF THE ISLAND, I HAVE A GOD FOR A FATHER, AND SO--
BEST YOU NEVER FIND OUT. IT'S NO DELIGHT, BELIEVE ME. IF I COULD GO BACK, I WOULD.
ENOUGH OF GRIM TOPICS. THERE ARE GOOD THINGS IN YOUR LIFE TOO, NO?
fn

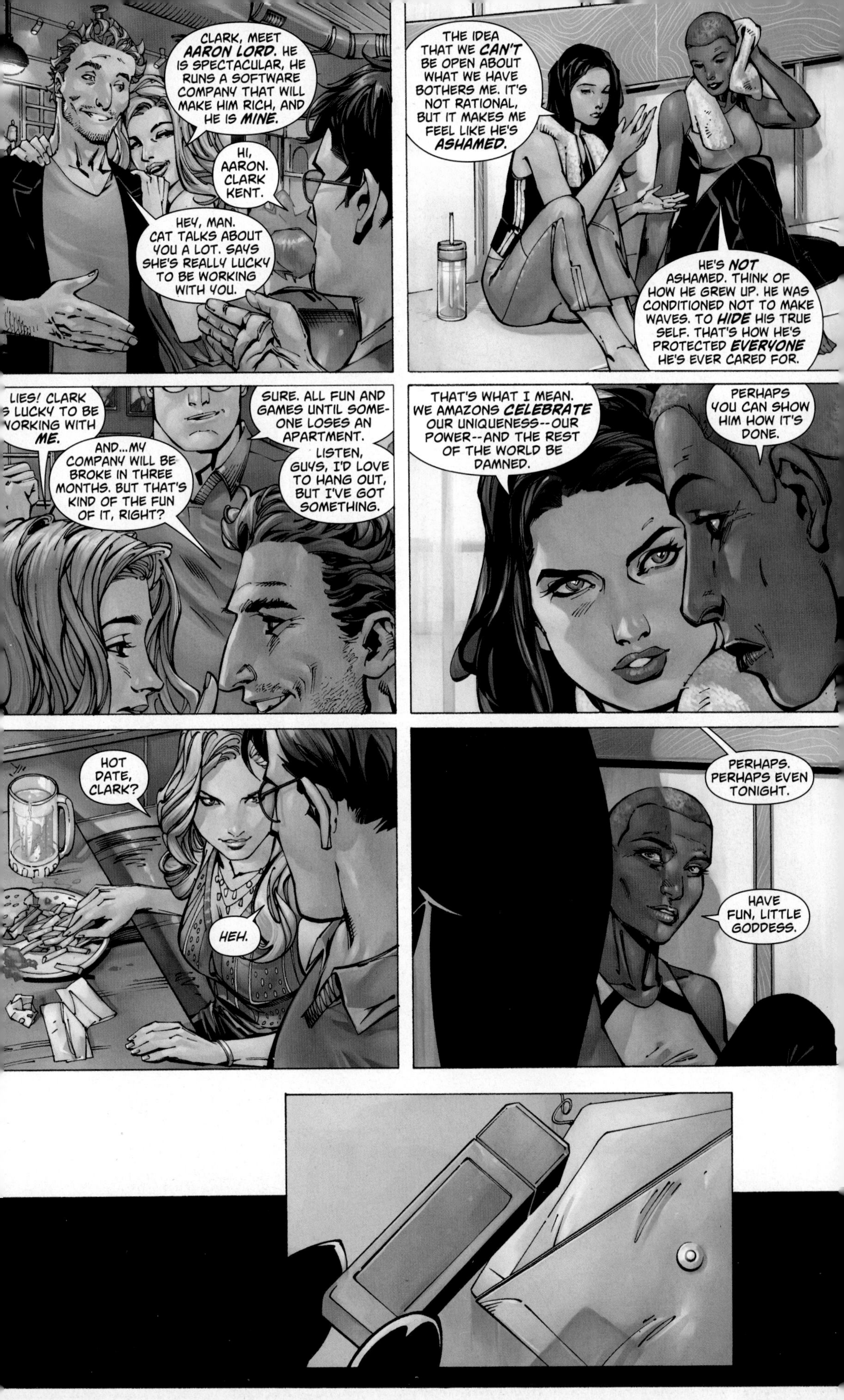
CLARK, MEET AARON LORD. HE IS SPECTACULAR, HE RUNS A SOFTWARE COMPANY THAT WILL MAKE HIM RICH, AND HE IS MINE.
HI, AARON. CLARK KENT.
HEY, MAN. CAT TALKS ABOUT YOU A LOT. SAYS SHE'S REALLY LUCKY TO BE WORKING WITH YOU.
THE IDEA THAT WE CAN'T BE OPEN ABOUT WHAT WE HAVE BOTHERS ME. IT'S NOT RATIONAL, BUT IT MAKES ME FEEL LIKE HE'S ASHAMED.
HE'S NOT ASHAMED. THINK OF HOW HE GREW UP. HE WAS CONDITIONED NOT TO MAKE WAVES. TO HIDE HIS TRUE SELF. THAT'S HOW HE'S PROTECTED EVERYONE HE'S EVER CARED FOR.
LIES! CLARK S LUCKY TO BE VORKING WITH ME.
AND...MY COMPANY WILL BE BROKE IN THREE MONTHS. BUT THAT'S KIND OF THE FUN OF IT, RIGHT?
SURE. ALL FUN AND GAMES UNTIL SOME-ONE LOSES AN APARTMENT.
LISTEN, GUYS, I'D LOVE TO HANG OUT, BUT I'VE GOT SOMETHING.
THAT'S WHAT I MEAN. WE AMAZONS CELEBRATE OUR UNIQUENESS--OUR POWER--AND THE REST OF THE WORLD BE DAMNED.
PERHAPS YOU CAN SHOW HIM HOW IT'S DONE.
HOT DATE, CLARK?
HEH.
PERHAPS. PERHAPS EVEN TONIGHT.
HAVE FUN, LITTLE GODDESS.

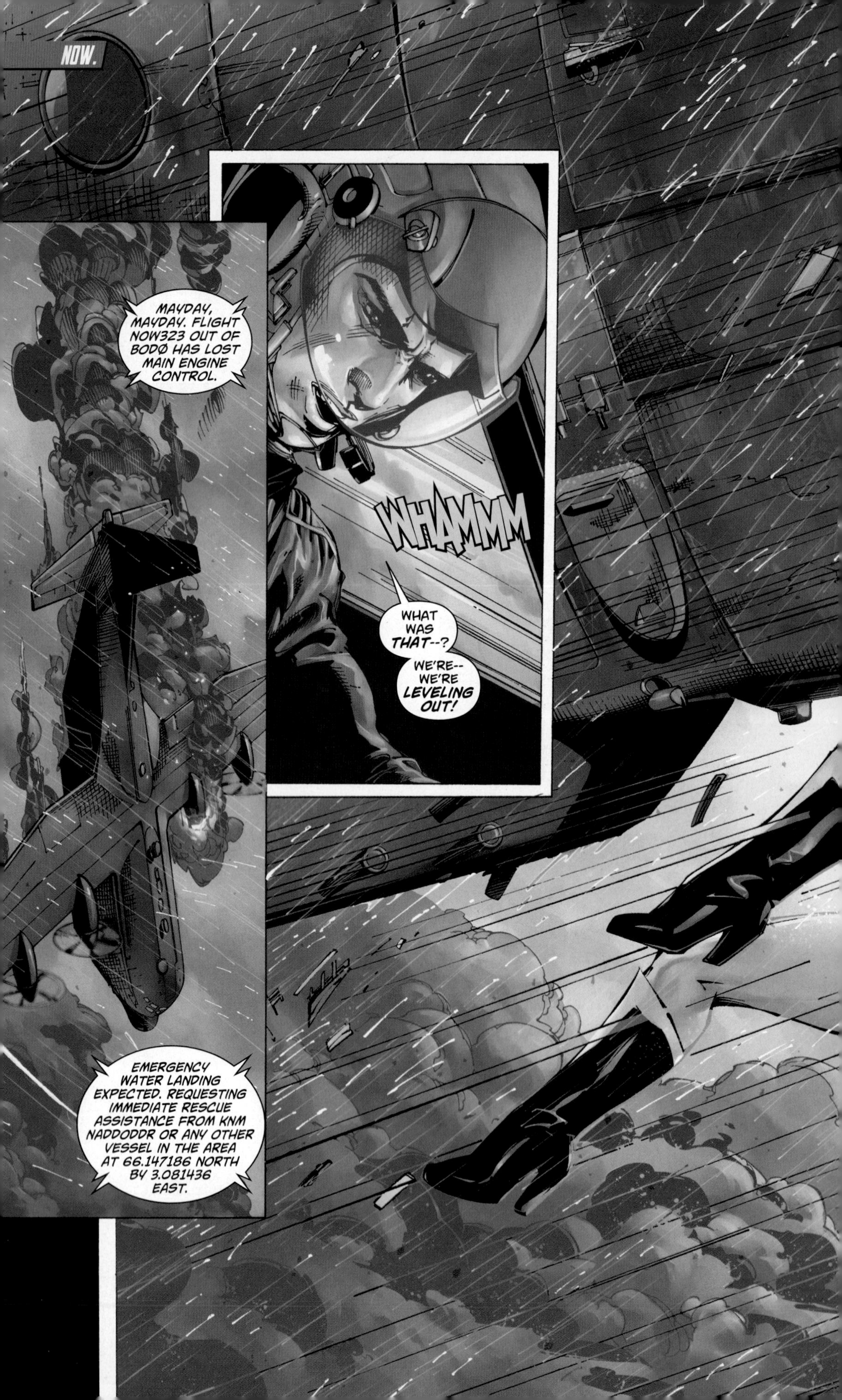
NOW.
MAYDAY, MAYDAY. FLIGHT NOW323 OUT OF BODØ HAS LOST MAIN ENGINE CONTROL.
WHAMMM
WHAT WAS THAT--?
WE'RE-- WE'RE LEVELING OUT!
EMERGENCY WATER LANDING EXPECTED. REQUESTING IMMEDIATE RESCUE ASSISTANCE FROM KNM NADDODDR OR ANY OTHER VESSEL IN THE AREA AT 66.147186 NORTH BY 3.081436 EAST.

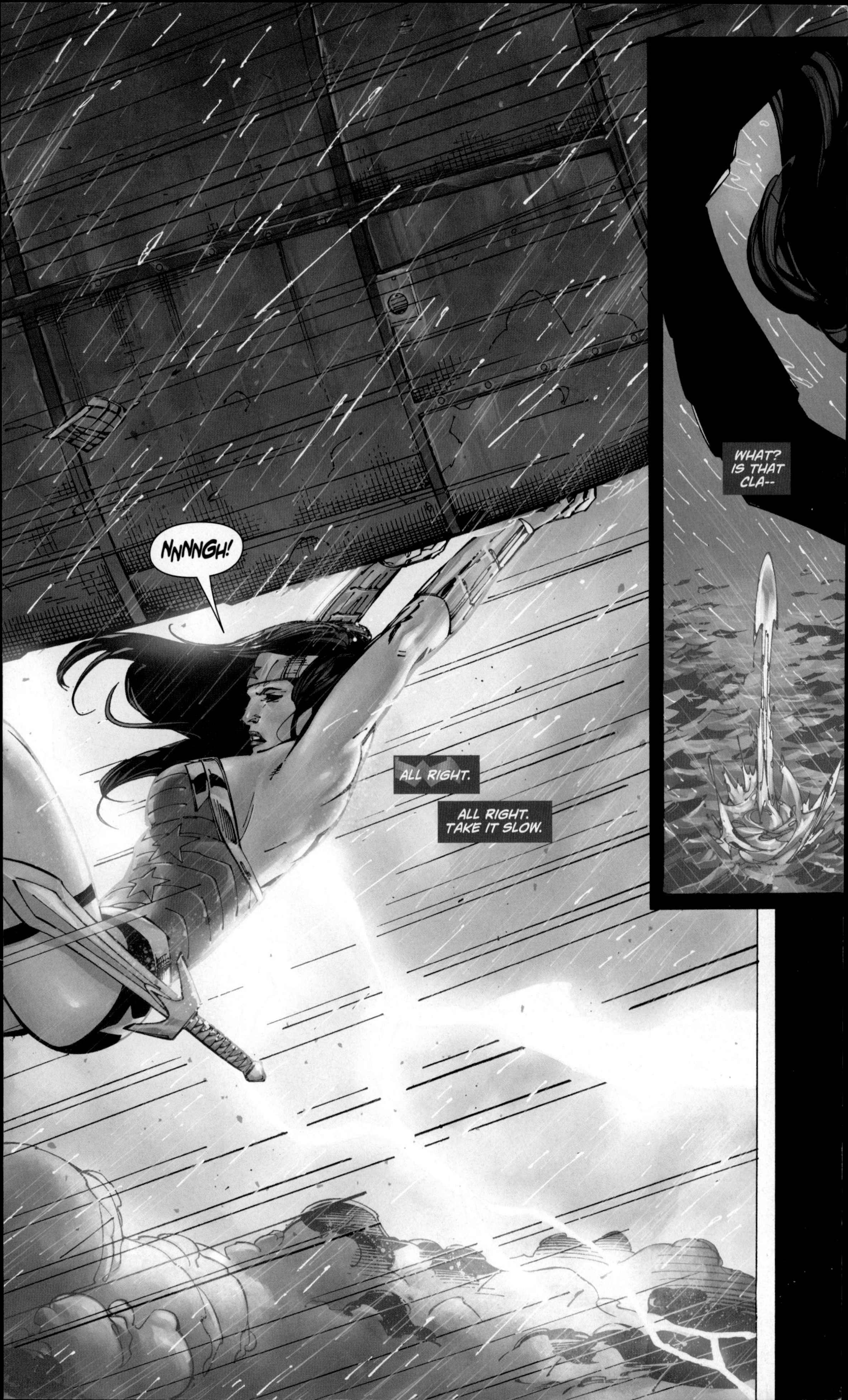
NNNNGH!
ALL RIGHT.
ALL RIGHT. TAKE IT SLOW.
WHAT? IS THAT CLA--

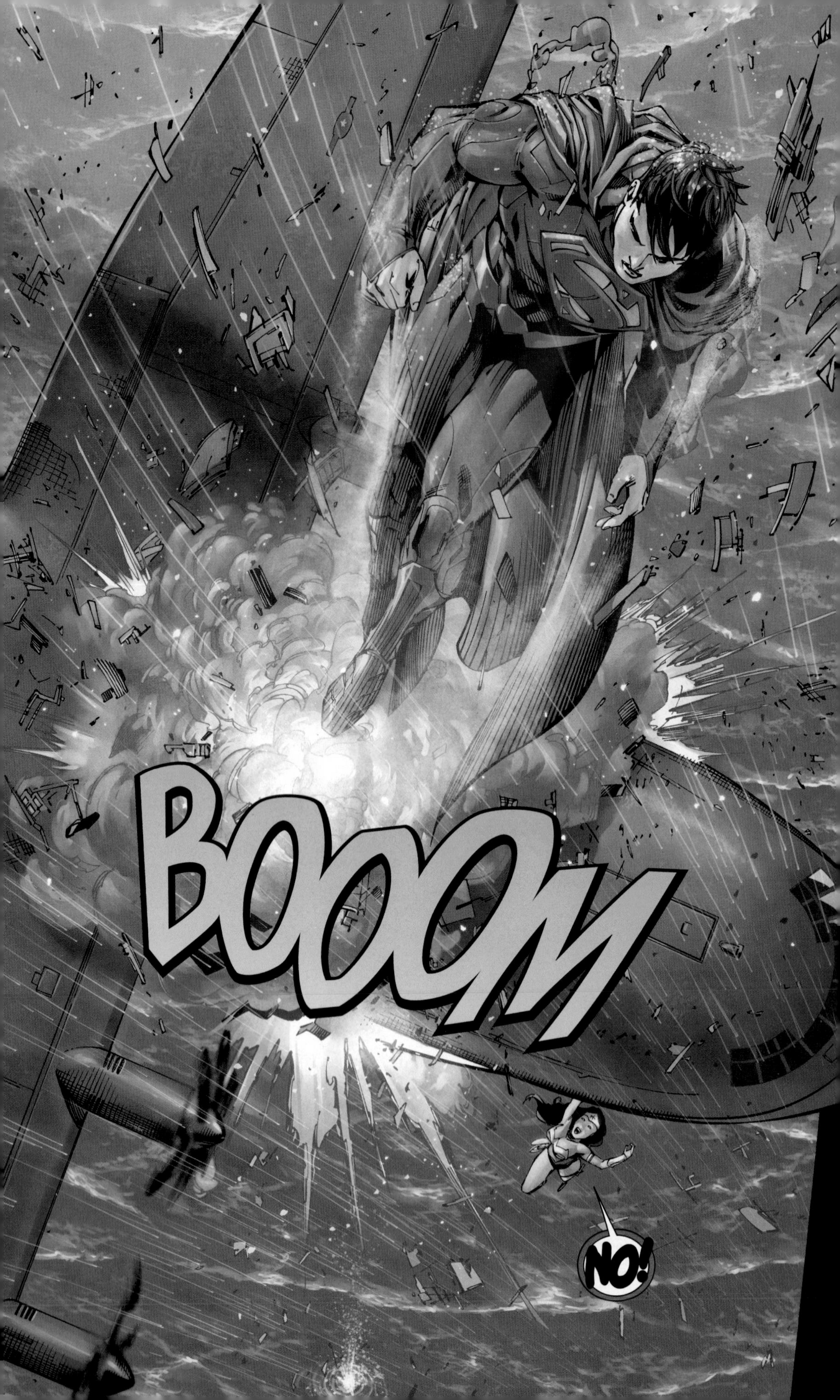
BOOOM
NO!

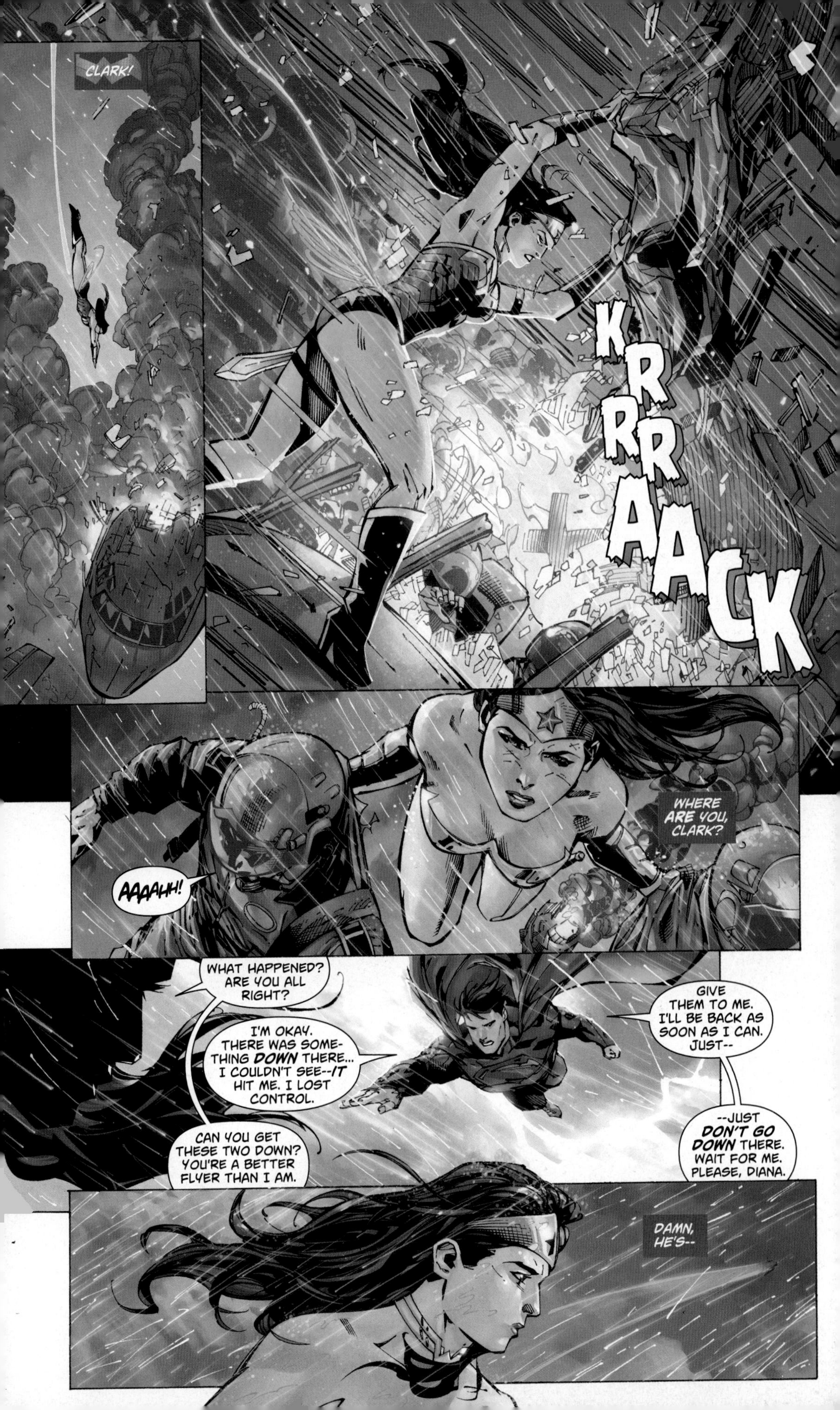
CLARK!
KRRRAACK
WHERE ARE YOU, CLARK?
AAAAHH!
WHAT HAPPENED? ARE YOU ALL RIGHT?
I'M OKAY. THERE WAS SOME-THING DOWN THERE... I COULDN'T SEE--IT HIT ME. I LOST CONTROL.
CAN YOU GET THESE TWO DOWN? YOU'RE A BETTER FLYER THAN I AM.
GIVE THEM TO ME. I'LL BE BACK AS SOON AS I CAN. JUST--
--JUST DON'T GO DOWN THERE. WAIT FOR ME. PLEASE, DIANA.
DAMN, HE'S--

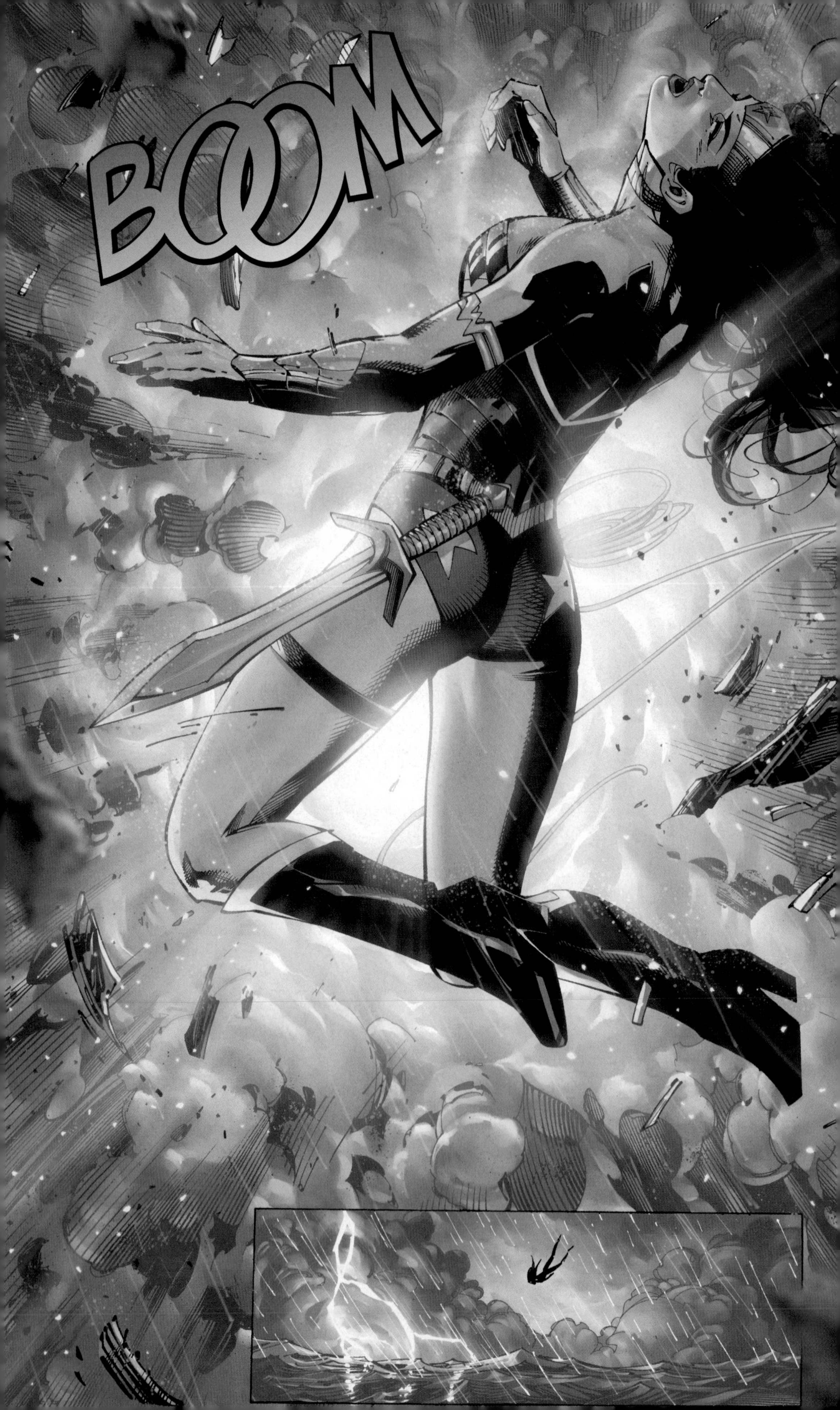
BOOM

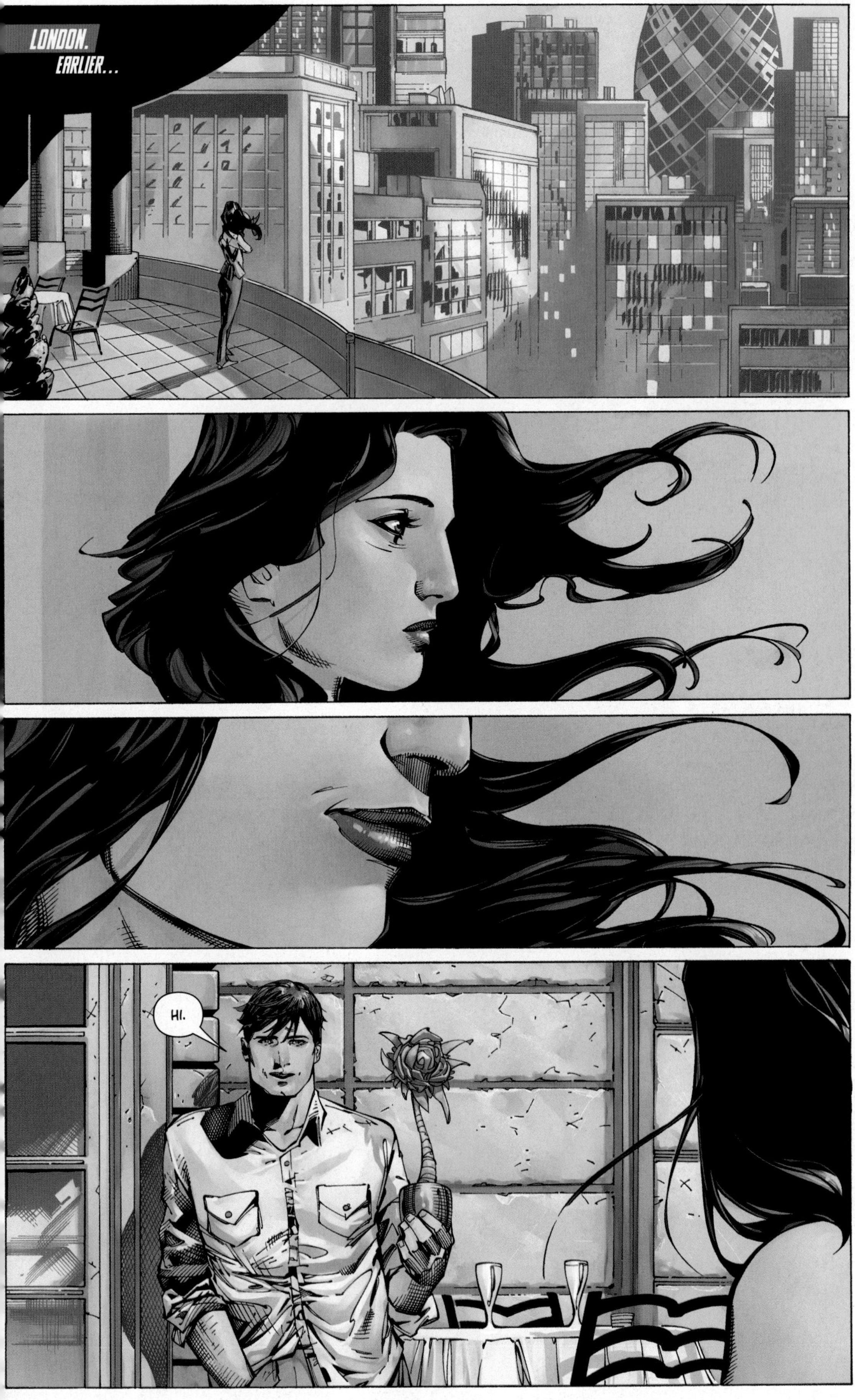
LONDON.
EARLIER...
HI.

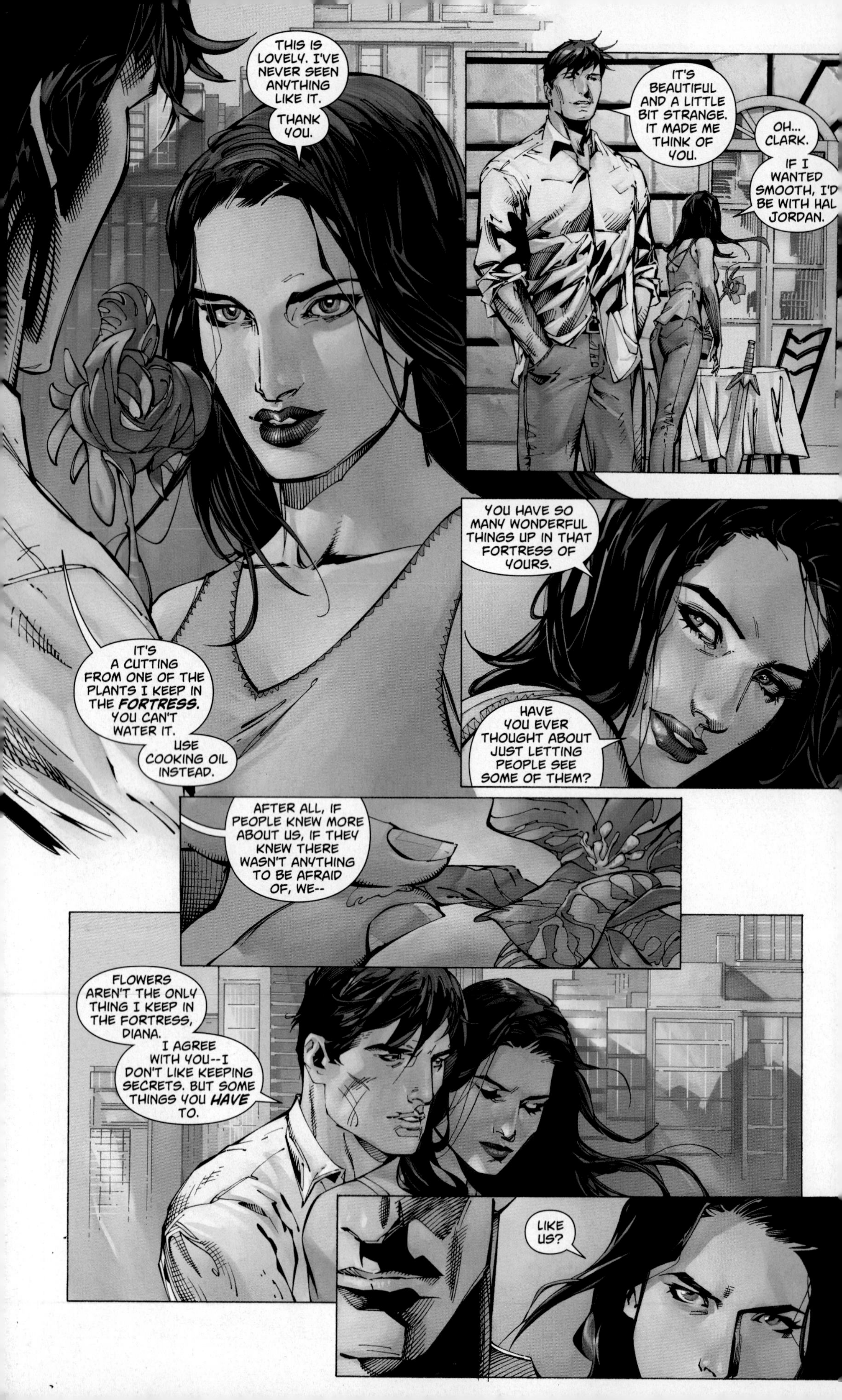
THIS IS LOVELY. I'VE NEVER SEEN ANYTHING LIKE IT.
THANK YOU.
IT'S BEAUTIFUL AND A LITTLE BIT STRANGE. IT MADE ME THINK OF YOU.
OH... CLARK.
IF I WANTED SMOOTH, I'D BE WITH HAL JORDAN.
IT'S A CUTTING FROM ONE OF THE PLANTS I KEEP IN THE **FORTRESS.** YOU CAN'T WATER IT.
USE COOKING OIL INSTEAD.
YOU HAVE SO MANY WONDERFUL THINGS UP IN THAT FORTRESS OF YOURS.
HAVE YOU EVER THOUGHT ABOUT JUST LETTING PEOPLE SEE SOME OF THEM?
AFTER ALL, IF PEOPLE KNEW MORE ABOUT US, IF THEY KNEW THERE WASN'T ANYTHING TO BE AFRAID OF, WE--
FLOWERS AREN'T THE ONLY THING I KEEP IN THE FORTRESS, DIANA.
I AGREE WITH YOU--I DON'T LIKE KEEPING SECRETS. BUT SOME THINGS YOU ***HAVE*** TO.
LIKE US?

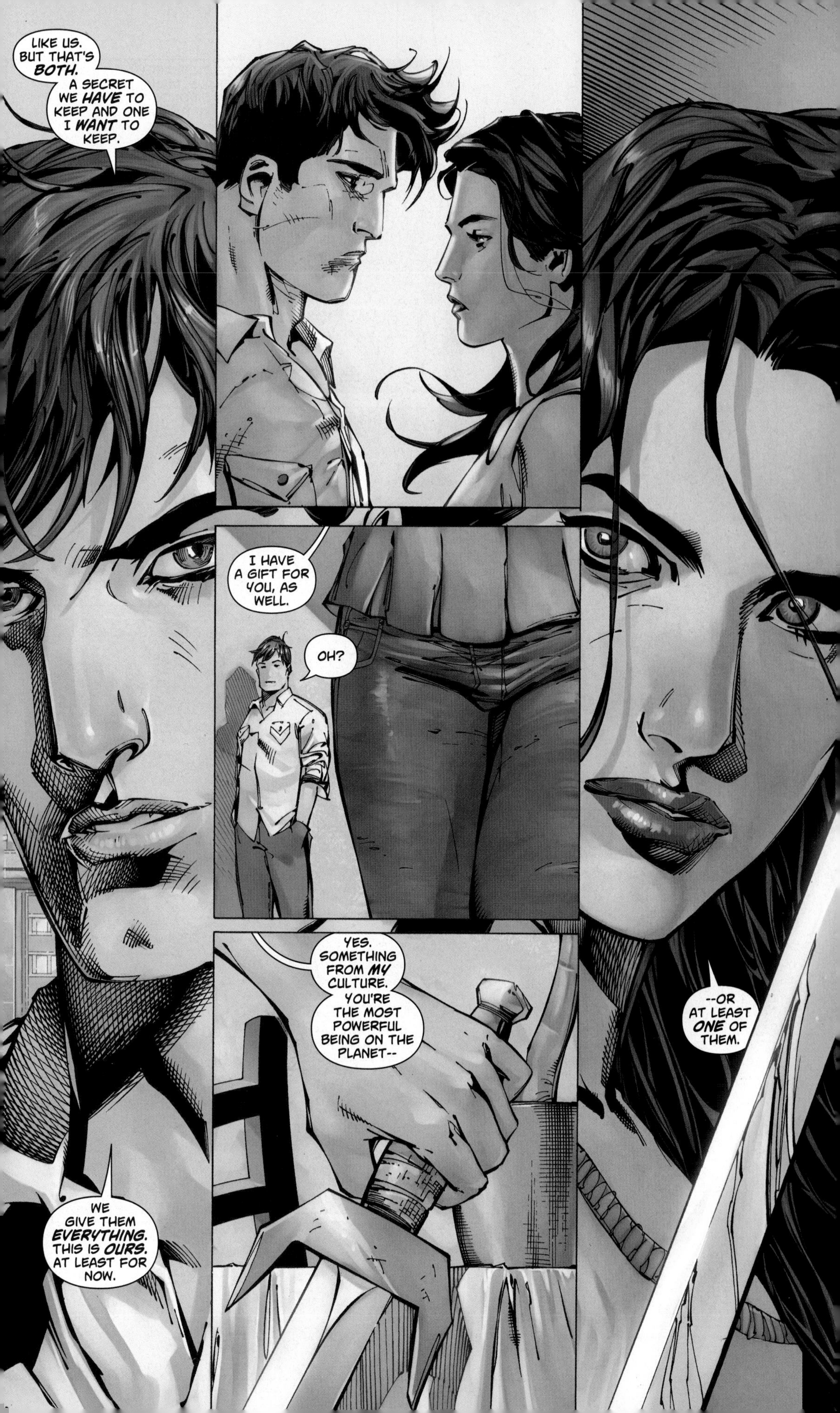

LIKE US. BUT THAT'S BOTH.
A SECRET WE HAVE TO KEEP AND ONE I WANT TO KEEP.
I HAVE A GIFT FOR YOU, AS WELL.
OH?
YES. SOMETHING FROM MY CULTURE.
YOU'RE THE MOST POWERFUL BEING ON THE PLANET--
--OR AT LEAST ONE OF THEM.
WE GIVE THEM EVERYTHING. THIS IS OURS. AT LEAST FOR NOW.

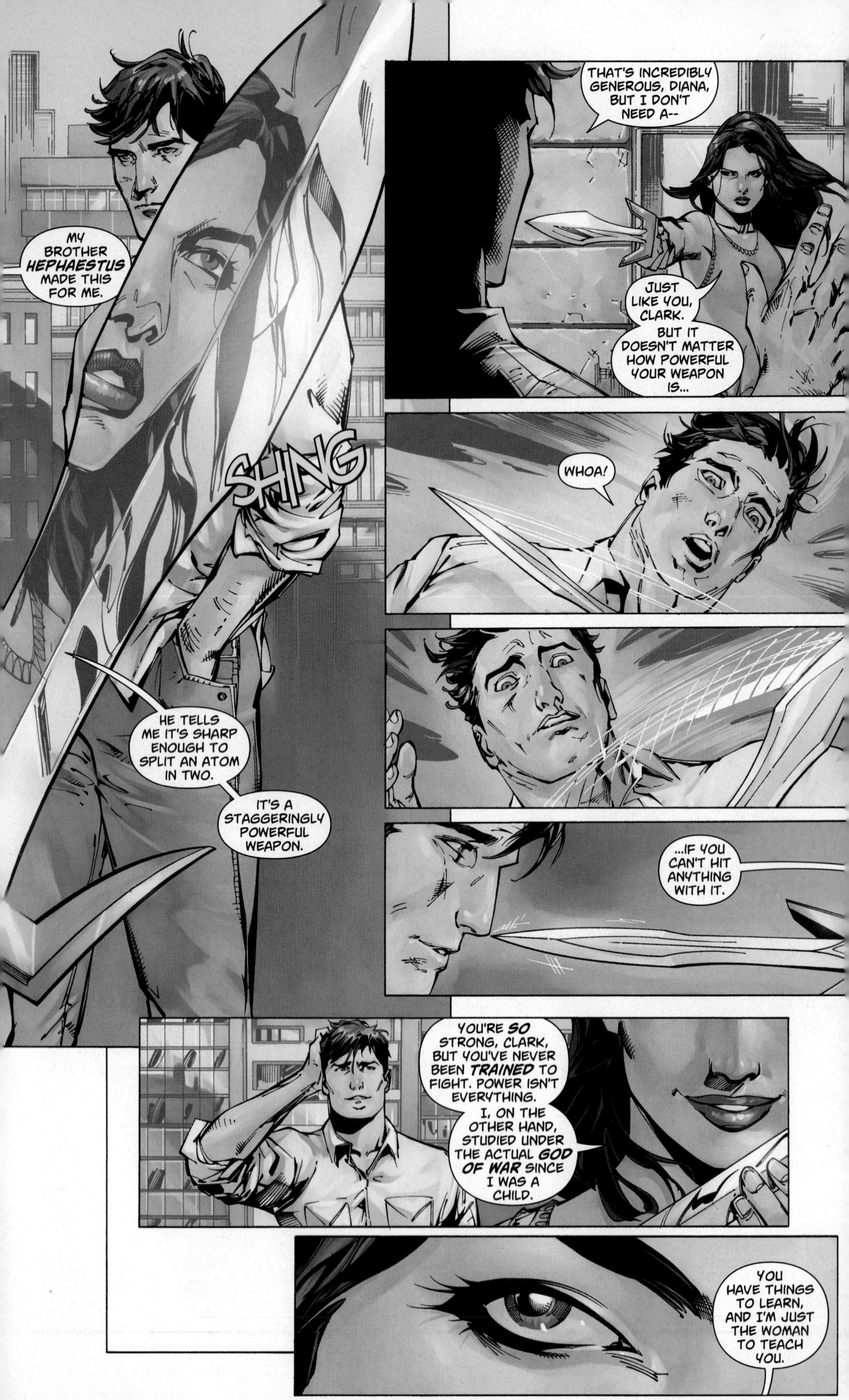
MY BROTHER HEPHAESTUS MADE THIS FOR ME.
SHING
HE TELLS ME IT'S SHARP ENOUGH TO SPLIT AN ATOM IN TWO.
IT'S A STAGGERINGLY POWERFUL WEAPON.
THAT'S INCREDIBLY GENEROUS, DIANA, BUT I DON'T NEED A--
JUST LIKE YOU, CLARK.
BUT IT DOESN'T MATTER HOW POWERFUL YOUR WEAPON IS...
WHOA!
...IF YOU CAN'T HIT ANYTHING WITH IT.
YOU'RE SO STRONG, CLARK, BUT YOU'VE NEVER BEEN TRAINED TO FIGHT. POWER ISN'T EVERYTHING.
I, ON THE OTHER HAND, STUDIED UNDER THE ACTUAL GOD OF WAR SINCE I WAS A CHILD.
YOU HAVE THINGS TO LEARN, AND I'M JUST THE WOMAN TO TEACH YOU.

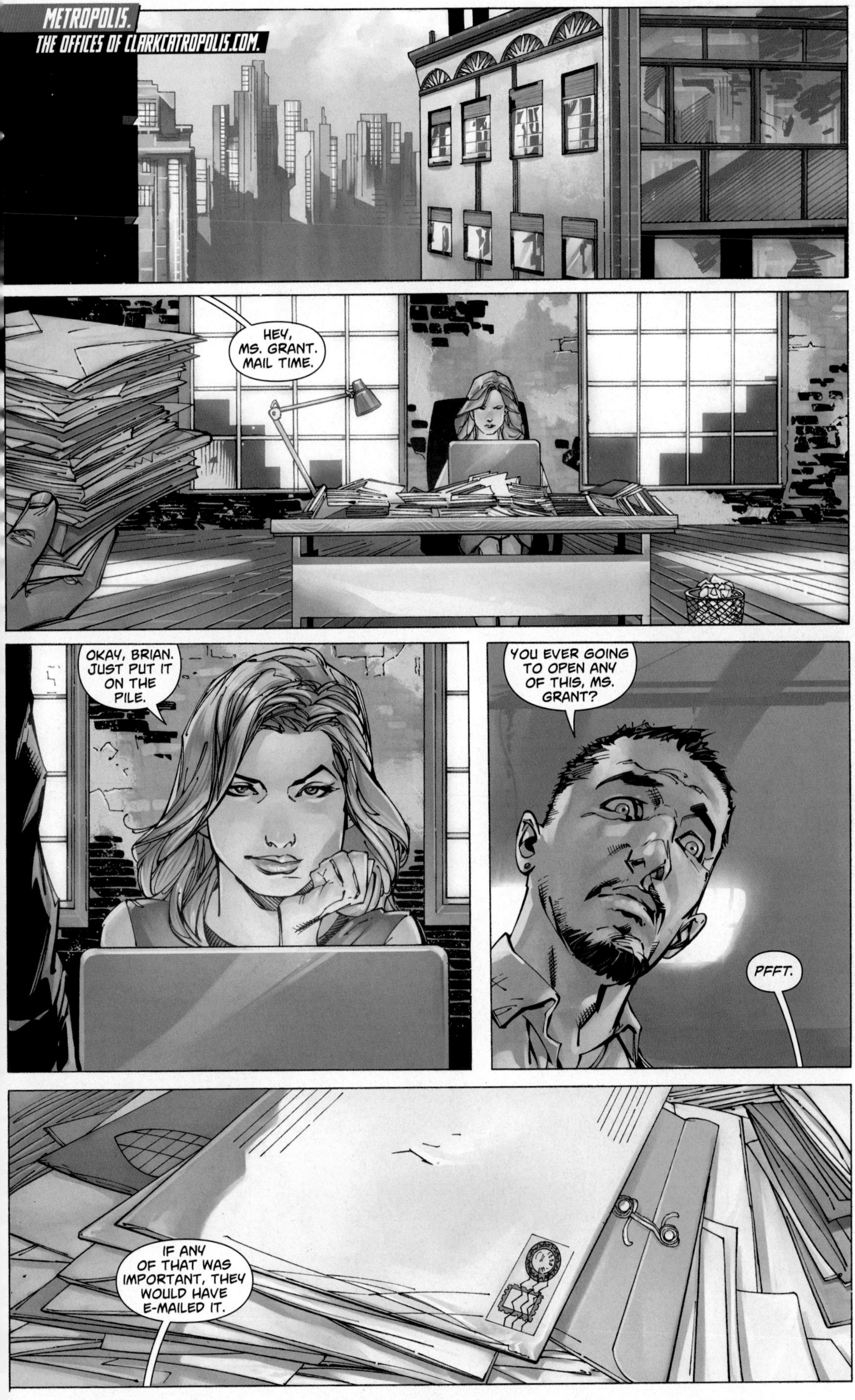
METROPOLIS.
THE OFFICES OF CLARKCATROPOLIS.COM.
HEY, MS. GRANT. MAIL TIME.
OKAY, BRIAN. JUST PUT IT ON THE PILE.
YOU EVER GOING TO OPEN ANY OF THIS, MS. GRANT?
PFFT.
IF ANY OF THAT WAS IMPORTANT, THEY WOULD HAVE E-MAILED IT.

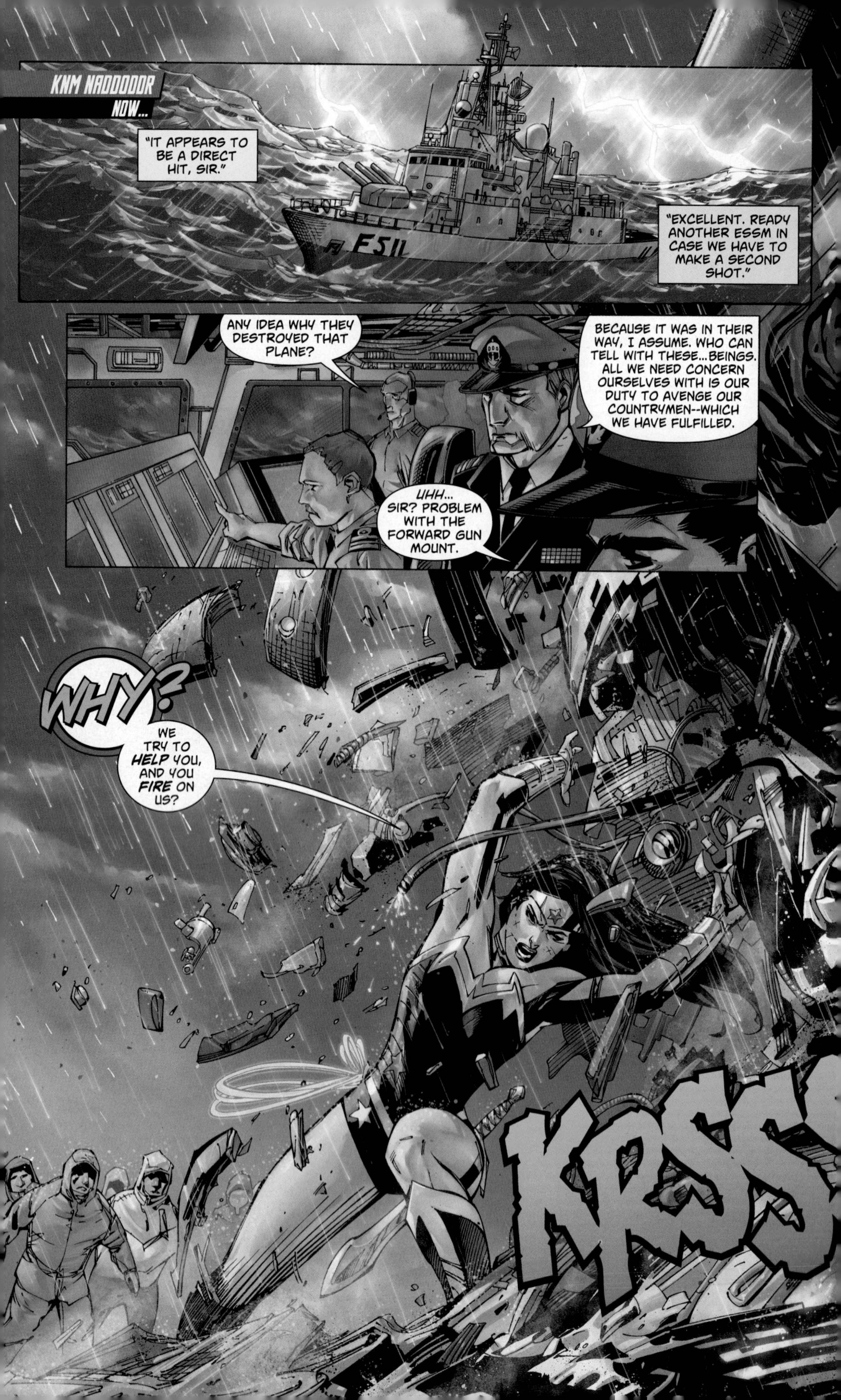
KNM NADDODOR
NOW...
"IT APPEARS TO BE A DIRECT HIT, SIR."
"EXCELLENT. READY ANOTHER ESSM IN CASE WE HAVE TO MAKE A SECOND SHOT."
ANY IDEA WHY THEY DESTROYED THAT PLANE?
BECAUSE IT WAS IN THEIR WAY, I ASSUME. WHO CAN TELL WITH THESE...BEINGS. ALL WE NEED CONCERN OURSELVES WITH IS OUR DUTY TO AVENGE OUR COUNTRYMEN--WHICH WE HAVE FULFILLED.
UHH... SIR? PROBLEM WITH THE FORWARD GUN MOUNT.
WHY?
WE TRY TO HELP YOU, AND YOU FIRE ON US?
KRSS

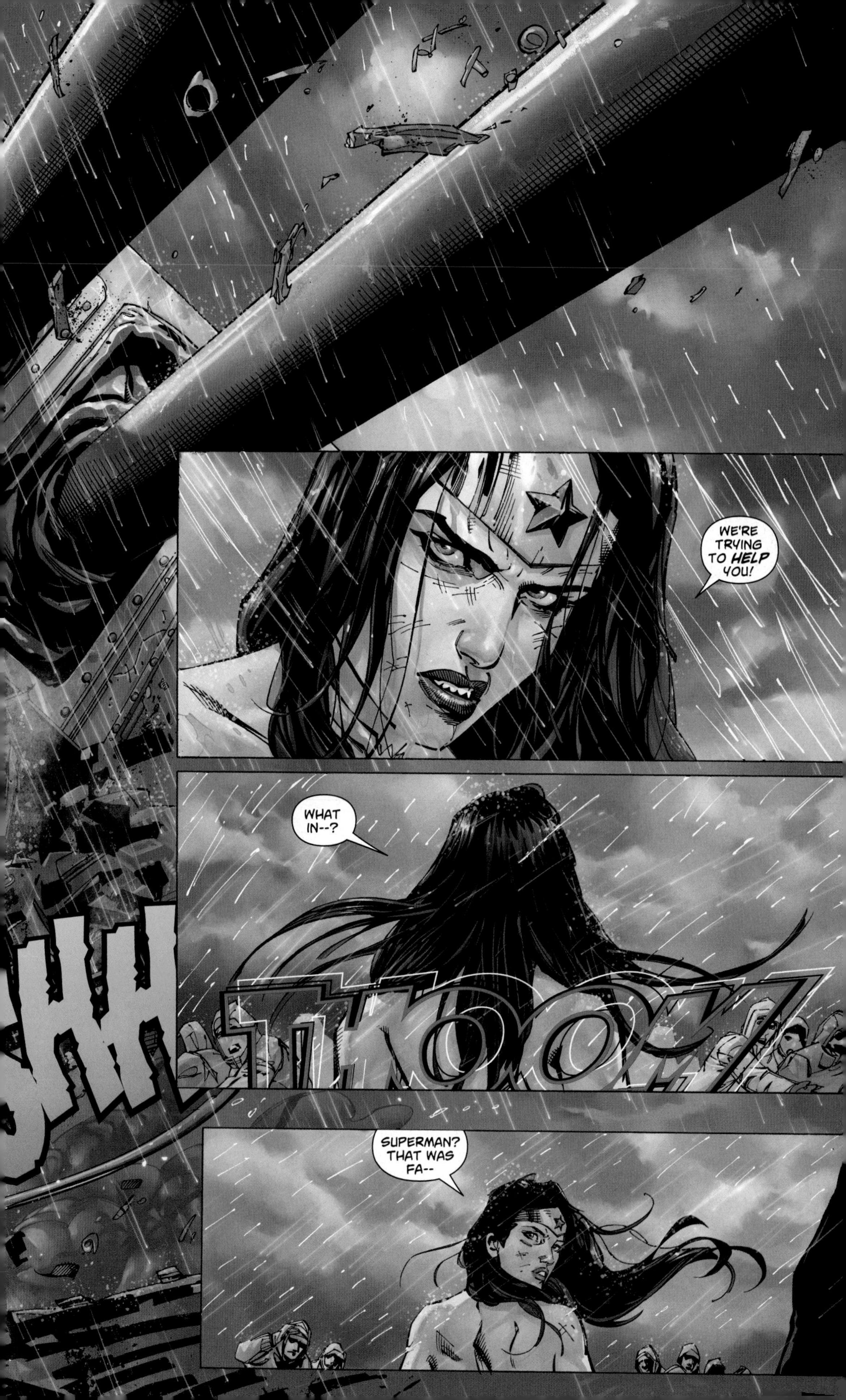
WE'RE TRYING TO HELP YOU!
WHAT IN--?
THOOM
SUPERMAN? THAT WAS FA--

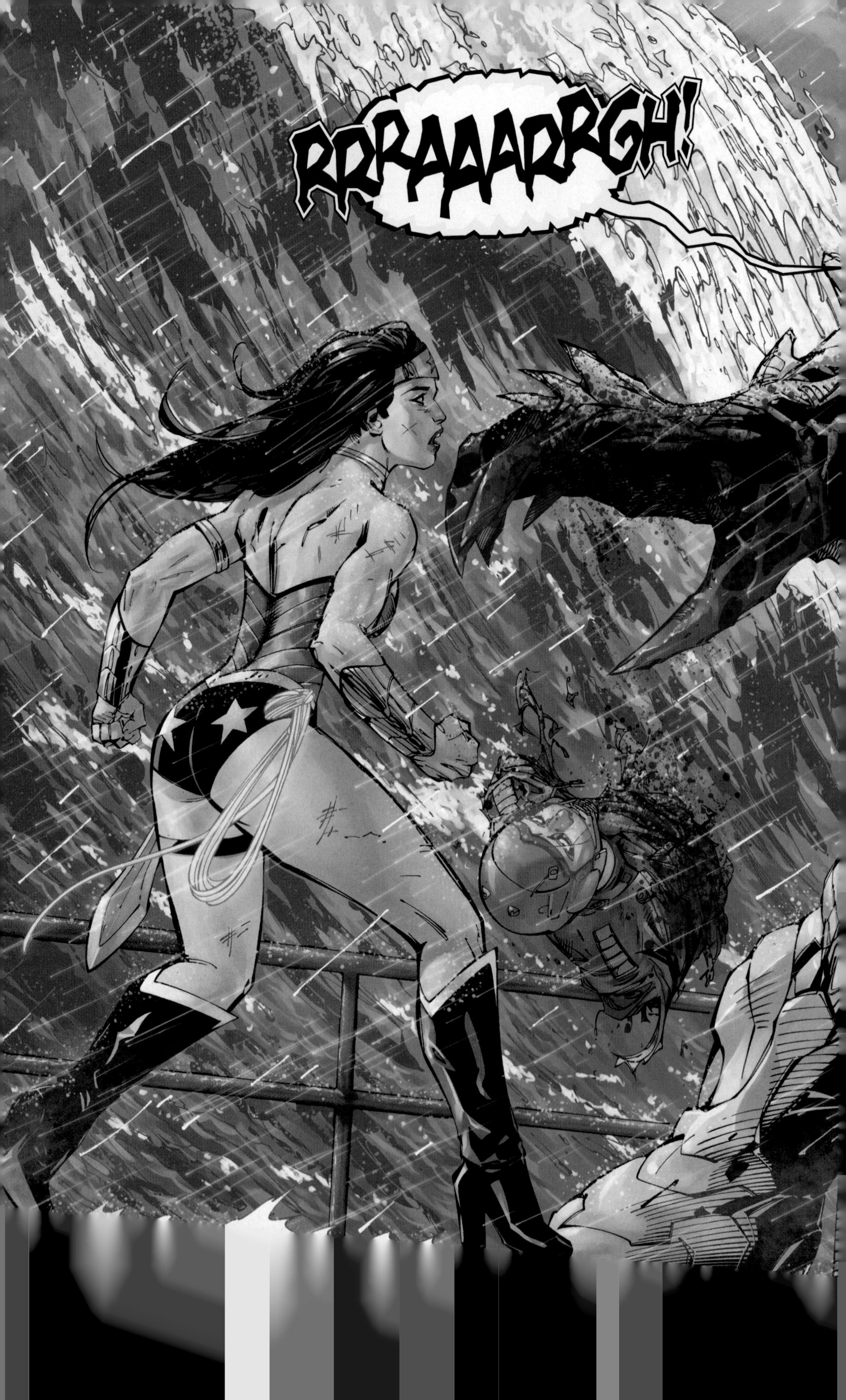
RRRAAAARRGH!

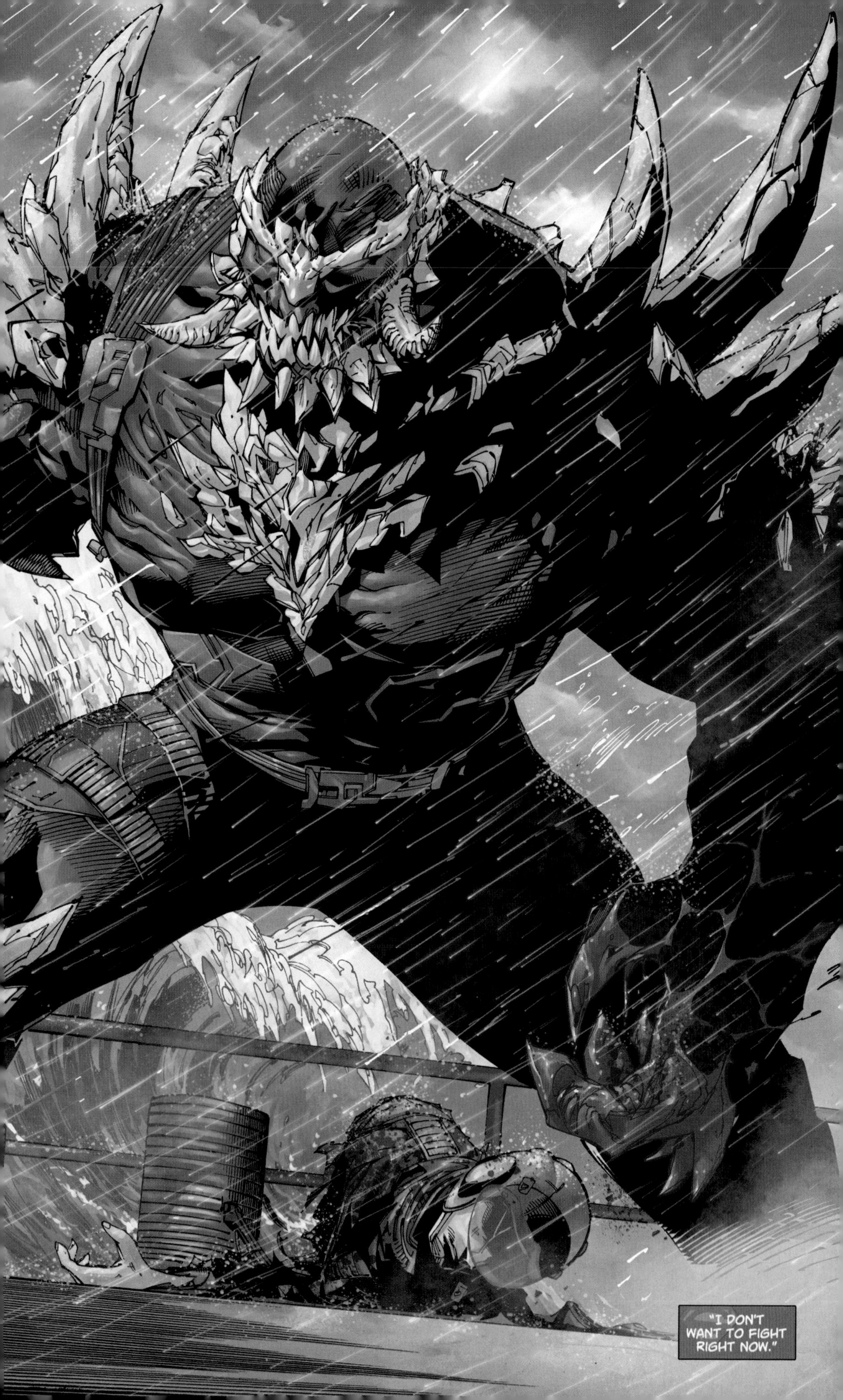
"I DON'T
WANT TO FIGHT
RIGHT NOW."

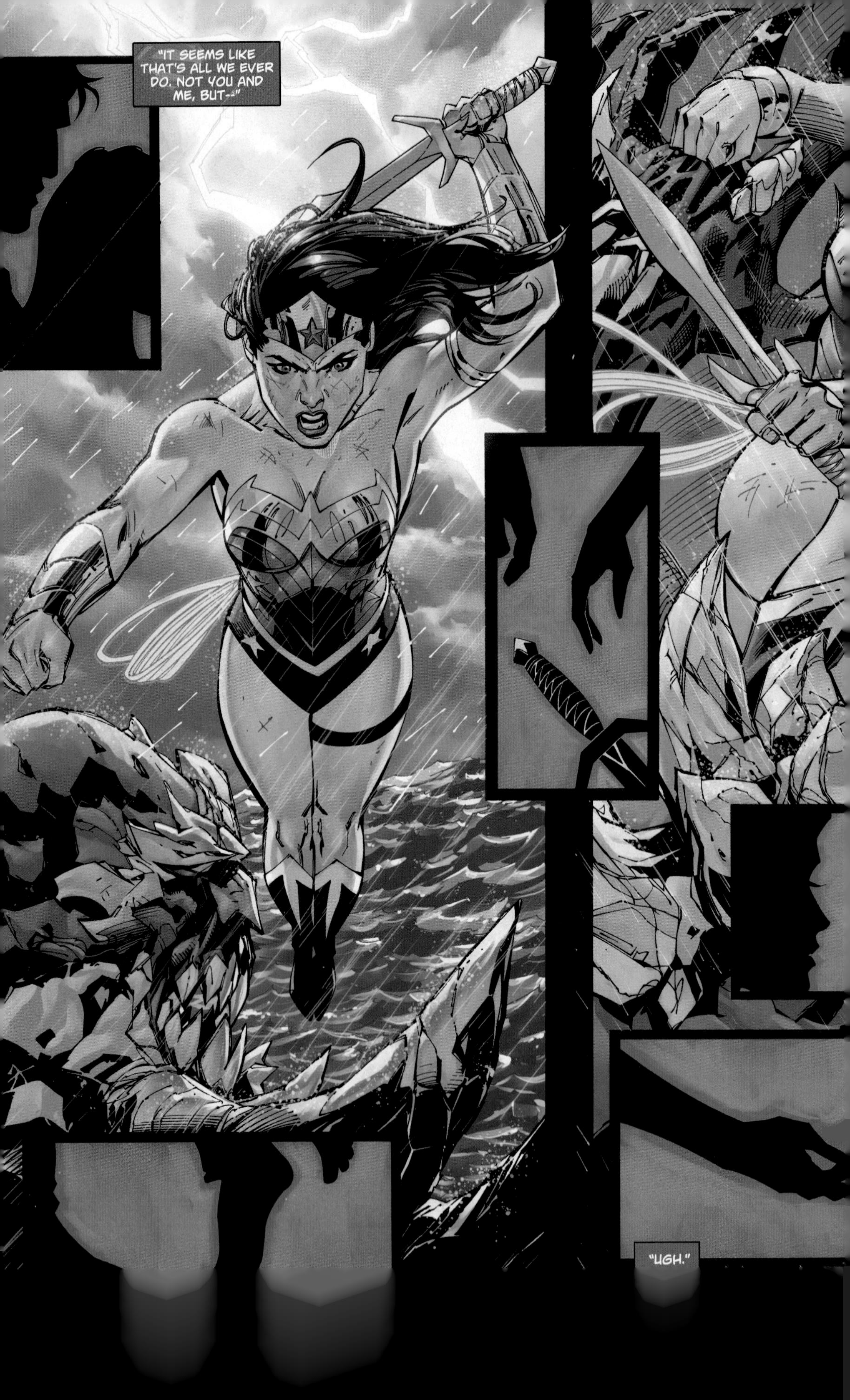
"IT SEEMS LIKE THAT'S ALL WE EVER DO. NOT YOU AND ME, BUT--"
"UGH."

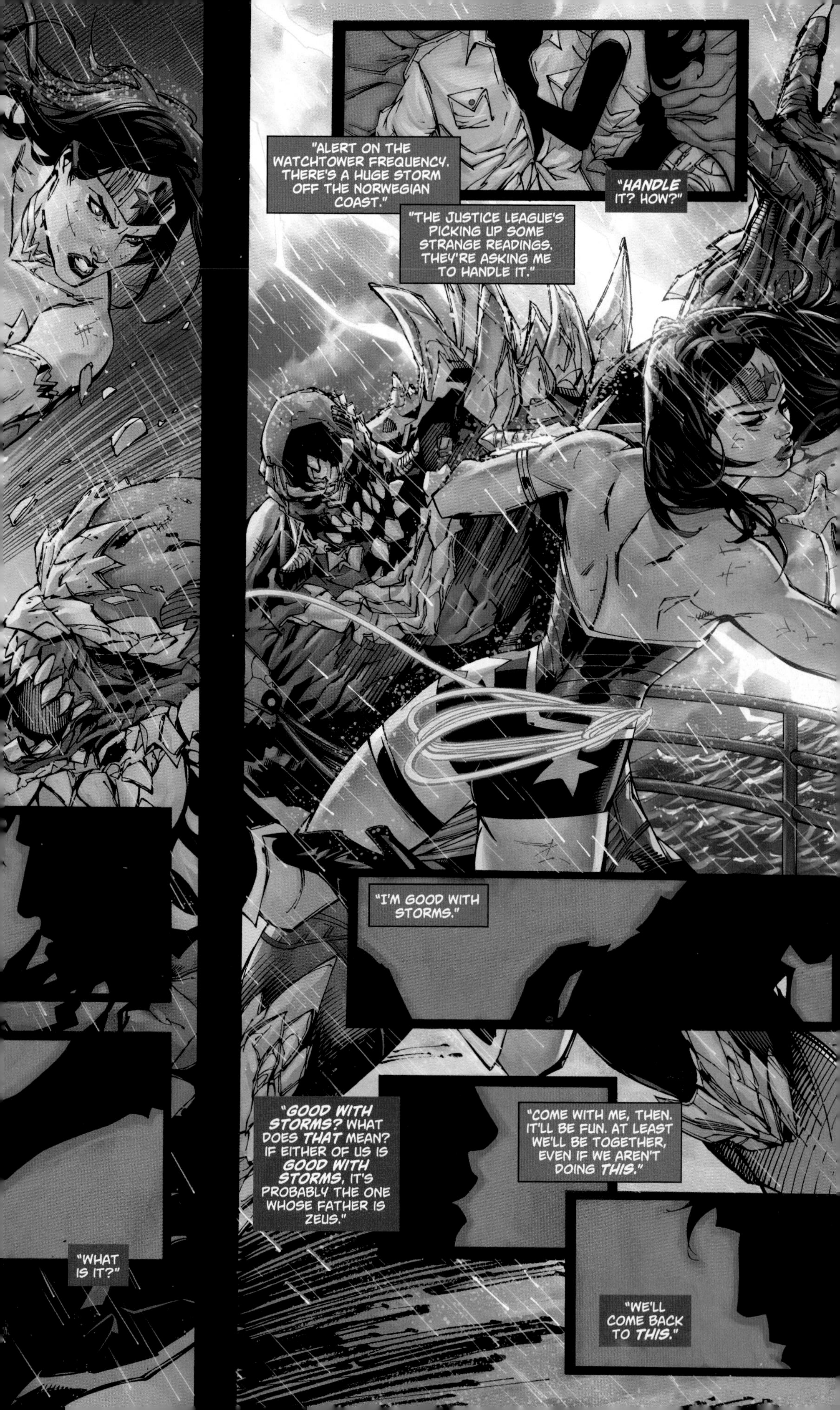

"ALERT ON THE WATCHTOWER FREQUENCY. THERE'S A HUGE STORM OFF THE NORWEGIAN COAST."
"THE JUSTICE LEAGUE'S PICKING UP SOME STRANGE READINGS. THEY'RE ASKING ME TO HANDLE IT."
"HANDLE IT? HOW?"
"I'M GOOD WITH STORMS."
"WHAT IS IT?"
"GOOD WITH STORMS? WHAT DOES THAT MEAN? IF EITHER OF US IS GOOD WITH STORMS, IT'S PROBABLY THE ONE WHOSE FATHER IS ZEUS."
"COME WITH ME, THEN. IT'LL BE FUN. AT LEAST WE'LL BE TOGETHER, EVEN IF WE AREN'T DOING THIS."
"WE'LL COME BACK TO THIS."

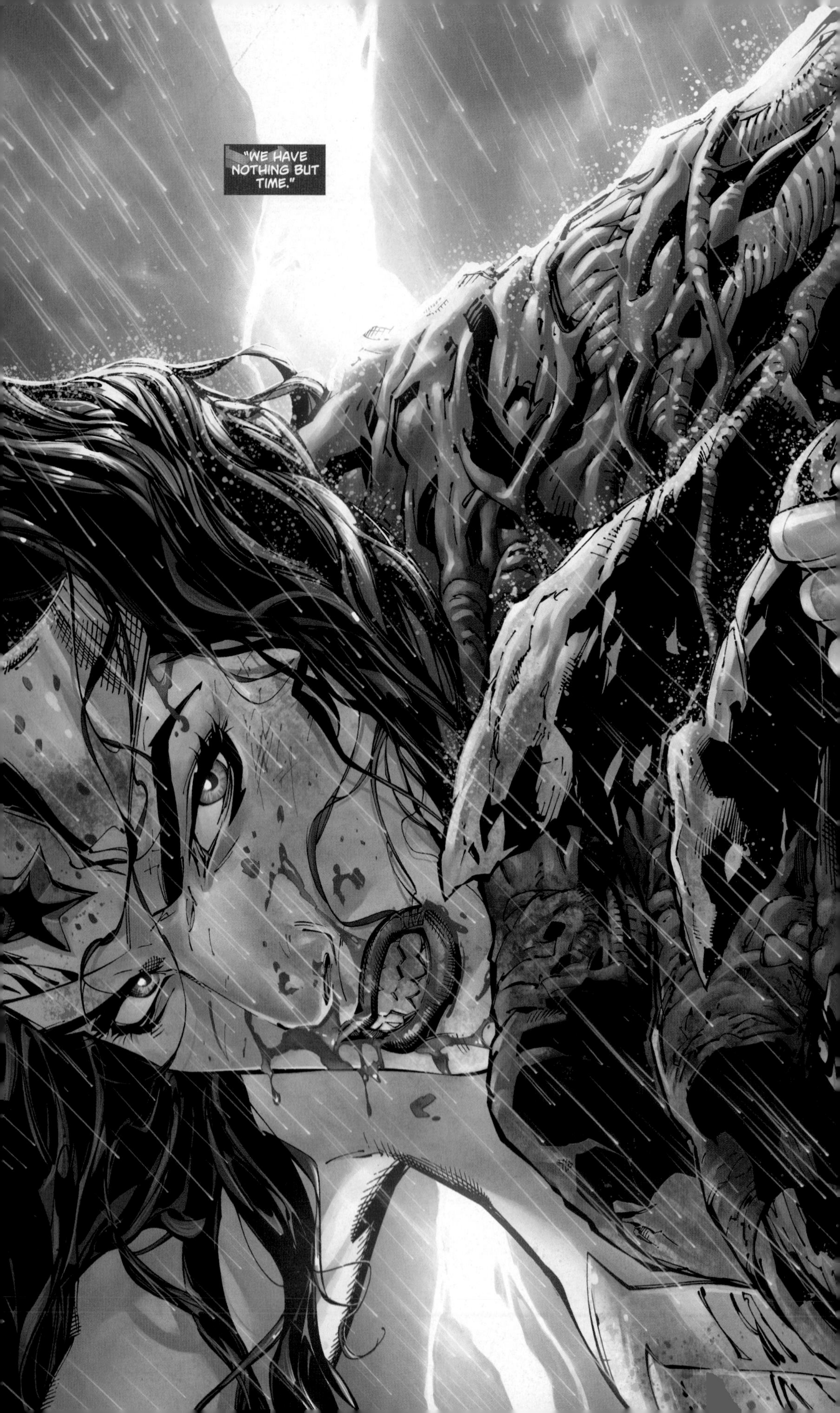
"WE HAVE NOTHING BUT TIME."

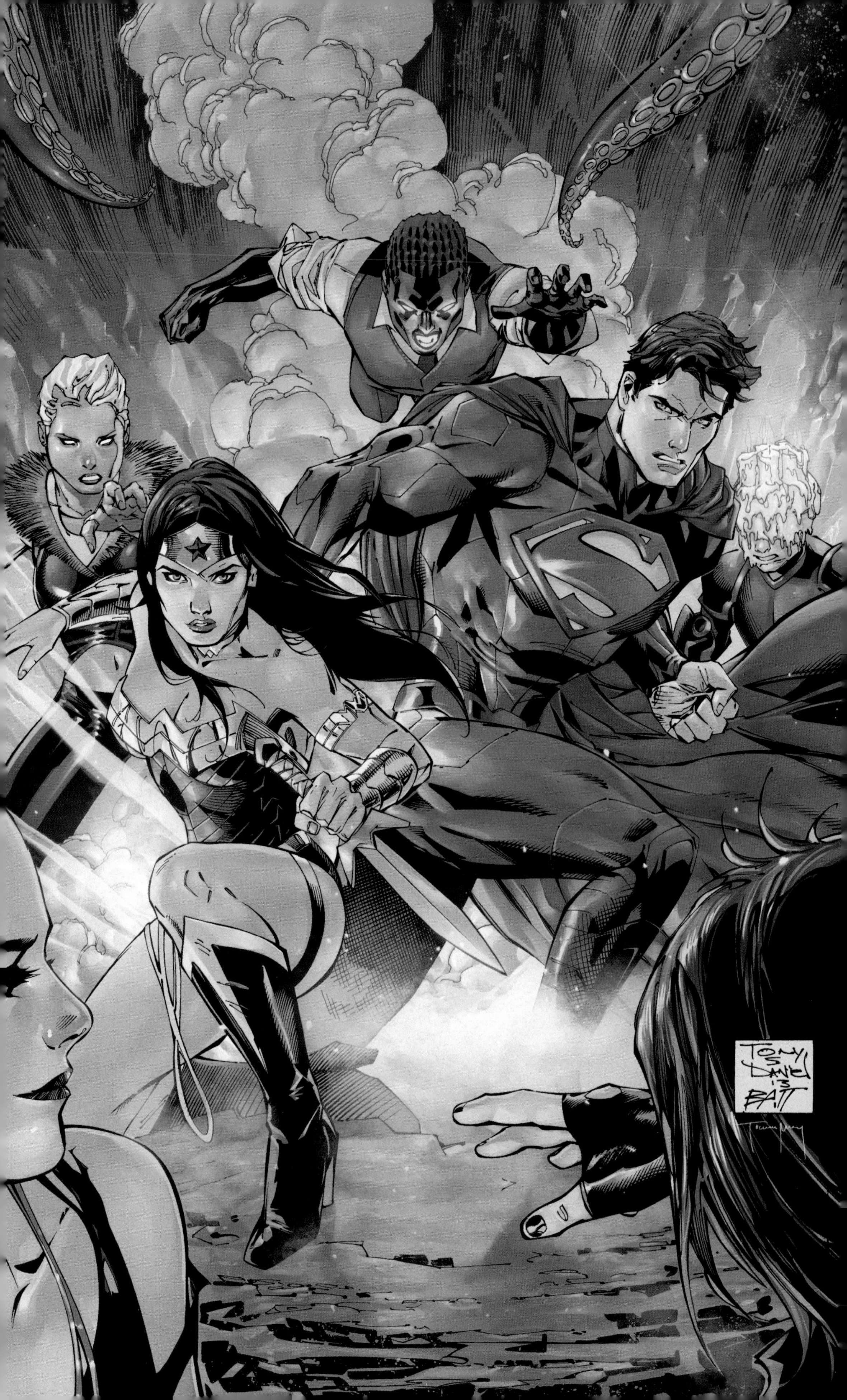
TONY S DANIEL '13 BATT

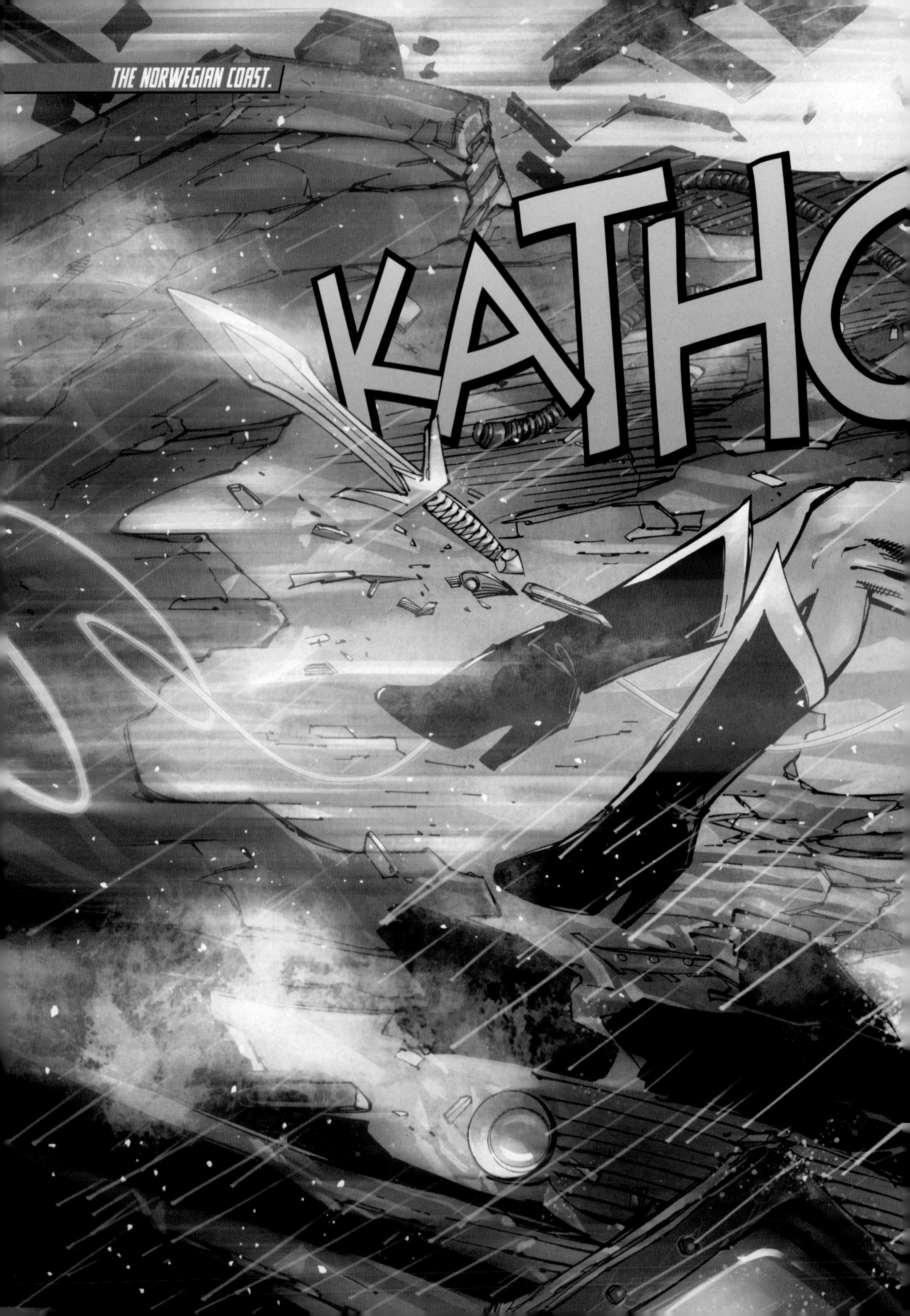
THE NORWEGIAN COAST.
KATHO

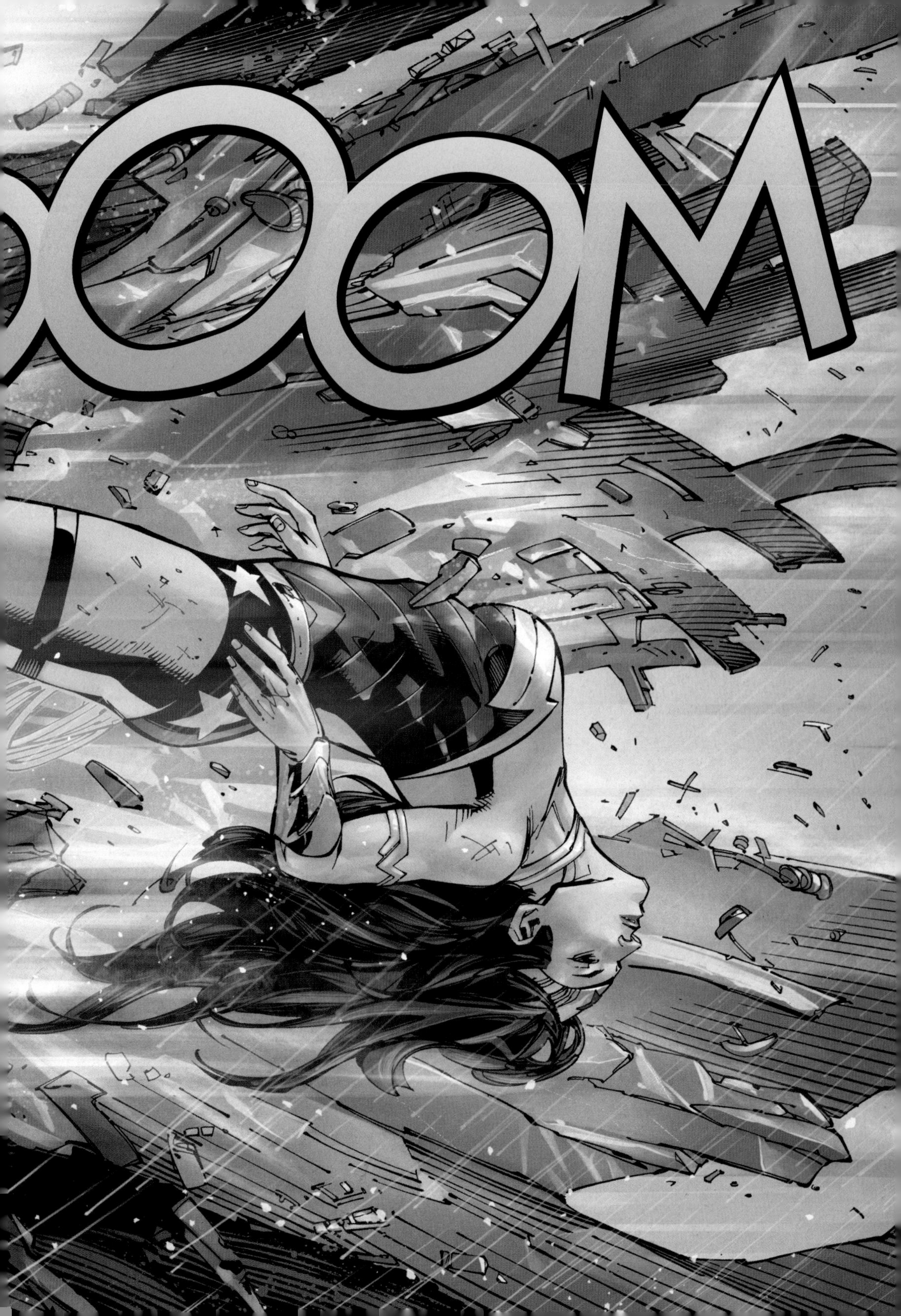
OOM

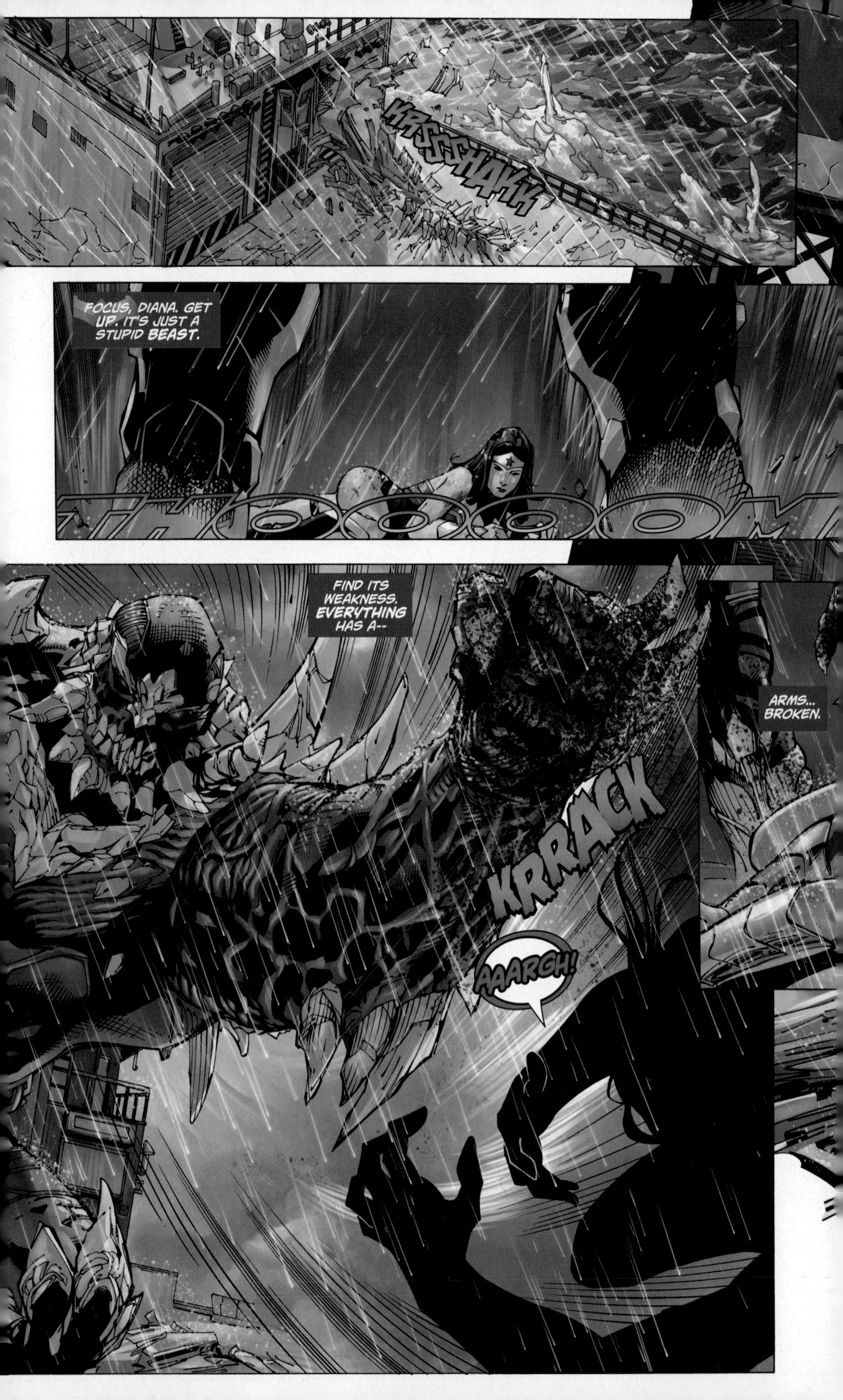
KRSSCHAKK
FOCUS, DIANA. GET UP. IT'S JUST A STUPID BEAST.
THOOOOOOM
FIND ITS WEAKNESS. EVERYTHING HAS A--
KRRACK
AAARGH!
ARMS... BROKEN.

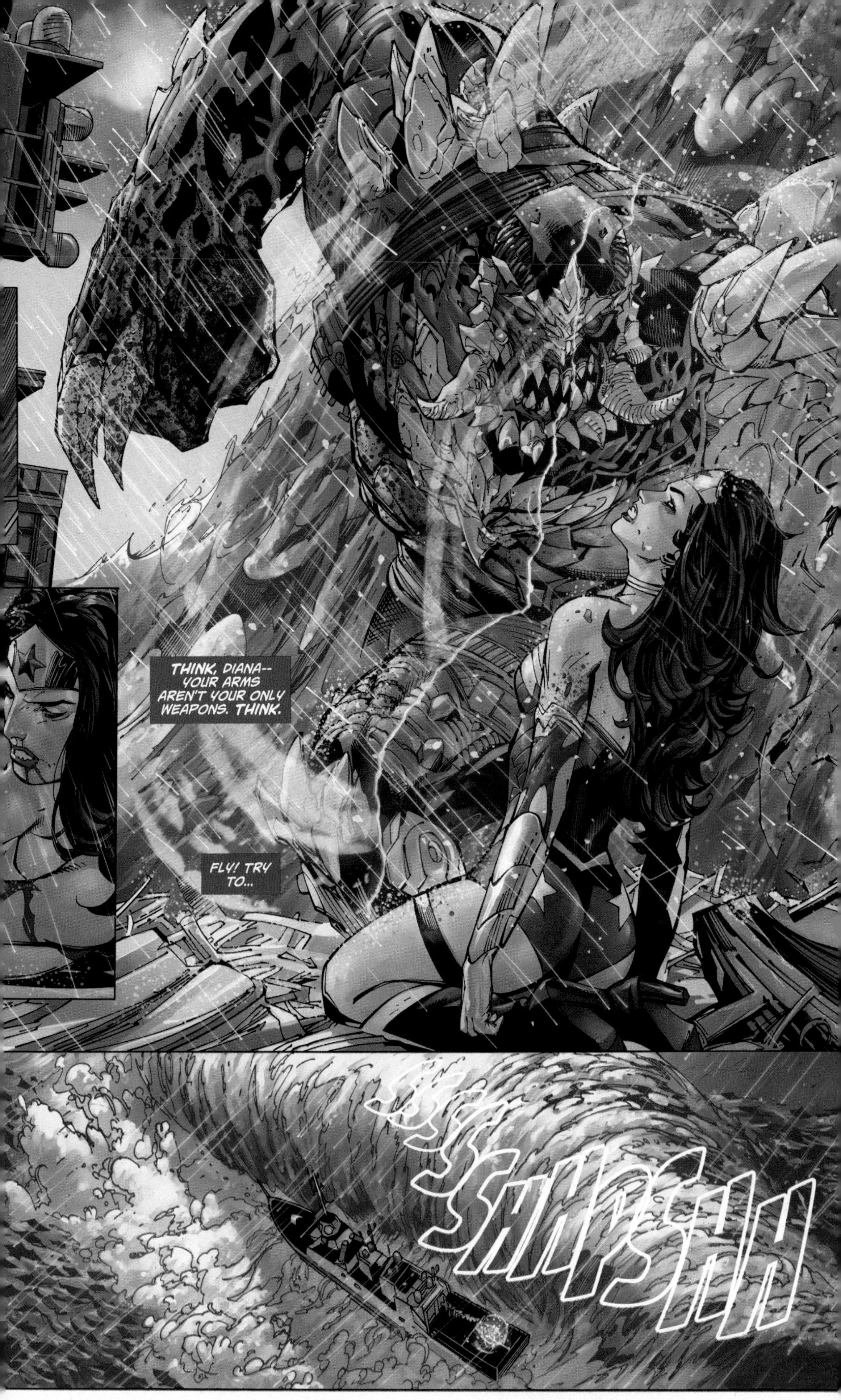
THINK, DIANA--
YOUR ARMS
AREN'T YOUR ONLY
WEAPONS. THINK.
FLY! TRY
TO...
SHHSHH

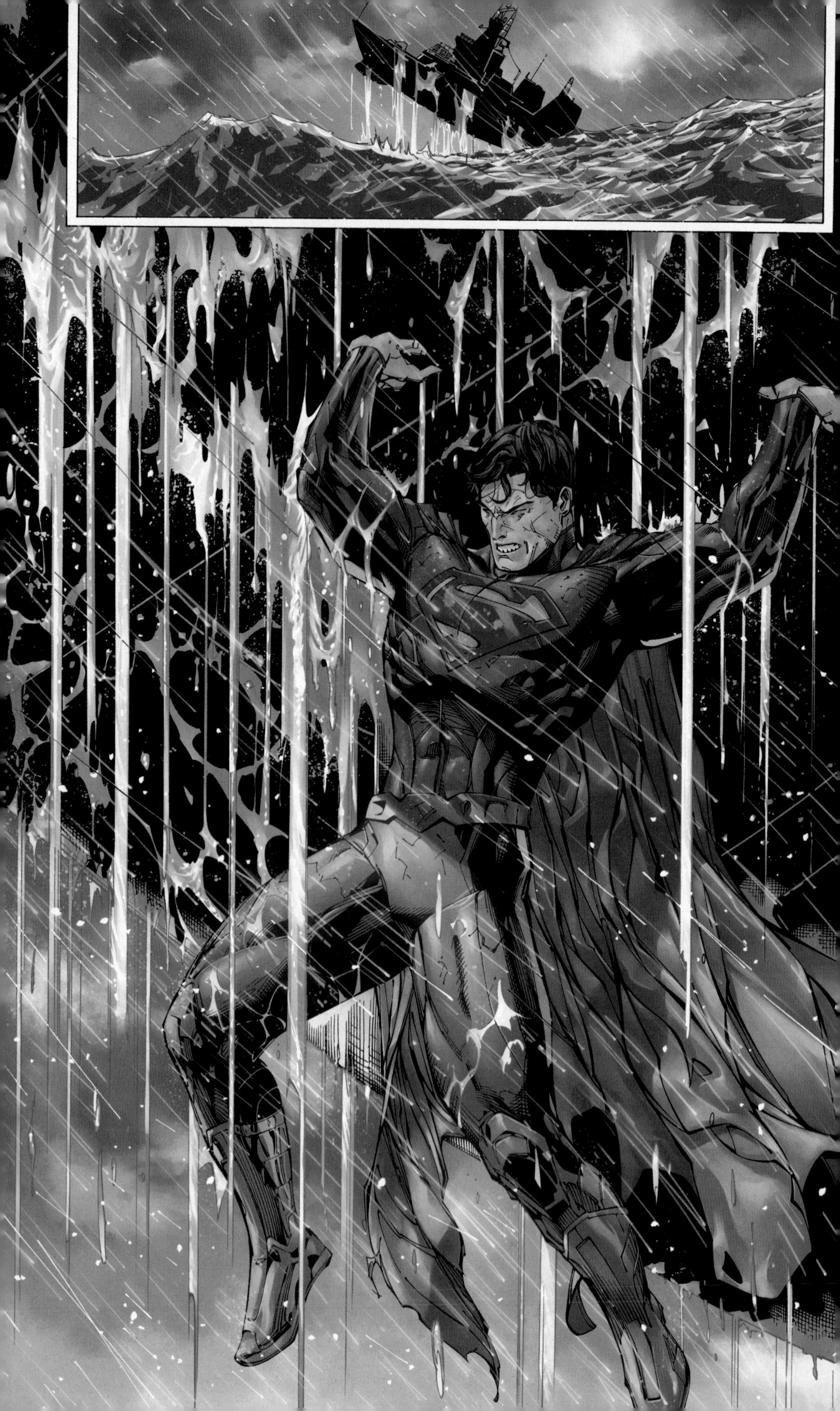

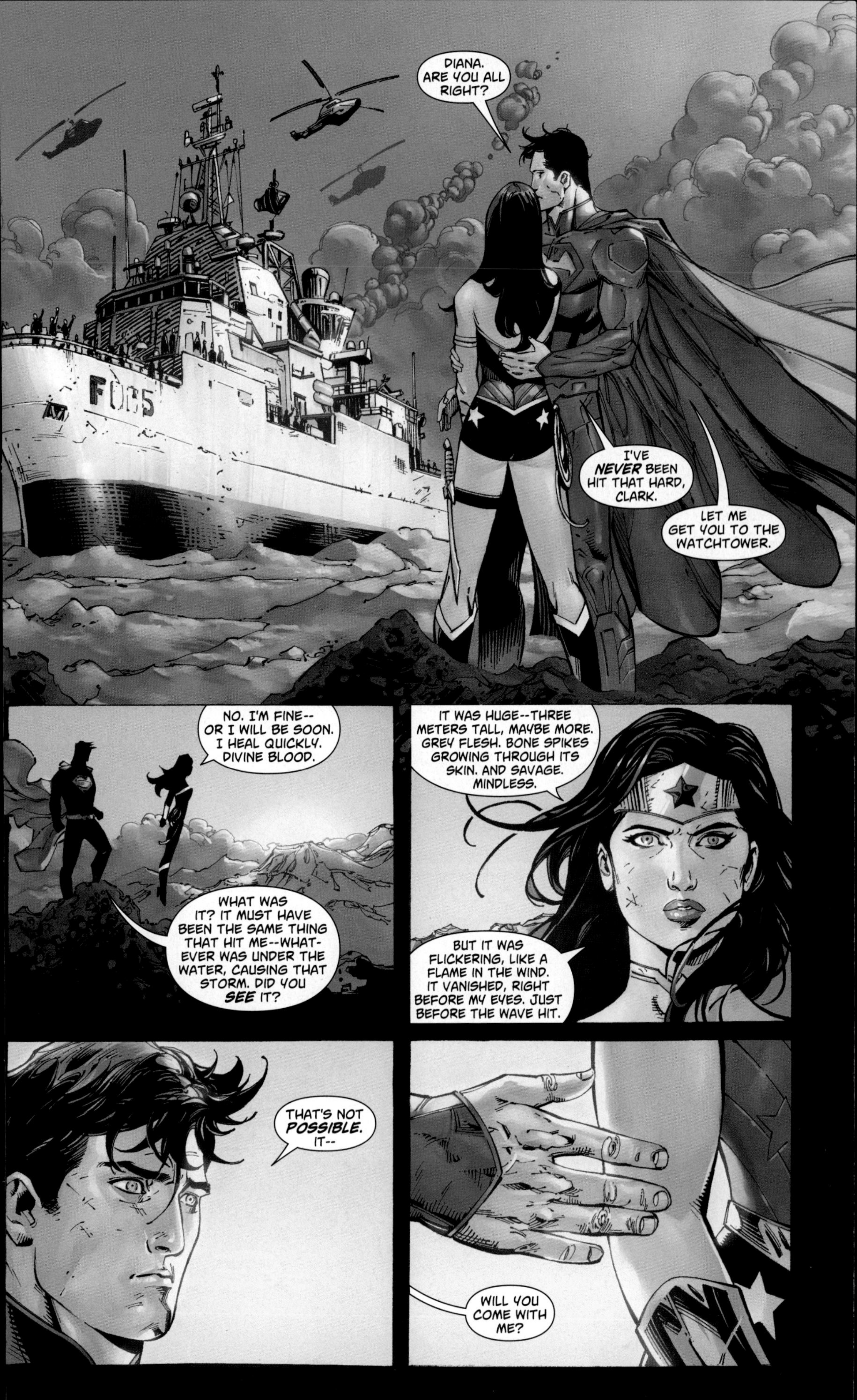

DIANA. ARE YOU ALL RIGHT?
I'VE NEVER BEEN HIT THAT HARD, CLARK.
LET ME GET YOU TO THE WATCHTOWER.
NO. I'M FINE-- OR I WILL BE SOON. I HEAL QUICKLY. DIVINE BLOOD.
WHAT WAS IT? IT MUST HAVE BEEN THE SAME THING THAT HIT ME--WHATEVER WAS UNDER THE WATER, CAUSING THAT STORM. DID YOU SEE IT?
IT WAS HUGE--THREE METERS TALL, MAYBE MORE. GREY FLESH. BONE SPIKES GROWING THROUGH ITS SKIN. AND SAVAGE. MINDLESS.
BUT IT WAS FLICKERING, LIKE A FLAME IN THE WIND. IT VANISHED, RIGHT BEFORE MY EYES. JUST BEFORE THE WAVE HIT.
THAT'S NOT POSSIBLE. IT--
WILL YOU COME WITH ME?

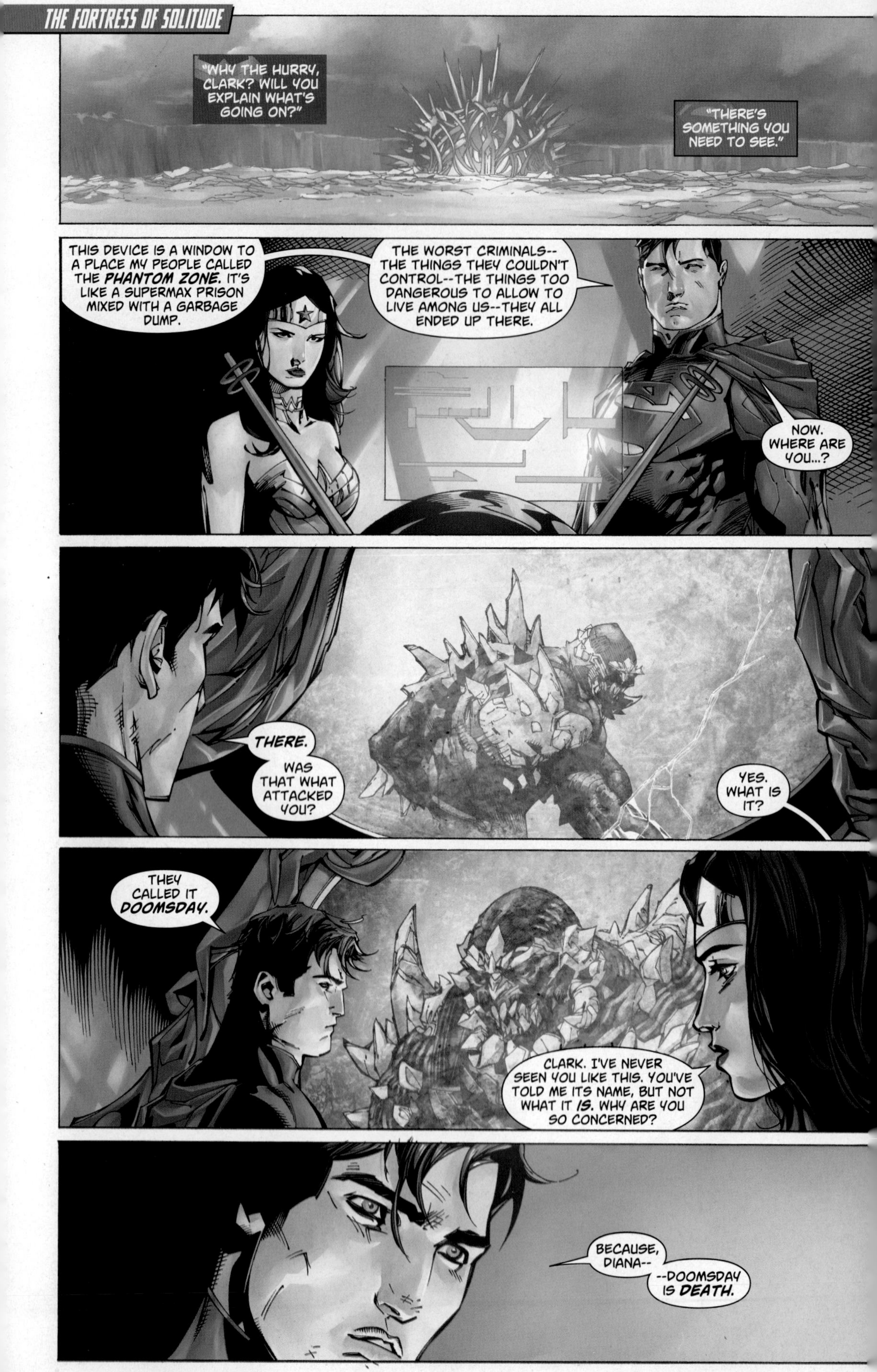
THE FORTRESS OF SOLITUDE
"WHY THE HURRY, CLARK? WILL YOU EXPLAIN WHAT'S GOING ON?"
"THERE'S SOMETHING YOU NEED TO SEE."
THIS DEVICE IS A WINDOW TO A PLACE MY PEOPLE CALLED THE PHANTOM ZONE. IT'S LIKE A SUPERMAX PRISON MIXED WITH A GARBAGE DUMP.
THE WORST CRIMINALS-- THE THINGS THEY COULDN'T CONTROL--THE THINGS TOO DANGEROUS TO ALLOW TO LIVE AMONG US--THEY ALL ENDED UP THERE.
NOW. WHERE ARE YOU...?
THERE.
WAS THAT WHAT ATTACKED YOU?
YES. WHAT IS IT?
THEY CALLED IT DOOMSDAY.
CLARK. I'VE NEVER SEEN YOU LIKE THIS. YOU'VE TOLD ME ITS NAME, BUT NOT WHAT IT IS. WHY ARE YOU SO CONCERNED?
BECAUSE, DIANA--
--DOOMSDAY IS DEATH.

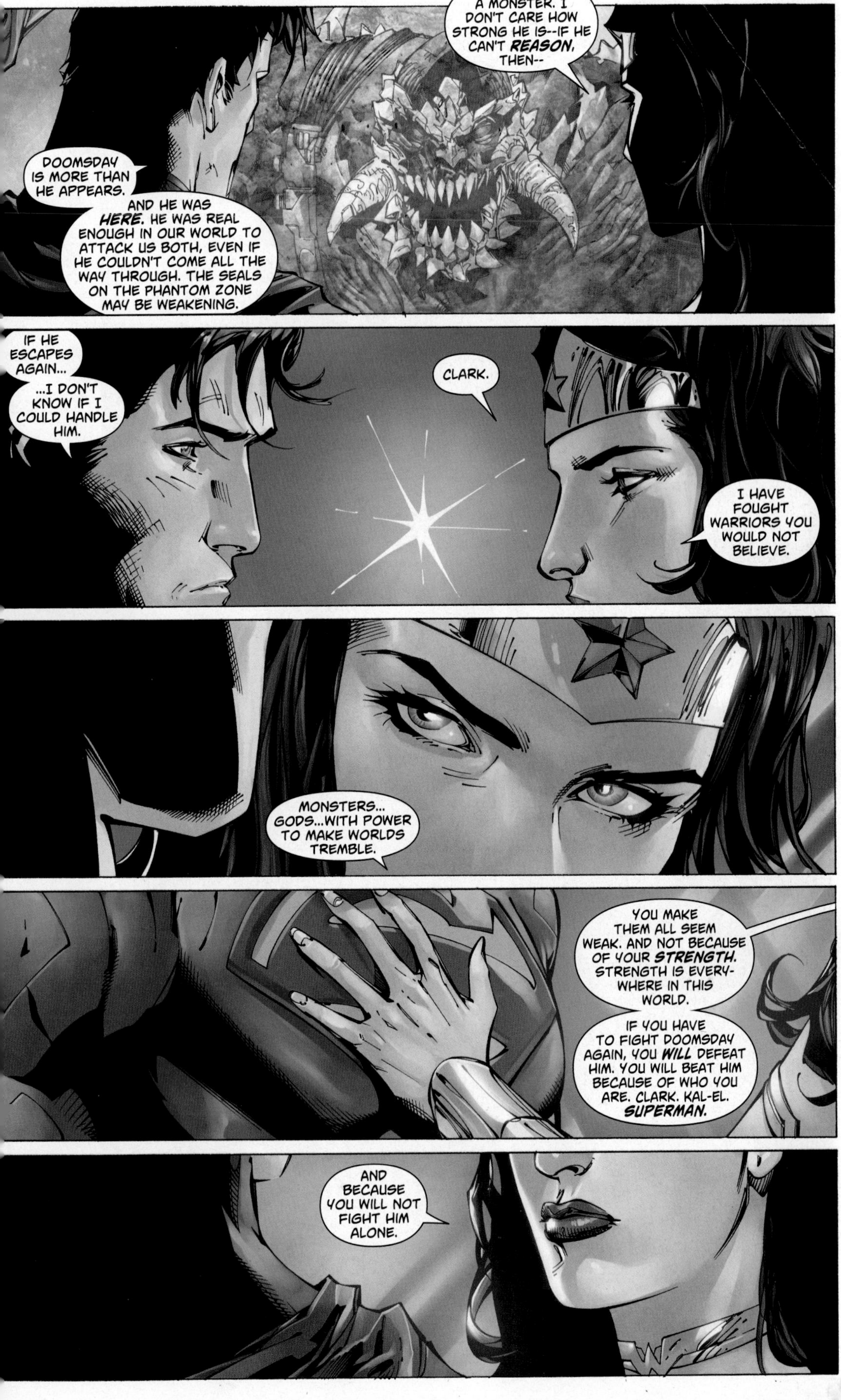
HE'S JUST A MONSTER. I DON'T CARE HOW STRONG HE IS--IF HE CAN'T **REASON**, THEN--
DOOMSDAY IS MORE THAN HE APPEARS.
AND HE WAS **HERE**. HE WAS REAL ENOUGH IN OUR WORLD TO ATTACK US BOTH, EVEN IF HE COULDN'T COME ALL THE WAY THROUGH. THE SEALS ON THE PHANTOM ZONE MAY BE WEAKENING.
IF HE ESCAPES AGAIN...
...I DON'T KNOW IF I COULD HANDLE HIM.
CLARK.
I HAVE FOUGHT WARRIORS YOU WOULD NOT BELIEVE.
MONSTERS... GODS...WITH POWER TO MAKE WORLDS TREMBLE.
YOU MAKE THEM ALL SEEM WEAK. AND NOT BECAUSE OF YOUR **STRENGTH**. STRENGTH IS EVERY-WHERE IN THIS WORLD.
IF YOU HAVE TO FIGHT DOOMSDAY AGAIN, YOU **WILL** DEFEAT HIM. YOU WILL BEAT HIM BECAUSE OF WHO YOU ARE. CLARK. KAL-EL. **SUPERMAN**.
AND BECAUSE YOU WILL NOT FIGHT HIM ALONE.

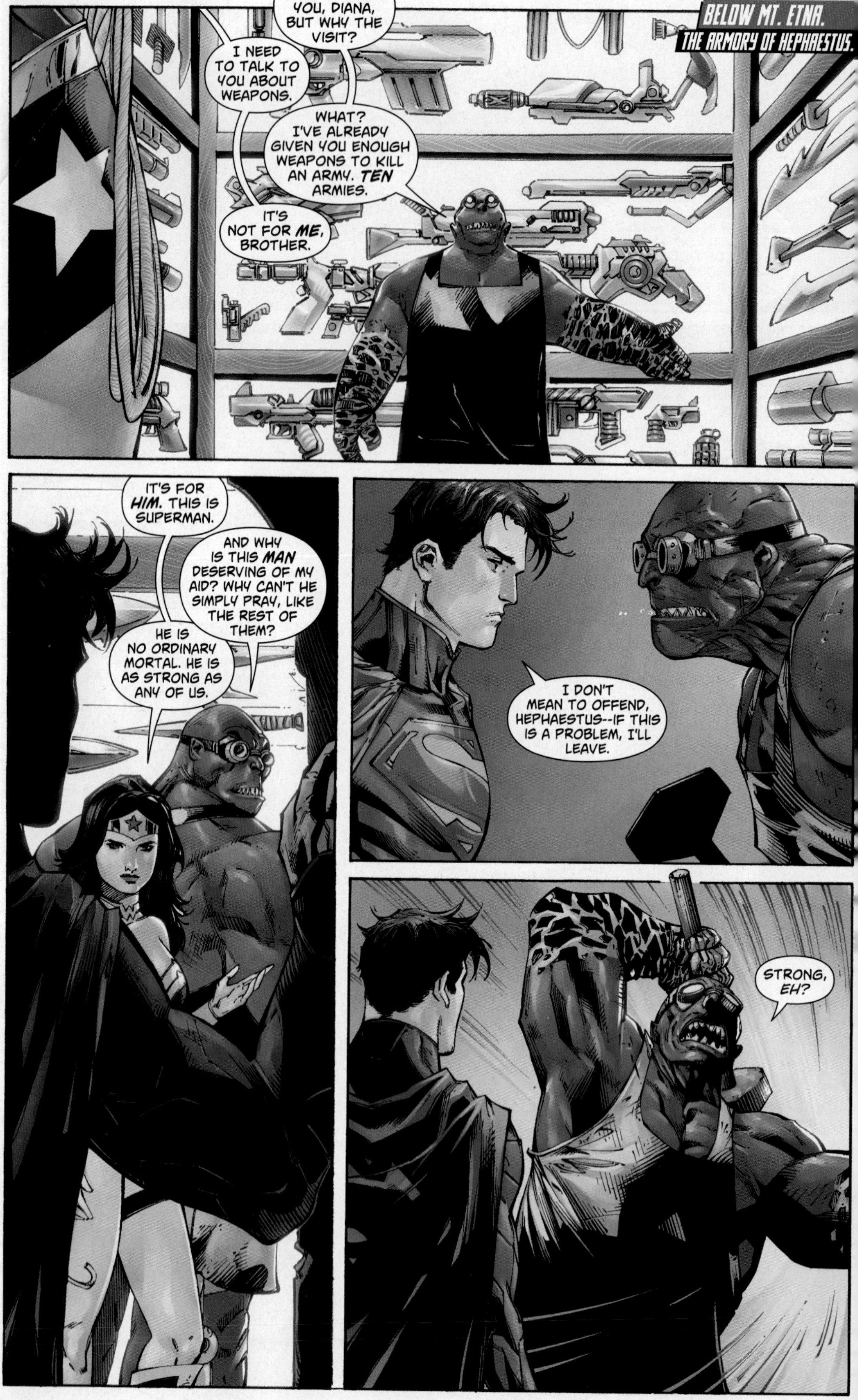
BELOW MT. ETNA.
THE ARMORY OF HEPHAESTUS.
ALWAYS GOOD TO SEE YOU, DIANA, BUT WHY THE VISIT?
I NEED TO TALK TO YOU ABOUT WEAPONS.
WHAT? I'VE ALREADY GIVEN YOU ENOUGH WEAPONS TO KILL AN ARMY. TEN ARMIES.
IT'S NOT FOR ME, BROTHER.
IT'S FOR HIM. THIS IS SUPERMAN.
AND WHY IS THIS MAN DESERVING OF MY AID? WHY CAN'T HE SIMPLY PRAY, LIKE THE REST OF THEM?
HE IS NO ORDINARY MORTAL. HE IS AS STRONG AS ANY OF US.
I DON'T MEAN TO OFFEND, HEPHAESTUS--IF THIS IS A PROBLEM, I'LL LEAVE.
STRONG, EH?

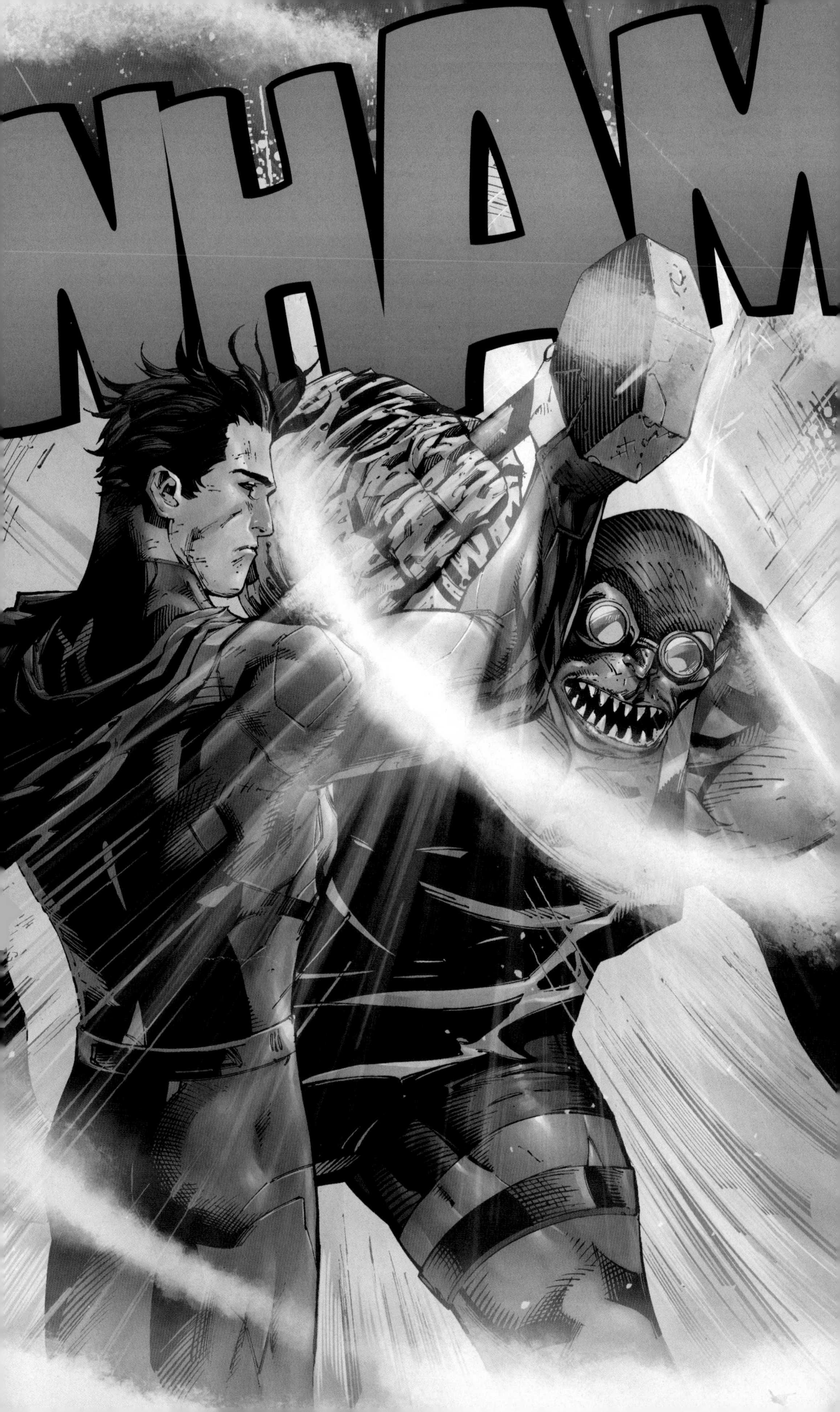
WHAM

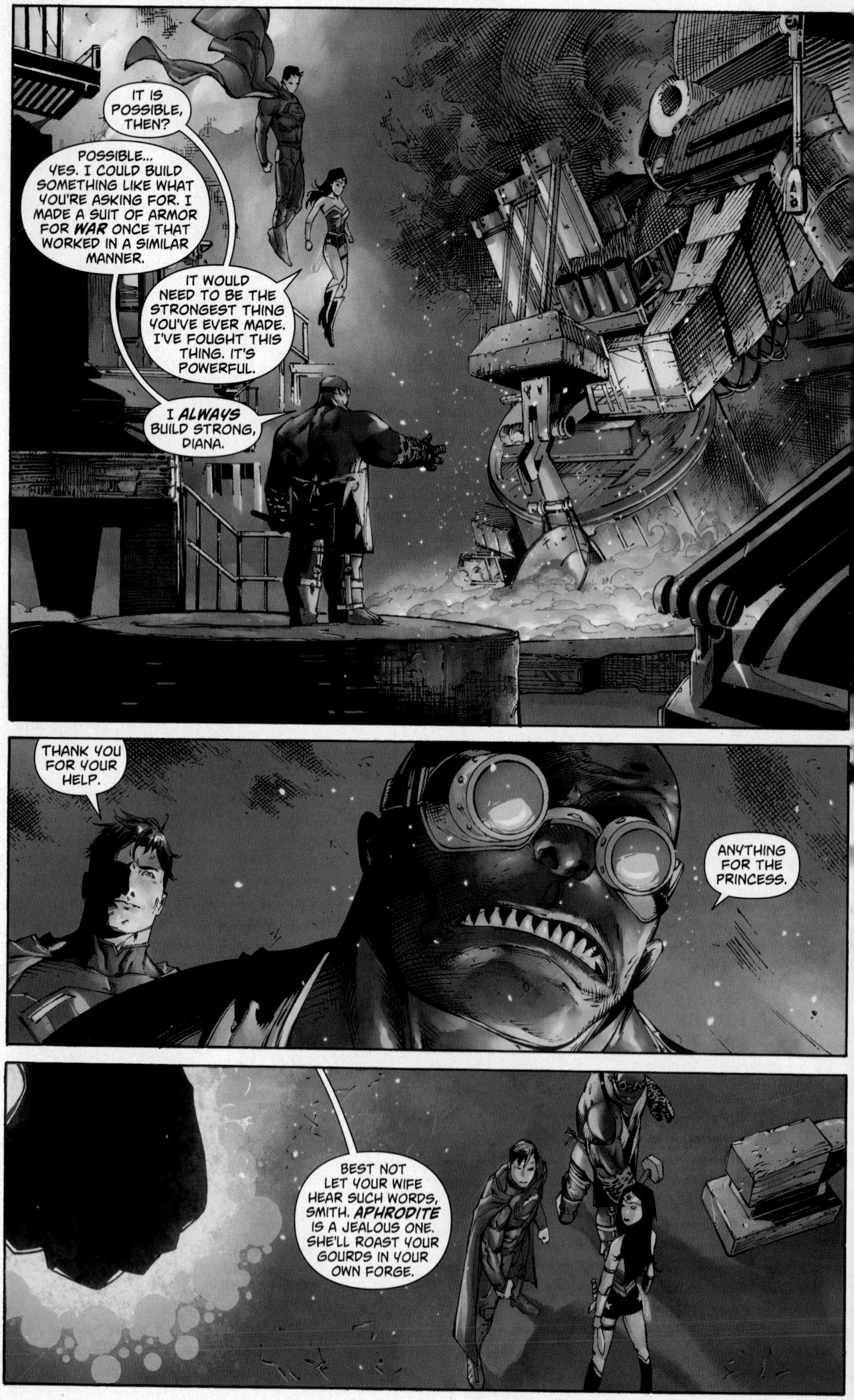
IT IS POSSIBLE, THEN?
POSSIBLE... YES. I COULD BUILD SOMETHING LIKE WHAT YOU'RE ASKING FOR. I MADE A SUIT OF ARMOR FOR WAR ONCE THAT WORKED IN A SIMILAR MANNER.
IT WOULD NEED TO BE THE STRONGEST THING YOU'VE EVER MADE. I'VE FOUGHT THIS THING. IT'S POWERFUL.
I ALWAYS BUILD STRONG, DIANA.
THANK YOU FOR YOUR HELP.
ANYTHING FOR THE PRINCESS.
BEST NOT LET YOUR WIFE HEAR SUCH WORDS, SMITH. APHRODITE IS A JEALOUS ONE. SHE'LL ROAST YOUR GOURDS IN YOUR OWN FORGE.

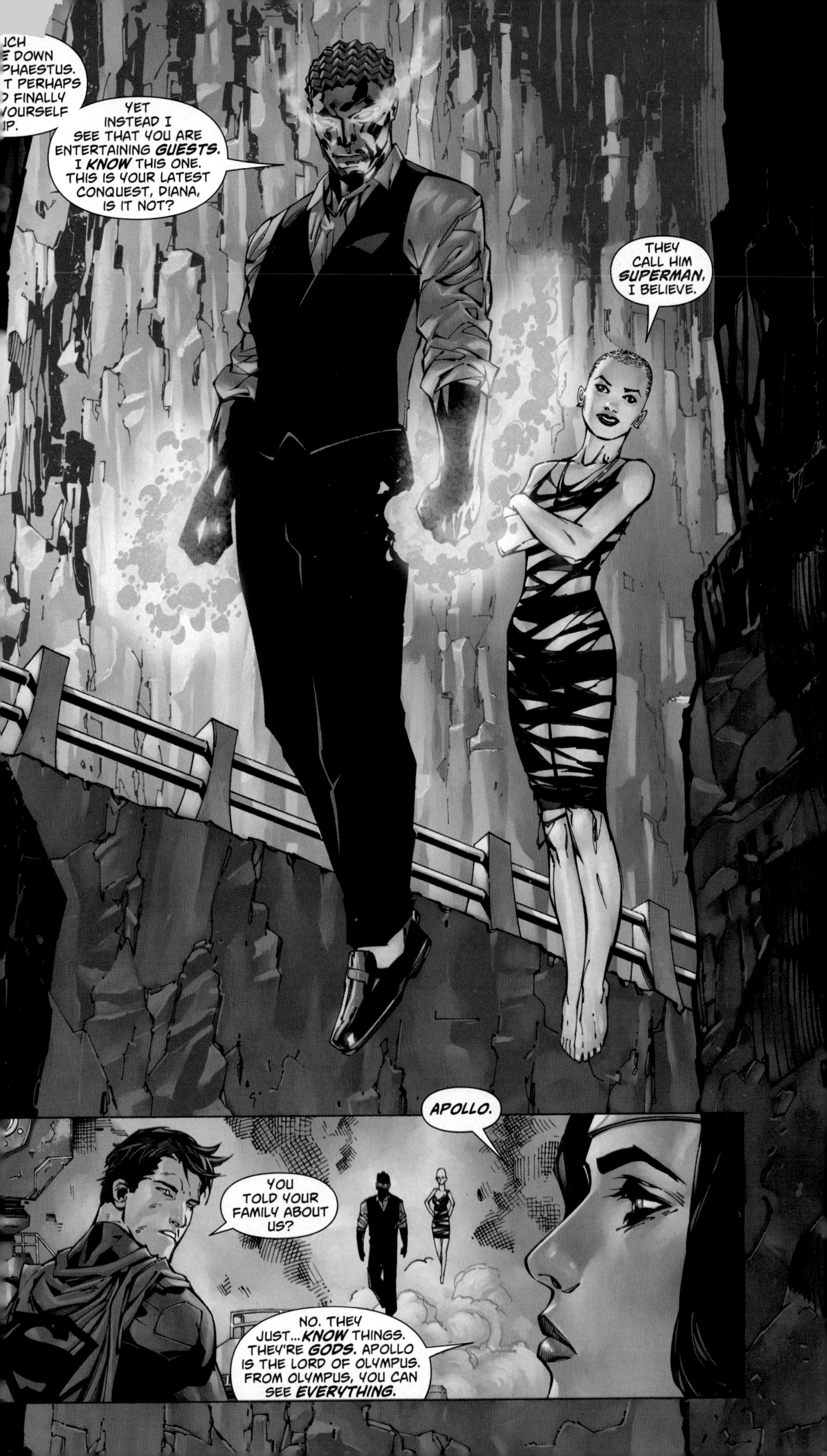

YET INSTEAD I SEE THAT YOU ARE ENTERTAINING GUESTS. I KNOW THIS ONE. THIS IS YOUR LATEST CONQUEST, DIANA, IS IT NOT?
THEY CALL HIM SUPERMAN, I BELIEVE.
APOLLO.
YOU TOLD YOUR FAMILY ABOUT US?
NO. THEY JUST...KNOW THINGS. THEY'RE GODS. APOLLO IS THE LORD OF OLYMPUS. FROM OLYMPUS, YOU CAN SEE EVERYTHING.

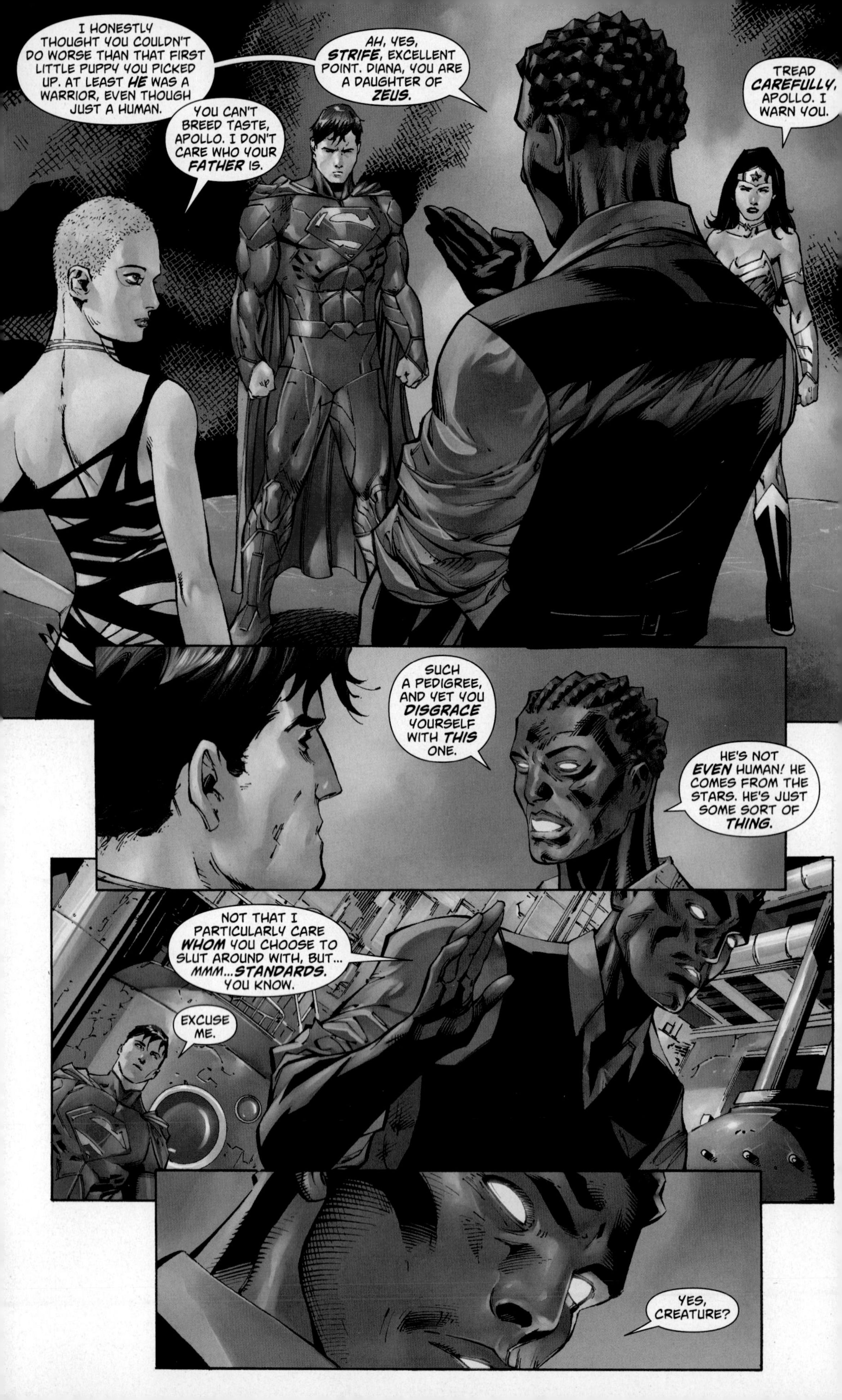
I HONESTLY THOUGHT YOU COULDN'T DO WORSE THAN THAT FIRST LITTLE PUPPY YOU PICKED UP. AT LEAST HE WAS A WARRIOR, EVEN THOUGH JUST A HUMAN.
AH, YES, STRIFE, EXCELLENT POINT. DIANA, YOU ARE A DAUGHTER OF ZEUS.
TREAD CAREFULLY, APOLLO. I WARN YOU.
YOU CAN'T BREED TASTE, APOLLO. I DON'T CARE WHO YOUR FATHER IS.
SUCH A PEDIGREE, AND YET YOU DISGRACE YOURSELF WITH THIS ONE.
HE'S NOT EVEN HUMAN! HE COMES FROM THE STARS. HE'S JUST SOME SORT OF THING.
NOT THAT I PARTICULARLY CARE WHOM YOU CHOOSE TO SLUT AROUND WITH, BUT... MMM...STANDARDS. YOU KNOW.
EXCUSE ME.
YES, CREATURE?

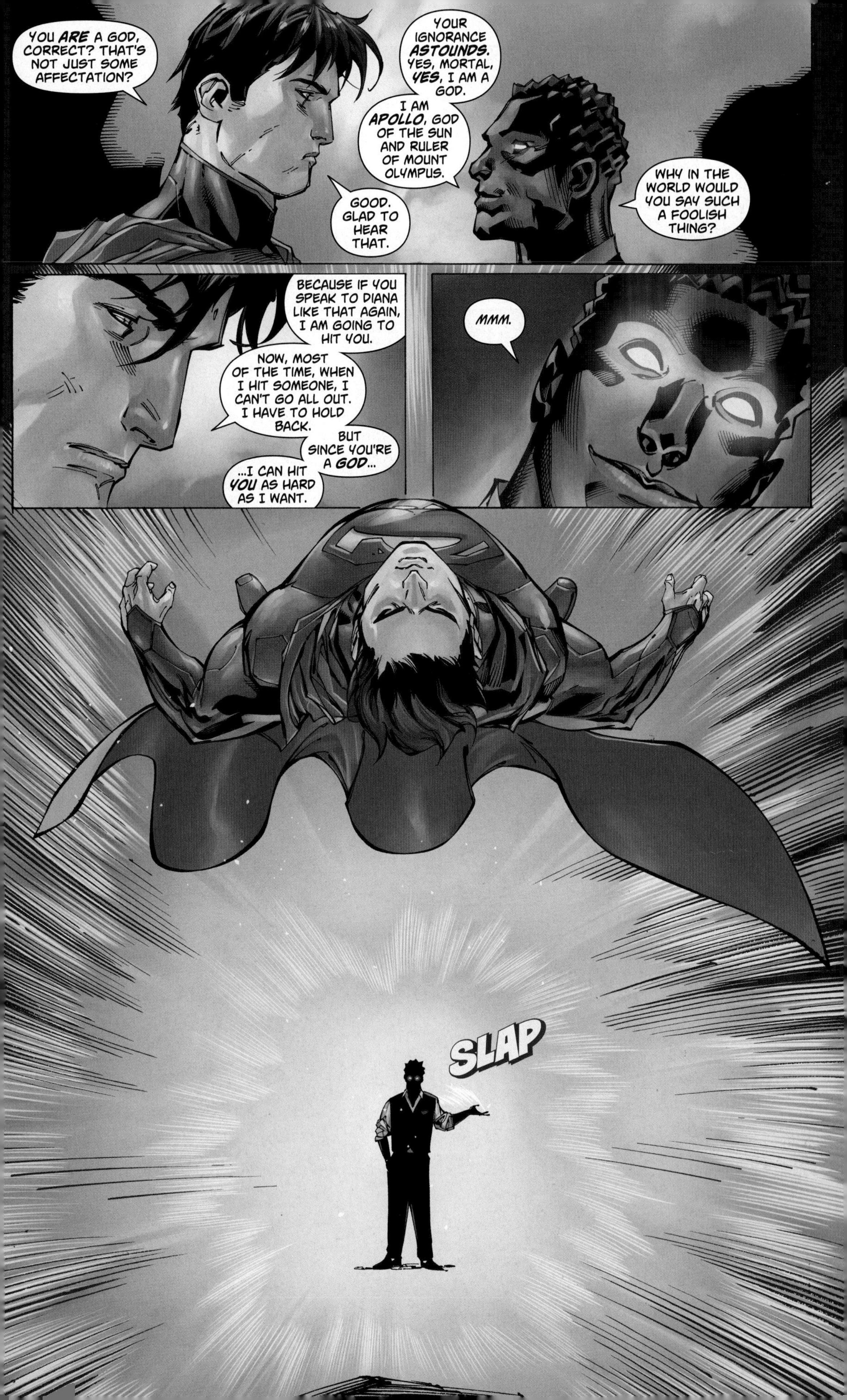
YOU ARE A GOD, CORRECT? THAT'S NOT JUST SOME AFFECTATION?
YOUR IGNORANCE ASTOUNDS. YES, MORTAL, YES, I AM A GOD.
I AM APOLLO, GOD OF THE SUN AND RULER OF MOUNT OLYMPUS.
GOOD. GLAD TO HEAR THAT.
WHY IN THE WORLD WOULD YOU SAY SUCH A FOOLISH THING?
BECAUSE IF YOU SPEAK TO DIANA LIKE THAT AGAIN, I AM GOING TO HIT YOU.
NOW, MOST OF THE TIME, WHEN I HIT SOMEONE, I CAN'T GO ALL OUT. I HAVE TO HOLD BACK.
BUT SINCE YOU'RE A GOD...
...I CAN HIT YOU AS HARD AS I WANT.
MMM.
SLAP

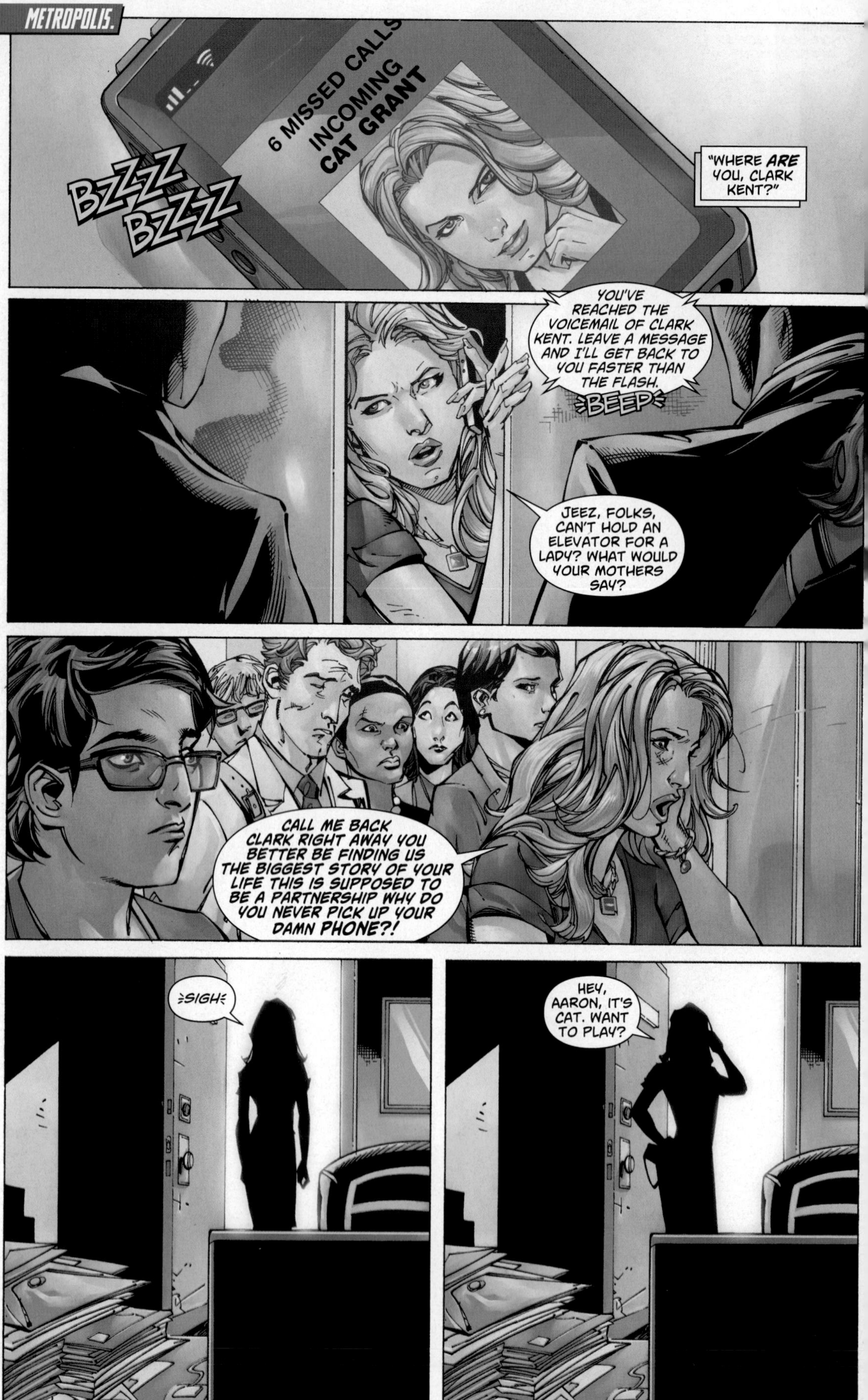

METROPOLIS.
6 MISSED CALLS
INCOMING
CAT GRANT
BZZZZ BZZZZ
"WHERE ARE YOU, CLARK KENT?"
YOU'VE REACHED THE VOICEMAIL OF CLARK KENT. LEAVE A MESSAGE AND I'LL GET BACK TO YOU FASTER THAN THE FLASH.
BEEP
JEEZ, FOLKS, CAN'T HOLD AN ELEVATOR FOR A LADY? WHAT WOULD YOUR MOTHERS SAY?
CALL ME BACK CLARK RIGHT AWAY YOU BETTER BE FINDING US THE BIGGEST STORY OF YOUR LIFE THIS IS SUPPOSED TO BE A PARTNERSHIP WHY DO YOU NEVER PICK UP YOUR DAMN PHONE?!
SIGH
HEY, AARON, IT'S CAT. WANT TO PLAY?

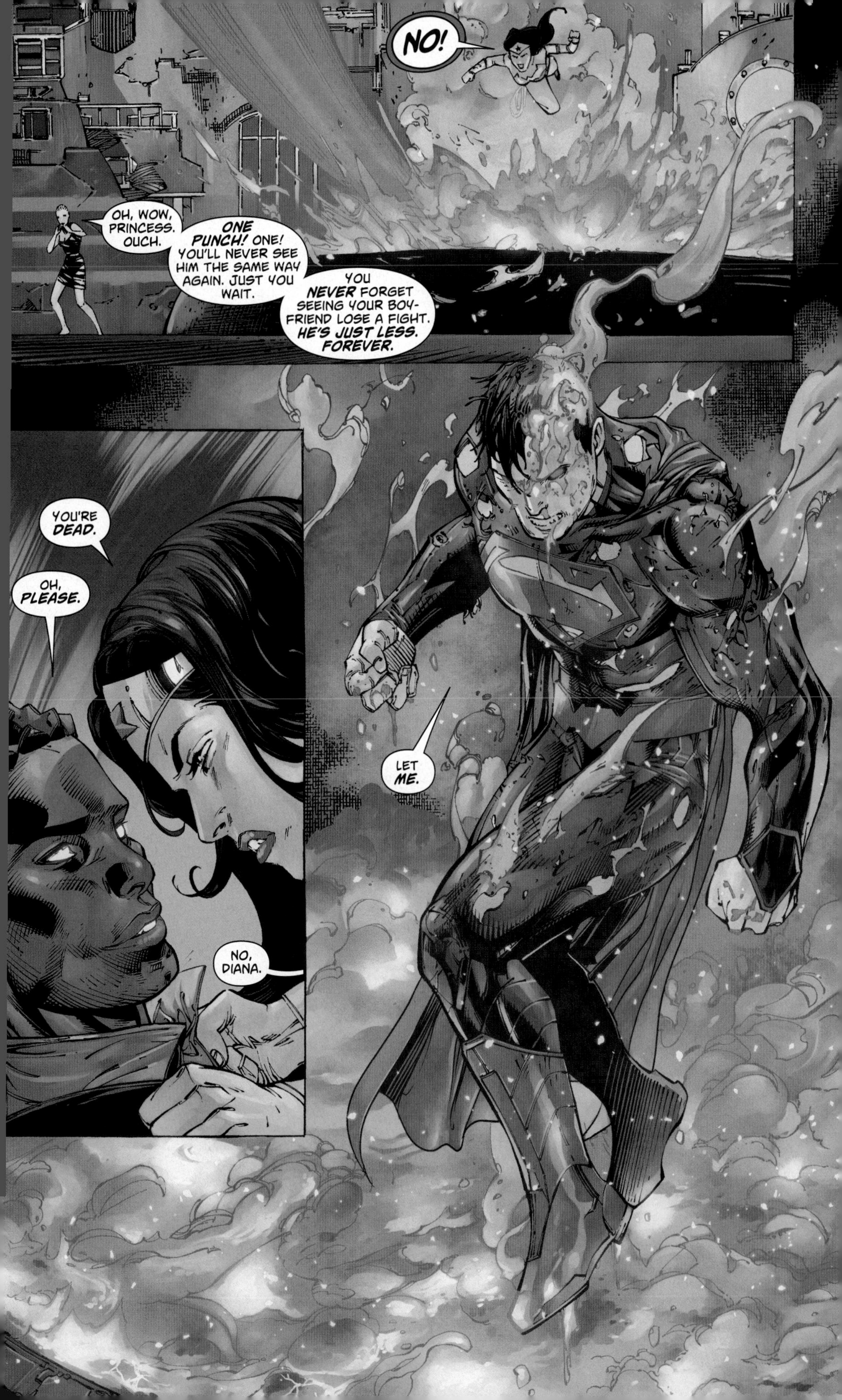
NO!
OH, WOW, PRINCESS. OUCH.
ONE PUNCH! ONE! YOU'LL NEVER SEE HIM THE SAME WAY AGAIN. JUST YOU WAIT.
YOU NEVER FORGET SEEING YOUR BOY-FRIEND LOSE A FIGHT. HE'S JUST LESS. FOREVER.
YOU'RE DEAD.
OH, PLEASE.
LET ME.
NO, DIANA.

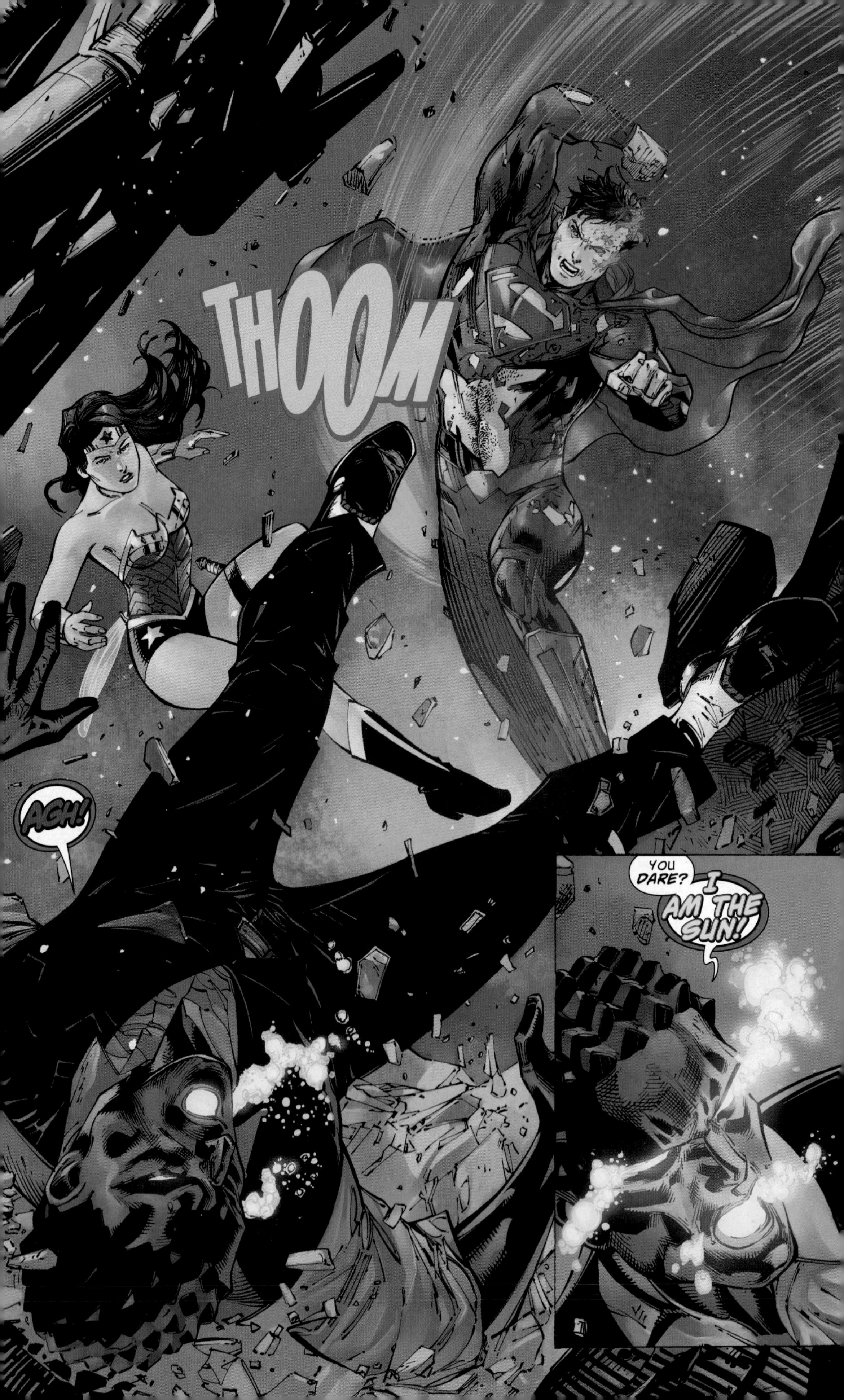
THOOM
AGH!
YOU DARE?
I AM THE SUN!

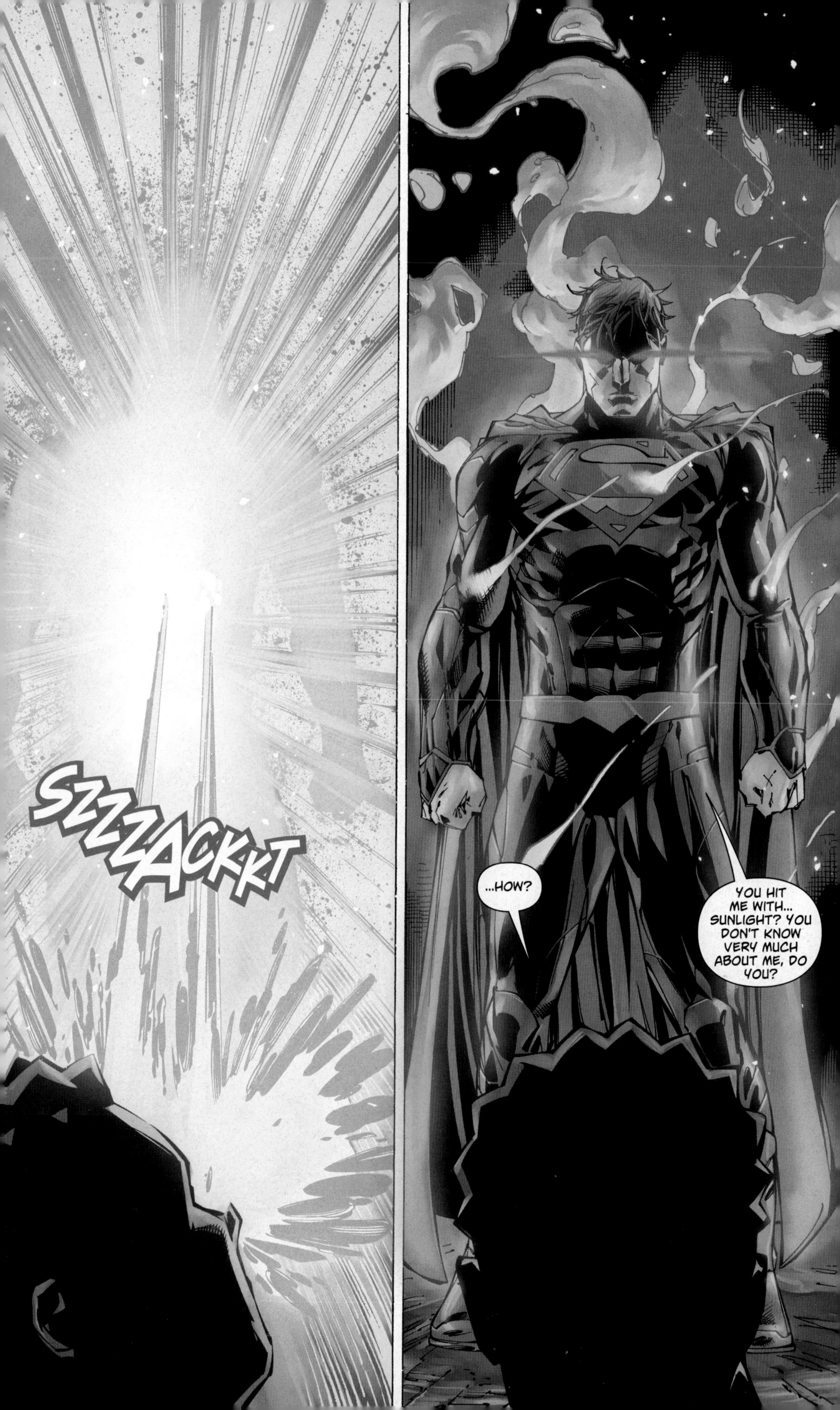
SZZZACKKT
...HOW?
YOU HIT ME WITH... SUNLIGHT? YOU DON'T KNOW VERY MUCH ABOUT ME, DO YOU?

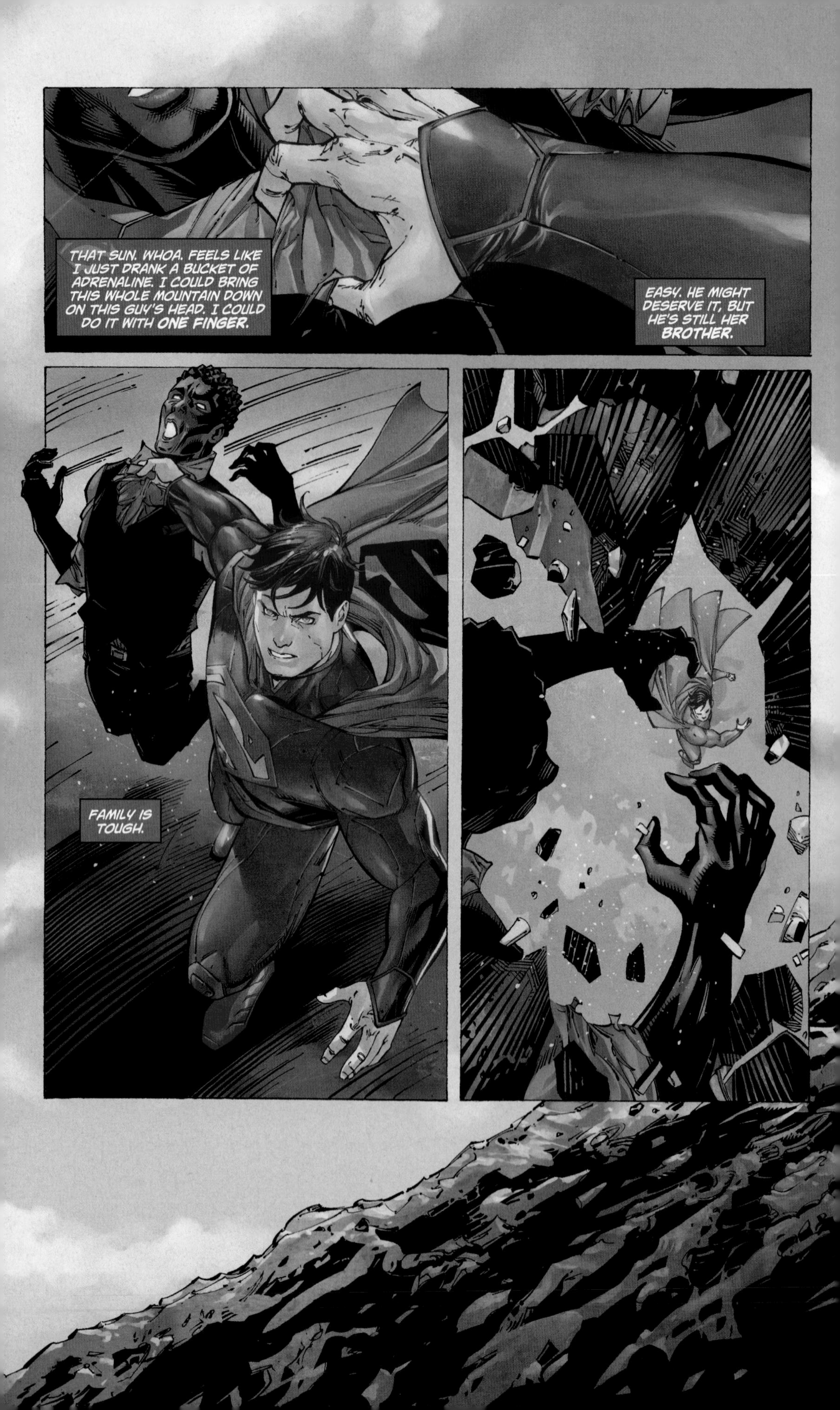
THAT SUN. WHOA. FEELS LIKE I JUST DRANK A BUCKET OF ADRENALINE. I COULD BRING THIS WHOLE MOUNTAIN DOWN ON THIS GUY'S HEAD. I COULD DO IT WITH ONE FINGER.
EASY. HE MIGHT DESERVE IT, BUT HE'S STILL HER BROTHER.
FAMILY IS TOUGH.

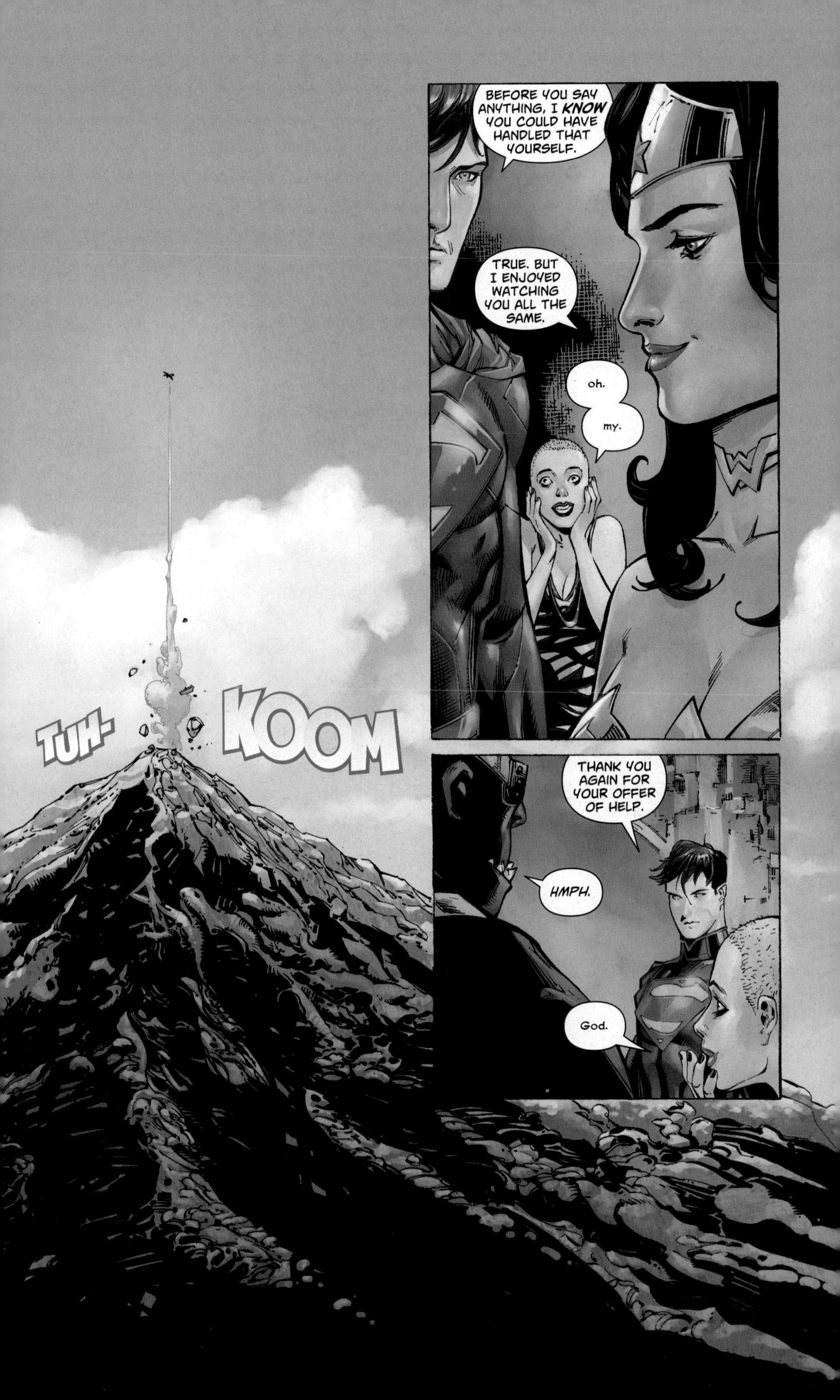
TUH-
KOOM
BEFORE YOU SAY ANYTHING, I KNOW YOU COULD HAVE HANDLED THAT YOURSELF.
TRUE. BUT I ENJOYED WATCHING YOU ALL THE SAME.
oh.
my.
THANK YOU AGAIN FOR YOUR OFFER OF HELP.
HMPH.
God.

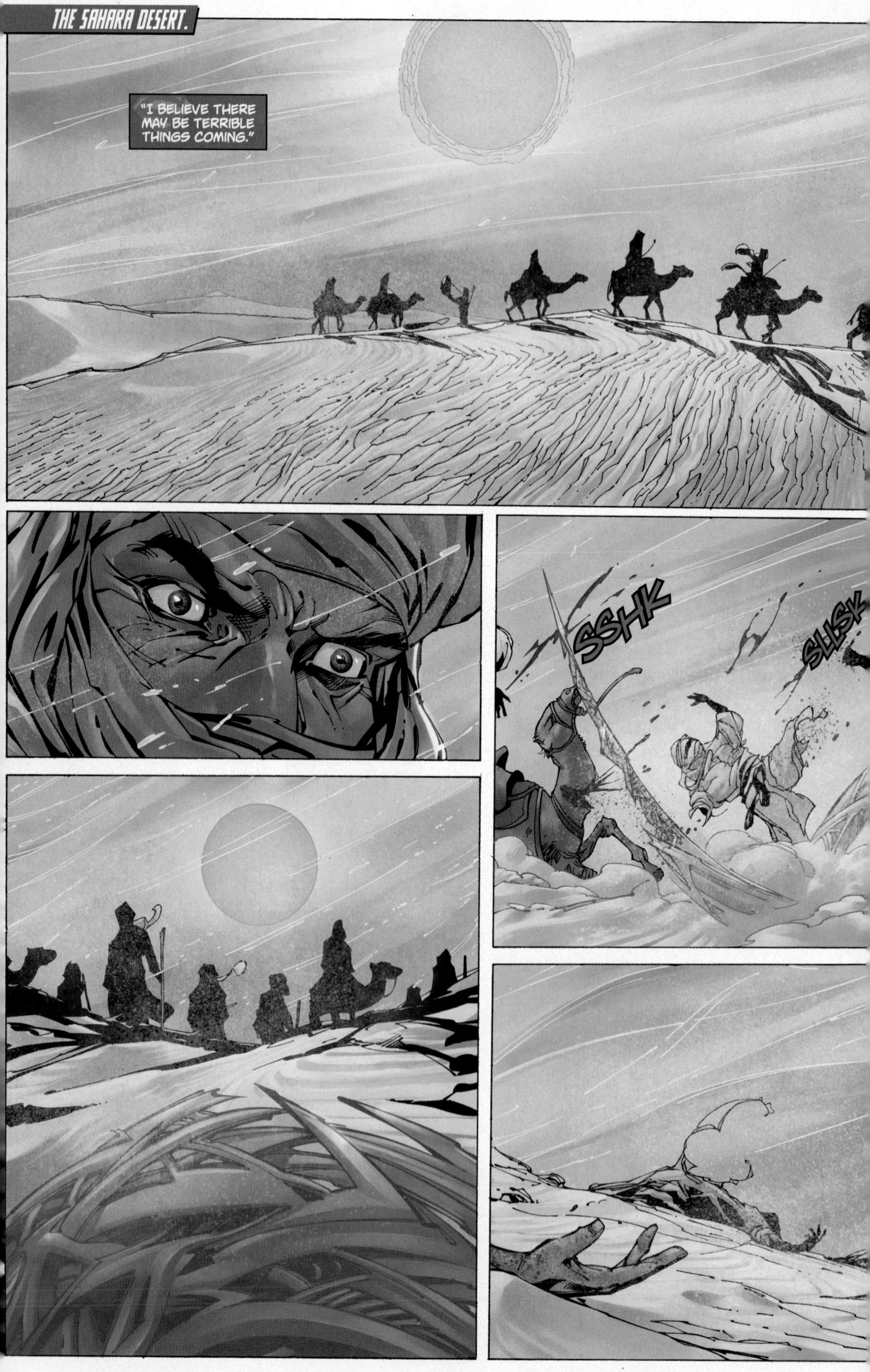
THE SAHARA DESERT.
"I BELIEVE THERE MAY BE TERRIBLE THINGS COMING."
SSHK
SLISK

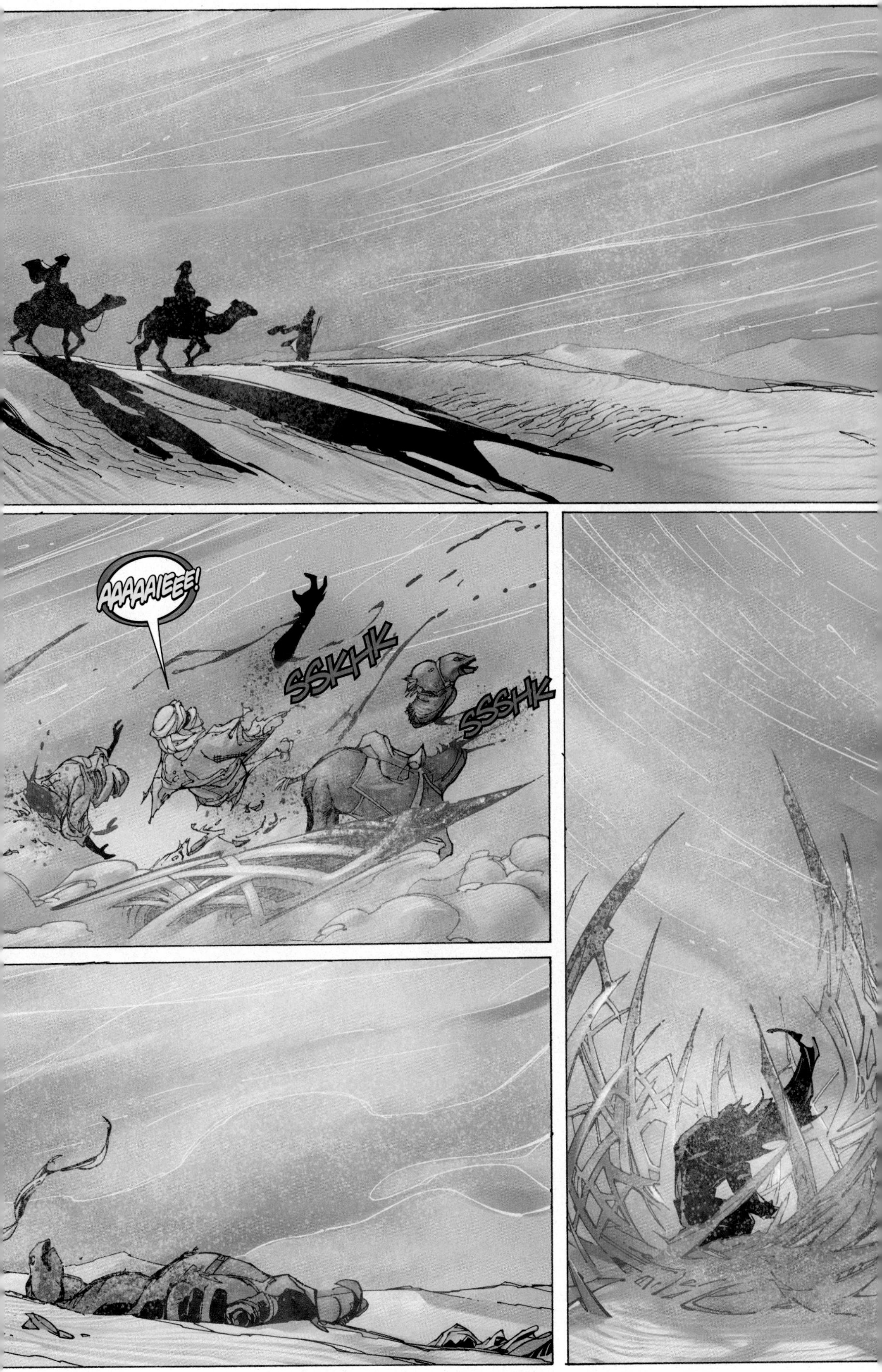
AAAAAIEEE!
SSKHK
SSSHK

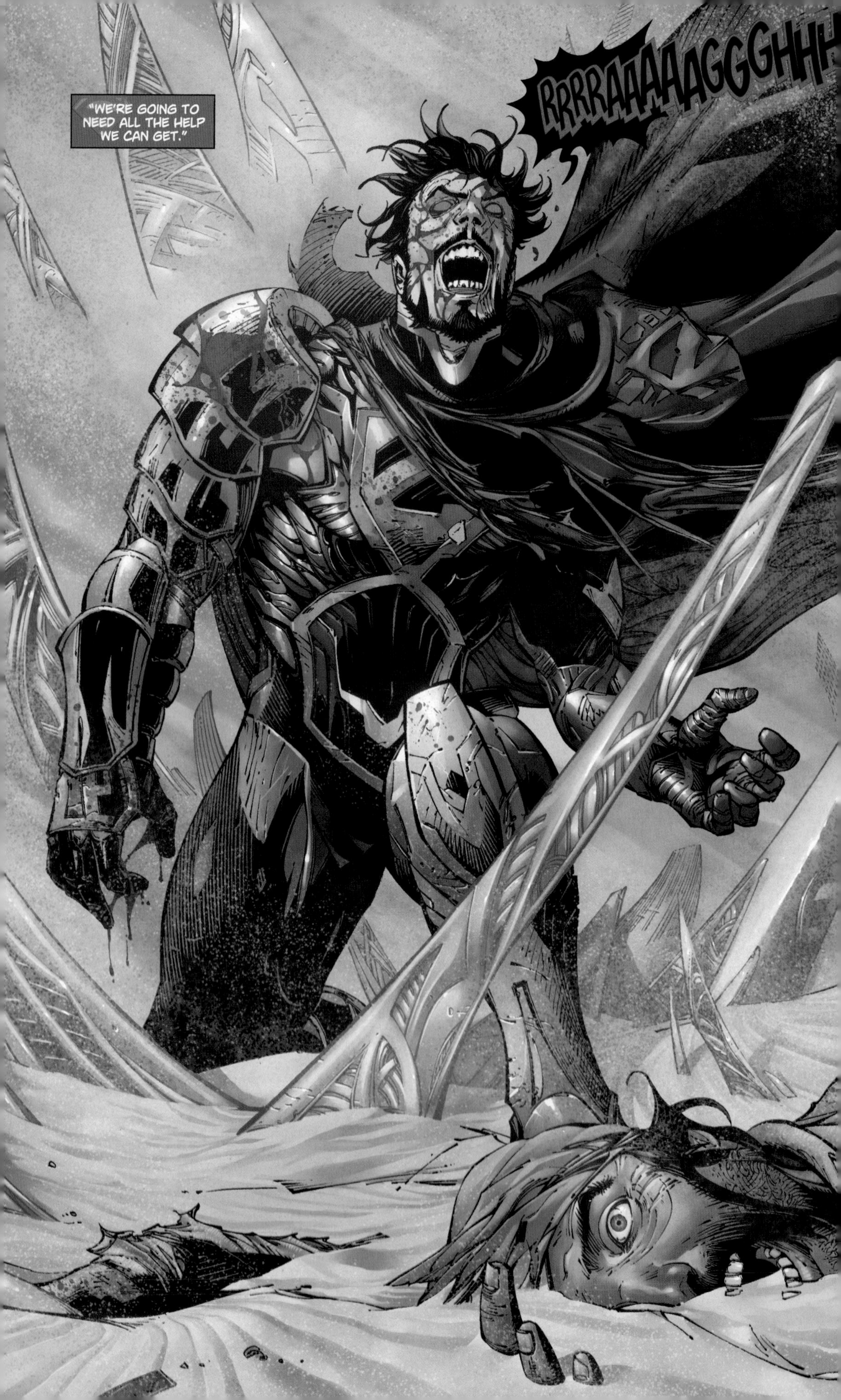
"WE'RE GOING TO NEED ALL THE HELP WE CAN GET."
RRRRAAAAAAGGGHHH

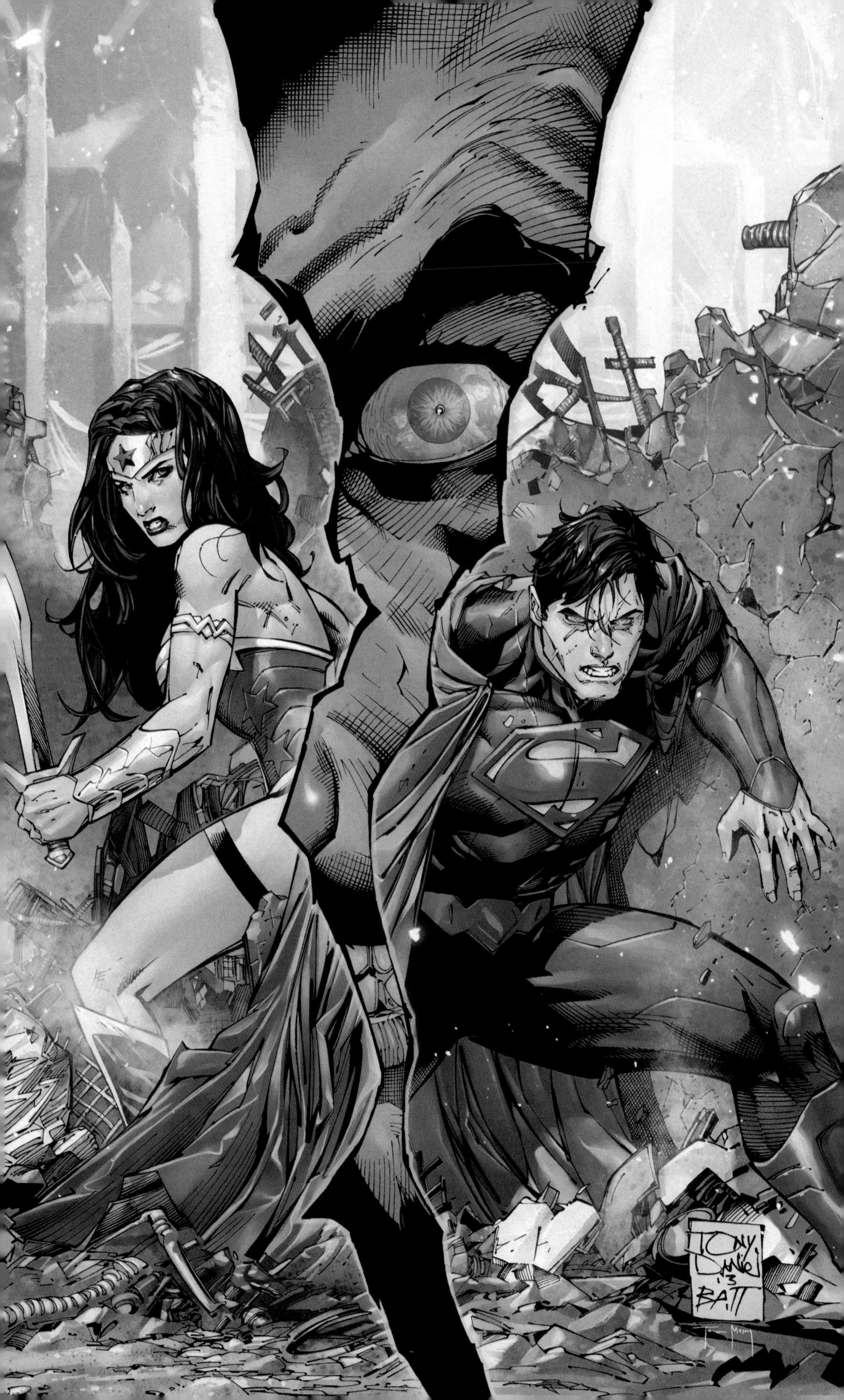

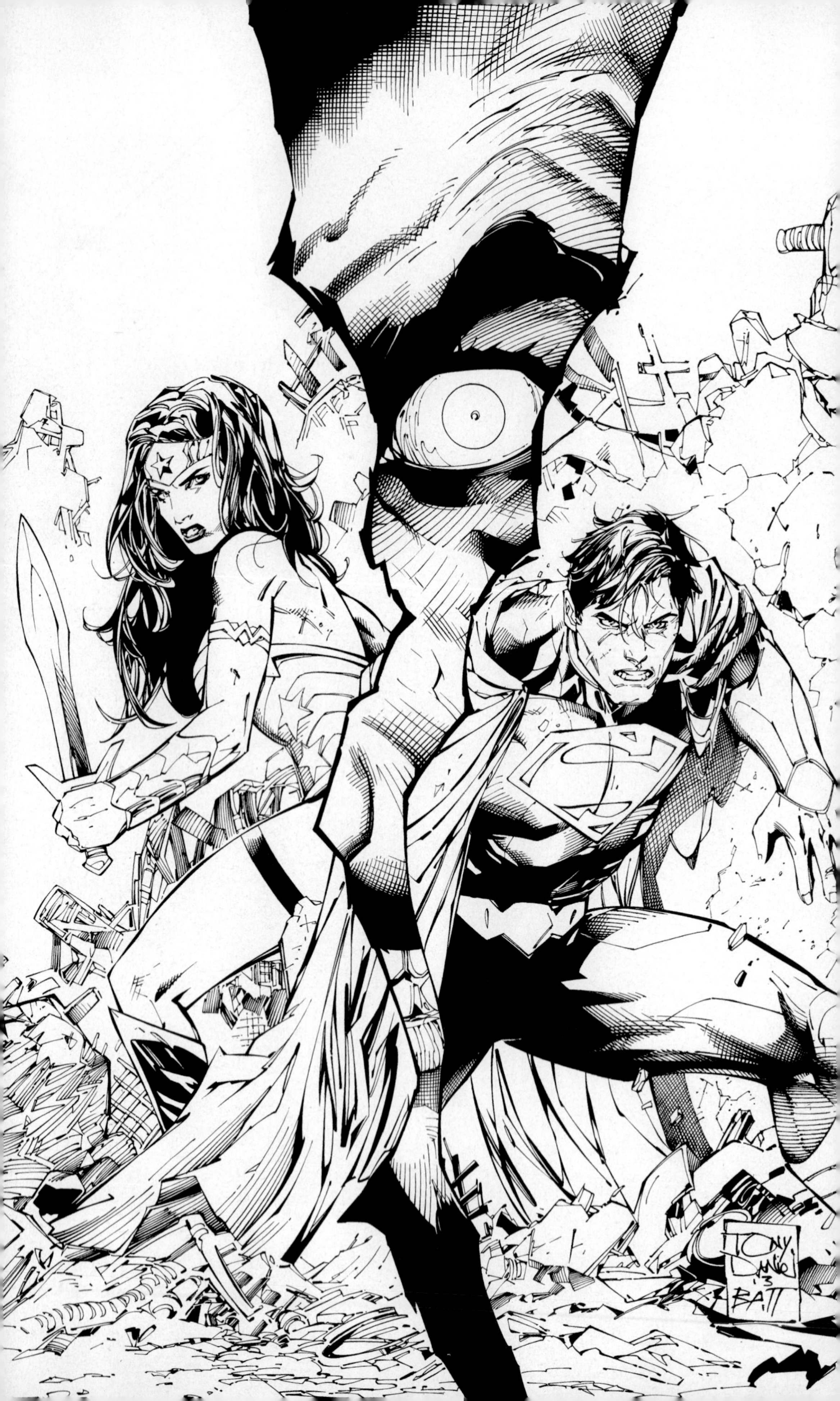

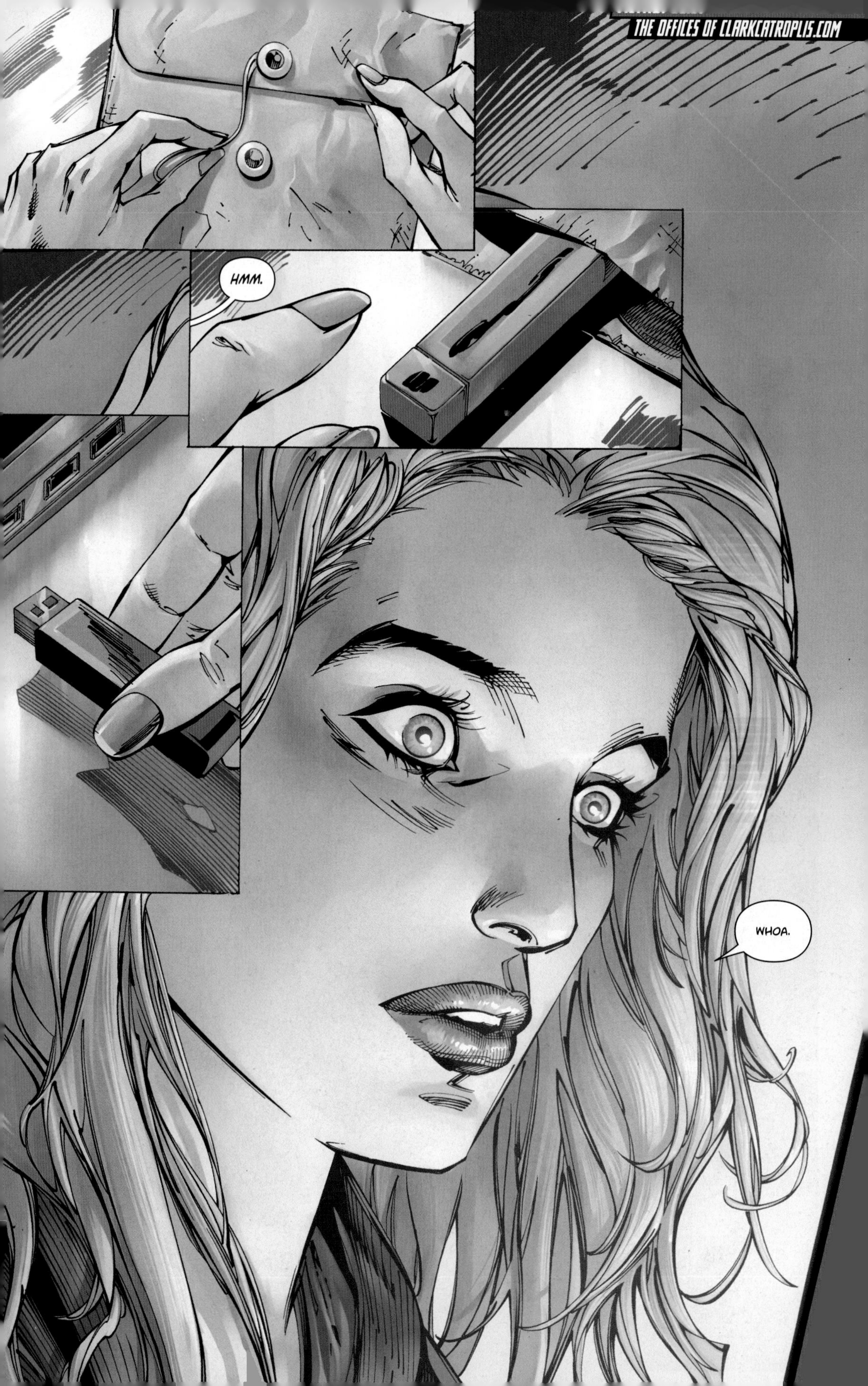
THE OFFICES OF CLARKCATROPLIS.COM
HMM.
WHOA.

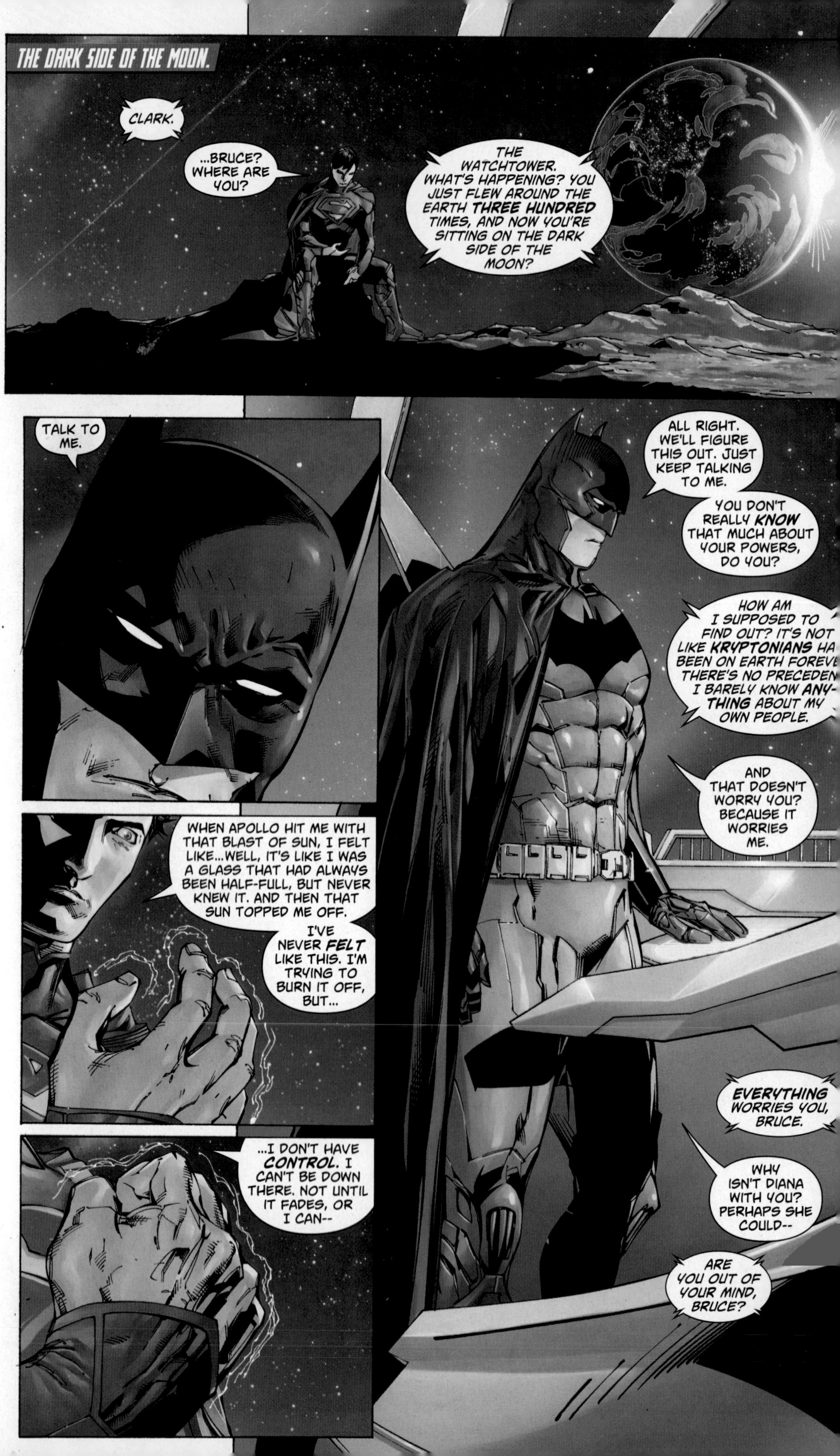

THE DARK SIDE OF THE MOON.
CLARK.
...BRUCE? WHERE ARE YOU?
THE WATCHTOWER. WHAT'S HAPPENING? YOU JUST FLEW AROUND THE EARTH THREE HUNDRED TIMES, AND NOW YOU'RE SITTING ON THE DARK SIDE OF THE MOON?
TALK TO ME.
WHEN APOLLO HIT ME WITH THAT BLAST OF SUN, I FELT LIKE...WELL, IT'S LIKE I WAS A GLASS THAT HAD ALWAYS BEEN HALF-FULL, BUT NEVER KNEW IT. AND THEN THAT SUN TOPPED ME OFF.
I'VE NEVER FELT LIKE THIS. I'M TRYING TO BURN IT OFF, BUT...
...I DON'T HAVE CONTROL. I CAN'T BE DOWN THERE. NOT UNTIL IT FADES, OR I CAN--
ALL RIGHT. WE'LL FIGURE THIS OUT. JUST KEEP TALKING TO ME.
YOU DON'T REALLY KNOW THAT MUCH ABOUT YOUR POWERS, DO YOU?
HOW AM I SUPPOSED TO FIND OUT? IT'S NOT LIKE KRYPTONIANS HA BEEN ON EARTH FOREVE THERE'S NO PRECEDEN I BARELY KNOW ANYTHING ABOUT MY OWN PEOPLE.
AND THAT DOESN'T WORRY YOU? BECAUSE IT WORRIES ME.
EVERYTHING WORRIES YOU, BRUCE.
WHY ISN'T DIANA WITH YOU? PERHAPS SHE COULD--
ARE YOU OUT OF YOUR MIND, BRUCE?

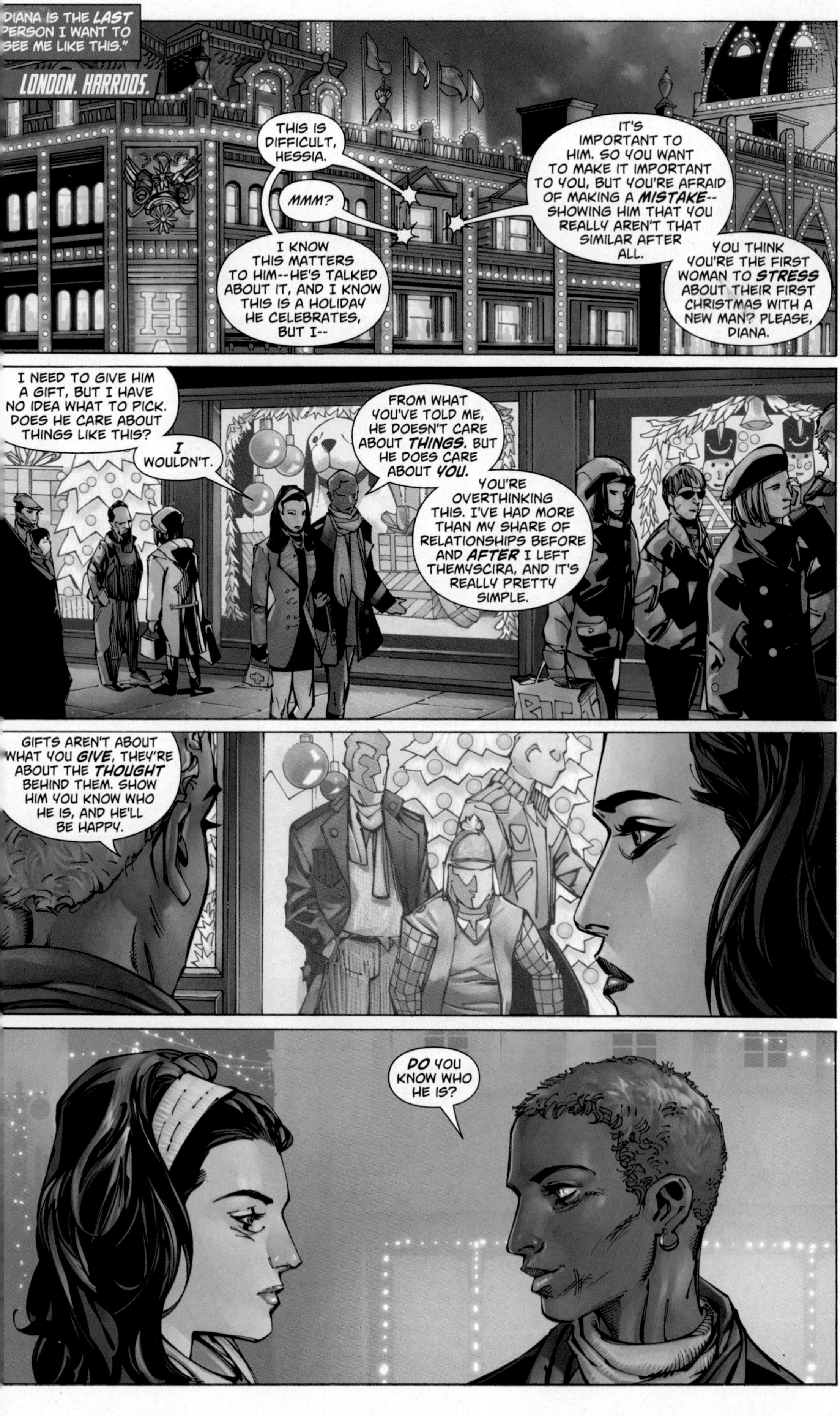
DIANA IS THE LAST PERSON I WANT TO SEE ME LIKE THIS."
LONDON. HARRODS.
THIS IS DIFFICULT, HESSIA.
MMM?
I KNOW THIS MATTERS TO HIM--HE'S TALKED ABOUT IT, AND I KNOW THIS IS A HOLIDAY HE CELEBRATES, BUT I--
IT'S IMPORTANT TO HIM. SO YOU WANT TO MAKE IT IMPORTANT TO YOU, BUT YOU'RE AFRAID OF MAKING A MISTAKE--SHOWING HIM THAT YOU REALLY AREN'T THAT SIMILAR AFTER ALL.
YOU THINK YOU'RE THE FIRST WOMAN TO STRESS ABOUT THEIR FIRST CHRISTMAS WITH A NEW MAN? PLEASE, DIANA.
I NEED TO GIVE HIM A GIFT, BUT I HAVE NO IDEA WHAT TO PICK. DOES HE CARE ABOUT THINGS LIKE THIS?
I WOULDN'T.
FROM WHAT YOU'VE TOLD ME, HE DOESN'T CARE ABOUT THINGS. BUT HE DOES CARE ABOUT YOU.
YOU'RE OVERTHINKING THIS. I'VE HAD MORE THAN MY SHARE OF RELATIONSHIPS BEFORE AND AFTER I LEFT THEMYSCIRA, AND IT'S REALLY PRETTY SIMPLE.
GIFTS AREN'T ABOUT WHAT YOU GIVE, THEY'RE ABOUT THE THOUGHT BEHIND THEM. SHOW HIM YOU KNOW WHO HE IS, AND HE'LL BE HAPPY.
DO YOU KNOW WHO HE IS?

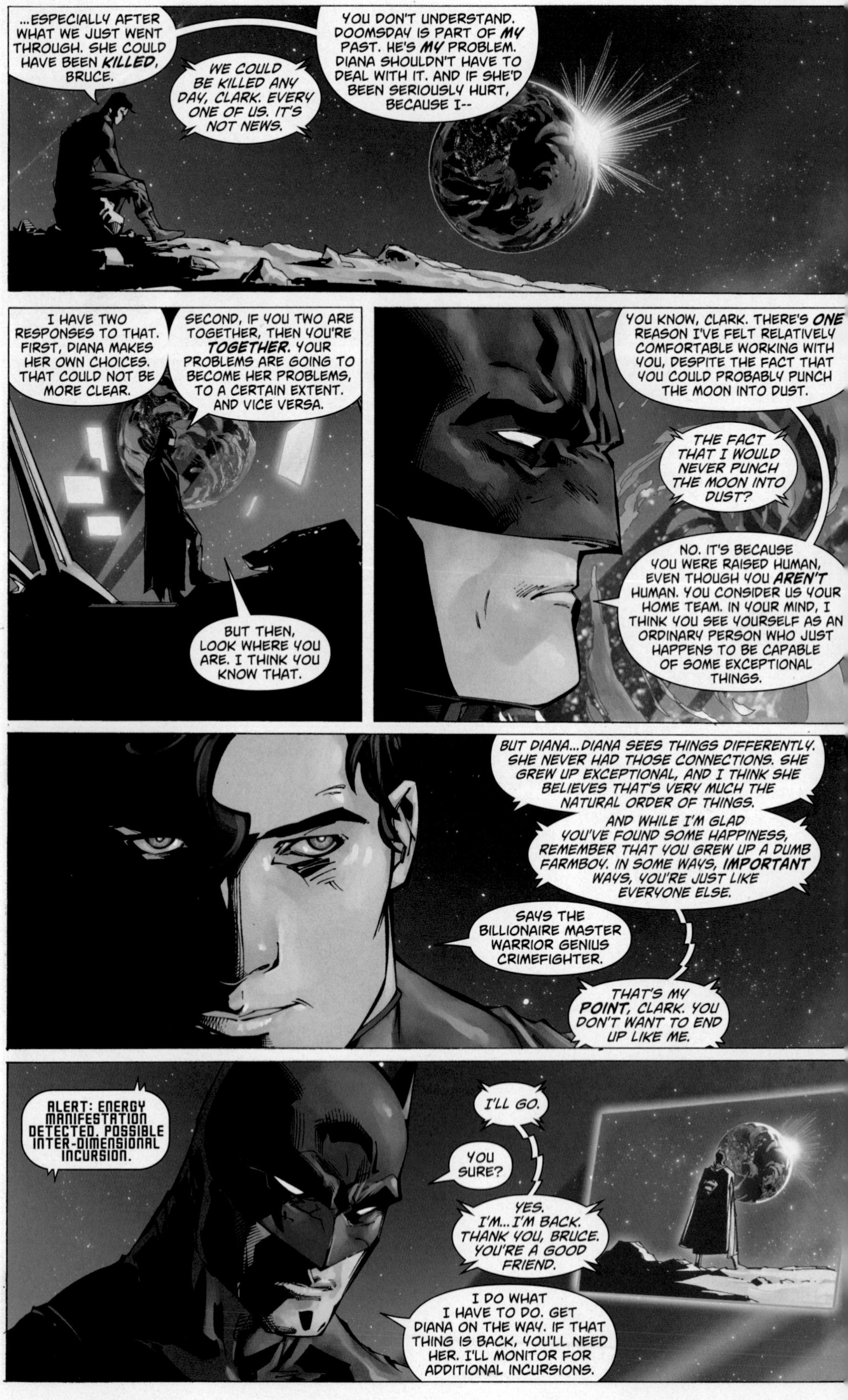
...ESPECIALLY AFTER WHAT WE JUST WENT THROUGH. SHE COULD HAVE BEEN KILLED, BRUCE.
WE COULD BE KILLED ANY DAY, CLARK. EVERY ONE OF US. IT'S NOT NEWS.
YOU DON'T UNDERSTAND. DOOMSDAY IS PART OF MY PAST. HE'S MY PROBLEM. DIANA SHOULDN'T HAVE TO DEAL WITH IT. AND IF SHE'D BEEN SERIOUSLY HURT, BECAUSE I--
I HAVE TWO RESPONSES TO THAT. FIRST, DIANA MAKES HER OWN CHOICES. THAT COULD NOT BE MORE CLEAR.
SECOND, IF YOU TWO ARE TOGETHER, THEN YOU'RE TOGETHER. YOUR PROBLEMS ARE GOING TO BECOME HER PROBLEMS, TO A CERTAIN EXTENT. AND VICE VERSA.
BUT THEN, LOOK WHERE YOU ARE. I THINK YOU KNOW THAT.
YOU KNOW, CLARK. THERE'S ONE REASON I'VE FELT RELATIVELY COMFORTABLE WORKING WITH YOU, DESPITE THE FACT THAT YOU COULD PROBABLY PUNCH THE MOON INTO DUST.
THE FACT THAT I WOULD NEVER PUNCH THE MOON INTO DUST?
NO. IT'S BECAUSE YOU WERE RAISED HUMAN, EVEN THOUGH YOU AREN'T HUMAN. YOU CONSIDER US YOUR HOME TEAM. IN YOUR MIND, I THINK YOU SEE YOURSELF AS AN ORDINARY PERSON WHO JUST HAPPENS TO BE CAPABLE OF SOME EXCEPTIONAL THINGS.
BUT DIANA...DIANA SEES THINGS DIFFERENTLY. SHE NEVER HAD THOSE CONNECTIONS. SHE GREW UP EXCEPTIONAL, AND I THINK SHE BELIEVES THAT'S VERY MUCH THE NATURAL ORDER OF THINGS.
AND WHILE I'M GLAD YOU'VE FOUND SOME HAPPINESS, REMEMBER THAT YOU GREW UP A DUMB FARMBOY. IN SOME WAYS, IMPORTANT WAYS, YOU'RE JUST LIKE EVERYONE ELSE.
SAYS THE BILLIONAIRE MASTER WARRIOR GENIUS CRIMEFIGHTER.
THAT'S MY POINT, CLARK. YOU DON'T WANT TO END UP LIKE ME.
ALERT: ENERGY MANIFESTATION DETECTED. POSSIBLE INTER-DIMENSIONAL INCURSION.
I'LL GO.
YOU SURE?
YES. I'M...I'M BACK. THANK YOU, BRUCE. YOU'RE A GOOD FRIEND.
I DO WHAT I HAVE TO DO. GET DIANA ON THE WAY. IF THAT THING IS BACK, YOU'LL NEED HER. I'LL MONITOR FOR ADDITIONAL INCURSIONS.

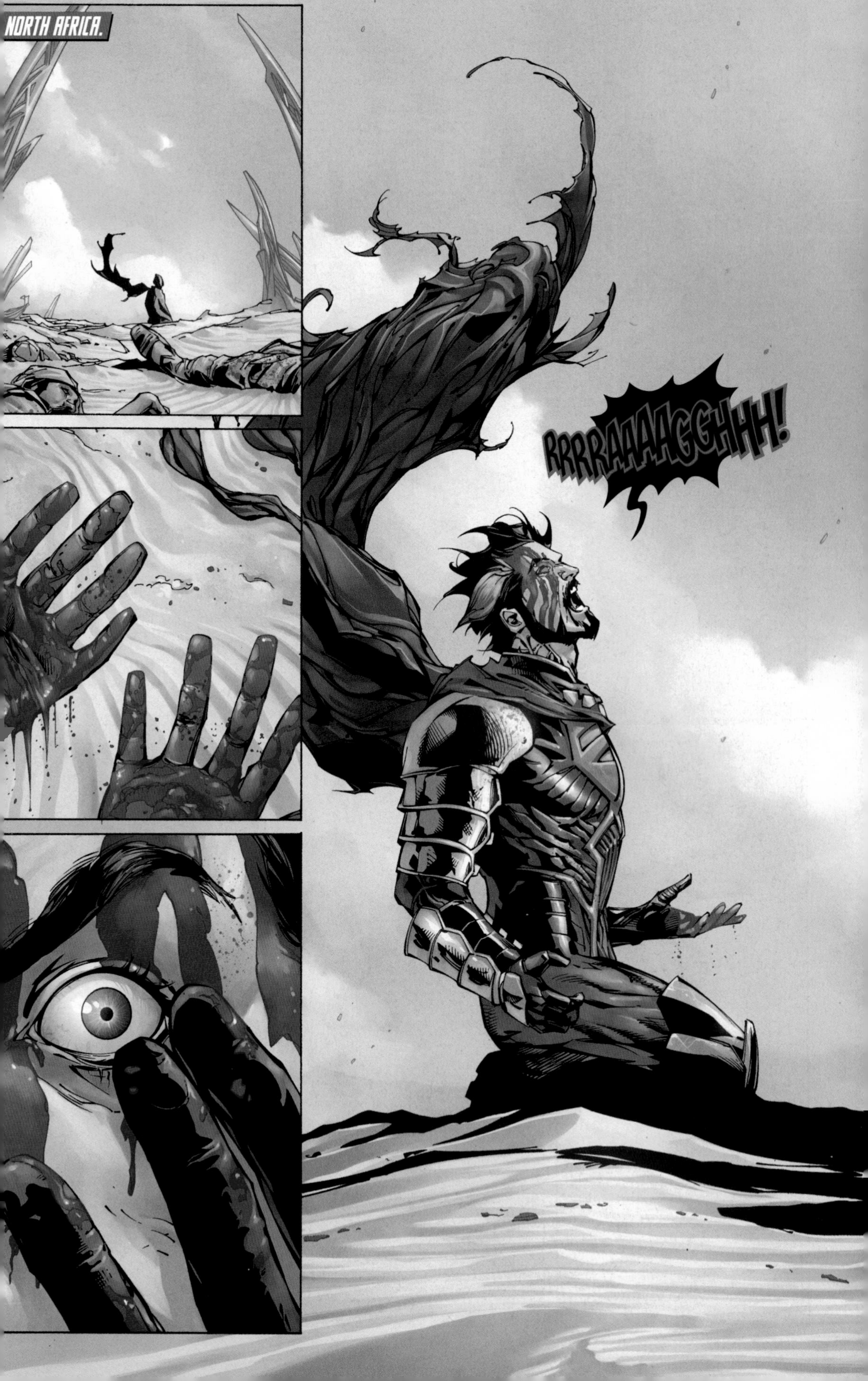
NORTH AFRICA.
RRRRAAAAGGHHH!

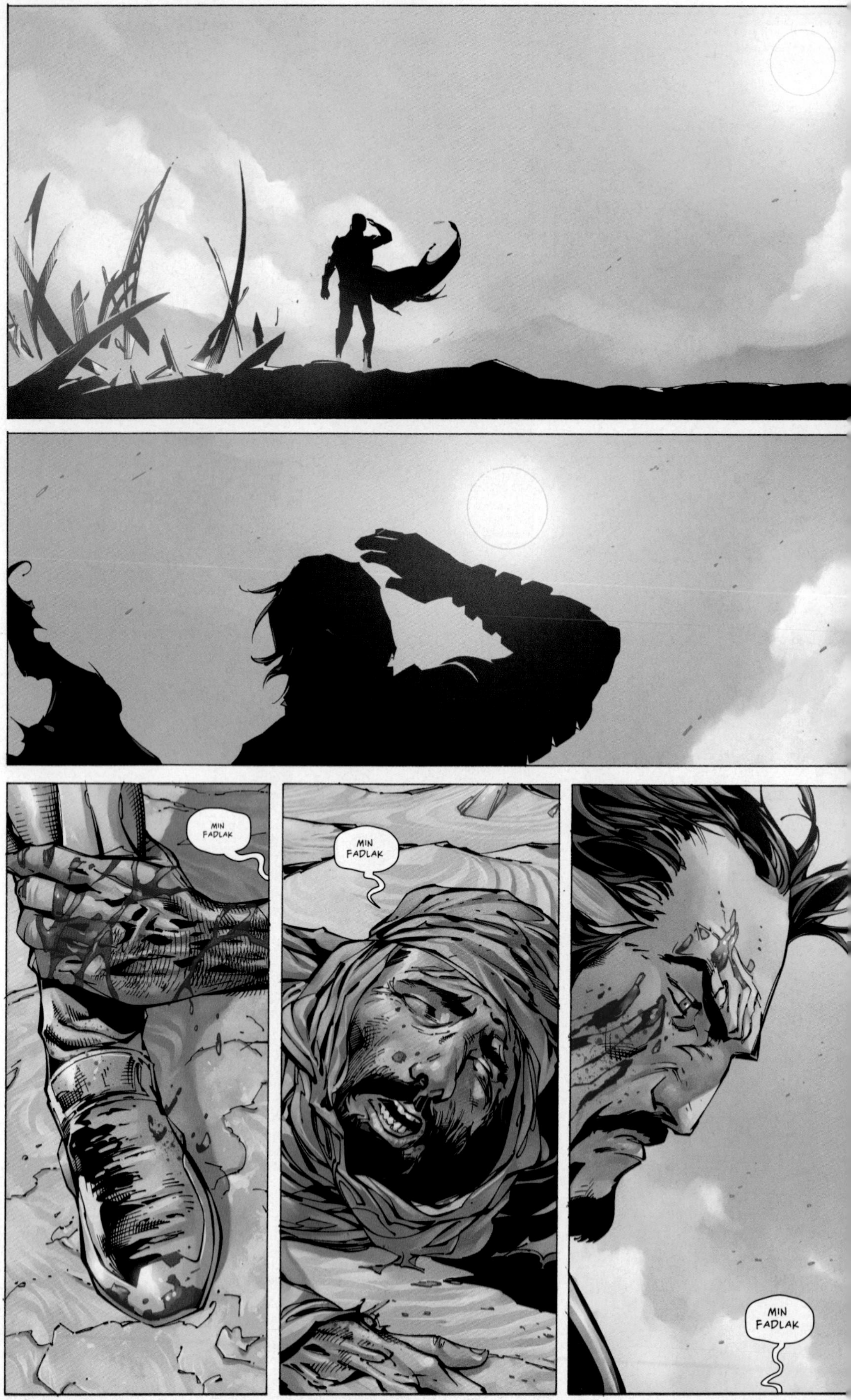
MIN FADLAK
MIN FADLAK
MIN FADLAK

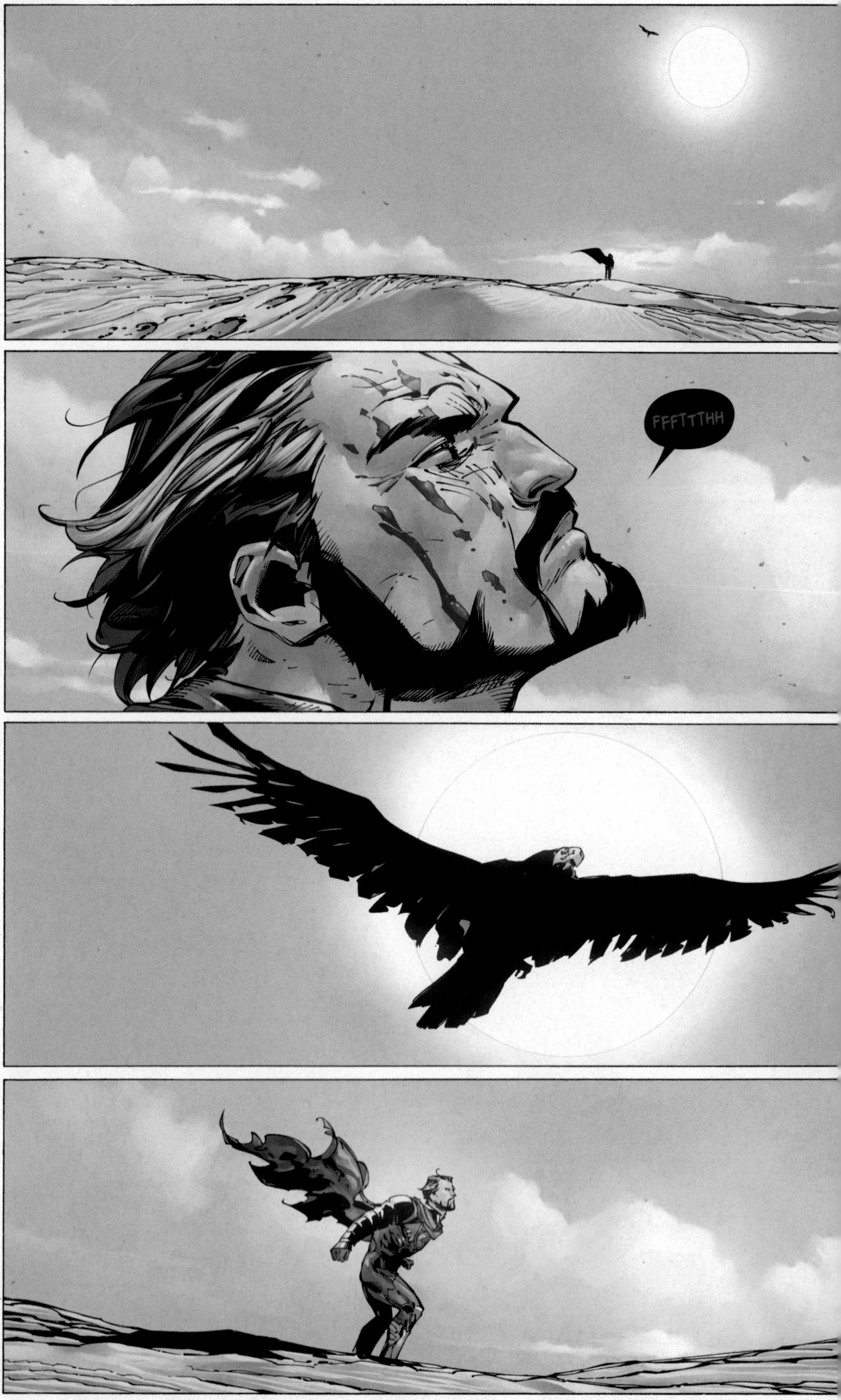
FFFTTTHH

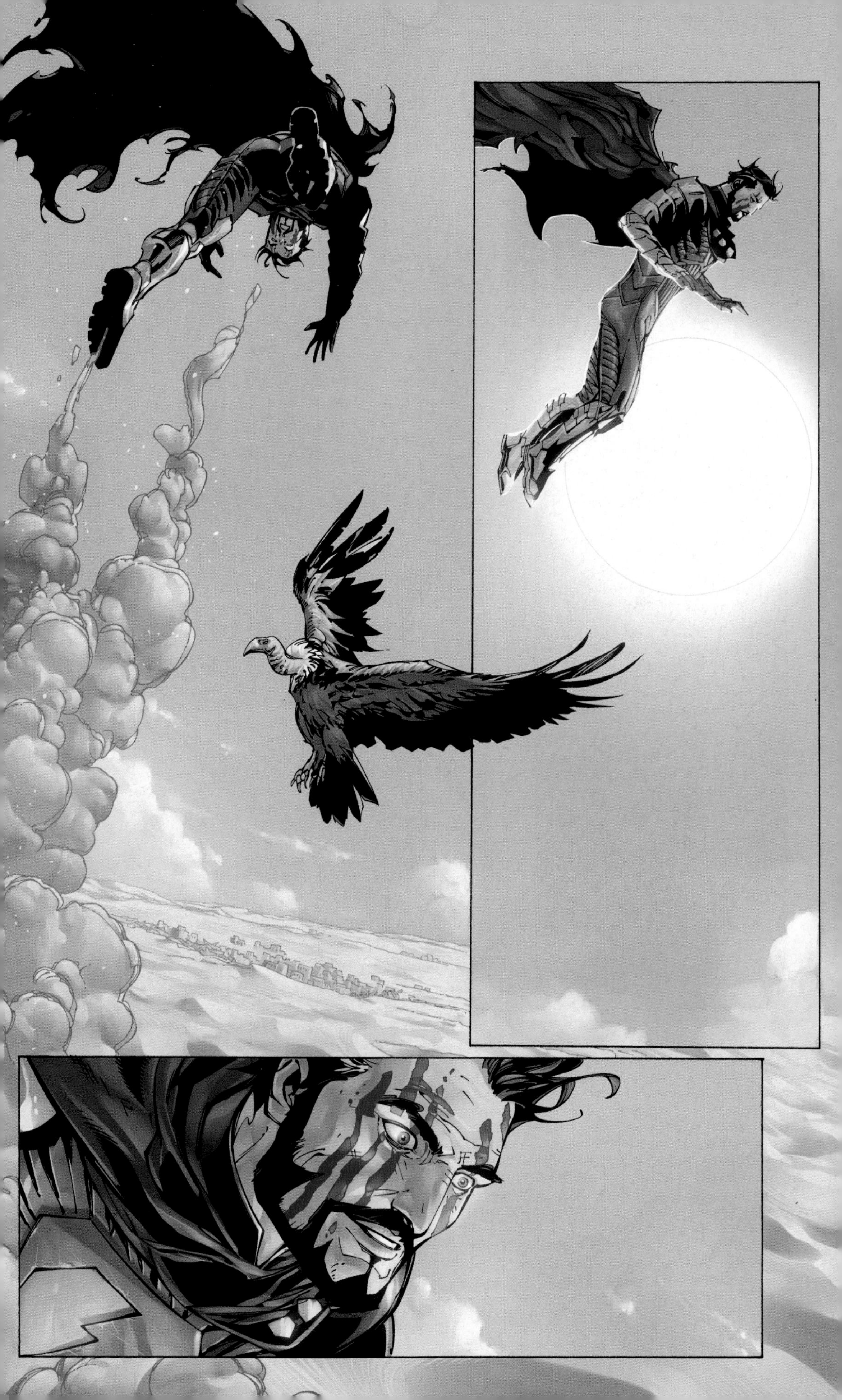

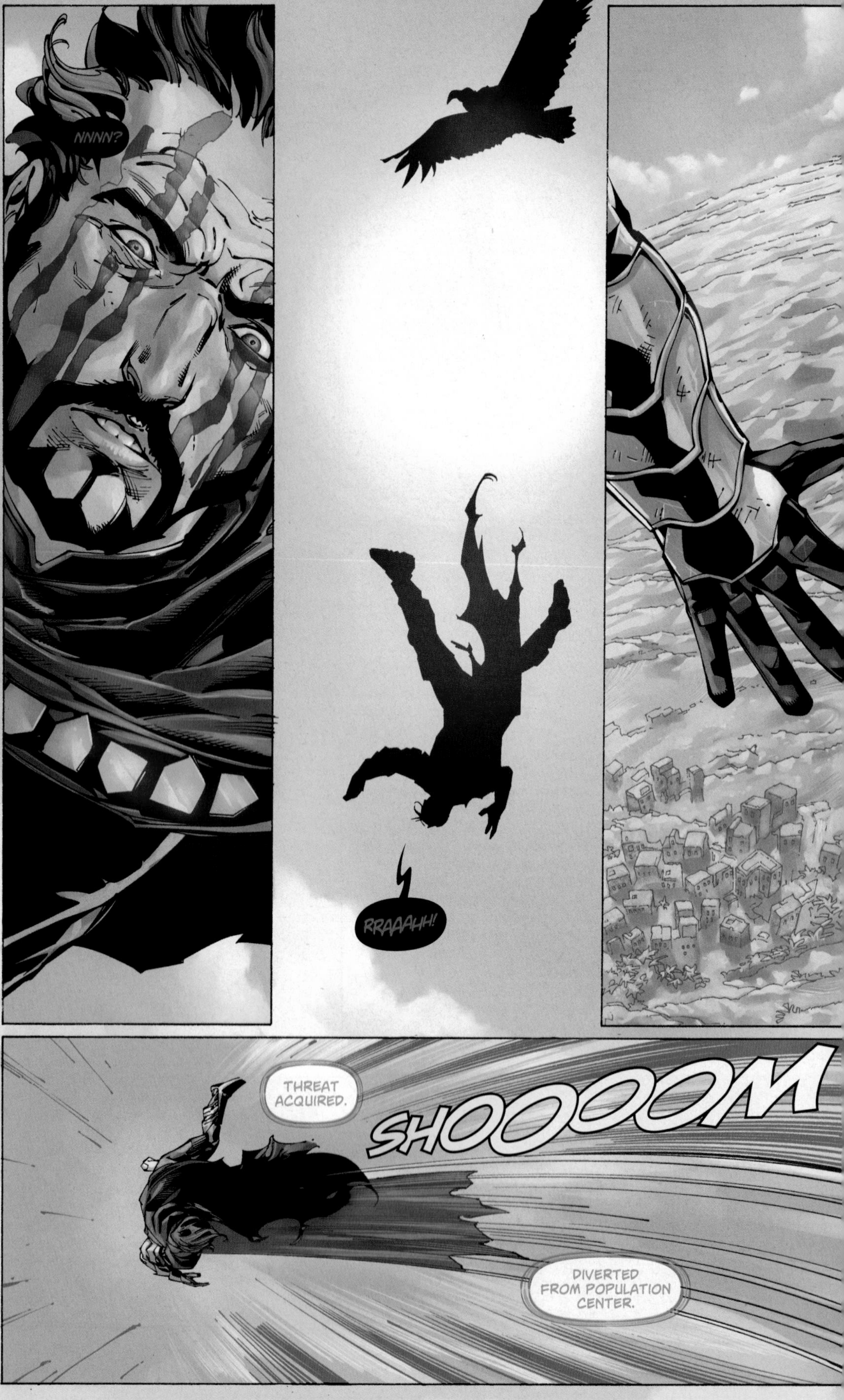

NNNN?
RRAAAHH!
THREAT ACQUIRED.
SHOOOOOM
DIVERTED FROM POPULATION CENTER.

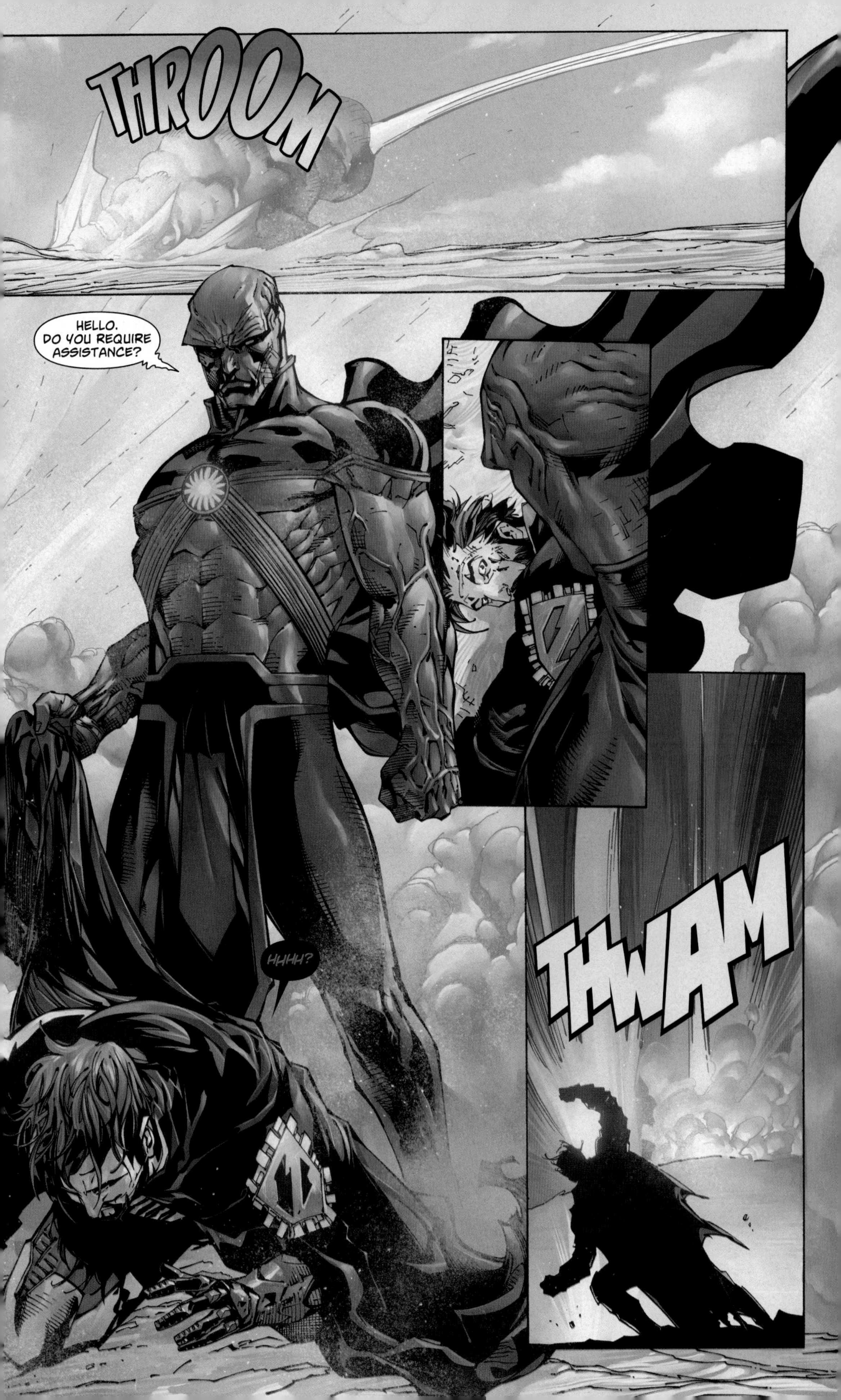
THROOM
HELLO. DO YOU REQUIRE ASSISTANCE?
HHHH?
THWAM

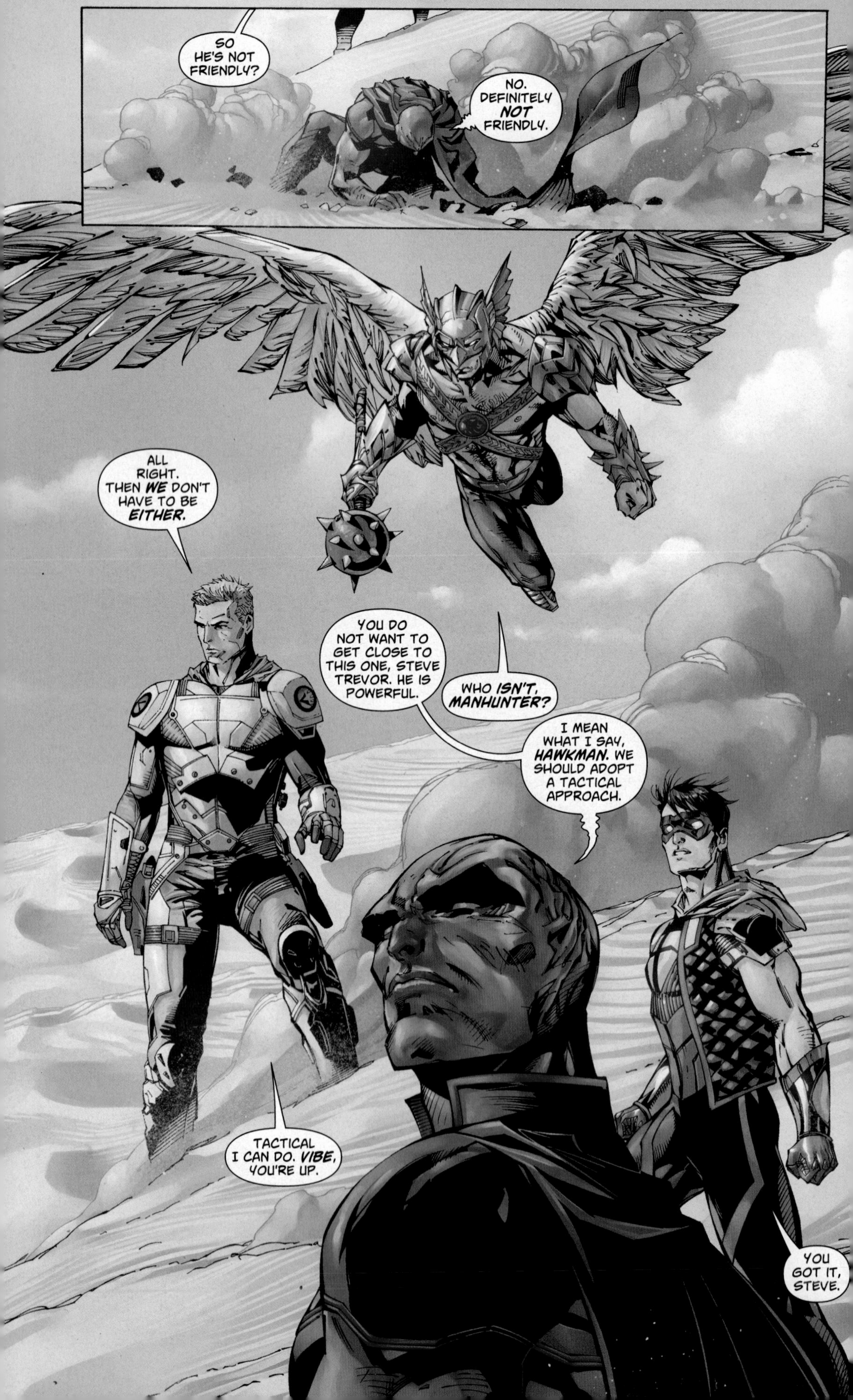

SO HE'S NOT FRIENDLY?
NO. DEFINITELY **NOT** FRIENDLY.
ALL RIGHT. THEN **WE** DON'T HAVE TO BE **EITHER**.
YOU DO NOT WANT TO GET CLOSE TO THIS ONE, STEVE TREVOR. HE IS POWERFUL.
WHO **ISN'T, MANHUNTER?**
I MEAN WHAT I SAY, **HAWKMAN**. WE SHOULD ADOPT A TACTICAL APPROACH.
TACTICAL I CAN DO. **VIBE**, YOU'RE UP.
YOU GOT IT, STEVE.

RRRMMMBBBLLE

PRMMMMBBBLLLE

MANHUNTER.
GO.
I KNOW
WHAT FLAMES
MEAN TO YOU,
BUT WE NEED
THE HEAT.

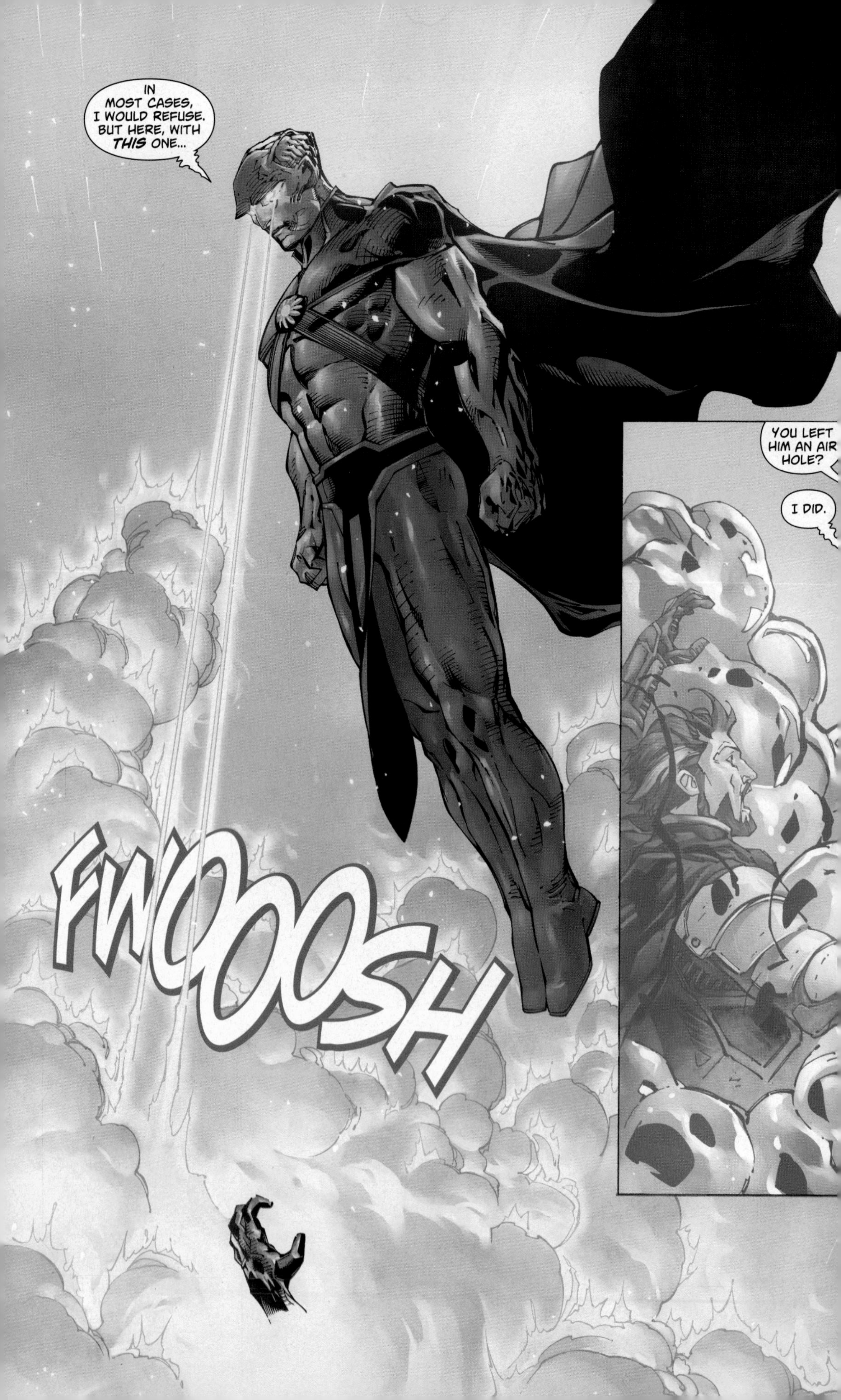
IN MOST CASES, I WOULD REFUSE. BUT HERE, WITH *THIS* ONE...
FWOOOOSH
YOU LEFT HIM AN AIR HOLE?
I DID.

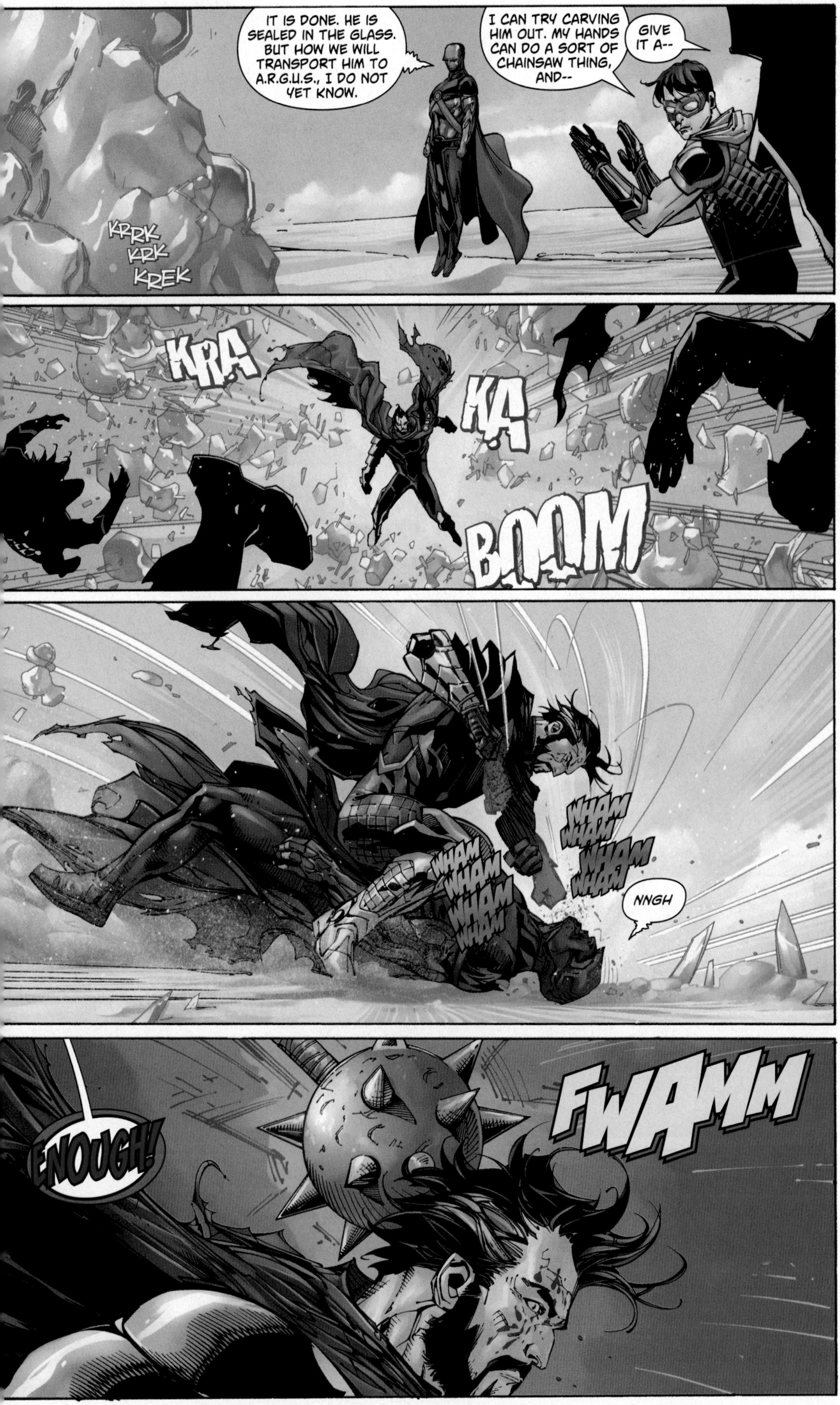

IT IS DONE. HE IS SEALED IN THE GLASS. BUT HOW WE WILL TRANSPORT HIM TO A.R.G.U.S., I DO NOT YET KNOW.
I CAN TRY CARVING HIM OUT. MY HANDS CAN DO A SORT OF CHAINSAW THING, AND--
GIVE IT A--
KRRK KRK KREK
KRA
KA
BOOM
WHAM WHAM WHAM WHAM
WHAM WHAM WHAM WHAM WHAM
NNGH
ENOUGH!
FWAMM

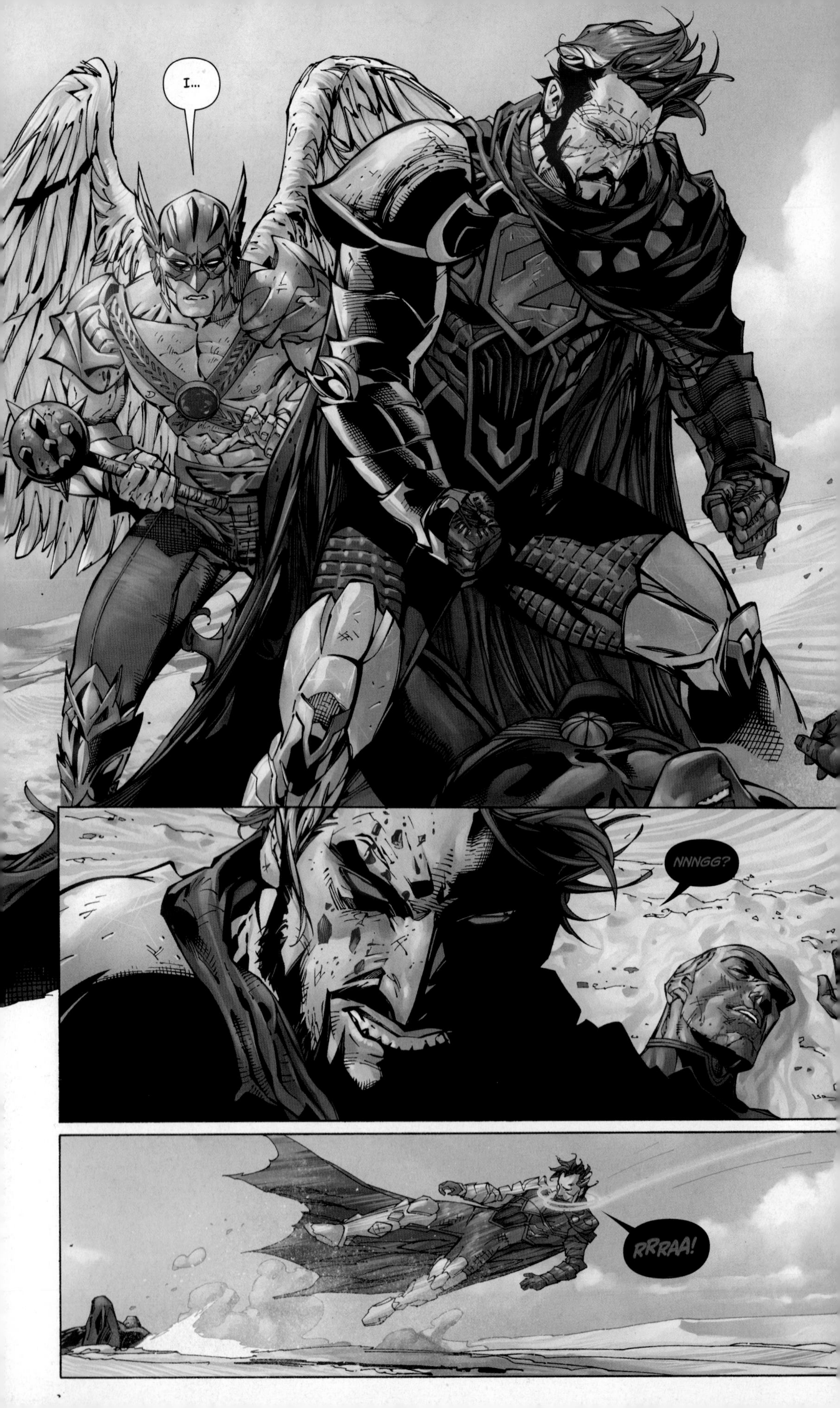
I...
NNNGG?
RRRAA!

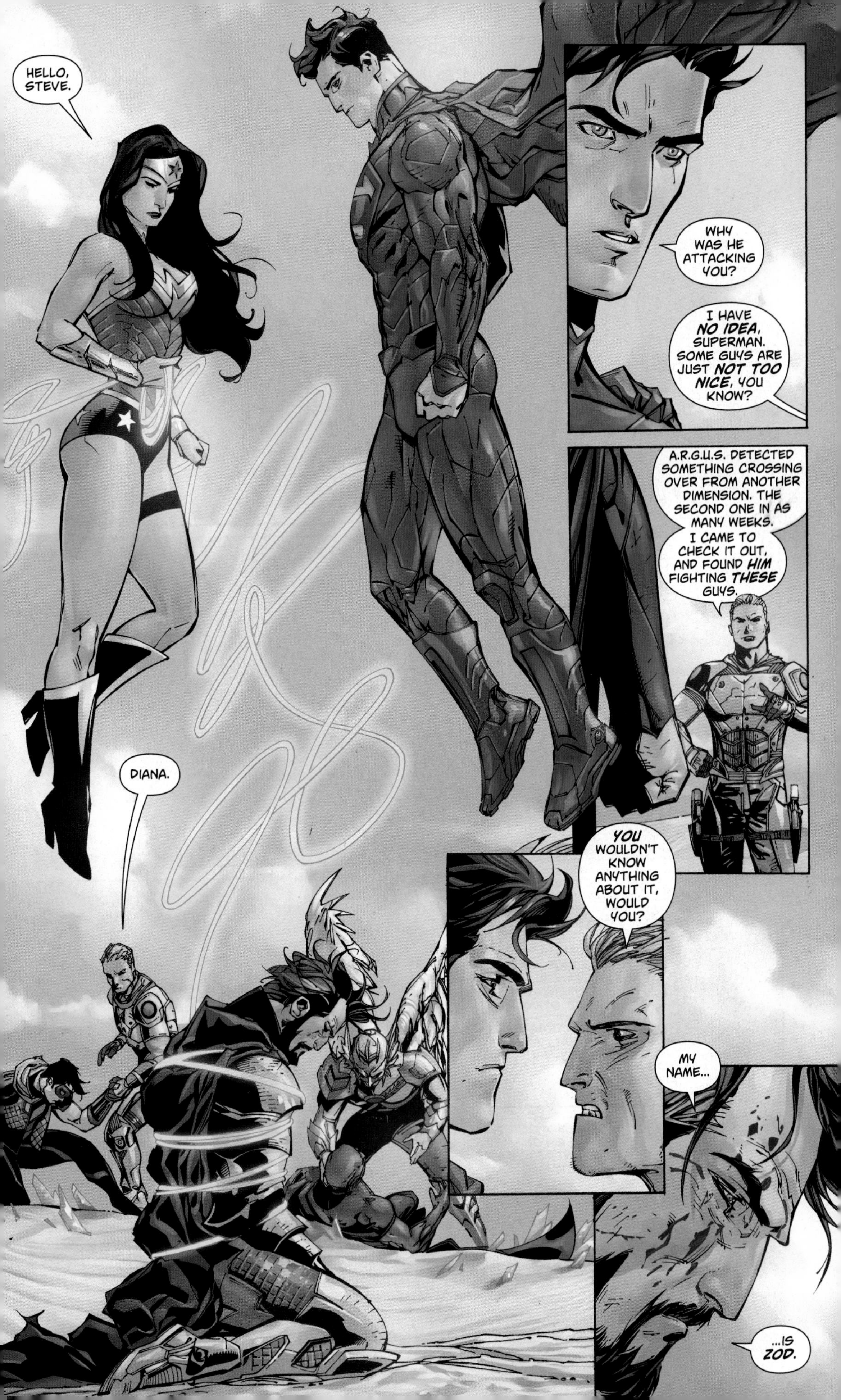
HELLO, STEVE.
DIANA.
WHY WAS HE ATTACKING YOU?
I HAVE NO IDEA, SUPERMAN. SOME GUYS ARE JUST NOT TOO NICE, YOU KNOW?
A.R.G.U.S. DETECTED SOMETHING CROSSING OVER FROM ANOTHER DIMENSION. THE SECOND ONE IN AS MANY WEEKS.
I CAME TO CHECK IT OUT, AND FOUND HIM FIGHTING THESE GUYS.
YOU WOULDN'T KNOW ANYTHING ABOUT IT, WOULD YOU?
MY NAME...
...IS ZOD.

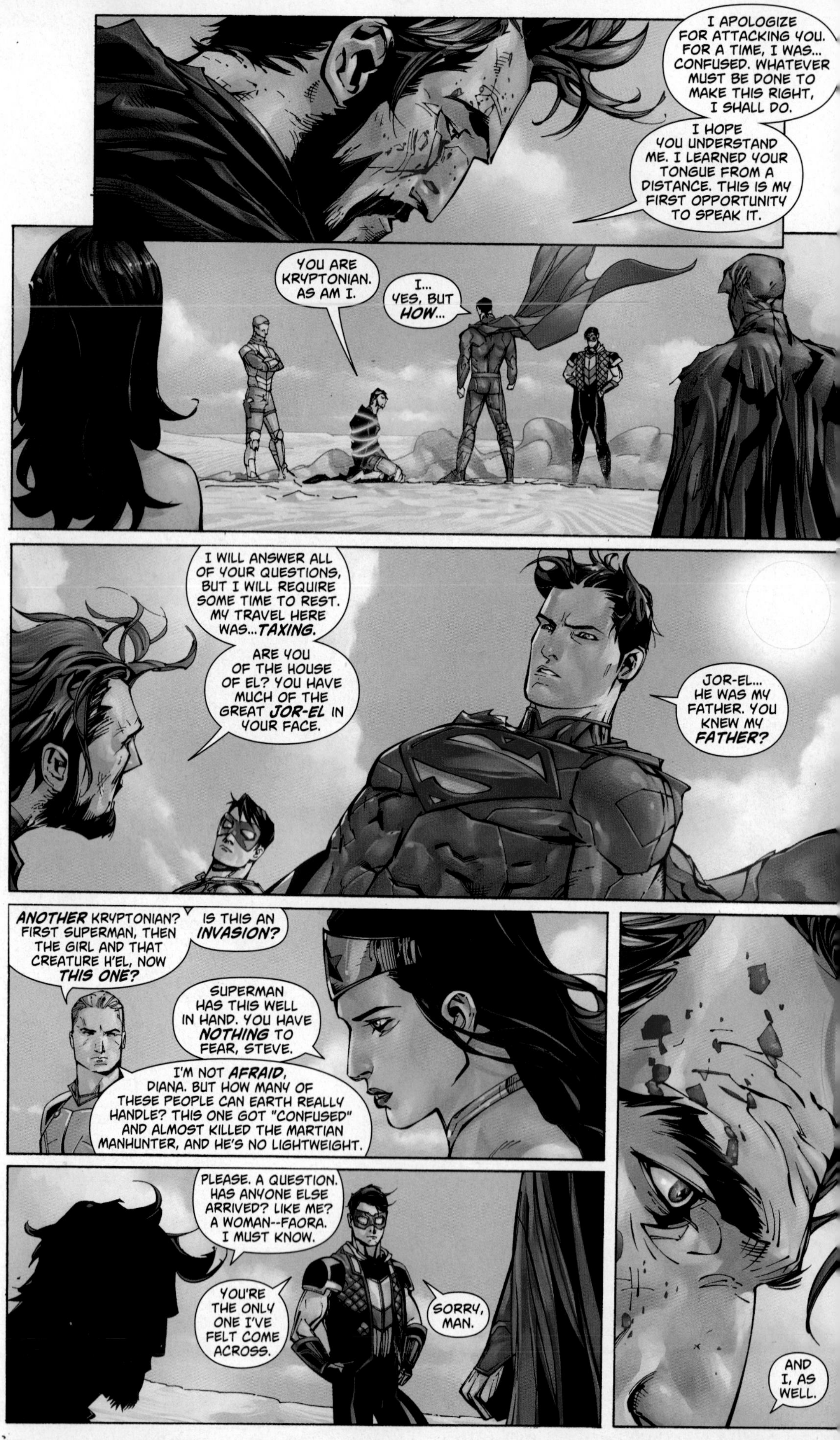

I APOLOGIZE FOR ATTACKING YOU. FOR A TIME, I WAS... CONFUSED. WHATEVER MUST BE DONE TO MAKE THIS RIGHT, I SHALL DO.
I HOPE YOU UNDERSTAND ME. I LEARNED YOUR TONGUE FROM A DISTANCE. THIS IS MY FIRST OPPORTUNITY TO SPEAK IT.
YOU ARE KRYPTONIAN. AS AM I.
I... YES, BUT HOW...
I WILL ANSWER ALL OF YOUR QUESTIONS, BUT I WILL REQUIRE SOME TIME TO REST. MY TRAVEL HERE WAS...TAXING.
ARE YOU OF THE HOUSE OF EL? YOU HAVE MUCH OF THE GREAT JOR-EL IN YOUR FACE.
JOR-EL... HE WAS MY FATHER. YOU KNEW MY FATHER?
ANOTHER KRYPTONIAN? FIRST SUPERMAN, THEN THE GIRL AND THAT CREATURE H'EL, NOW THIS ONE?
IS THIS AN INVASION?
SUPERMAN HAS THIS WELL IN HAND. YOU HAVE NOTHING TO FEAR, STEVE.
I'M NOT AFRAID, DIANA. BUT HOW MANY OF THESE PEOPLE CAN EARTH REALLY HANDLE? THIS ONE GOT "CONFUSED" AND ALMOST KILLED THE MARTIAN MANHUNTER, AND HE'S NO LIGHTWEIGHT.
PLEASE. A QUESTION. HAS ANYONE ELSE ARRIVED? LIKE ME? A WOMAN--FAORA. I MUST KNOW.
YOU'RE THE ONLY ONE I'VE FELT COME ACROSS.
SORRY, MAN.
AND I, AS WELL.

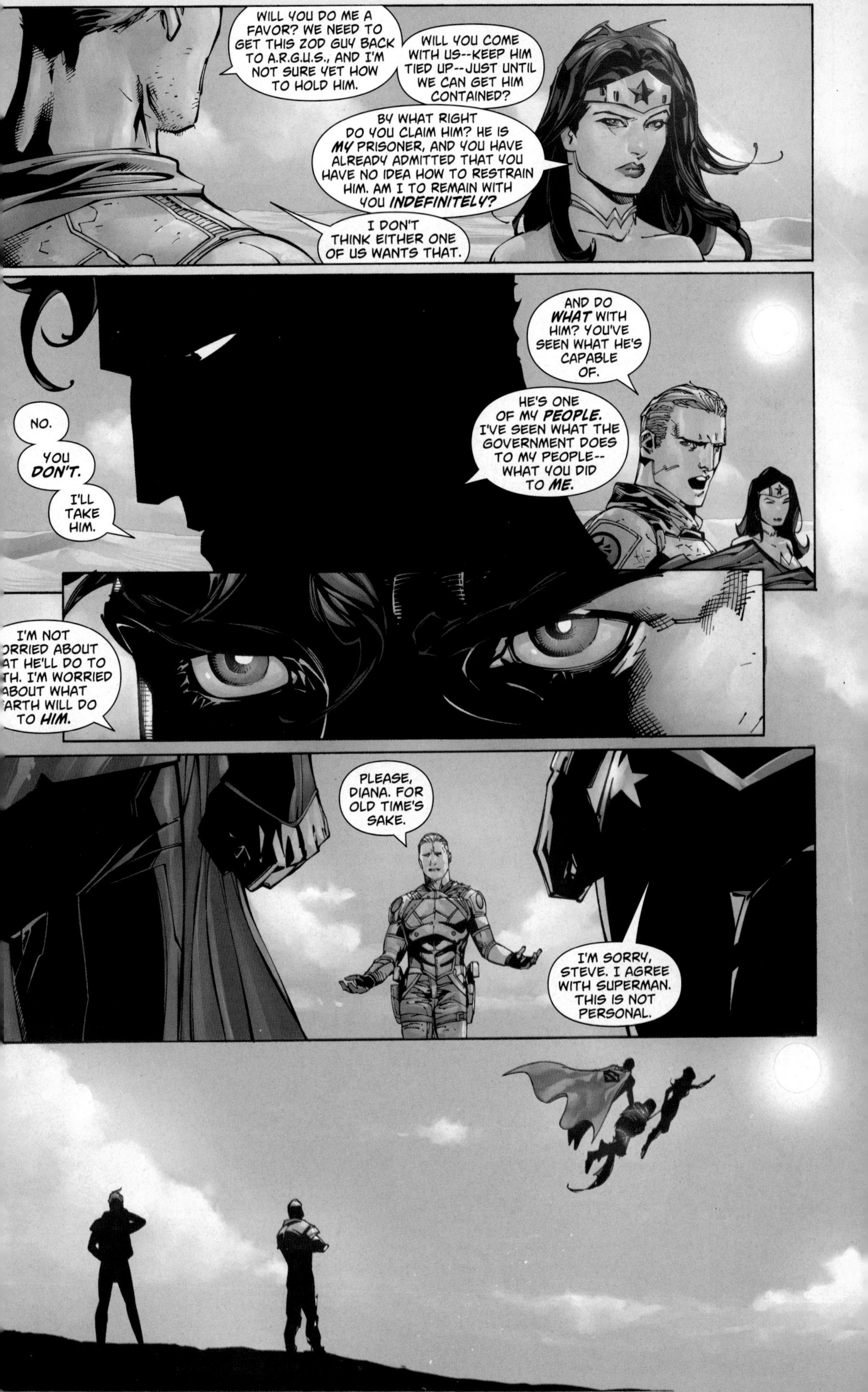

WILL YOU DO ME A FAVOR? WE NEED TO GET THIS ZOD GUY BACK TO A.R.G.U.S., AND I'M NOT SURE YET HOW TO HOLD HIM.
WILL YOU COME WITH US--KEEP HIM TIED UP--JUST UNTIL WE CAN GET HIM CONTAINED?
BY WHAT RIGHT DO YOU CLAIM HIM? HE IS MY PRISONER, AND YOU HAVE ALREADY ADMITTED THAT YOU HAVE NO IDEA HOW TO RESTRAIN HIM. AM I TO REMAIN WITH YOU INDEFINITELY?
I DON'T THINK EITHER ONE OF US WANTS THAT.
AND DO WHAT WITH HIM? YOU'VE SEEN WHAT HE'S CAPABLE OF.
HE'S ONE OF MY PEOPLE. I'VE SEEN WHAT THE GOVERNMENT DOES TO MY PEOPLE-- WHAT YOU DID TO ME.
NO.
YOU DON'T.
I'LL TAKE HIM.
I'M NOT ORRIED ABOUT AT HE'LL DO TO TH. I'M WORRIED ABOUT WHAT ARTH WILL DO TO HIM.
PLEASE, DIANA. FOR OLD TIME'S SAKE.
I'M SORRY, STEVE. I AGREE WITH SUPERMAN. THIS IS NOT PERSONAL.

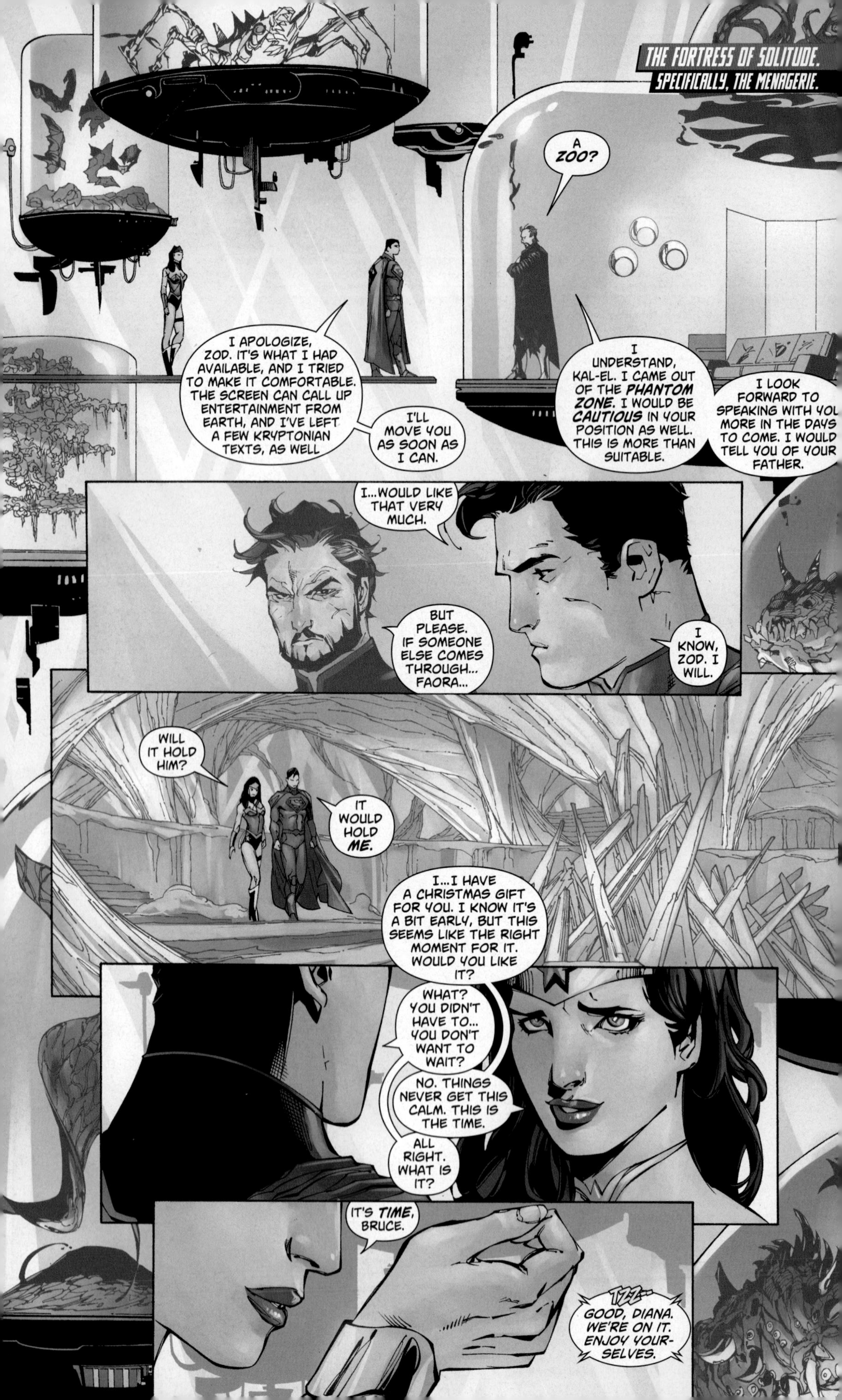
THE FORTRESS OF SOLITUDE. SPECIFICALLY, THE MENAGERIE.
A ZOO?
I APOLOGIZE, ZOD. IT'S WHAT I HAD AVAILABLE, AND I TRIED TO MAKE IT COMFORTABLE. THE SCREEN CAN CALL UP ENTERTAINMENT FROM EARTH, AND I'VE LEFT A FEW KRYPTONIAN TEXTS, AS WELL
I'LL MOVE YOU AS SOON AS I CAN.
I UNDERSTAND, KAL-EL. I CAME OUT OF THE PHANTOM ZONE. I WOULD BE CAUTIOUS IN YOUR POSITION AS WELL. THIS IS MORE THAN SUITABLE.
I LOOK FORWARD TO SPEAKING WITH YOU MORE IN THE DAYS TO COME. I WOULD TELL YOU OF YOUR FATHER.
I...WOULD LIKE THAT VERY MUCH.
BUT PLEASE. IF SOMEONE ELSE COMES THROUGH... FAORA...
I KNOW, ZOD. I WILL.
WILL IT HOLD HIM?
IT WOULD HOLD ME.
I...I HAVE A CHRISTMAS GIFT FOR YOU. I KNOW IT'S A BIT EARLY, BUT THIS SEEMS LIKE THE RIGHT MOMENT FOR IT. WOULD YOU LIKE IT?
WHAT? YOU DIDN'T HAVE TO... YOU DON'T WANT TO WAIT?
NO. THINGS NEVER GET THIS CALM. THIS IS THE TIME.
ALL RIGHT. WHAT IS IT?
IT'S TIME, BRUCE.
TZZZ
GOOD, DIANA. WE'RE ON IT. ENJOY YOURSELVES.

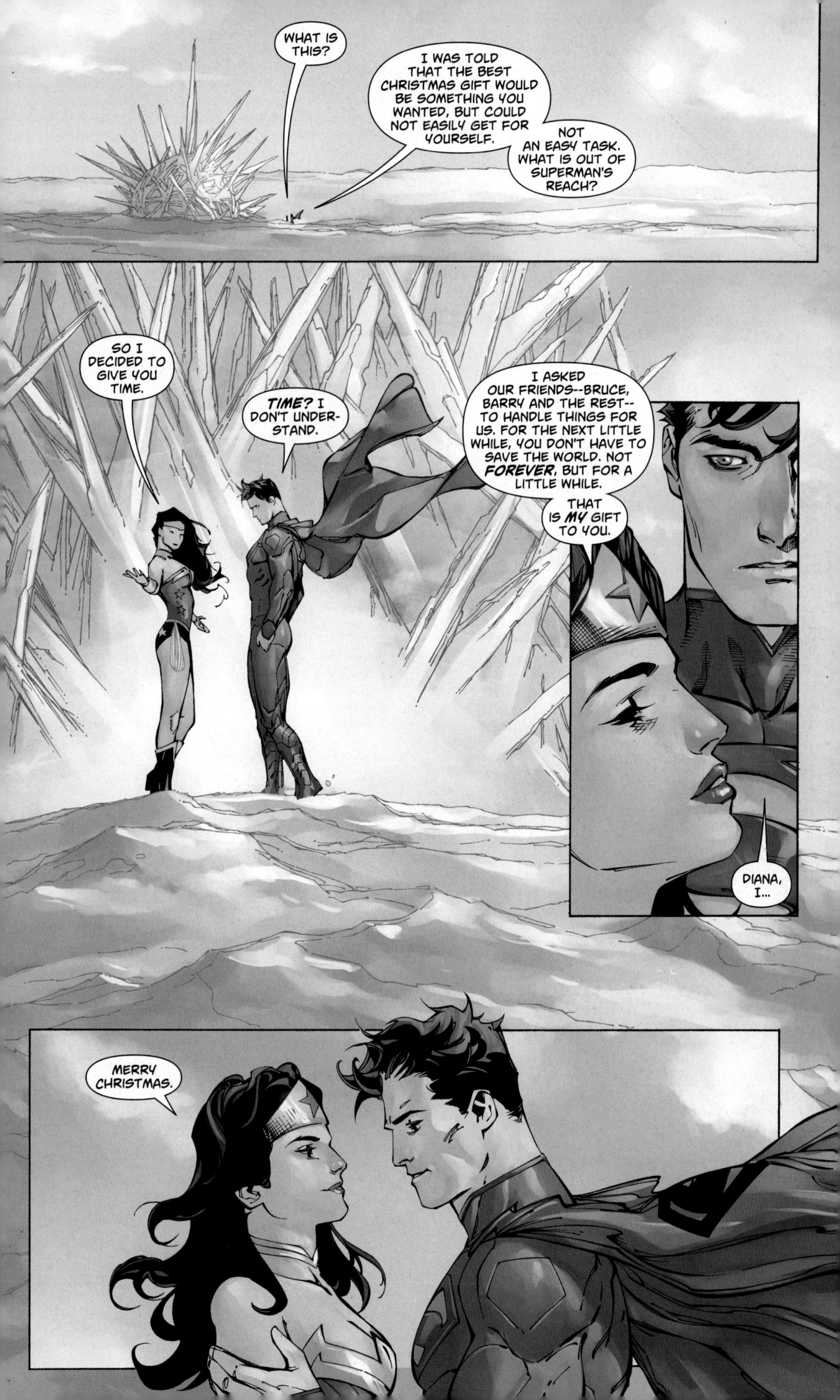

WHAT IS THIS?
I WAS TOLD THAT THE BEST CHRISTMAS GIFT WOULD BE SOMETHING YOU WANTED, BUT COULD NOT EASILY GET FOR YOURSELF.
NOT AN EASY TASK. WHAT IS OUT OF SUPERMAN'S REACH?
SO I DECIDED TO GIVE YOU TIME.
TIME? I DON'T UNDER-STAND.
I ASKED OUR FRIENDS--BRUCE, BARRY AND THE REST--TO HANDLE THINGS FOR US. FOR THE NEXT LITTLE WHILE, YOU DON'T HAVE TO SAVE THE WORLD. NOT *FOREVER*, BUT FOR A LITTLE WHILE.
THAT IS *MY* GIFT TO YOU.
DIANA, I...
MERRY CHRISTMAS.

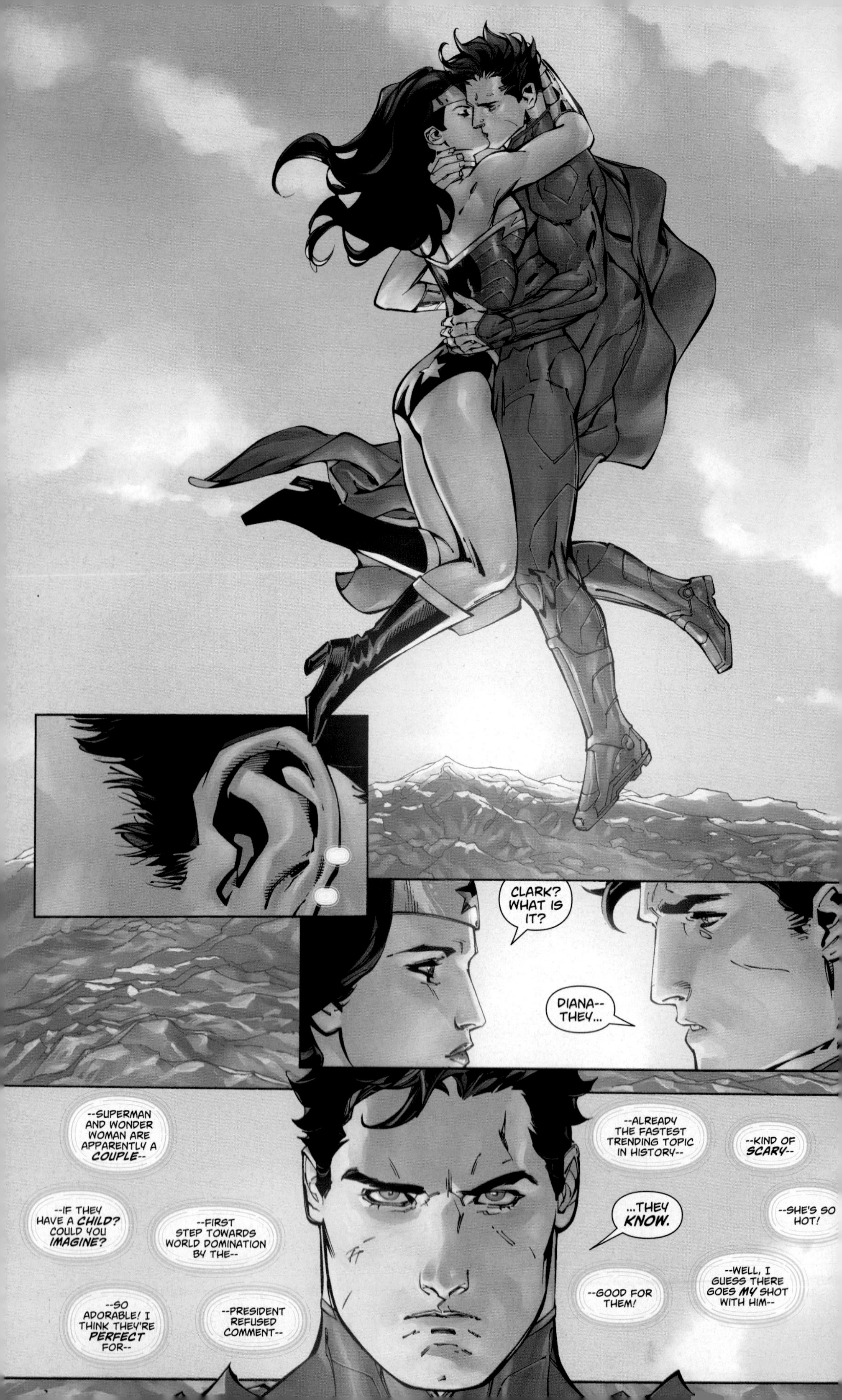
CLARK? WHAT IS IT?
DIANA-- THEY...
--SUPERMAN AND WONDER WOMAN ARE APPARENTLY A COUPLE--
--IF THEY HAVE A CHILD? COULD YOU IMAGINE?
--FIRST STEP TOWARDS WORLD DOMINATION BY THE--
--SO ADORABLE! I THINK THEY'RE PERFECT FOR--
--PRESIDENT REFUSED COMMENT--
--ALREADY THE FASTEST TRENDING TOPIC IN HISTORY--
--KIND OF SCARY--
...THEY KNOW.
--SHE'S SO HOT!
--GOOD FOR THEM!
--WELL, I GUESS THERE GOES MY SHOT WITH HIM--

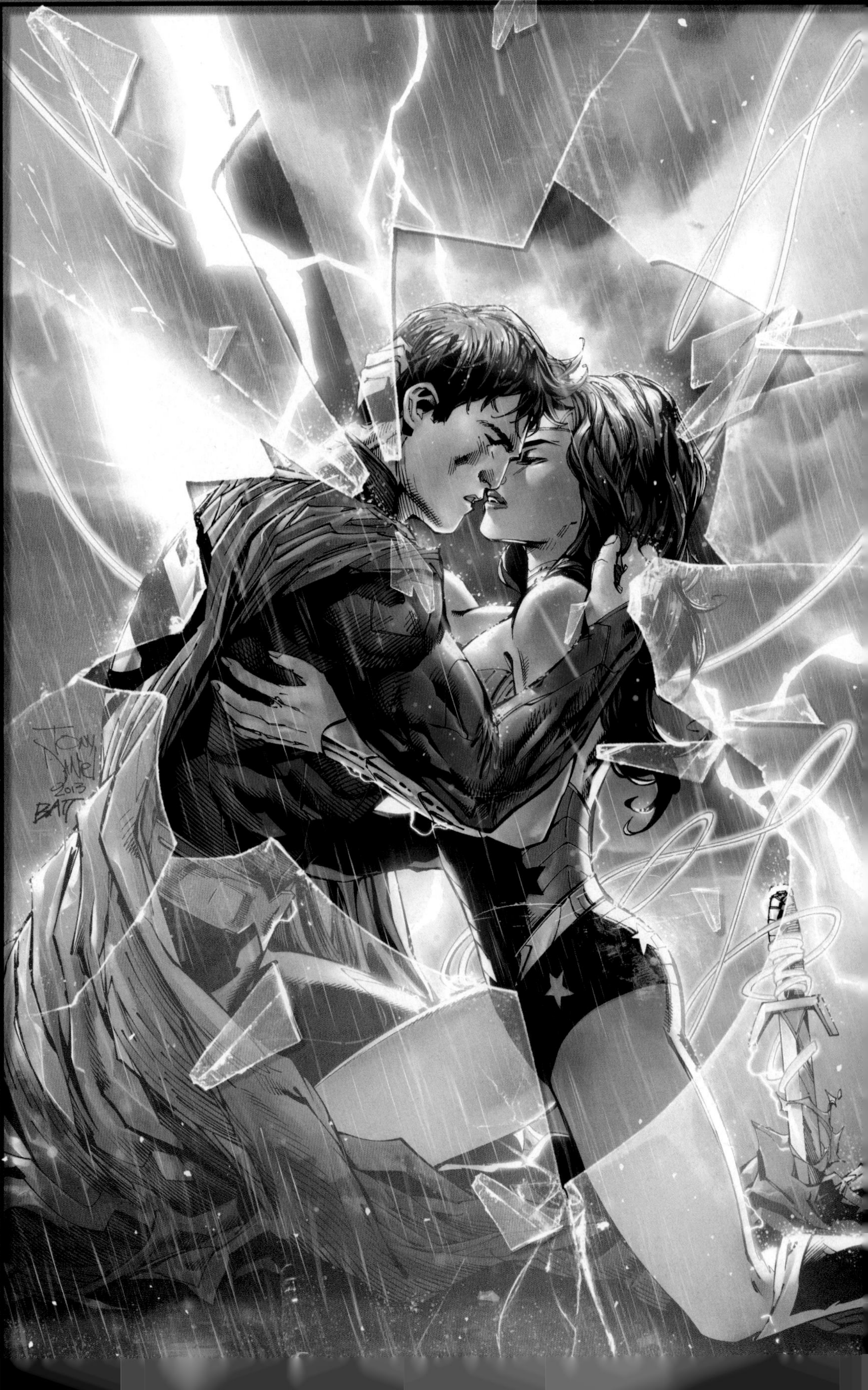

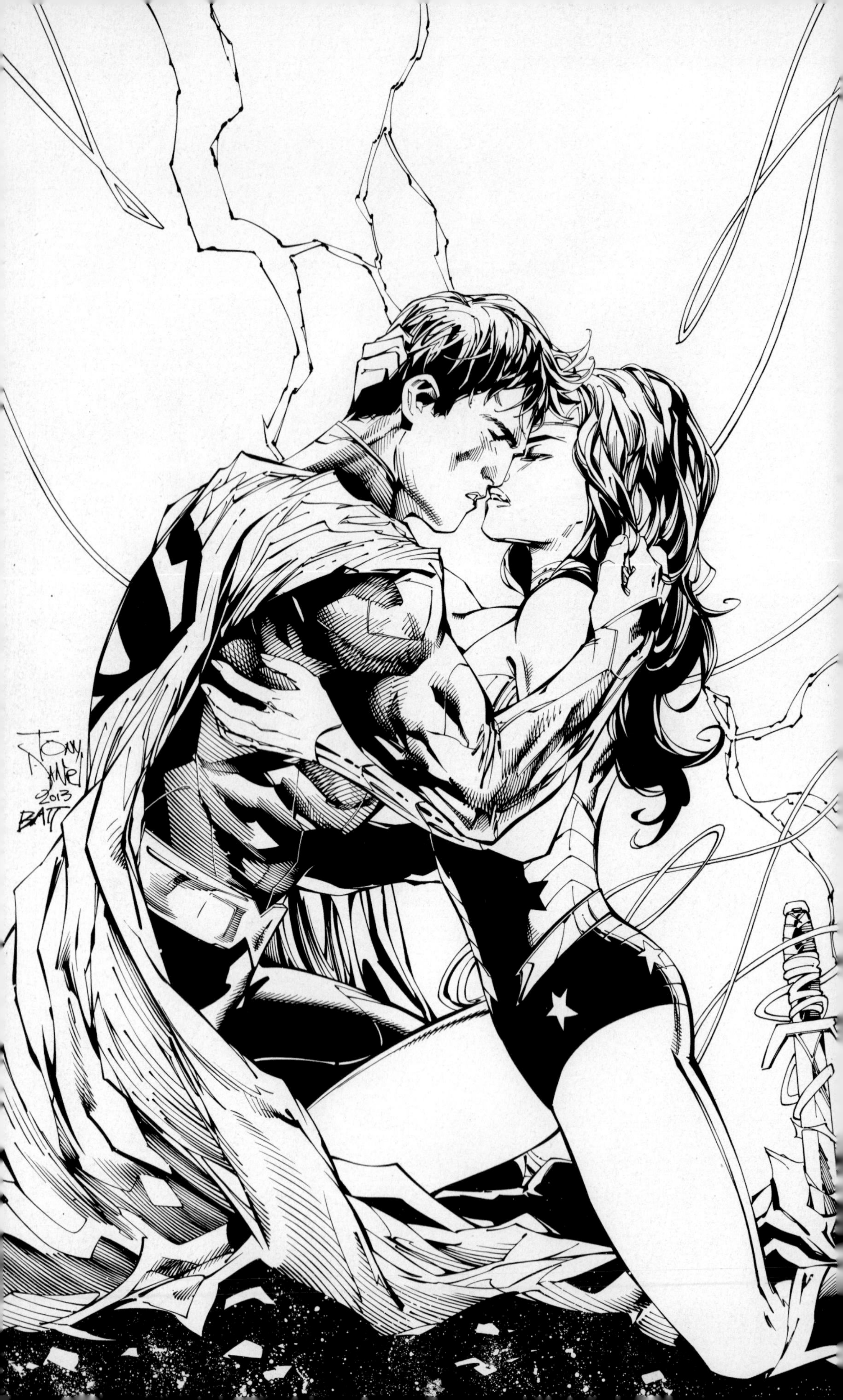
Tony Daniel
2013
BATT

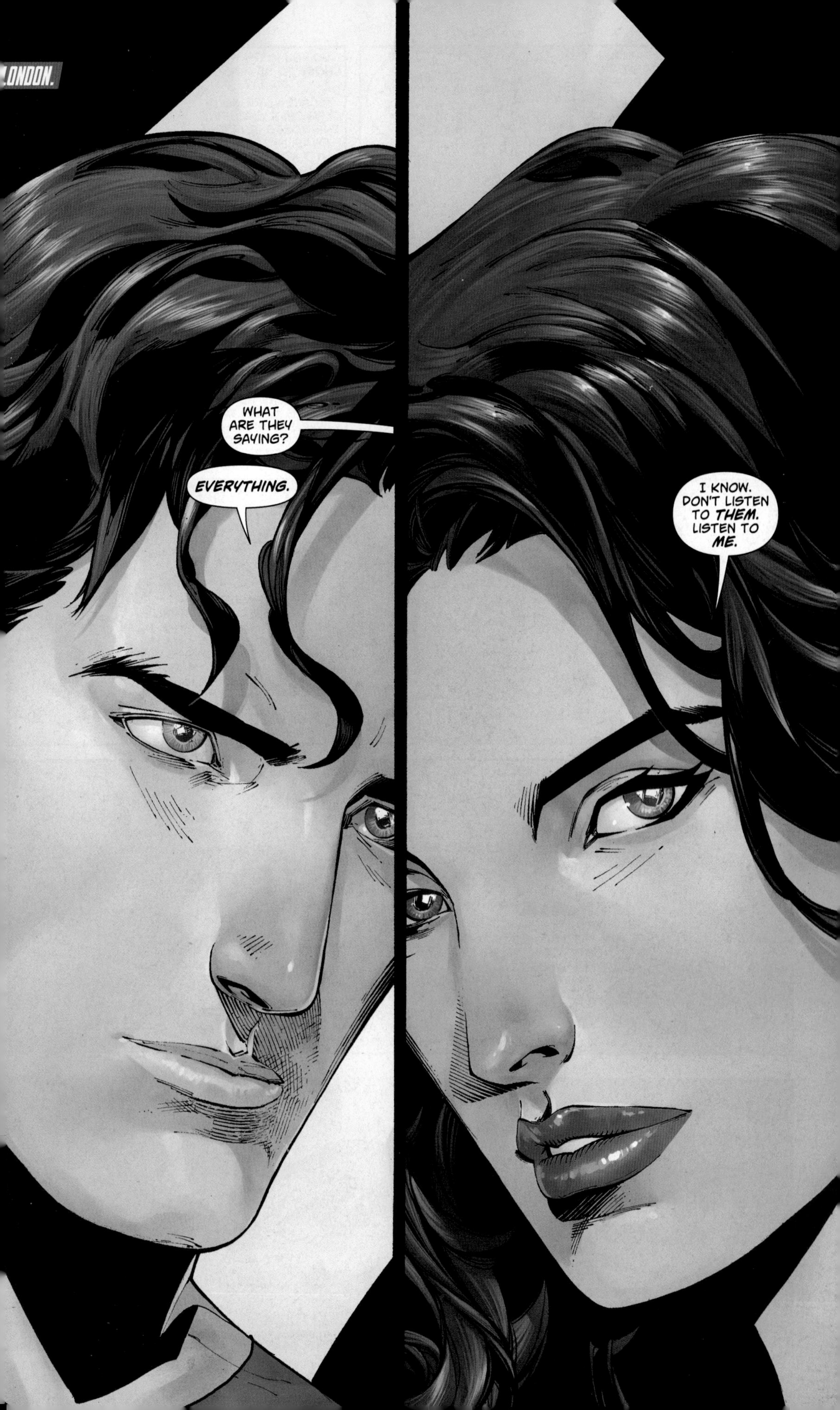

LONDON.
WHAT ARE THEY SAYING?
EVERYTHING.
I KNOW. DON'T LISTEN TO THEM. LISTEN TO ME.

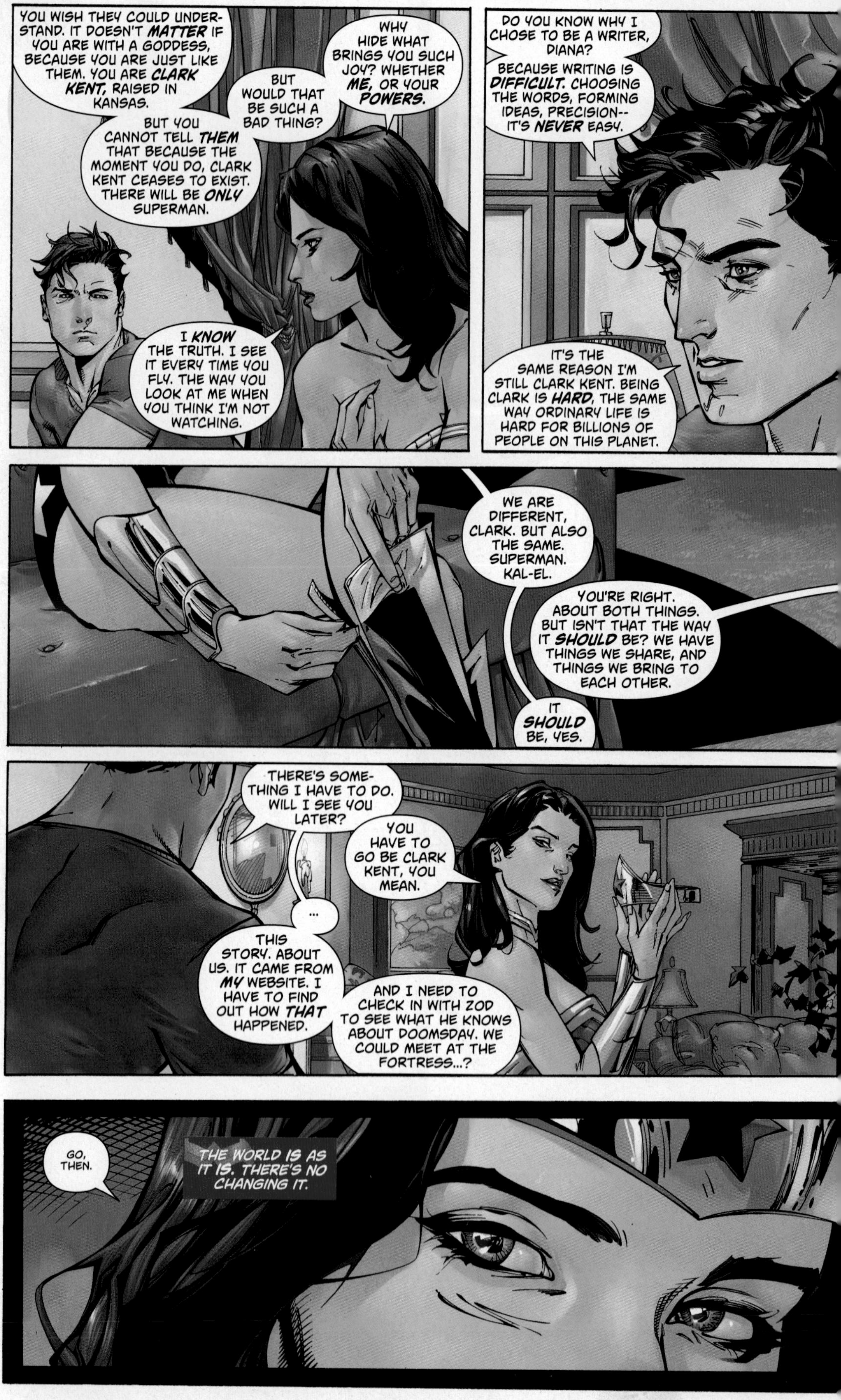

YOU WISH THEY COULD UNDERSTAND. IT DOESN'T MATTER IF YOU ARE WITH A GODDESS, BECAUSE YOU ARE JUST LIKE THEM. YOU ARE CLARK KENT, RAISED IN KANSAS.
BUT YOU CANNOT TELL THEM THAT BECAUSE THE MOMENT YOU DO, CLARK KENT CEASES TO EXIST. THERE WILL BE ONLY SUPERMAN.
BUT WOULD THAT BE SUCH A BAD THING?
WHY HIDE WHAT BRINGS YOU SUCH JOY? WHETHER ME, OR YOUR POWERS.
I KNOW THE TRUTH. I SEE IT EVERY TIME YOU FLY. THE WAY YOU LOOK AT ME WHEN YOU THINK I'M NOT WATCHING.
DO YOU KNOW WHY I CHOSE TO BE A WRITER, DIANA?
BECAUSE WRITING IS DIFFICULT. CHOOSING THE WORDS, FORMING IDEAS, PRECISION-- IT'S NEVER EASY.
IT'S THE SAME REASON I'M STILL CLARK KENT. BEING CLARK IS HARD, THE SAME WAY ORDINARY LIFE IS HARD FOR BILLIONS OF PEOPLE ON THIS PLANET.
WE ARE DIFFERENT, CLARK. BUT ALSO THE SAME. SUPERMAN. KAL-EL.
YOU'RE RIGHT. ABOUT BOTH THINGS. BUT ISN'T THAT THE WAY IT SHOULD BE? WE HAVE THINGS WE SHARE, AND THINGS WE BRING TO EACH OTHER.
IT SHOULD BE, YES.
THERE'S SOMETHING I HAVE TO DO. WILL I SEE YOU LATER?
YOU HAVE TO GO BE CLARK KENT, YOU MEAN.
...
THIS STORY. ABOUT US. IT CAME FROM MY WEBSITE. I HAVE TO FIND OUT HOW THAT HAPPENED.
AND I NEED TO CHECK IN WITH ZOD TO SEE WHAT HE KNOWS ABOUT DOOMSDAY. WE COULD MEET AT THE FORTRESS...?
GO, THEN.
THE WORLD IS AS IT IS. THERE'S NO CHANGING IT.

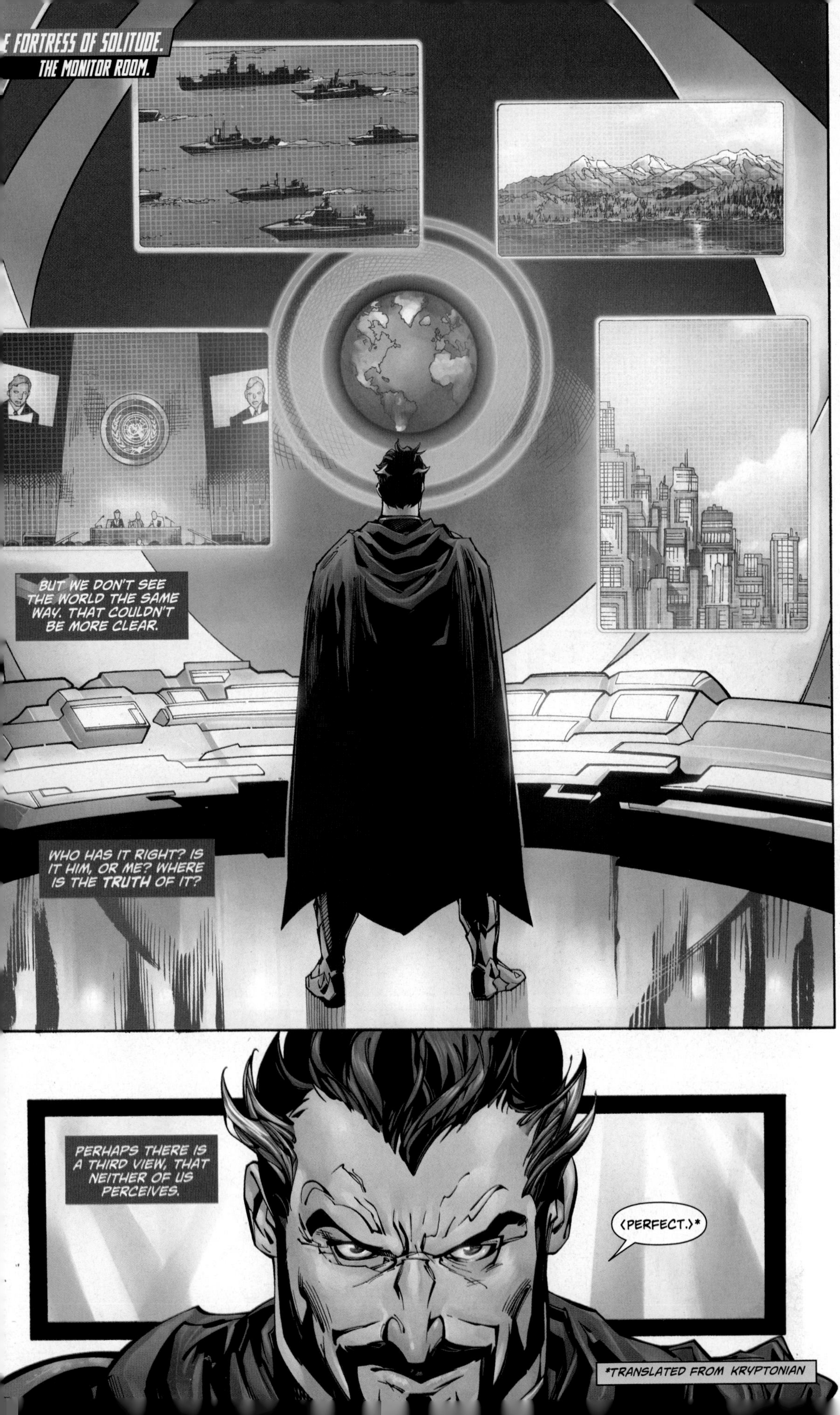
E FORTRESS OF SOLITUDE.
THE MONITOR ROOM.
BUT WE DON'T SEE THE WORLD THE SAME WAY. THAT COULDN'T BE MORE CLEAR.
WHO HAS IT RIGHT? IS IT HIM, OR ME? WHERE IS THE TRUTH OF IT?
PERHAPS THERE IS A THIRD VIEW, THAT NEITHER OF US PERCEIVES.
‹PERFECT.›*
*TRANSLATED FROM KRYPTONIAN

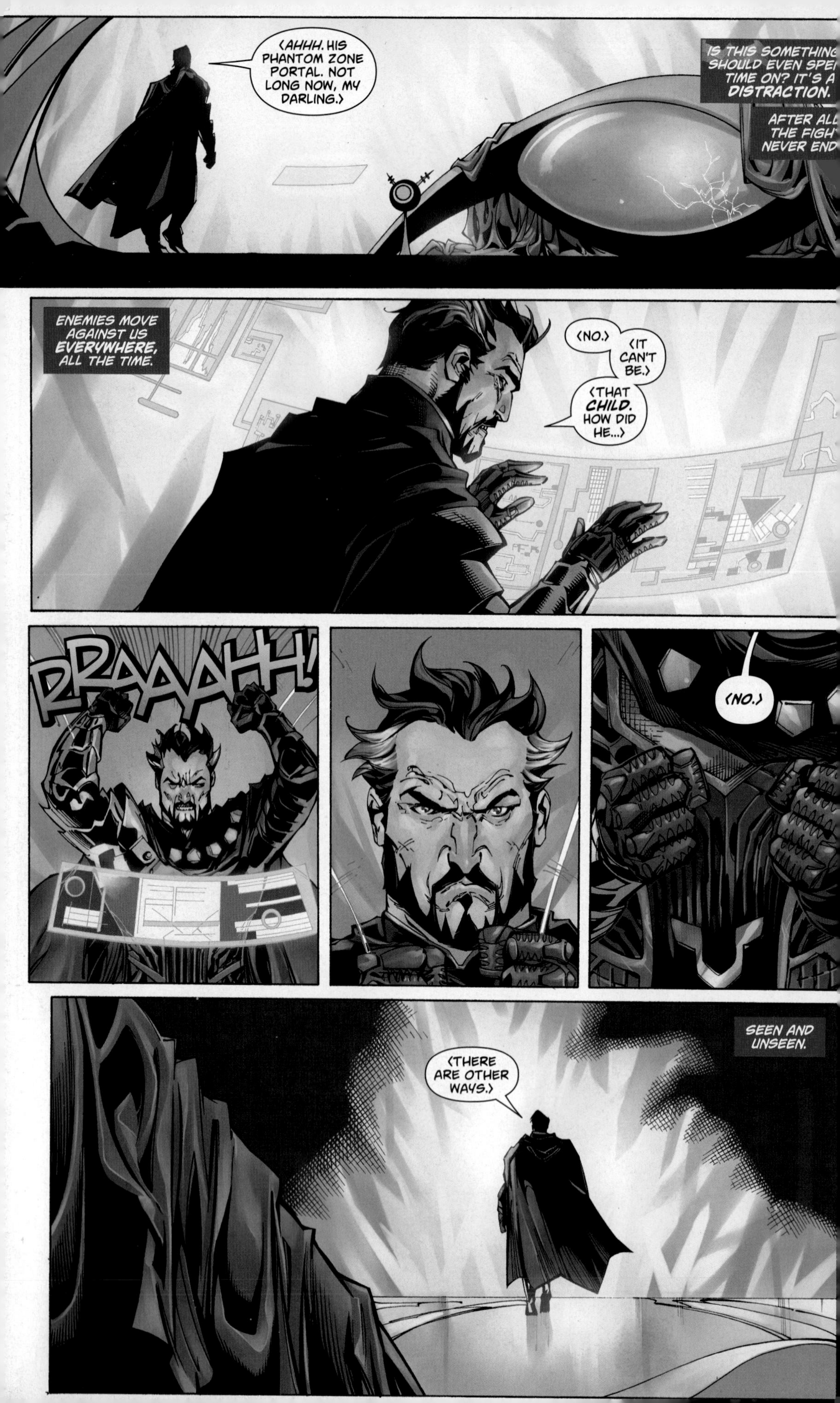
‹AHHH. HIS PHANTOM ZONE PORTAL. NOT LONG NOW, MY DARLING.›
IS THIS SOMETHING SHOULD EVEN SPE TIME ON? IT'S A DISTRACTION.
AFTER ALL THE FIGH NEVER END
ENEMIES MOVE AGAINST US EVERYWHERE, ALL THE TIME.
‹NO.›
‹IT CAN'T BE.›
‹THAT CHILD. HOW DID HE...›
RRAAAHH!
‹NO.›
SEEN AND UNSEEN.
‹THERE ARE OTHER WAYS.›

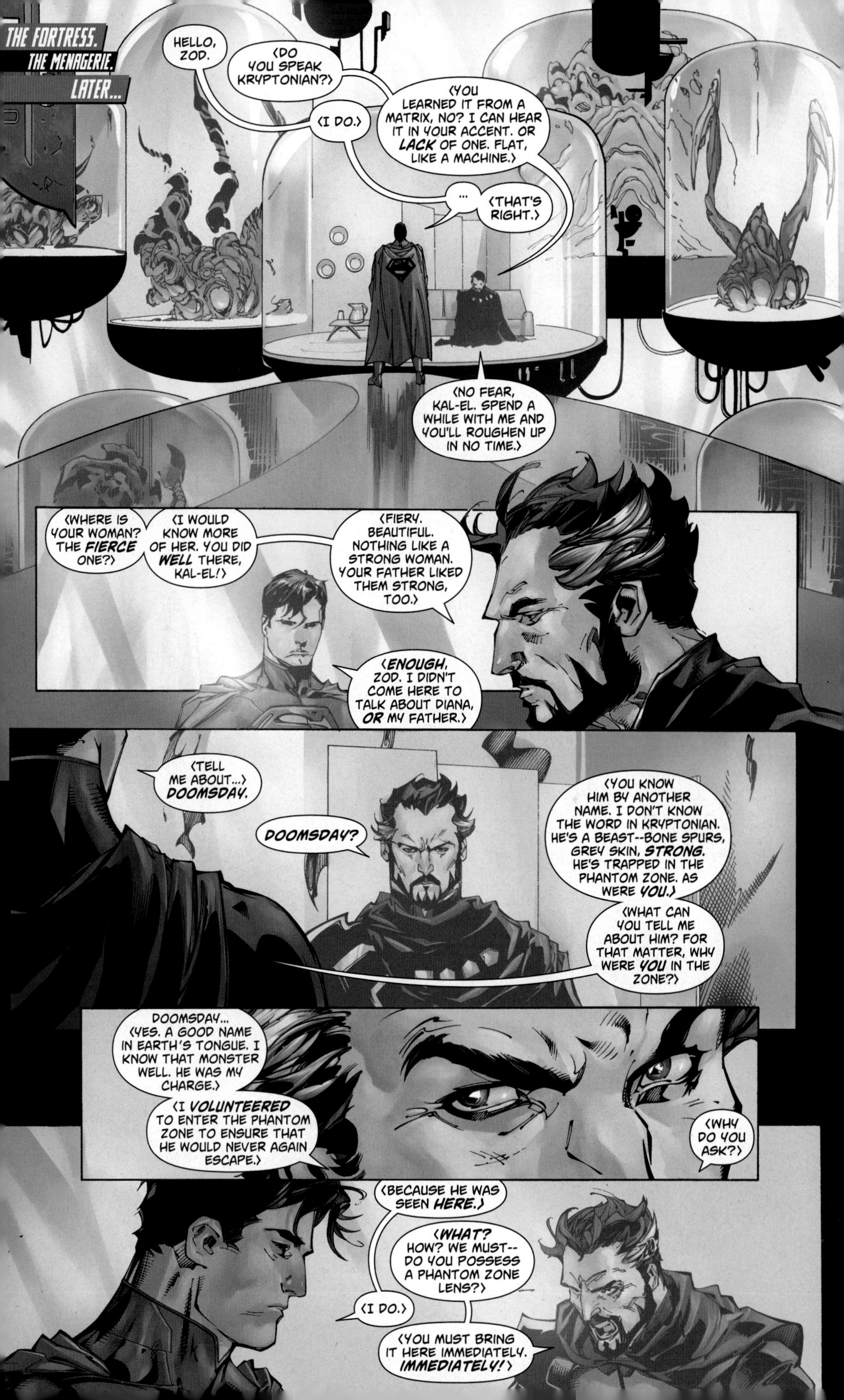
THE FORTRESS.
THE MENAGERIE.
LATER...
HELLO, ZOD.
⟨DO YOU SPEAK KRYPTONIAN?⟩
⟨I DO.⟩
⟨YOU LEARNED IT FROM A MATRIX, NO? I CAN HEAR IT IN YOUR ACCENT. OR LACK OF ONE. FLAT, LIKE A MACHINE.⟩
...
⟨THAT'S RIGHT.⟩
⟨NO FEAR, KAL-EL. SPEND A WHILE WITH ME AND YOU'LL ROUGHEN UP IN NO TIME.⟩
⟨WHERE IS YOUR WOMAN? THE FIERCE ONE?⟩
⟨I WOULD KNOW MORE OF HER. YOU DID WELL THERE, KAL-EL!⟩
⟨FIERY. BEAUTIFUL. NOTHING LIKE A STRONG WOMAN. YOUR FATHER LIKED THEM STRONG, TOO.⟩
⟨ENOUGH, ZOD. I DIDN'T COME HERE TO TALK ABOUT DIANA, OR MY FATHER.⟩
⟨TELL ME ABOUT...⟩ DOOMSDAY.
DOOMSDAY?
⟨YOU KNOW HIM BY ANOTHER NAME. I DON'T KNOW THE WORD IN KRYPTONIAN. HE'S A BEAST--BONE SPURS, GREY SKIN, STRONG. HE'S TRAPPED IN THE PHANTOM ZONE. AS WERE YOU.⟩
⟨WHAT CAN YOU TELL ME ABOUT HIM? FOR THAT MATTER, WHY WERE YOU IN THE ZONE?⟩
DOOMSDAY... ⟨YES. A GOOD NAME IN EARTH'S TONGUE. I KNOW THAT MONSTER WELL. HE WAS MY CHARGE.⟩
⟨I VOLUNTEERED TO ENTER THE PHANTOM ZONE TO ENSURE THAT HE WOULD NEVER AGAIN ESCAPE.⟩
⟨WHY DO YOU ASK?⟩
⟨BECAUSE HE WAS SEEN HERE.⟩
⟨WHAT? HOW? WE MUST-- DO YOU POSSESS A PHANTOM ZONE LENS?⟩
⟨I DO.⟩
⟨YOU MUST BRING IT HERE IMMEDIATELY. IMMEDIATELY!⟩

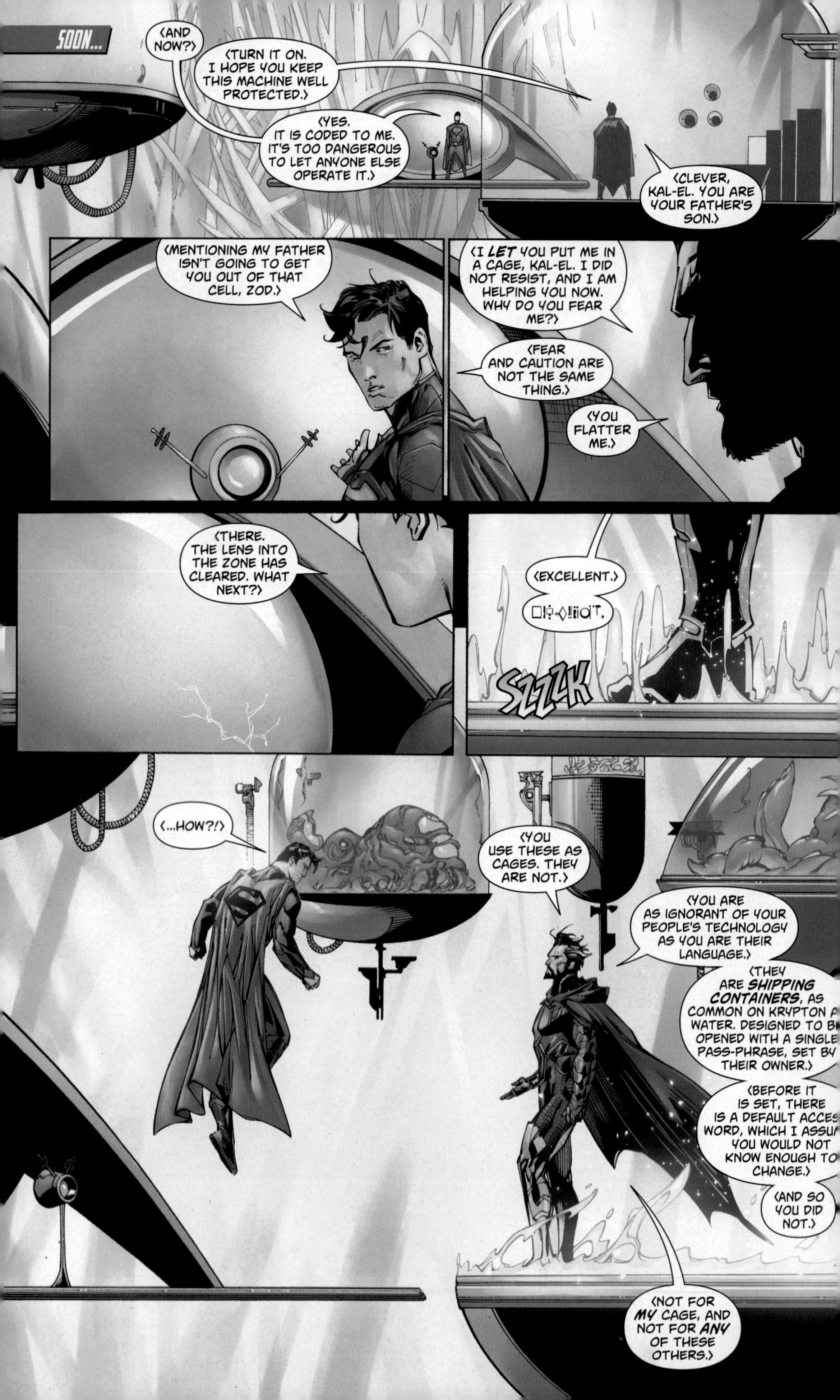
SOON...
⟨AND NOW?⟩
⟨TURN IT ON. I HOPE YOU KEEP THIS MACHINE WELL PROTECTED.⟩
⟨YES. IT IS CODED TO ME. IT'S TOO DANGEROUS TO LET ANYONE ELSE OPERATE IT.⟩
⟨CLEVER, KAL-EL. YOU ARE YOUR FATHER'S SON.⟩
⟨MENTIONING MY FATHER ISN'T GOING TO GET YOU OUT OF THAT CELL, ZOD.⟩
⟨I LET YOU PUT ME IN A CAGE, KAL-EL. I DID NOT RESIST, AND I AM HELPING YOU NOW. WHY DO YOU FEAR ME?⟩
⟨FEAR AND CAUTION ARE NOT THE SAME THING.⟩
⟨YOU FLATTER ME.⟩
⟨THERE. THE LENS INTO THE ZONE HAS CLEARED. WHAT NEXT?⟩
⟨EXCELLENT.⟩
SZZZK
⟨...HOW?!⟩
⟨YOU USE THESE AS CAGES. THEY ARE NOT.⟩
⟨YOU ARE AS IGNORANT OF YOUR PEOPLE'S TECHNOLOGY AS YOU ARE THEIR LANGUAGE.⟩
⟨THEY ARE SHIPPING CONTAINERS, AS COMMON ON KRYPTON A WATER. DESIGNED TO B OPENED WITH A SINGLE PASS-PHRASE, SET BY THEIR OWNER.⟩
⟨BEFORE IT IS SET, THERE IS A DEFAULT ACCES WORD, WHICH I ASSU YOU WOULD NOT KNOW ENOUGH TO CHANGE.⟩
⟨AND SO YOU DID NOT.⟩
⟨NOT FOR MY CAGE, AND NOT FOR ANY OF THESE OTHERS.⟩

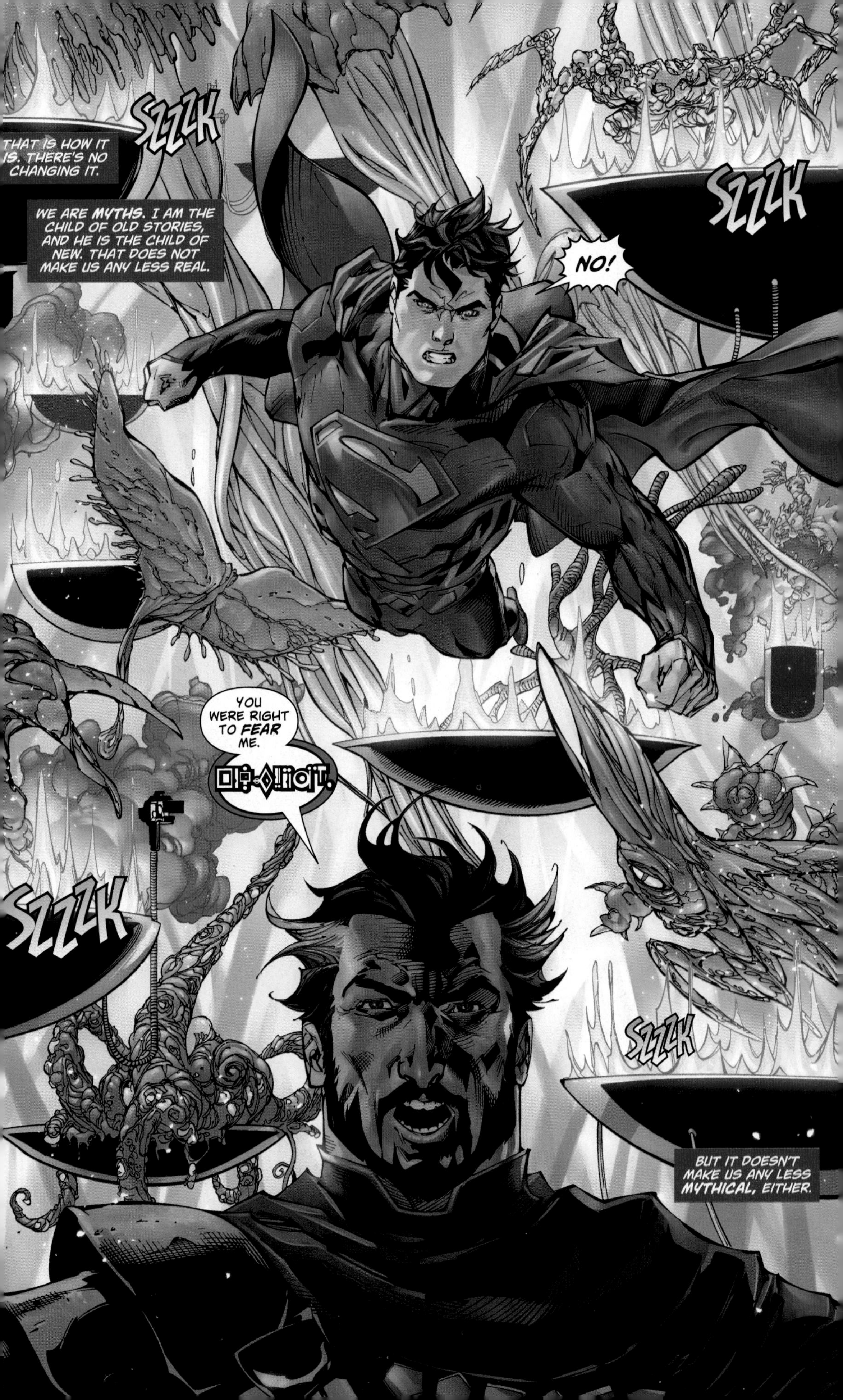

SZZZK
THAT IS HOW IT IS. THERE'S NO CHANGING IT.
WE ARE MYTHS. I AM THE CHILD OF OLD STORIES, AND HE IS THE CHILD OF NEW. THAT DOES NOT MAKE US ANY LESS REAL.
SZZZK
NO!
YOU WERE RIGHT TO FEAR ME.
SZZZK
SZZZK
BUT IT DOESN'T MAKE US ANY LESS MYTHICAL, EITHER.

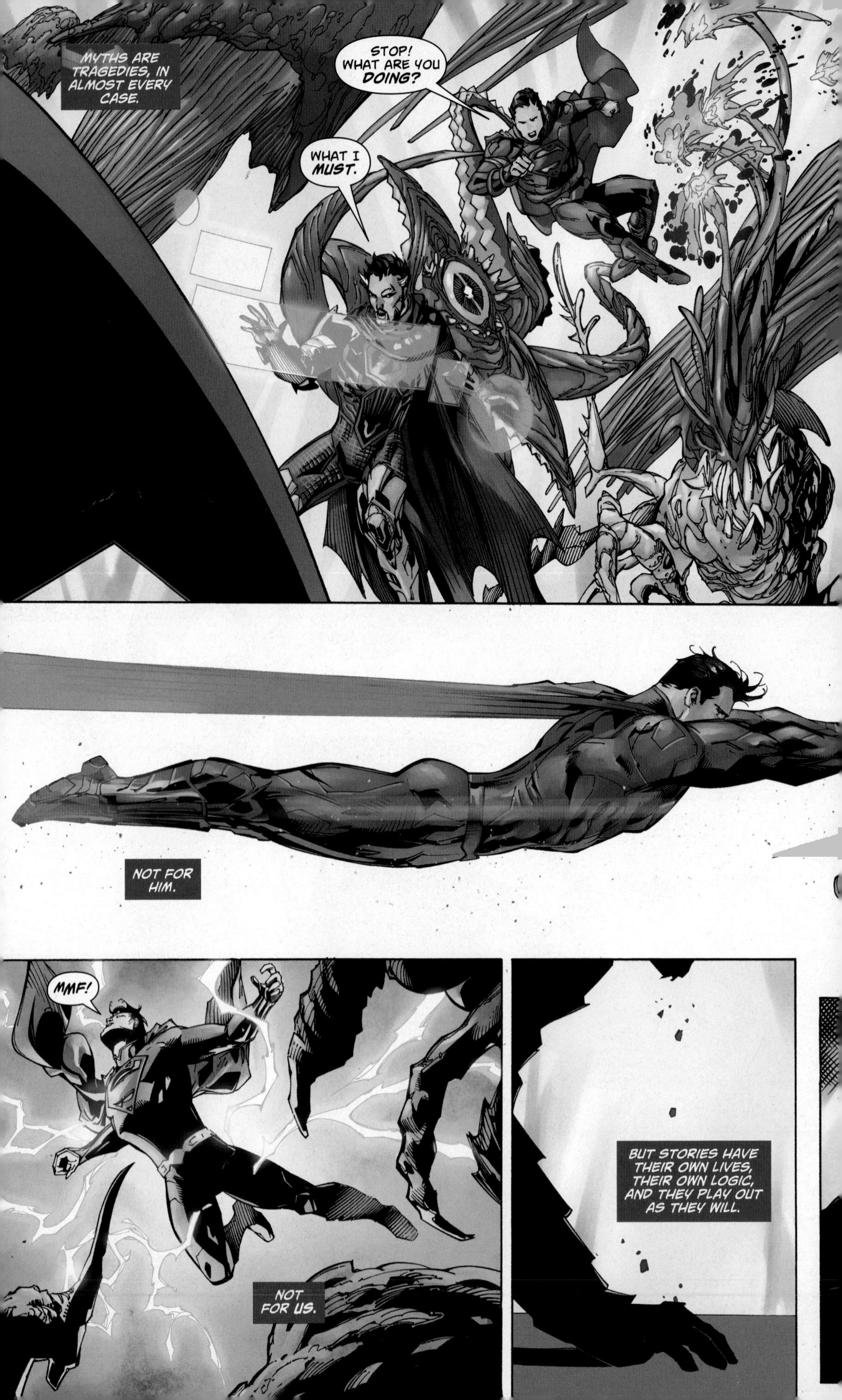

MYTHS ARE TRAGEDIES, IN ALMOST EVERY CASE.
STOP! WHAT ARE YOU DOING?
WHAT I MUST.
NOT FOR HIM.
MMF!
NOT FOR US.
BUT STORIES HAVE THEIR OWN LIVES, THEIR OWN LOGIC, AND THEY PLAY OUT AS THEY WILL.

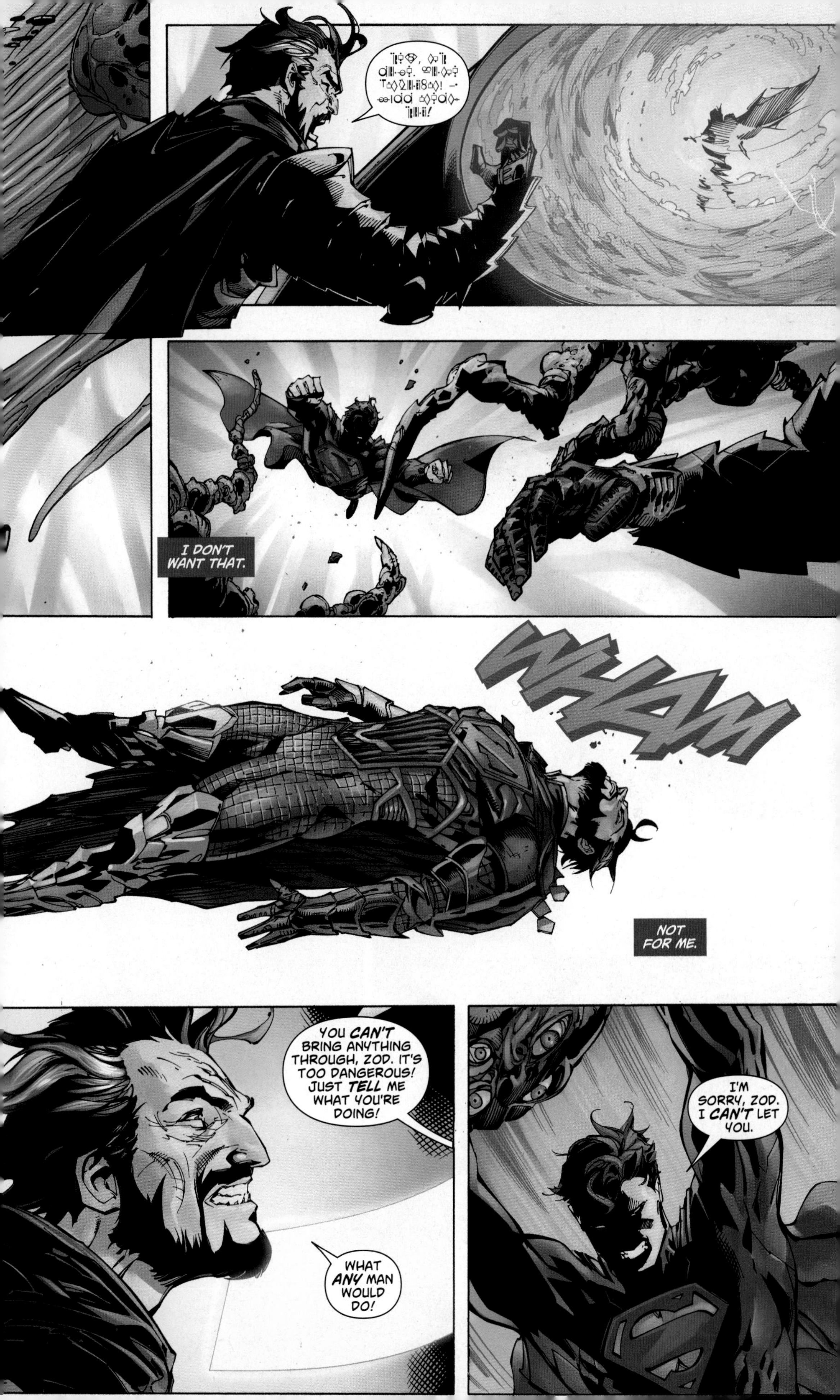
I DON'T WANT THAT.
WHAM
NOT FOR ME.
YOU CAN'T BRING ANYTHING THROUGH, ZOD. IT'S TOO DANGEROUS! JUST TELL ME WHAT YOU'RE DOING!
WHAT ANY MAN WOULD DO!
I'M SORRY, ZOD. I CAN'T LET YOU.

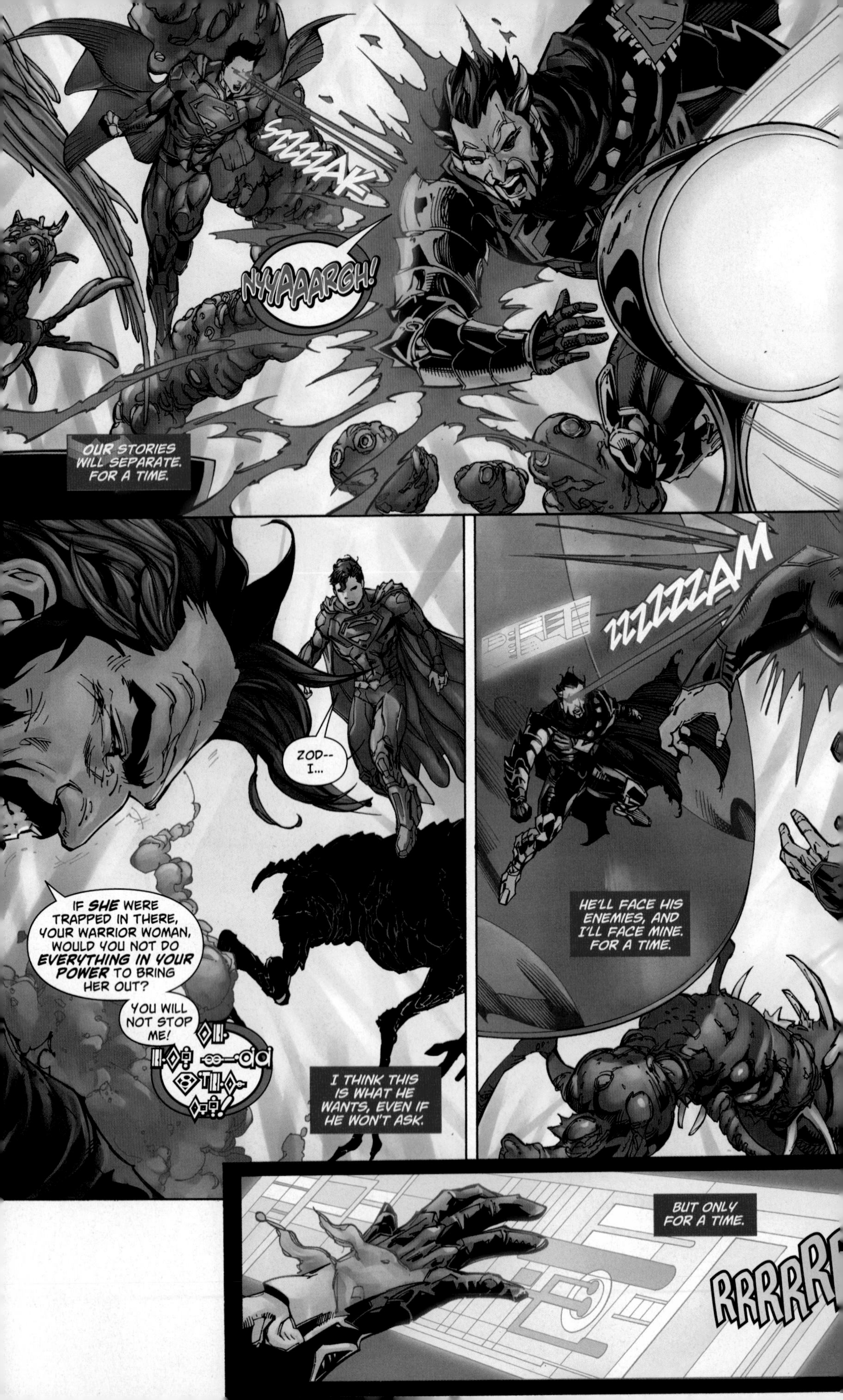
SZZZZAK
NYYAAARGH!
OUR STORIES WILL SEPARATE. FOR A TIME.
ZOD-- I...
IF SHE WERE TRAPPED IN THERE, YOUR WARRIOR WOMAN, WOULD YOU NOT DO EVERYTHING IN YOUR POWER TO BRING HER OUT?
YOU WILL NOT STOP ME!
I THINK THIS IS WHAT HE WANTS, EVEN IF HE WON'T ASK.
ZZZZZZAM
HE'LL FACE HIS ENEMIES, AND I'LL FACE MINE. FOR A TIME.
BUT ONLY FOR A TIME.
RRRRR

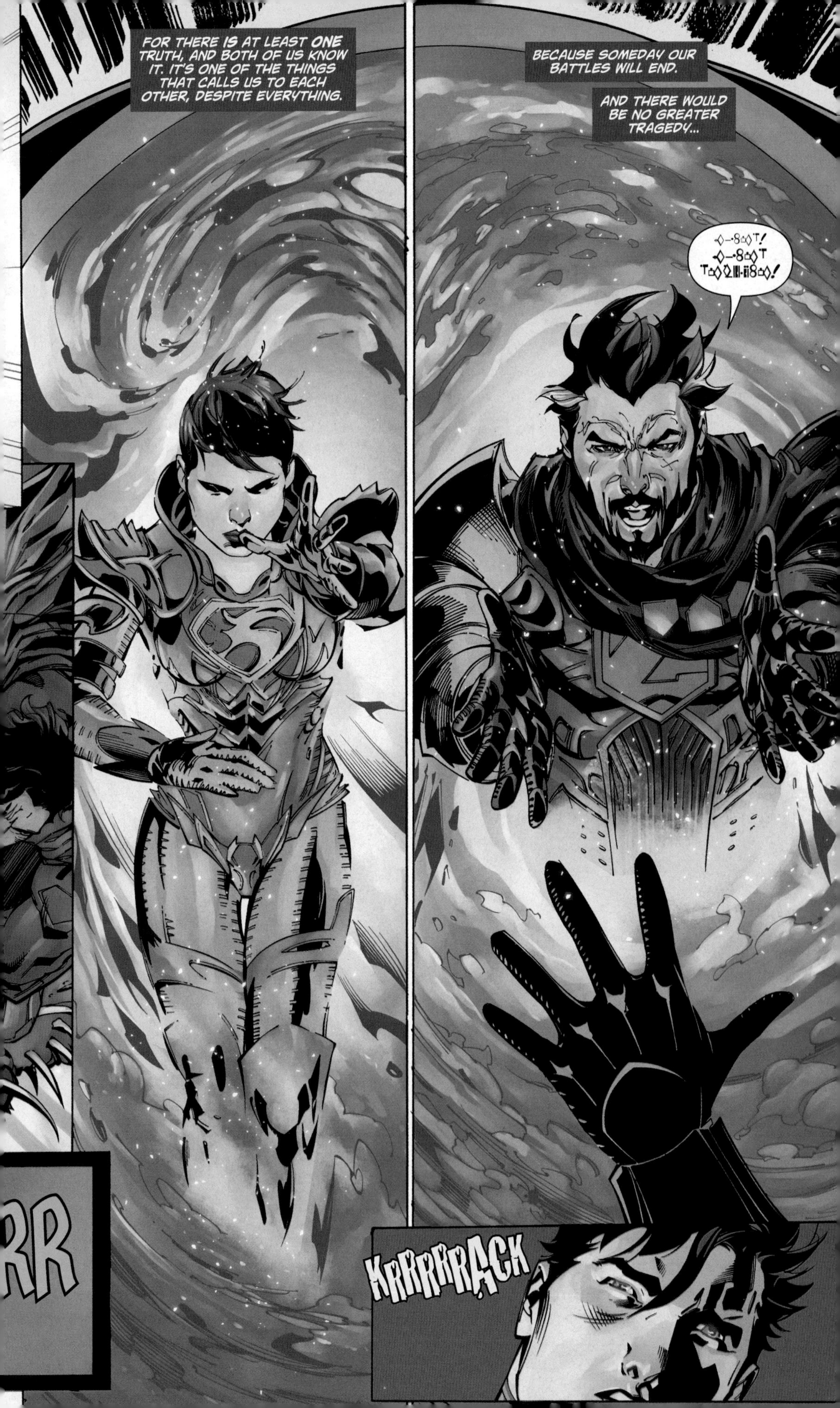
FOR THERE IS AT LEAST ONE TRUTH, AND BOTH OF US KNOW IT. IT'S ONE OF THE THINGS THAT CALLS US TO EACH OTHER, DESPITE EVERYTHING.
BECAUSE SOMEDAY OUR BATTLES WILL END.
AND THERE WOULD BE NO GREATER TRAGEDY...
RR
KRRRRRACK

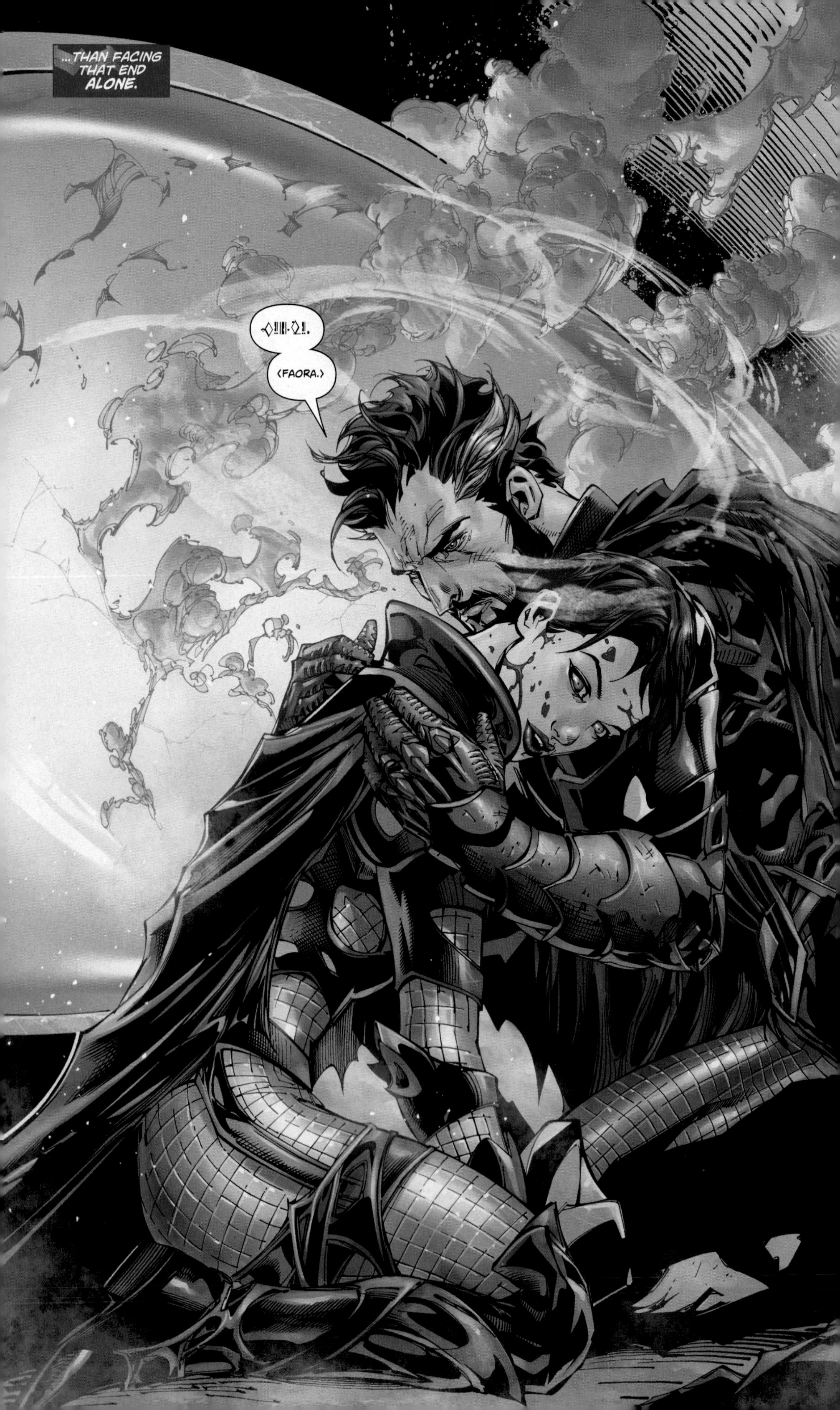
...THAN FACING THAT END ALONE.
<FAORA.>

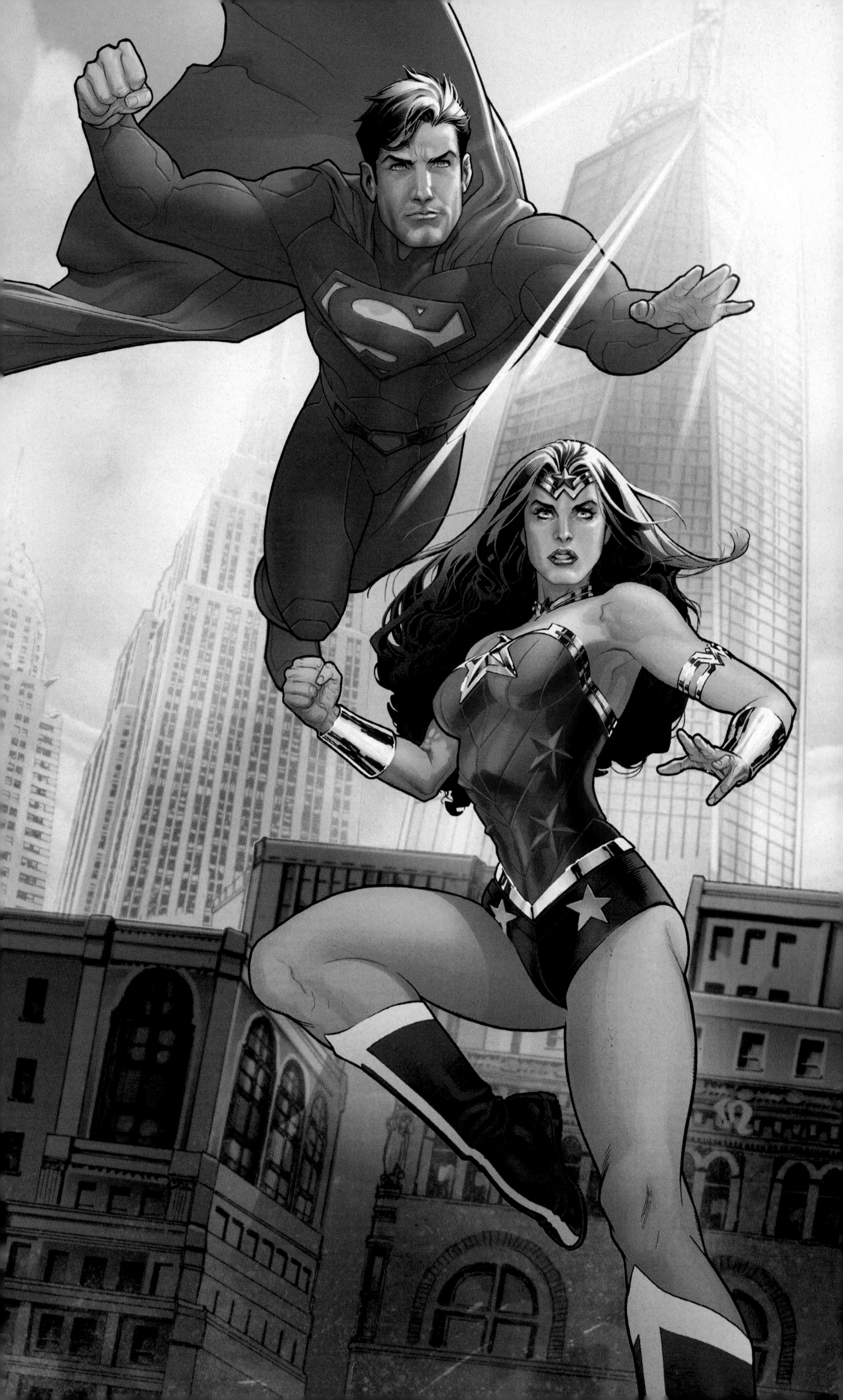

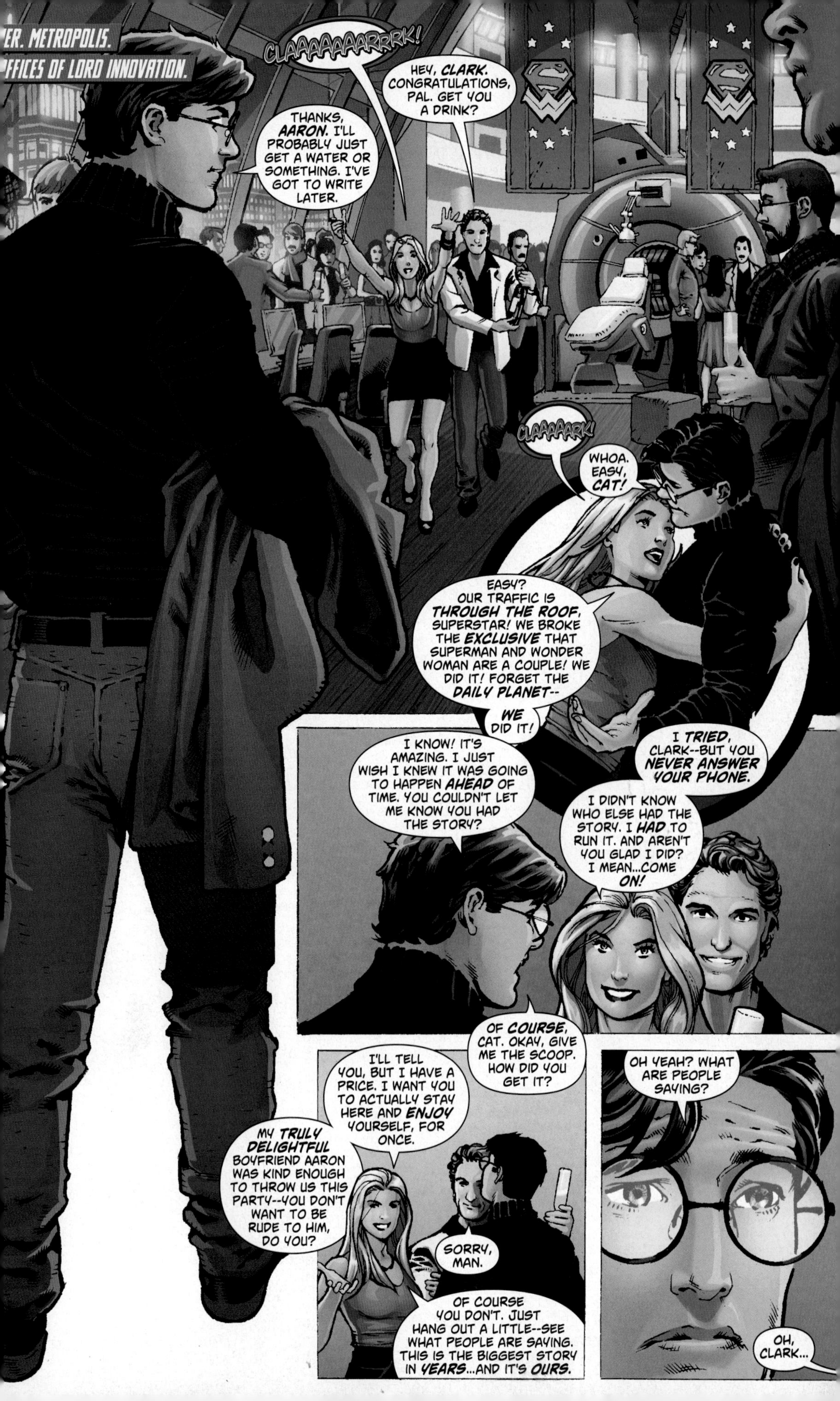
ER. METROPOLIS.
FFICES OF LORD INNOVATION.
CLAAAAAAARRRK!
HEY, CLARK. CONGRATULATIONS, PAL. GET YOU A DRINK?
THANKS, AARON. I'LL PROBABLY JUST GET A WATER OR SOMETHING. I'VE GOT TO WRITE LATER.
CLAAAAARK!
WHOA. EASY, CAT!
EASY? OUR TRAFFIC IS THROUGH THE ROOF, SUPERSTAR! WE BROKE THE EXCLUSIVE THAT SUPERMAN AND WONDER WOMAN ARE A COUPLE! WE DID IT! FORGET THE DAILY PLANET--
WE DID IT!
I KNOW! IT'S AMAZING. I JUST WISH I KNEW IT WAS GOING TO HAPPEN AHEAD OF TIME. YOU COULDN'T LET ME KNOW YOU HAD THE STORY?
I TRIED, CLARK--BUT YOU NEVER ANSWER YOUR PHONE.
I DIDN'T KNOW WHO ELSE HAD THE STORY. I HAD TO RUN IT. AND AREN'T YOU GLAD I DID? I MEAN...COME ON!
OF COURSE, CAT. OKAY, GIVE ME THE SCOOP. HOW DID YOU GET IT?
I'LL TELL YOU, BUT I HAVE A PRICE. I WANT YOU TO ACTUALLY STAY HERE AND ENJOY YOURSELF, FOR ONCE.
MY TRULY DELIGHTFUL BOYFRIEND AARON WAS KIND ENOUGH TO THROW US THIS PARTY--YOU DON'T WANT TO BE RUDE TO HIM, DO YOU?
SORRY, MAN.
OF COURSE YOU DON'T. JUST HANG OUT A LITTLE--SEE WHAT PEOPLE ARE SAYING. THIS IS THE BIGGEST STORY IN YEARS...AND IT'S OURS.
OH YEAH? WHAT ARE PEOPLE SAYING?
OH, CLARK...

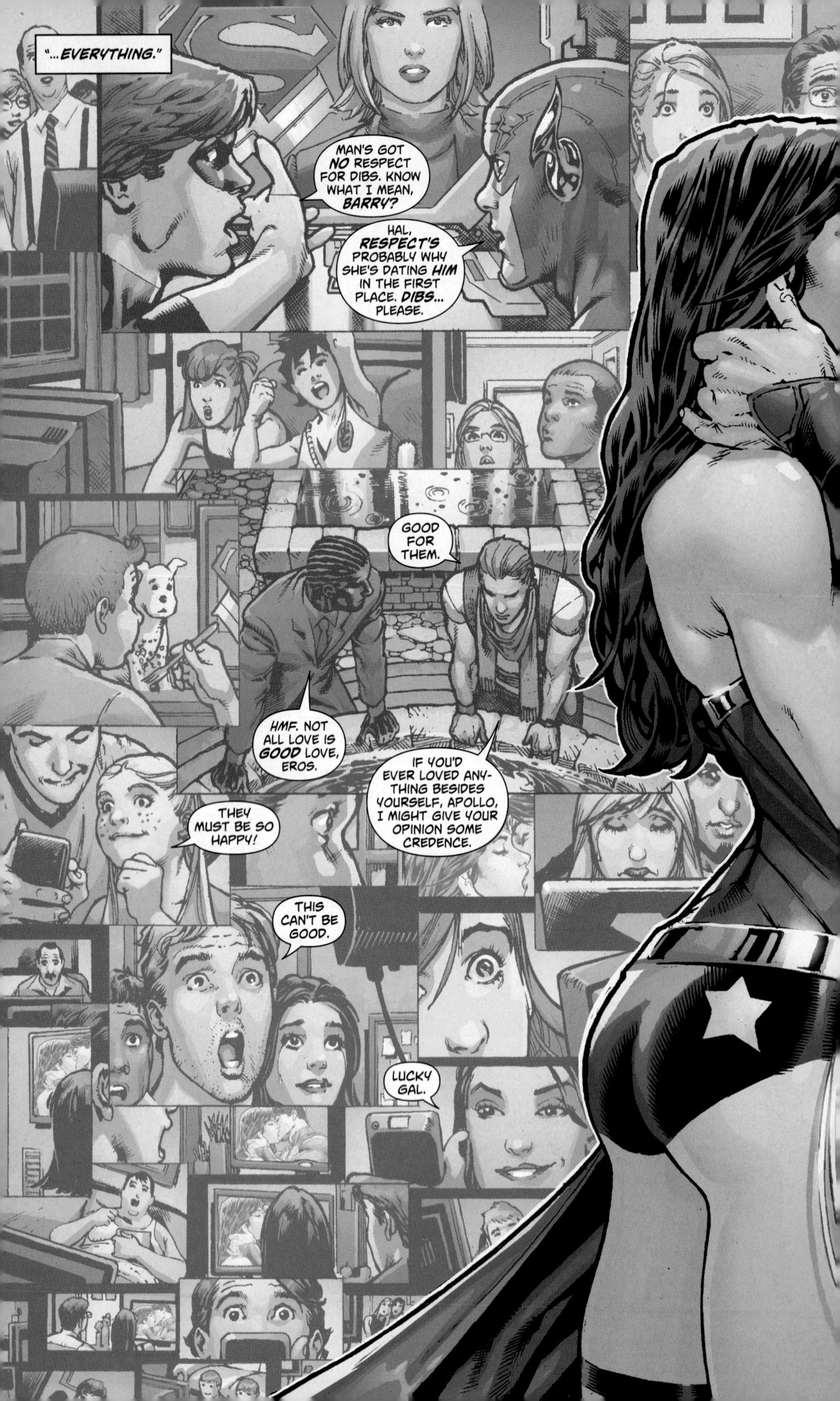
"...EVERYTHING."
MAN'S GOT NO RESPECT FOR DIBS. KNOW WHAT I MEAN, BARRY?
HAL, RESPECT'S PROBABLY WHY SHE'S DATING HIM IN THE FIRST PLACE. DIBS... PLEASE.
GOOD FOR THEM.
HMF. NOT ALL LOVE IS GOOD LOVE, EROS.
IF YOU'D EVER LOVED ANYTHING BESIDES YOURSELF, APOLLO, I MIGHT GIVE YOUR OPINION SOME CREDENCE.
THEY MUST BE SO HAPPY!
THIS CAN'T BE GOOD.
LUCKY GAL.

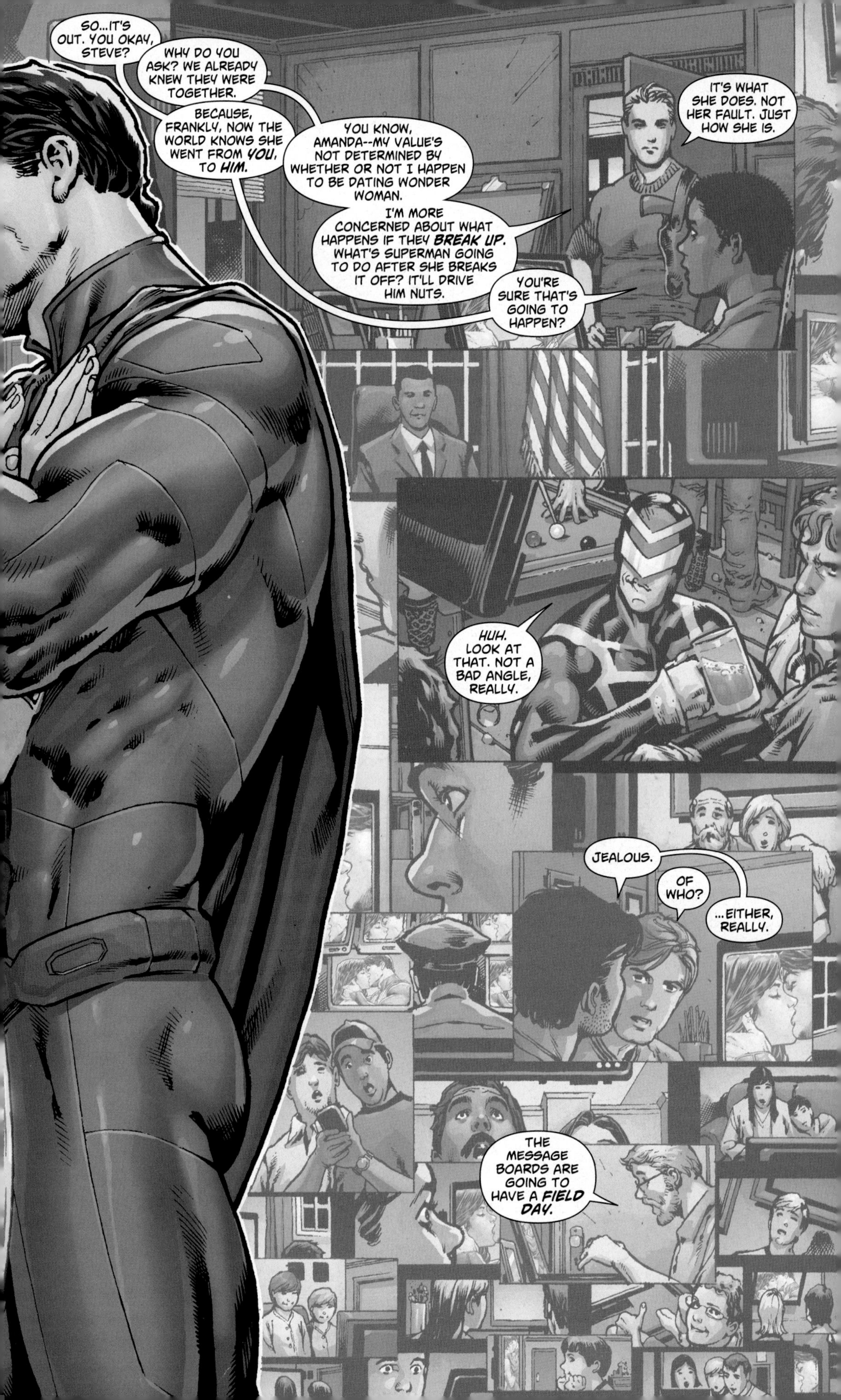
SO...IT'S OUT. YOU OKAY, STEVE?
WHY DO YOU ASK? WE ALREADY KNEW THEY WERE TOGETHER.
BECAUSE, FRANKLY, NOW THE WORLD KNOWS SHE WENT FROM *YOU*, TO *HIM*.
YOU KNOW, AMANDA--MY VALUE'S NOT DETERMINED BY WHETHER OR NOT I HAPPEN TO BE DATING WONDER WOMAN.
I'M MORE CONCERNED ABOUT WHAT HAPPENS IF THEY *BREAK UP*. WHAT'S SUPERMAN GOING TO DO AFTER SHE BREAKS IT OFF? IT'LL DRIVE HIM NUTS.
YOU'RE SURE THAT'S GOING TO HAPPEN?
IT'S WHAT SHE DOES. NOT HER FAULT. JUST HOW SHE IS.
HUH. LOOK AT THAT. NOT A BAD ANGLE, REALLY.
JEALOUS.
OF WHO?
...EITHER, REALLY.
THE MESSAGE BOARDS ARE GOING TO HAVE A *FIELD DAY*.

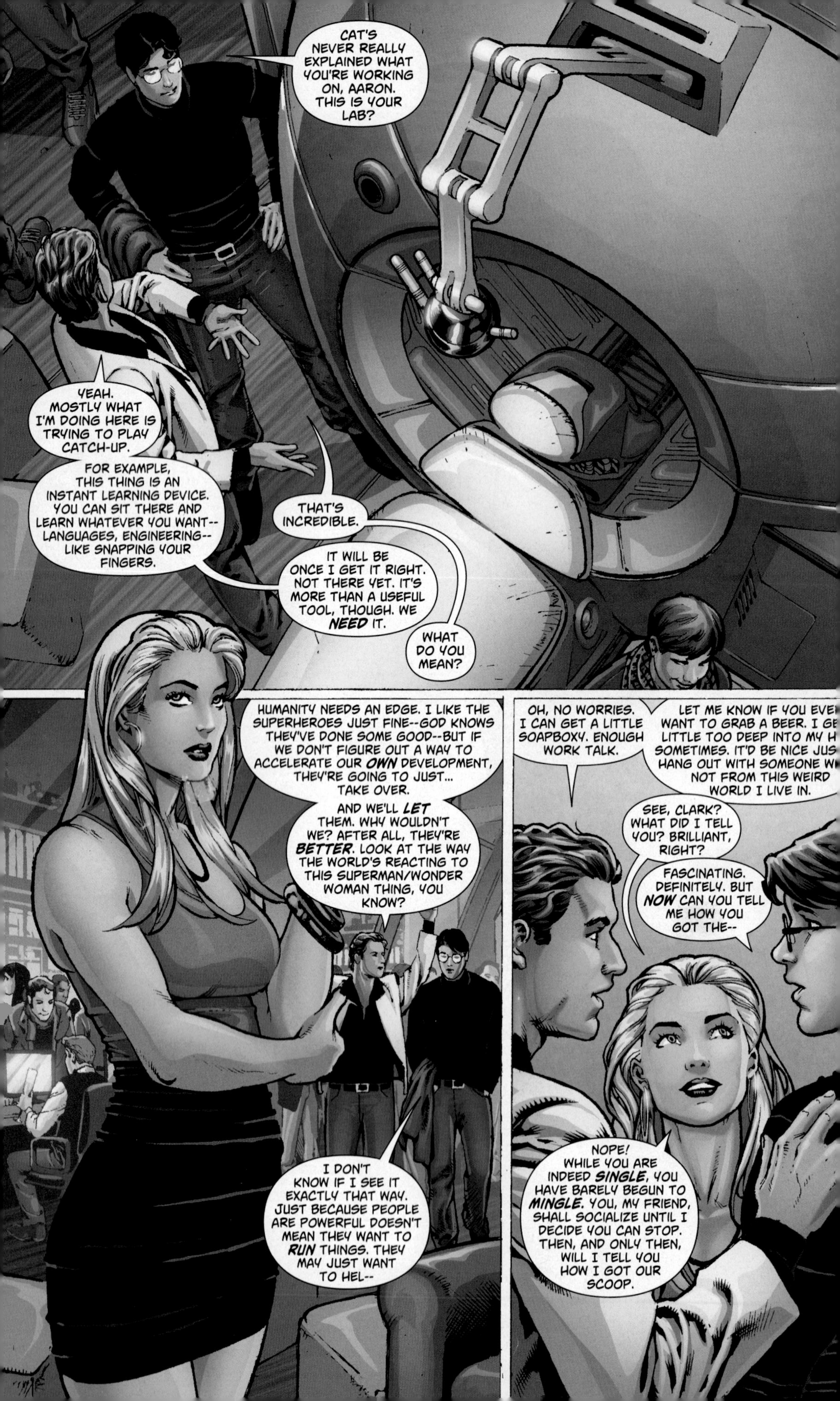
CAT'S NEVER REALLY EXPLAINED WHAT YOU'RE WORKING ON, AARON. THIS IS YOUR LAB?
YEAH. MOSTLY WHAT I'M DOING HERE IS TRYING TO PLAY CATCH-UP.
FOR EXAMPLE, THIS THING IS AN INSTANT LEARNING DEVICE. YOU CAN SIT THERE AND LEARN WHATEVER YOU WANT-- LANGUAGES, ENGINEERING-- LIKE SNAPPING YOUR FINGERS.
THAT'S INCREDIBLE.
IT WILL BE ONCE I GET IT RIGHT. NOT THERE YET. IT'S MORE THAN A USEFUL TOOL, THOUGH. WE **NEED** IT.
WHAT DO YOU MEAN?
HUMANITY NEEDS AN EDGE. I LIKE THE SUPERHEROES JUST FINE--GOD KNOWS THEY'VE DONE SOME GOOD--BUT IF WE DON'T FIGURE OUT A WAY TO ACCELERATE OUR **OWN** DEVELOPMENT, THEY'RE GOING TO JUST... TAKE OVER.
AND WE'LL **LET** THEM. WHY WOULDN'T WE? AFTER ALL, THEY'RE **BETTER**. LOOK AT THE WAY THE WORLD'S REACTING TO THIS SUPERMAN/WONDER WOMAN THING, YOU KNOW?
I DON'T KNOW IF I SEE IT EXACTLY THAT WAY. JUST BECAUSE PEOPLE ARE POWERFUL DOESN'T MEAN THEY WANT TO **RUN** THINGS. THEY MAY JUST WANT TO HEL--
OH, NO WORRIES. I CAN GET A LITTLE SOAPBOXY. ENOUGH WORK TALK.
LET ME KNOW IF YOU EVE WANT TO GRAB A BEER. I GE LITTLE TOO DEEP INTO MY H SOMETIMES. IT'D BE NICE JUS HANG OUT WITH SOMEONE W NOT FROM THIS WEIRD WORLD I LIVE IN.
SEE, CLARK? WHAT DID I TELL YOU? BRILLIANT, RIGHT?
FASCINATING. DEFINITELY. BUT **NOW** CAN YOU TELL ME HOW YOU GOT THE--
NOPE! WHILE YOU ARE INDEED **SINGLE**, YOU HAVE BARELY BEGUN TO **MINGLE**. YOU, MY FRIEND, SHALL SOCIALIZE UNTIL I DECIDE YOU CAN STOP. THEN, AND ONLY THEN, WILL I TELL YOU HOW I GOT OUR SCOOP.

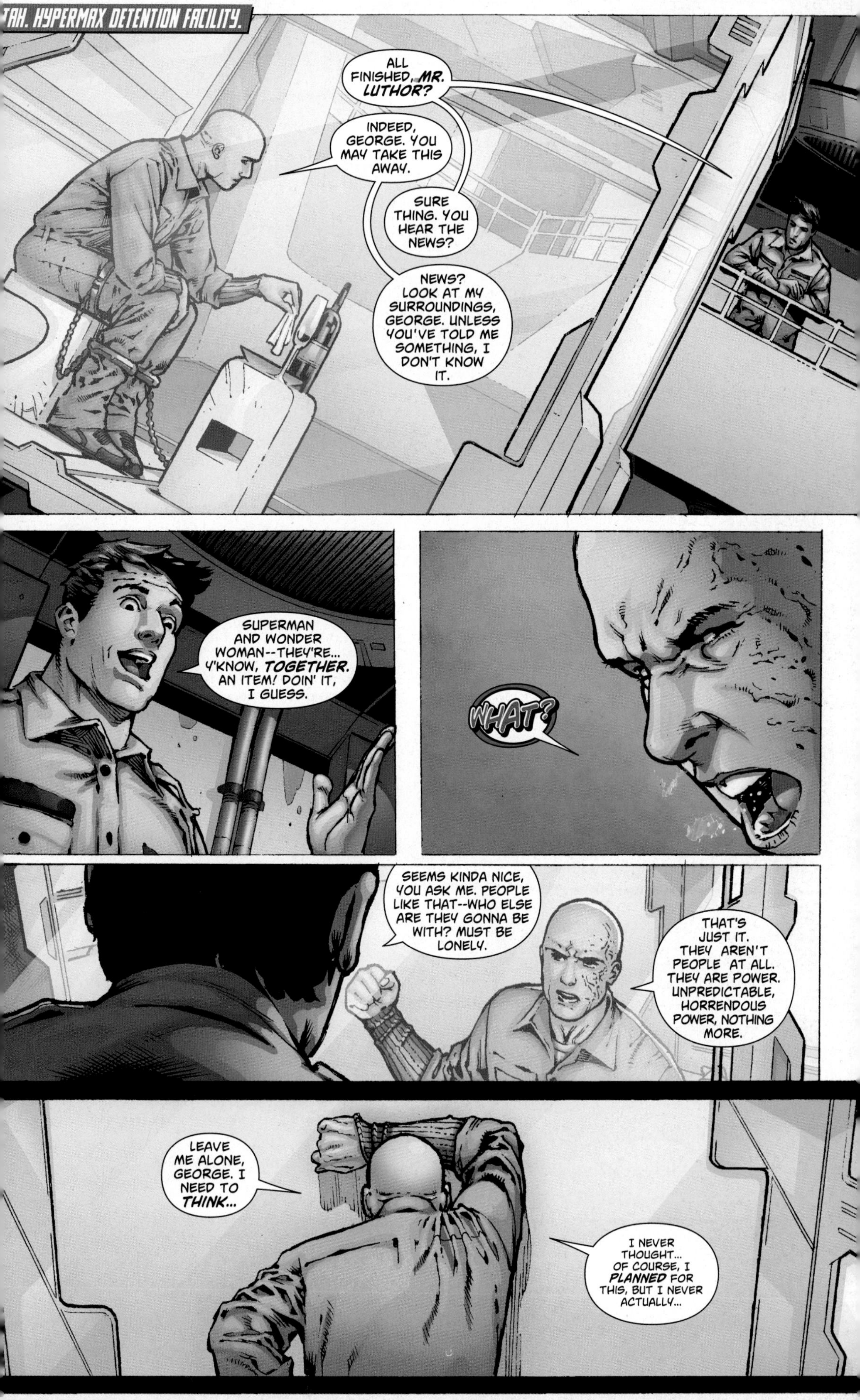
TAH. HYPERMAX DETENTION FACILITY.
ALL FINISHED, MR. LUTHOR?
INDEED, GEORGE. YOU MAY TAKE THIS AWAY.
SURE THING. YOU HEAR THE NEWS?
NEWS? LOOK AT MY SURROUNDINGS, GEORGE. UNLESS YOU'VE TOLD ME SOMETHING, I DON'T KNOW IT.
SUPERMAN AND WONDER WOMAN--THEY'RE... Y'KNOW, TOGETHER. AN ITEM! DOIN' IT, I GUESS.
WHAT?
SEEMS KINDA NICE, YOU ASK ME. PEOPLE LIKE THAT--WHO ELSE ARE THEY GONNA BE WITH? MUST BE LONELY.
THAT'S JUST IT. THEY AREN'T PEOPLE AT ALL. THEY ARE POWER. UNPREDICTABLE, HORRENDOUS POWER, NOTHING MORE.
LEAVE ME ALONE, GEORGE. I NEED TO THINK...
I NEVER THOUGHT... OF COURSE, I PLANNED FOR THIS, BUT I NEVER ACTUALLY...

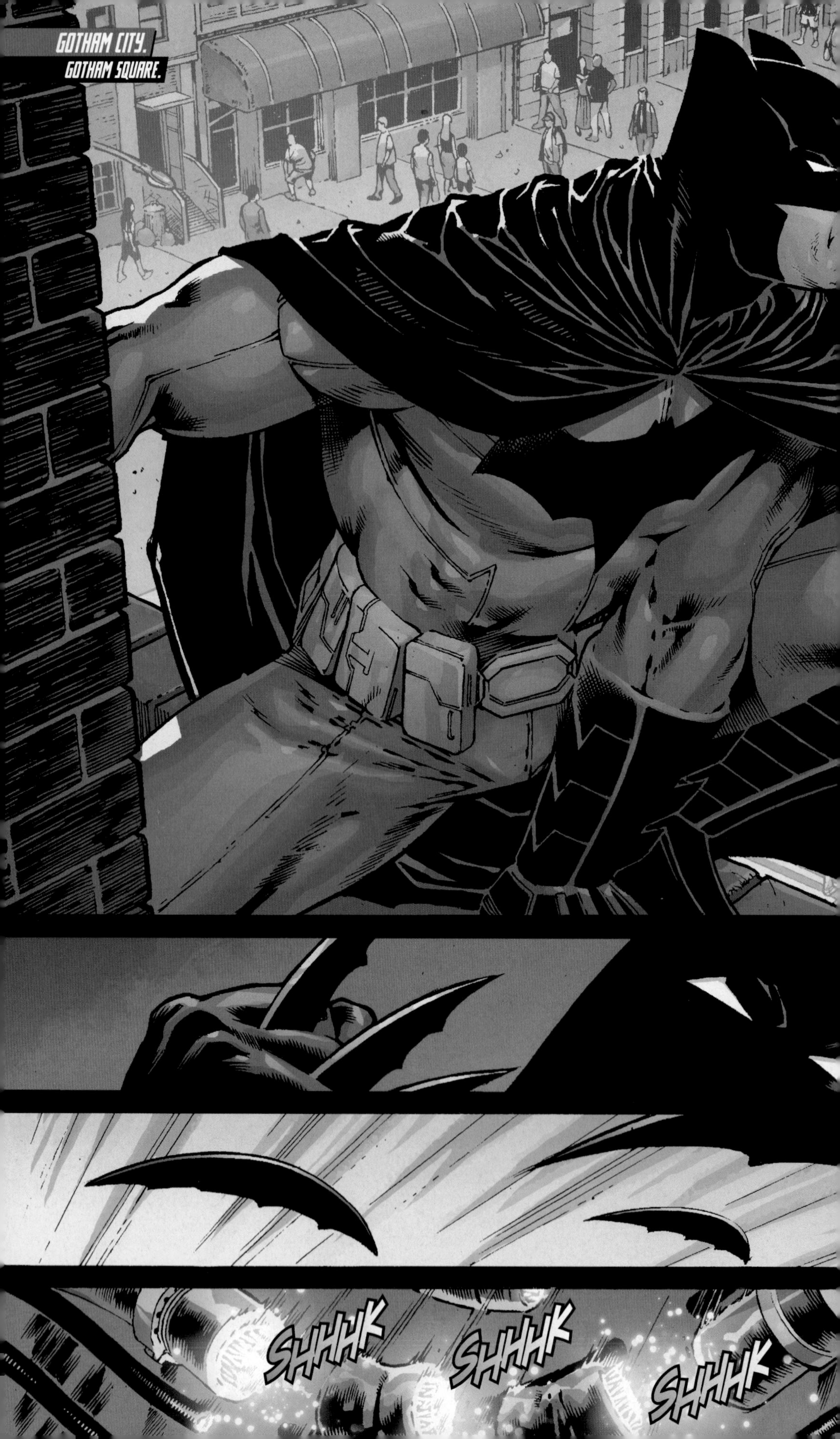
GOTHAM CITY.
GOTHAM SQUARE.
SHHHK
SHHHK
SHHHK

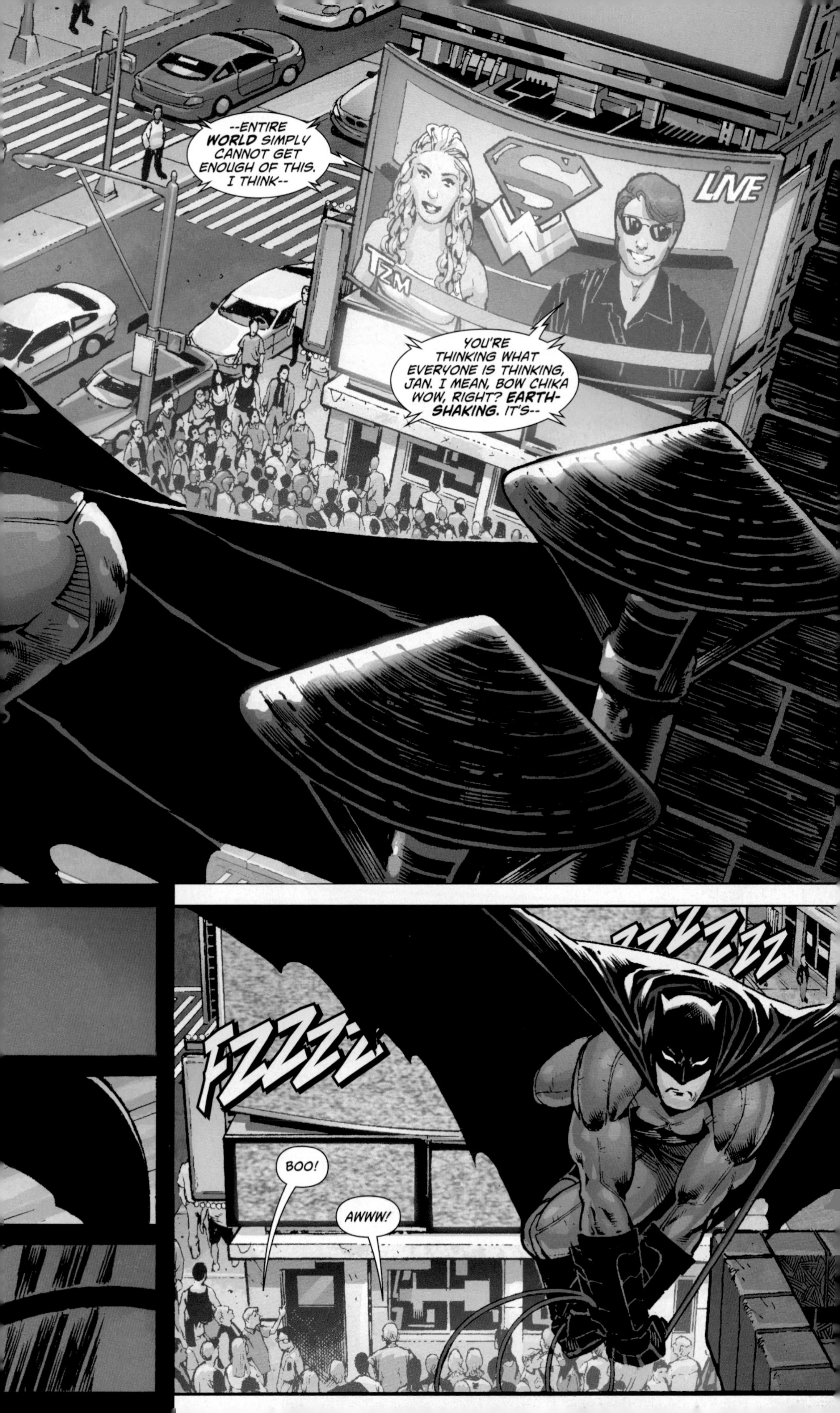
--ENTIRE WORLD SIMPLY CANNOT GET ENOUGH OF THIS. I THINK--
LIVE
TZM
YOU'RE THINKING WHAT EVERYONE IS THINKING, JAN. I MEAN, BOW CHIKA WOW, RIGHT? EARTH-SHAKING. IT'S--
ZZZZZZ
FZZZZZ
BOO!
AWWW!

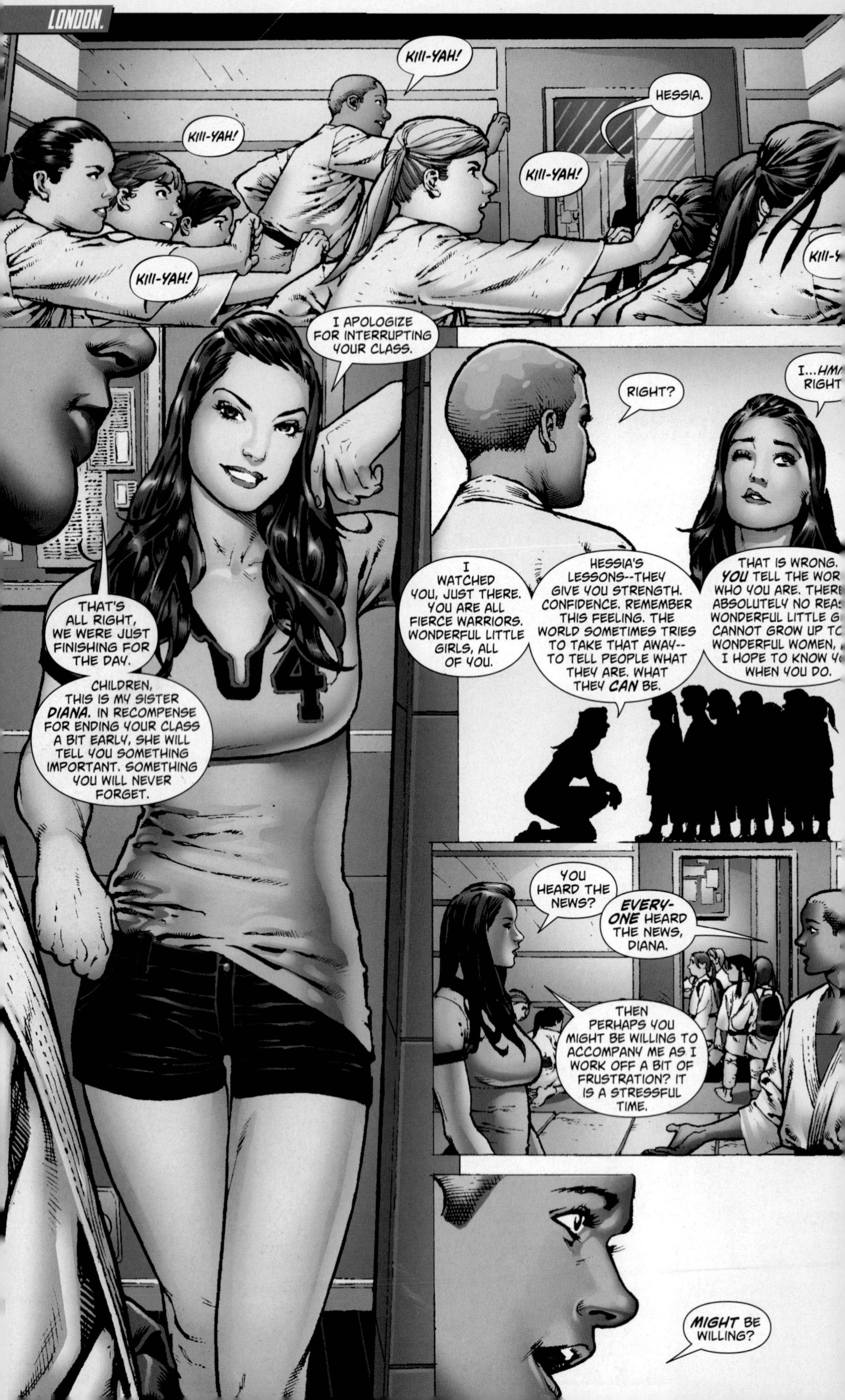
LONDON.
KIII-YAH!
HESSIA.
KIII-YAH!
KIII-YAH!
KIII-YAH!
I APOLOGIZE FOR INTERRUPTING YOUR CLASS.
THAT'S ALL RIGHT, WE WERE JUST FINISHING FOR THE DAY.
CHILDREN, THIS IS MY SISTER DIANA. IN RECOMPENSE FOR ENDING YOUR CLASS A BIT EARLY, SHE WILL TELL YOU SOMETHING IMPORTANT. SOMETHING YOU WILL NEVER FORGET.
RIGHT?
I...HM/ RIGHT
I WATCHED YOU, JUST THERE. YOU ARE ALL FIERCE WARRIORS. WONDERFUL LITTLE GIRLS, ALL OF YOU.
HESSIA'S LESSONS--THEY GIVE YOU STRENGTH. CONFIDENCE. REMEMBER THIS FEELING. THE WORLD SOMETIMES TRIES TO TAKE THAT AWAY-- TO TELL PEOPLE WHAT THEY ARE. WHAT THEY CAN BE.
THAT IS WRONG. YOU TELL THE WOR WHO YOU ARE. THER ABSOLUTELY NO REA WONDERFUL LITTLE G CANNOT GROW UP TO WONDERFUL WOMEN, I HOPE TO KNOW Y WHEN YOU DO.
YOU HEARD THE NEWS?
EVERYONE HEARD THE NEWS, DIANA.
THEN PERHAPS YOU MIGHT BE WILLING TO ACCOMPANY ME AS I WORK OFF A BIT OF FRUSTRATION? IT IS A STRESSFUL TIME.
MIGHT BE WILLING?

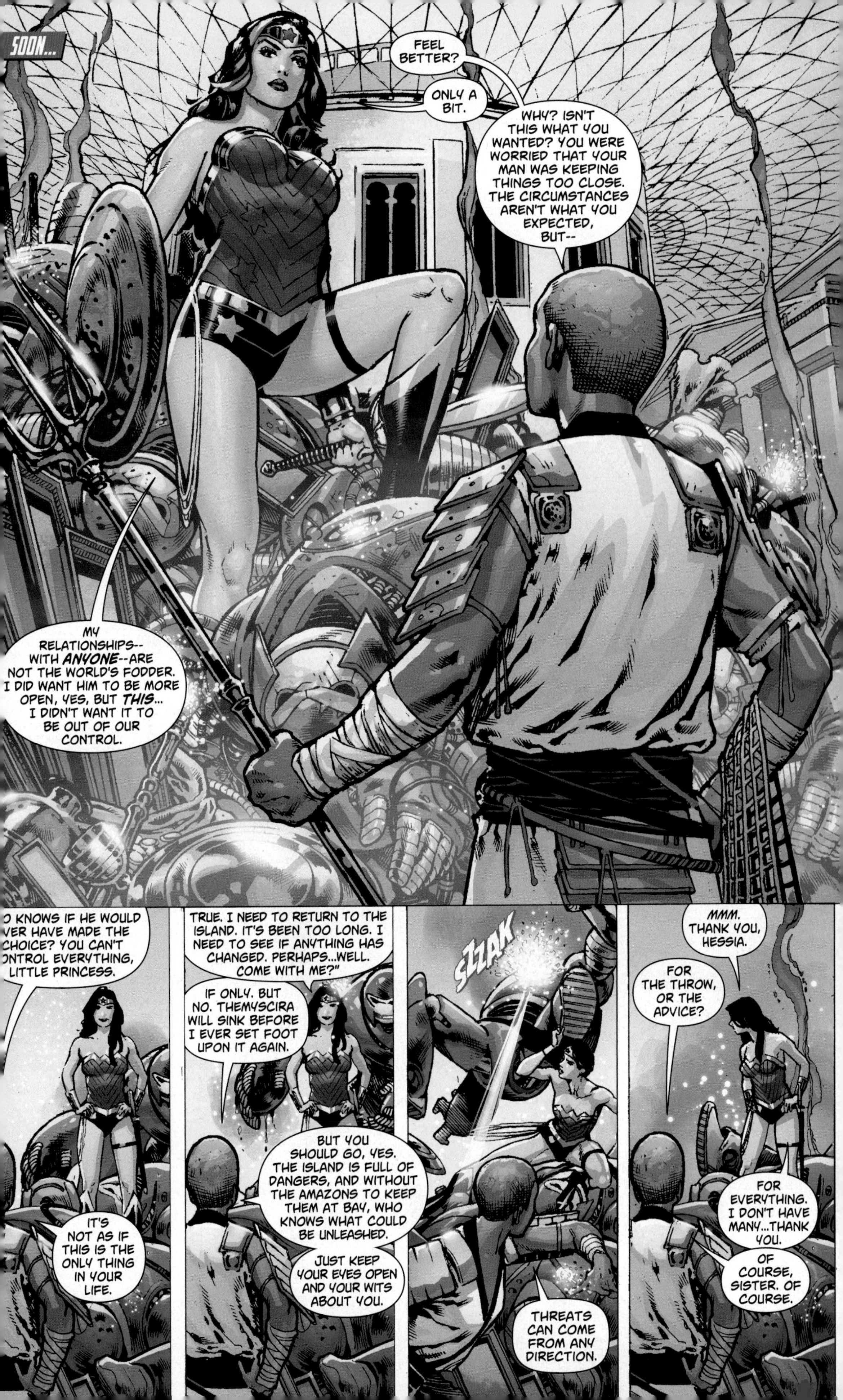
SOON...
FEEL BETTER?
ONLY A BIT.
WHY? ISN'T THIS WHAT YOU WANTED? YOU WERE WORRIED THAT YOUR MAN WAS KEEPING THINGS TOO CLOSE. THE CIRCUMSTANCES AREN'T WHAT YOU EXPECTED, BUT--
MY RELATIONSHIPS--WITH ANYONE--ARE NOT THE WORLD'S FODDER. I DID WANT HIM TO BE MORE OPEN, YES, BUT THIS... I DIDN'T WANT IT TO BE OUT OF OUR CONTROL.
O KNOWS IF HE WOULD VER HAVE MADE THE CHOICE? YOU CAN'T ONTROL EVERYTHING, LITTLE PRINCESS.
IT'S NOT AS IF THIS IS THE ONLY THING IN YOUR LIFE.
TRUE. I NEED TO RETURN TO THE ISLAND. IT'S BEEN TOO LONG. I NEED TO SEE IF ANYTHING HAS CHANGED. PERHAPS...WELL. COME WITH ME?"
IF ONLY. BUT NO. THEMYSCIRA WILL SINK BEFORE I EVER SET FOOT UPON IT AGAIN.
BUT YOU SHOULD GO, YES. THE ISLAND IS FULL OF DANGERS, AND WITHOUT THE AMAZONS TO KEEP THEM AT BAY, WHO KNOWS WHAT COULD BE UNLEASHED.
JUST KEEP YOUR EYES OPEN AND YOUR WITS ABOUT YOU.
SZZAK
THREATS CAN COME FROM ANY DIRECTION.
MMM. THANK YOU, HESSIA.
FOR THE THROW, OR THE ADVICE?
FOR EVERYTHING. I DON'T HAVE MANY...THANK YOU.
OF COURSE, SISTER. OF COURSE.

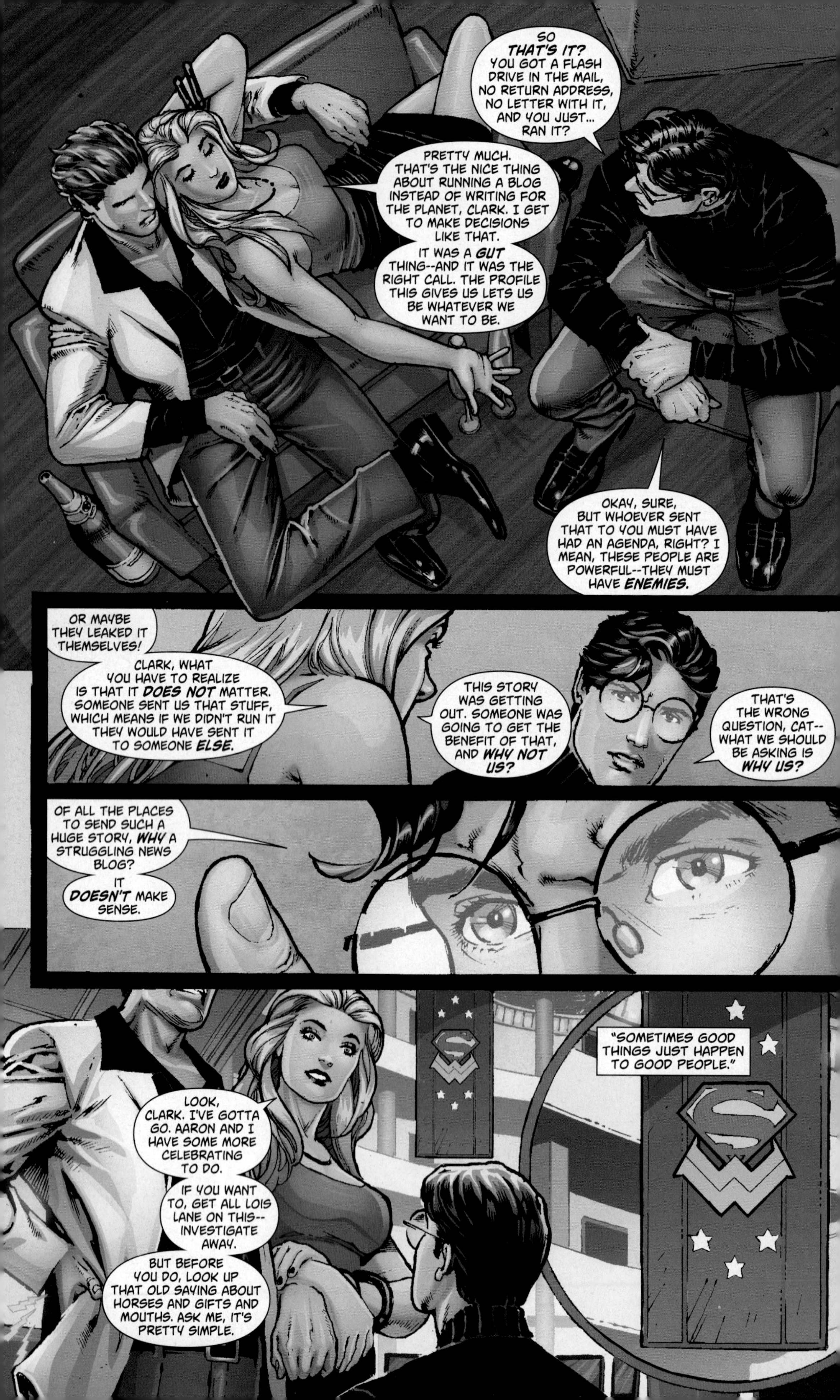
SO THAT'S IT? YOU GOT A FLASH DRIVE IN THE MAIL, NO RETURN ADDRESS, NO LETTER WITH IT, AND YOU JUST... RAN IT?
PRETTY MUCH. THAT'S THE NICE THING ABOUT RUNNING A BLOG INSTEAD OF WRITING FOR THE PLANET, CLARK. I GET TO MAKE DECISIONS LIKE THAT.
IT WAS A GUT THING--AND IT WAS THE RIGHT CALL. THE PROFILE THIS GIVES US LETS US BE WHATEVER WE WANT TO BE.
OKAY, SURE, BUT WHOEVER SENT THAT TO YOU MUST HAVE HAD AN AGENDA, RIGHT? I MEAN, THESE PEOPLE ARE POWERFUL--THEY MUST HAVE ENEMIES.
OR MAYBE THEY LEAKED IT THEMSELVES!
CLARK, WHAT YOU HAVE TO REALIZE IS THAT IT DOES NOT MATTER. SOMEONE SENT US THAT STUFF, WHICH MEANS IF WE DIDN'T RUN IT THEY WOULD HAVE SENT IT TO SOMEONE ELSE.
THIS STORY WAS GETTING OUT. SOMEONE WAS GOING TO GET THE BENEFIT OF THAT, AND WHY NOT US?
THAT'S THE WRONG QUESTION, CAT--WHAT WE SHOULD BE ASKING IS WHY US?
OF ALL THE PLACES TO SEND SUCH A HUGE STORY, WHY A STRUGGLING NEWS BLOG?
IT DOESN'T MAKE SENSE.
"SOMETIMES GOOD THINGS JUST HAPPEN TO GOOD PEOPLE."
LOOK, CLARK. I'VE GOTTA GO. AARON AND I HAVE SOME MORE CELEBRATING TO DO.
IF YOU WANT TO, GET ALL LOIS LANE ON THIS--INVESTIGATE AWAY.
BUT BEFORE YOU DO, LOOK UP THAT OLD SAYING ABOUT HORSES AND GIFTS AND MOUTHS. ASK ME, IT'S PRETTY SIMPLE.

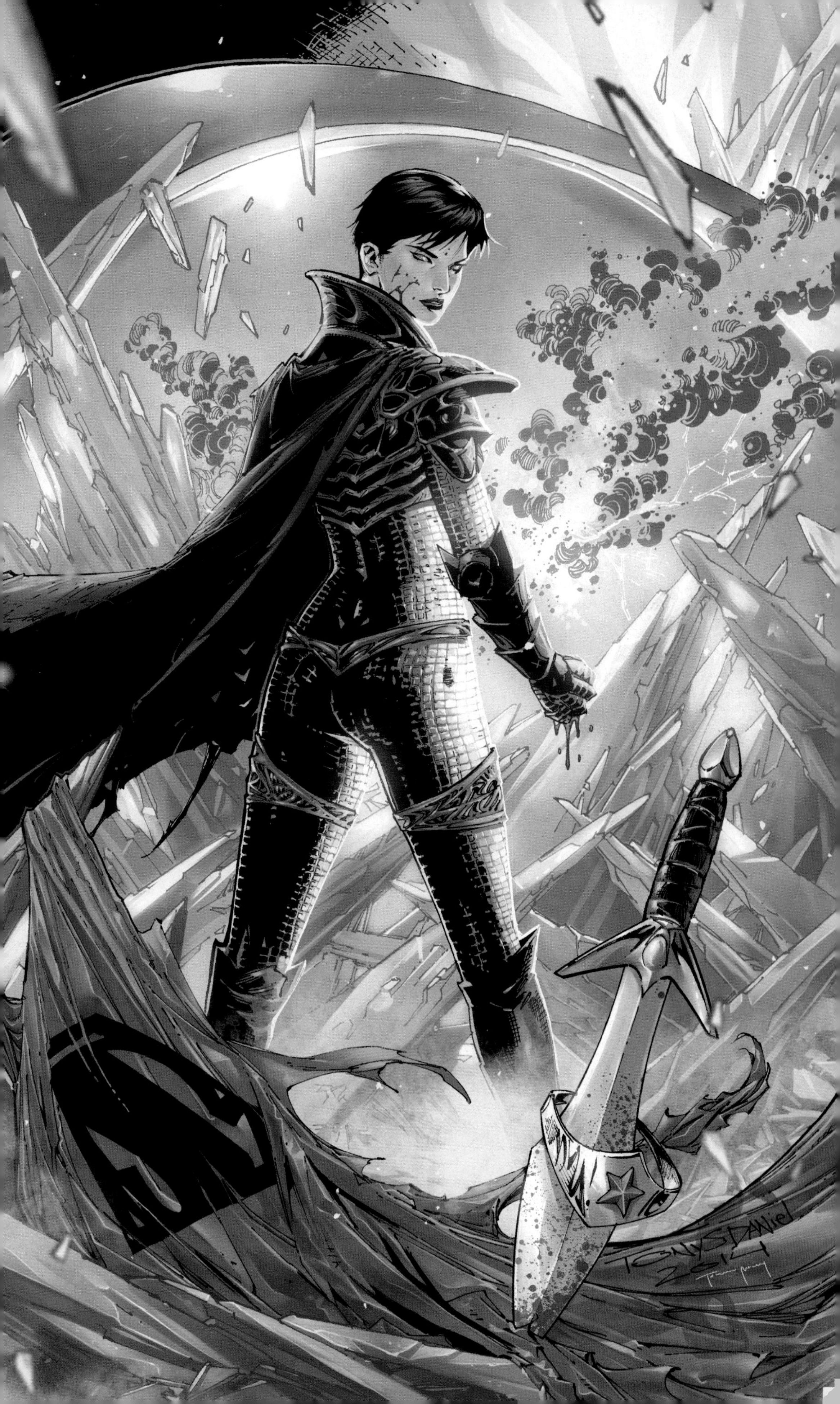

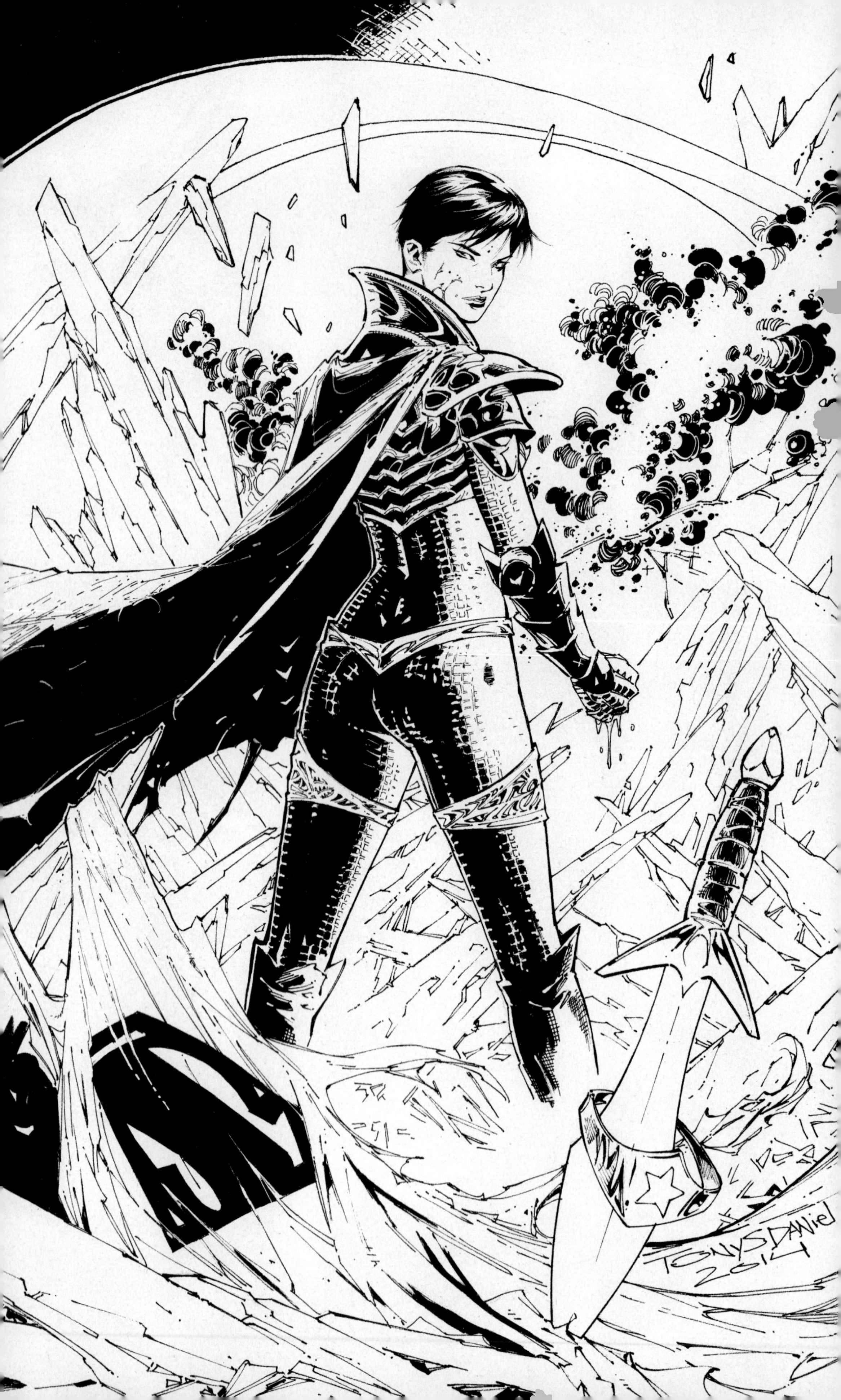
TONY S DANIEL
2014

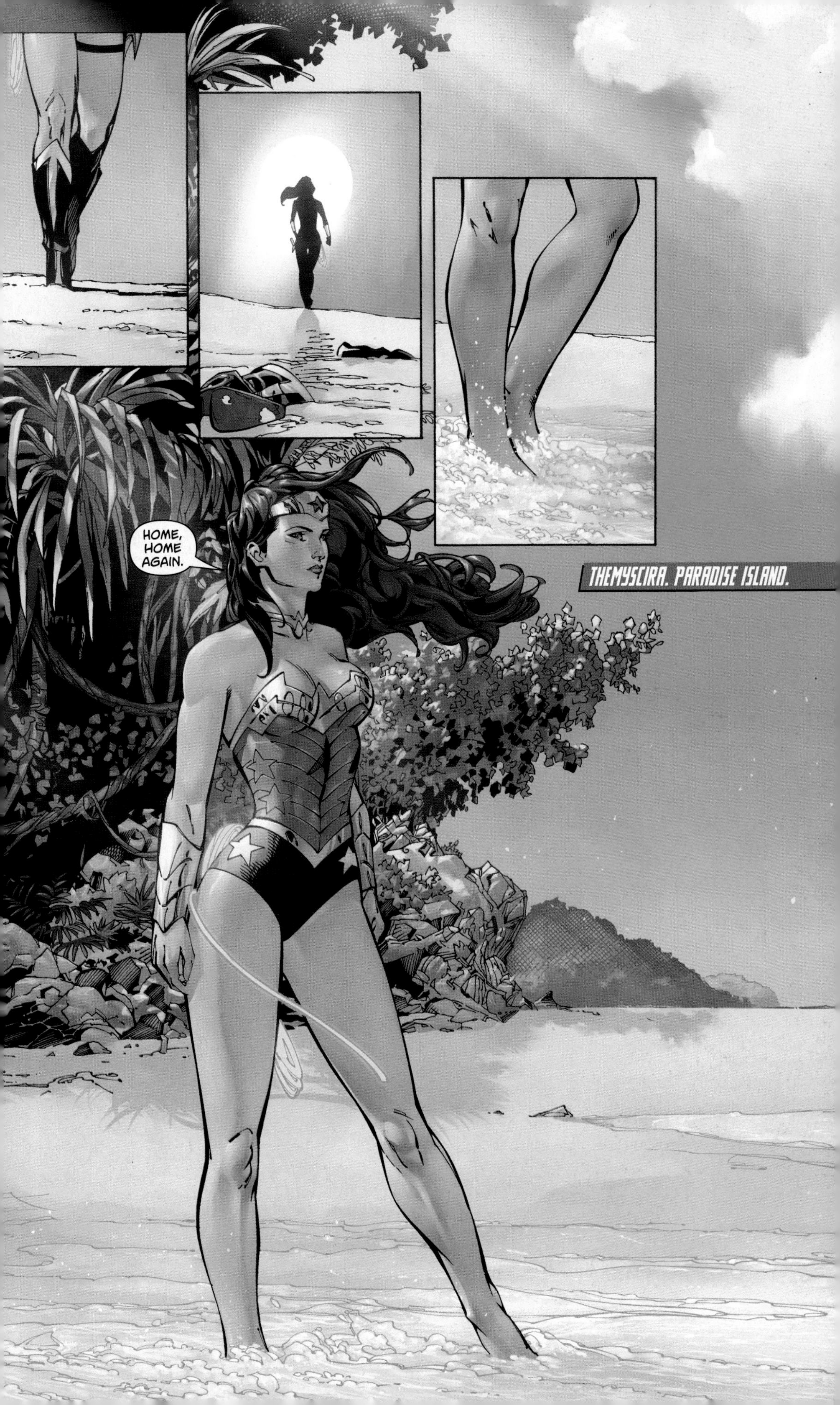

HOME, HOME AGAIN.
THEMYSCIRA. PARADISE ISLAND.

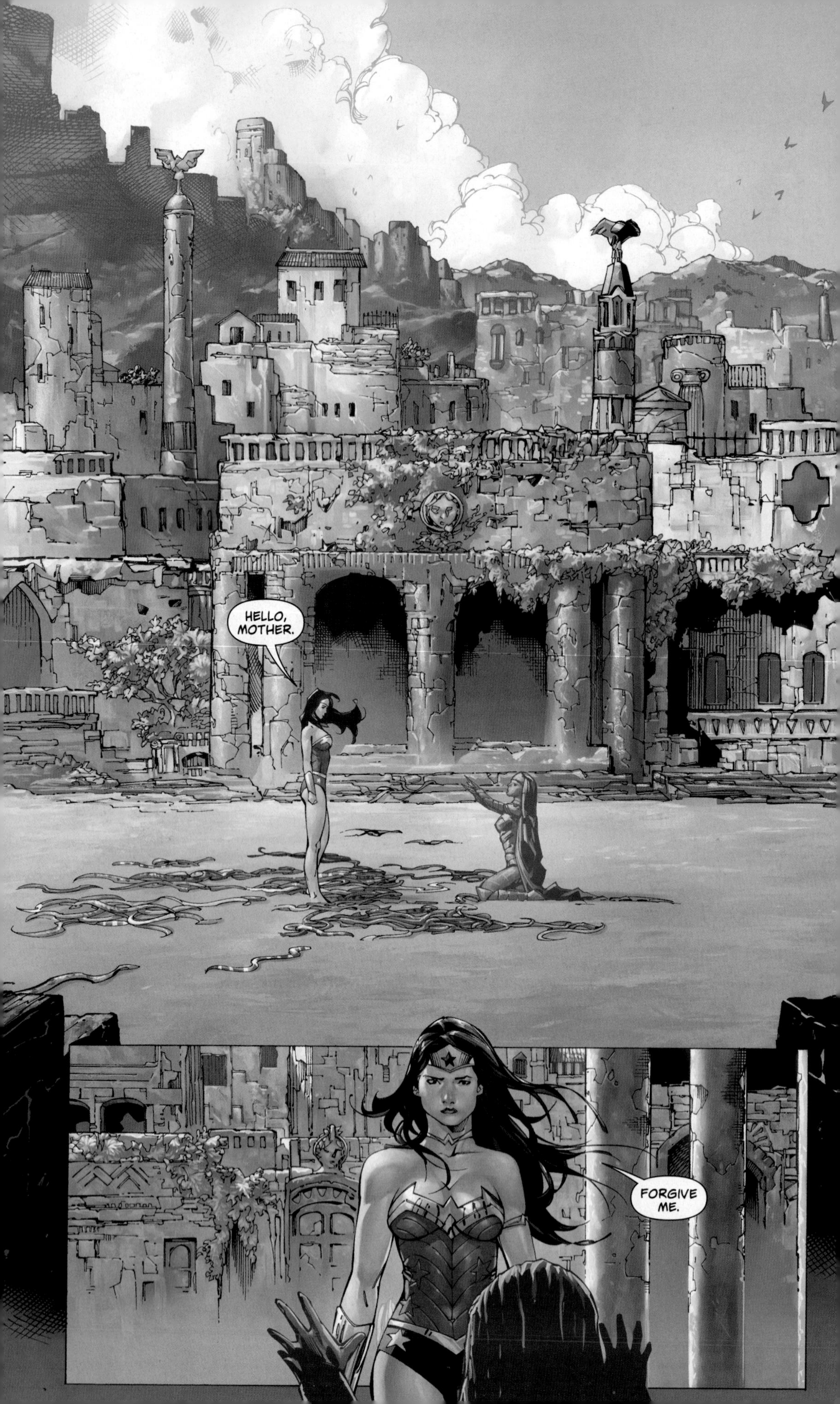

HELLO, MOTHER.
FORGIVE ME.

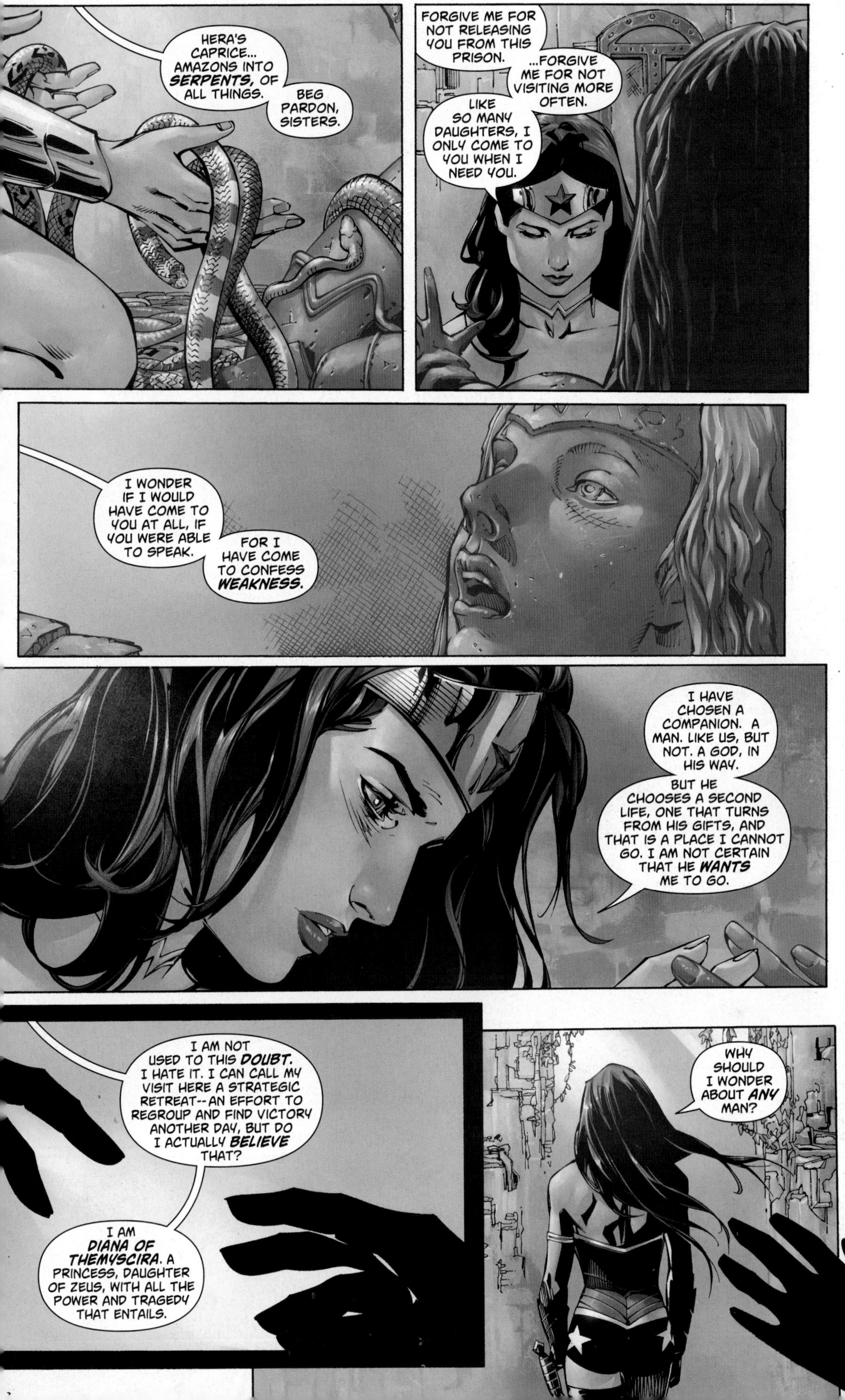
HERA'S CAPRICE... AMAZONS INTO SERPENTS, OF ALL THINGS.
BEG PARDON, SISTERS.
FORGIVE ME FOR NOT RELEASING YOU FROM THIS PRISON.
...FORGIVE ME FOR NOT VISITING MORE OFTEN.
LIKE SO MANY DAUGHTERS, I ONLY COME TO YOU WHEN I NEED YOU.
I WONDER IF I WOULD HAVE COME TO YOU AT ALL, IF YOU WERE ABLE TO SPEAK.
FOR I HAVE COME TO CONFESS WEAKNESS.
I HAVE CHOSEN A COMPANION. A MAN. LIKE US, BUT NOT. A GOD, IN HIS WAY.
BUT HE CHOOSES A SECOND LIFE, ONE THAT TURNS FROM HIS GIFTS, AND THAT IS A PLACE I CANNOT GO. I AM NOT CERTAIN THAT HE WANTS ME TO GO.
I AM NOT USED TO THIS DOUBT. I HATE IT. I CAN CALL MY VISIT HERE A STRATEGIC RETREAT--AN EFFORT TO REGROUP AND FIND VICTORY ANOTHER DAY, BUT DO I ACTUALLY BELIEVE THAT?
I AM DIANA OF THEMYSCIRA. A PRINCESS, DAUGHTER OF ZEUS, WITH ALL THE POWER AND TRAGEDY THAT ENTAILS.
WHY SHOULD I WONDER ABOUT ANY MAN?

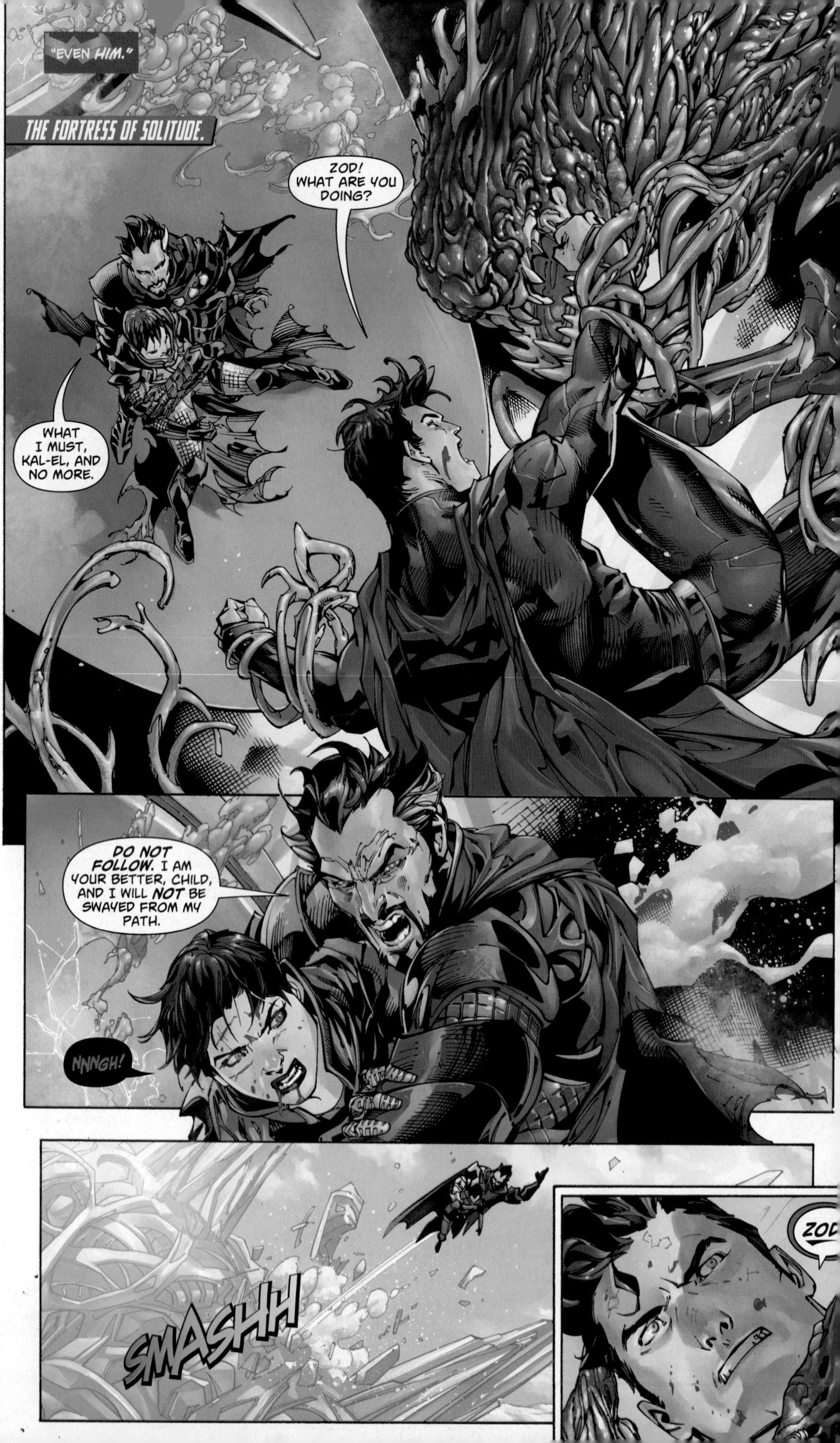
"EVEN HIM."
THE FORTRESS OF SOLITUDE.
ZOD! WHAT ARE YOU DOING?
WHAT I MUST, KAL-EL, AND NO MORE.
DO NOT FOLLOW. I AM YOUR BETTER, CHILD, AND I WILL NOT BE SWAYED FROM MY PATH.
NNNGH!
SMASHH
ZOD

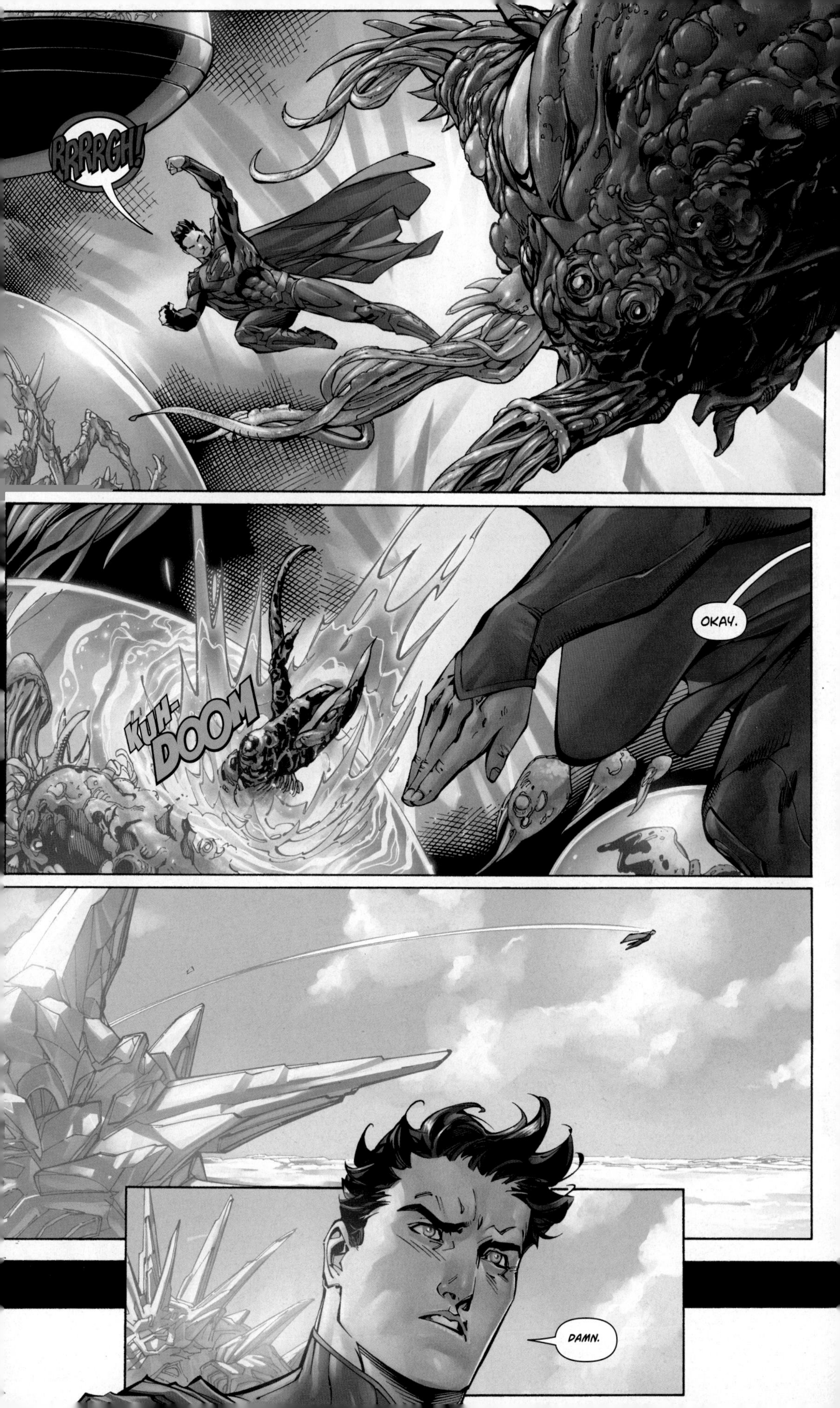
RRRRGH!
OKAY.
KUH-DOOM
DAMN.

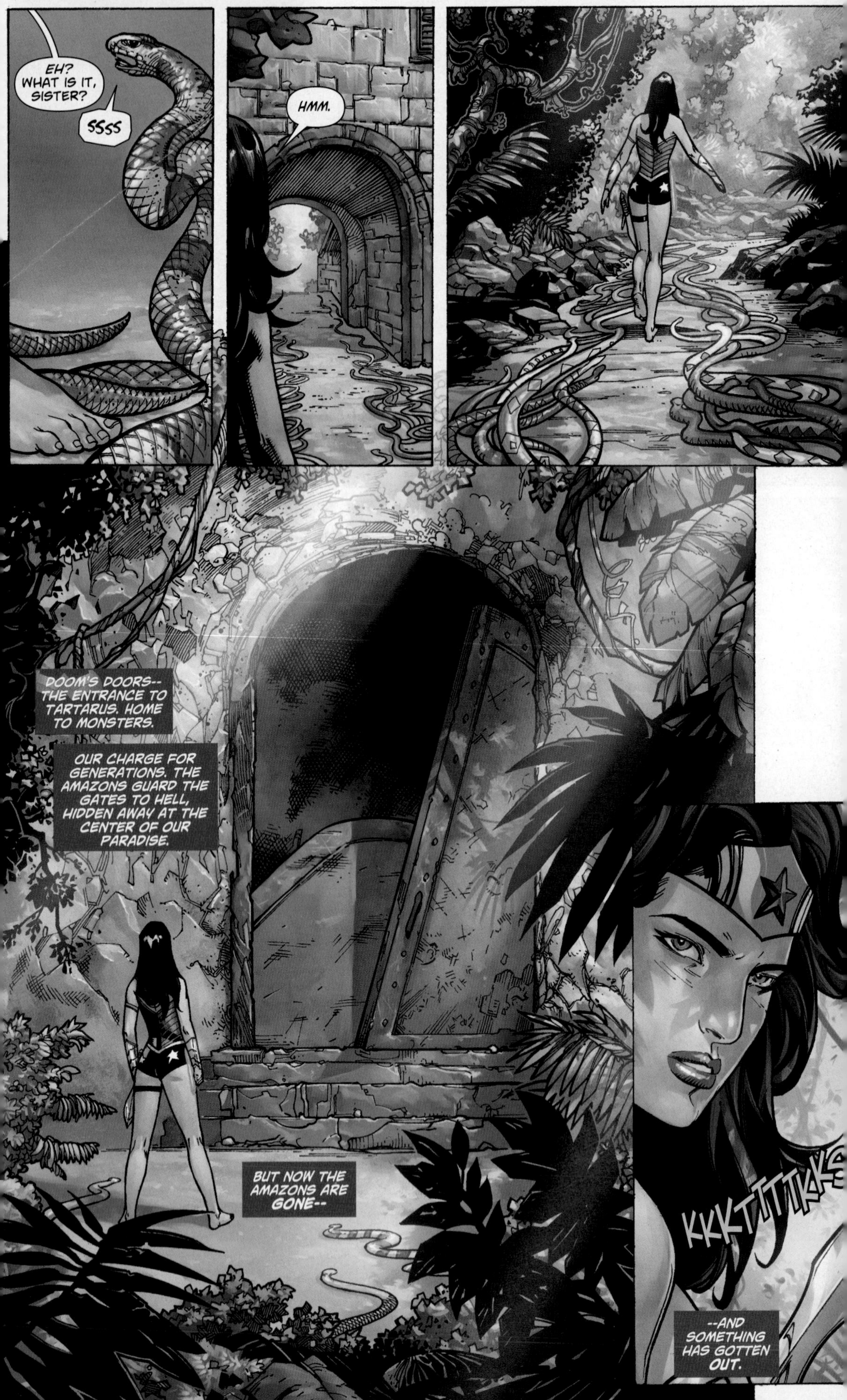
EH? WHAT IS IT, SISTER?
SSSS
HMM.
DOOM'S DOORS-- THE ENTRANCE TO TARTARUS. HOME TO MONSTERS.
OUR CHARGE FOR GENERATIONS. THE AMAZONS GUARD THE GATES TO HELL, HIDDEN AWAY AT THE CENTER OF OUR PARADISE.
BUT NOW THE AMAZONS ARE GONE--
KKKTTTTKKK
--AND SOMETHING HAS GOTTEN OUT.

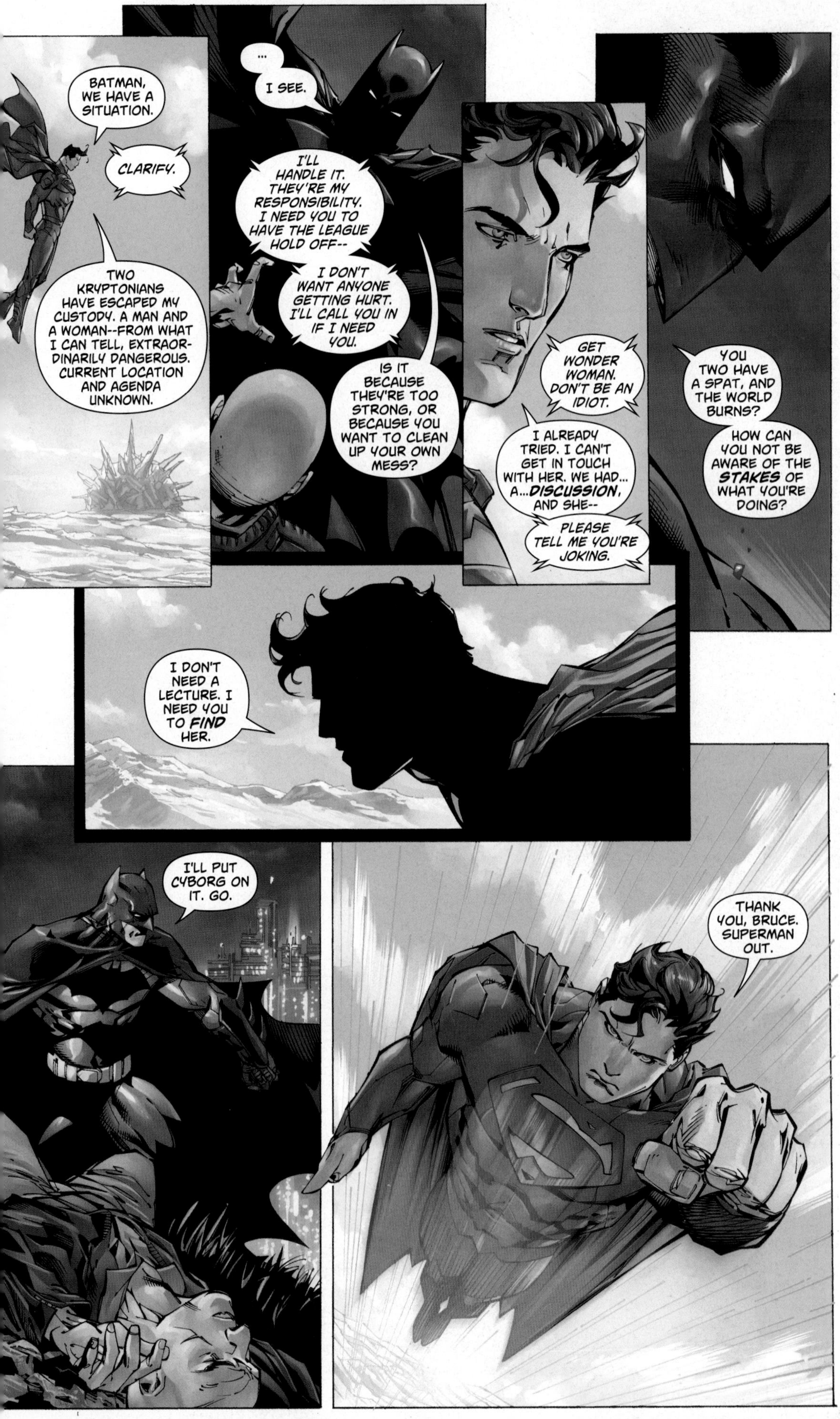
BATMAN, WE HAVE A SITUATION.
CLARIFY.
TWO KRYPTONIANS HAVE ESCAPED MY CUSTODY. A MAN AND A WOMAN--FROM WHAT I CAN TELL, EXTRAOR-DINARILY DANGEROUS. CURRENT LOCATION AND AGENDA UNKNOWN.
...
I SEE.
I'LL HANDLE IT. THEY'RE MY RESPONSIBILITY. I NEED YOU TO HAVE THE LEAGUE HOLD OFF--
I DON'T WANT ANYONE GETTING HURT. I'LL CALL YOU IN IF I NEED YOU.
IS IT BECAUSE THEY'RE TOO STRONG, OR BECAUSE YOU WANT TO CLEAN UP YOUR OWN MESS?
GET WONDER WOMAN. DON'T BE AN IDIOT.
I ALREADY TRIED. I CAN'T GET IN TOUCH WITH HER. WE HAD... A...DISCUSSION, AND SHE--
PLEASE TELL ME YOU'RE JOKING.
YOU TWO HAVE A SPAT, AND THE WORLD BURNS?
HOW CAN YOU NOT BE AWARE OF THE STAKES OF WHAT YOU'RE DOING?
I DON'T NEED A LECTURE. I NEED YOU TO FIND HER.
I'LL PUT CYBORG ON IT. GO.
THANK YOU, BRUCE. SUPERMAN OUT.

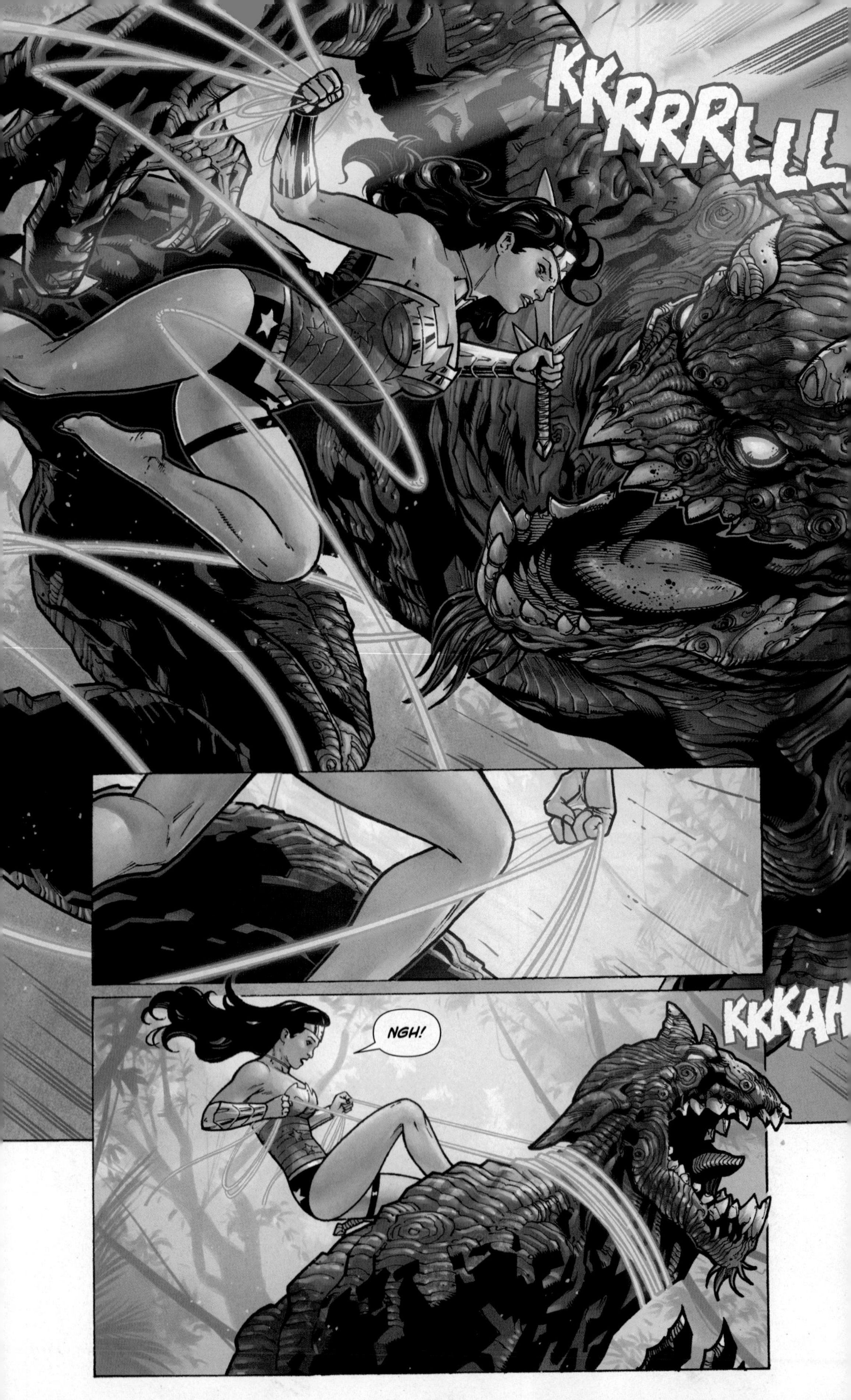
KKRRRLLL
NGH!
KKKAH

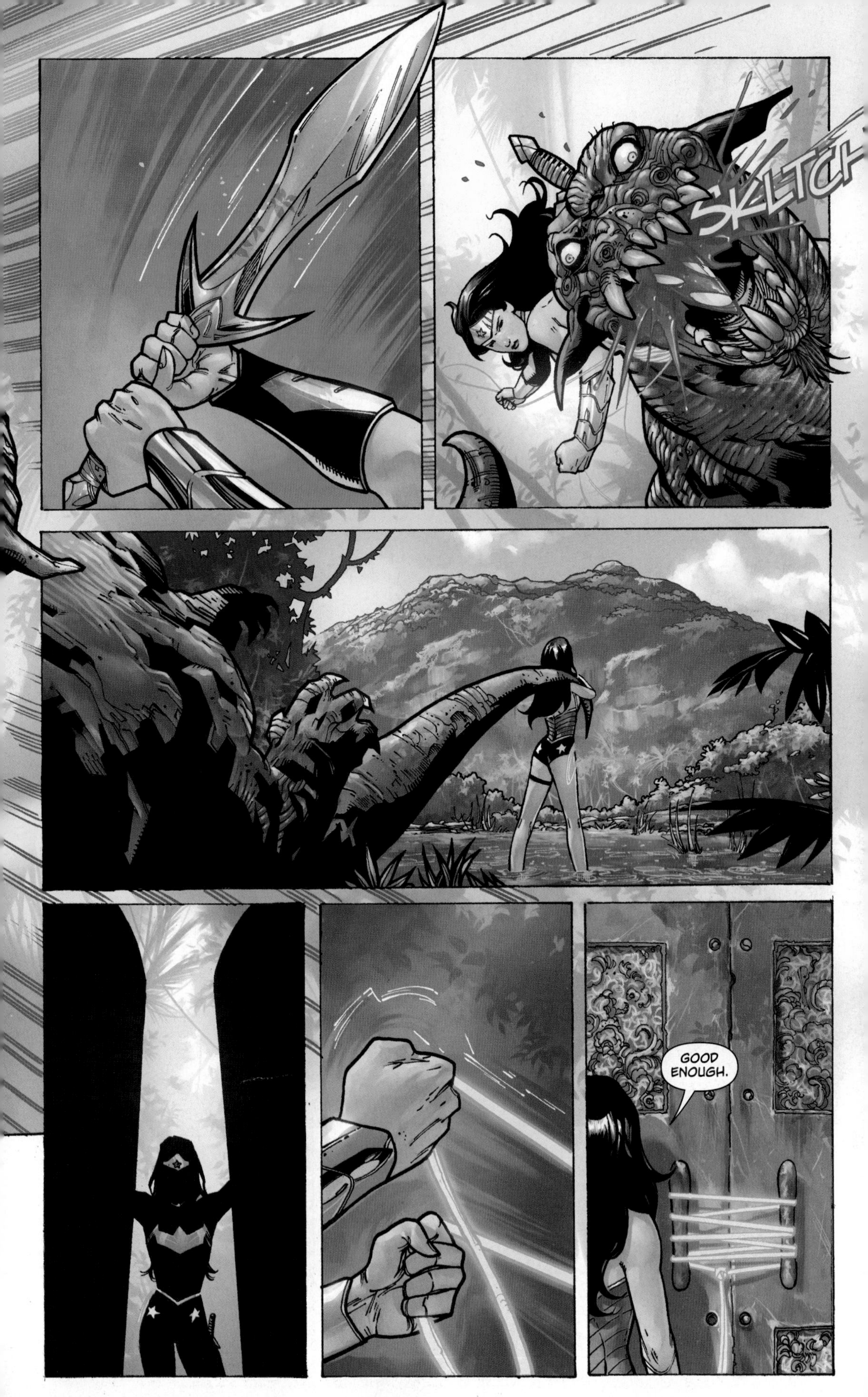
SKLTCH
GOOD ENOUGH.

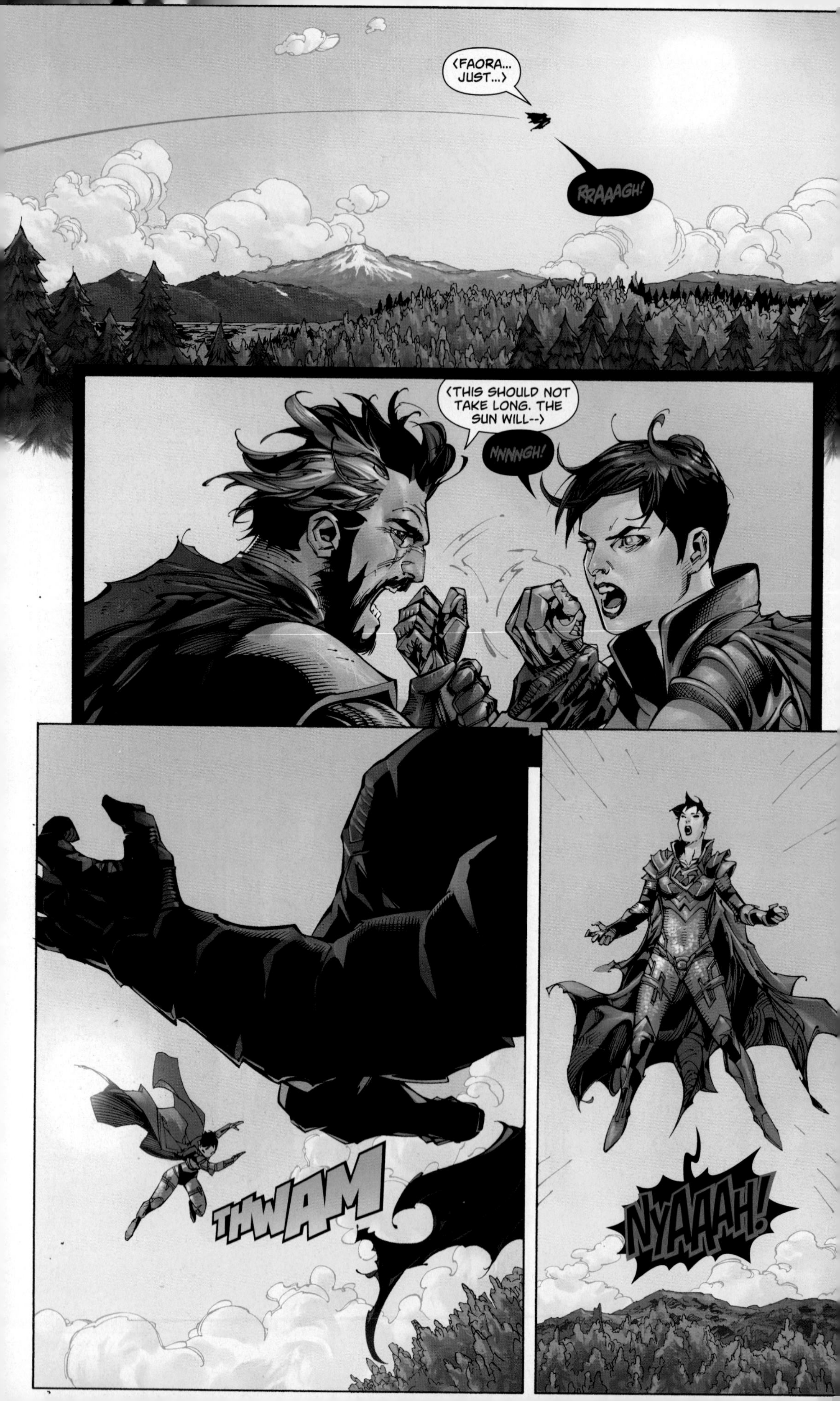

‹FAORA... JUST...›
RRAAAGH!
‹THIS SHOULD NOT TAKE LONG. THE SUN WILL--›
NNNNGH!
THWAM
NYAAAH!

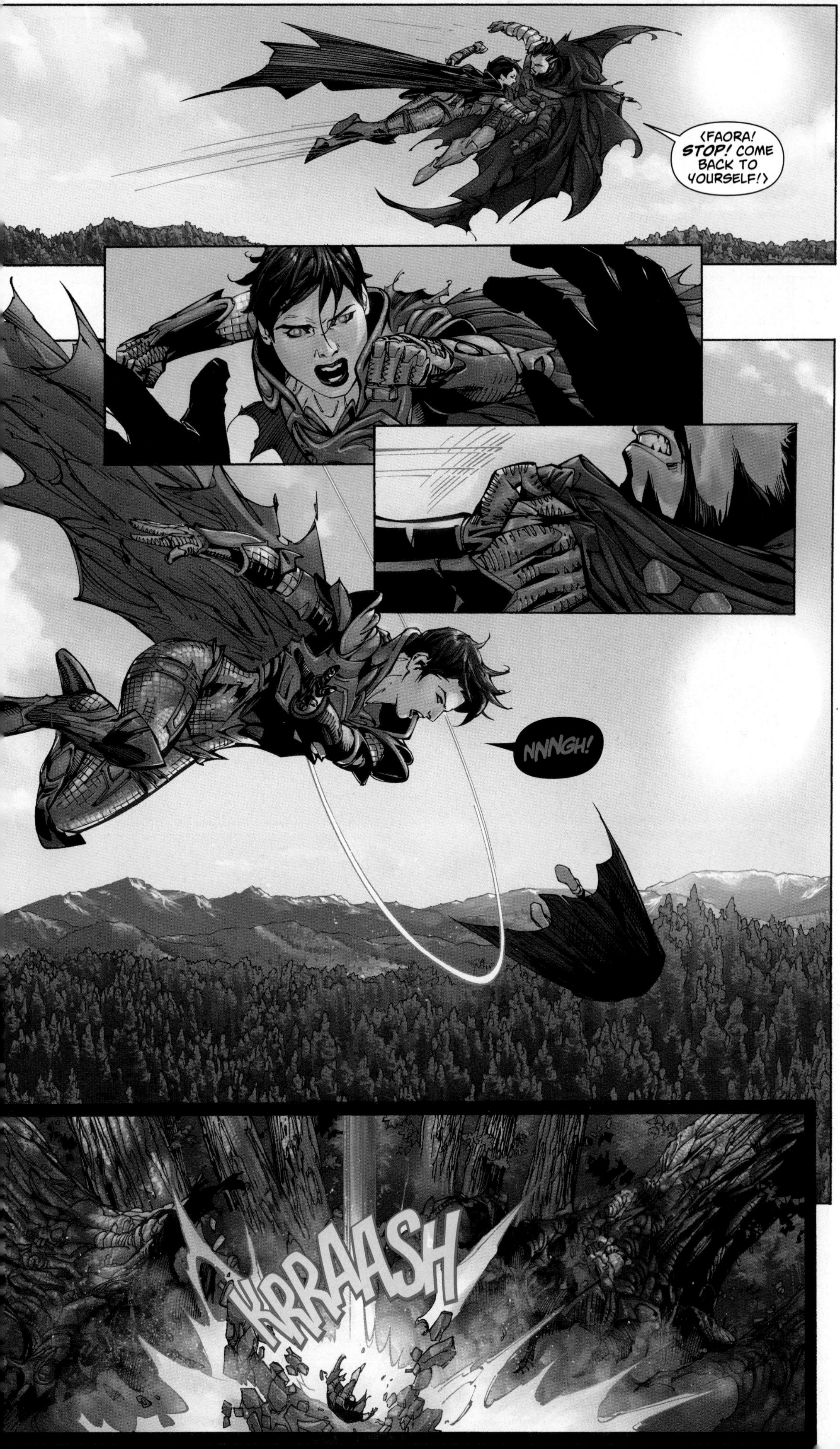

⟨FAORA! STOP! COME BACK TO YOURSELF!⟩
NNNGH!
KRRAASH

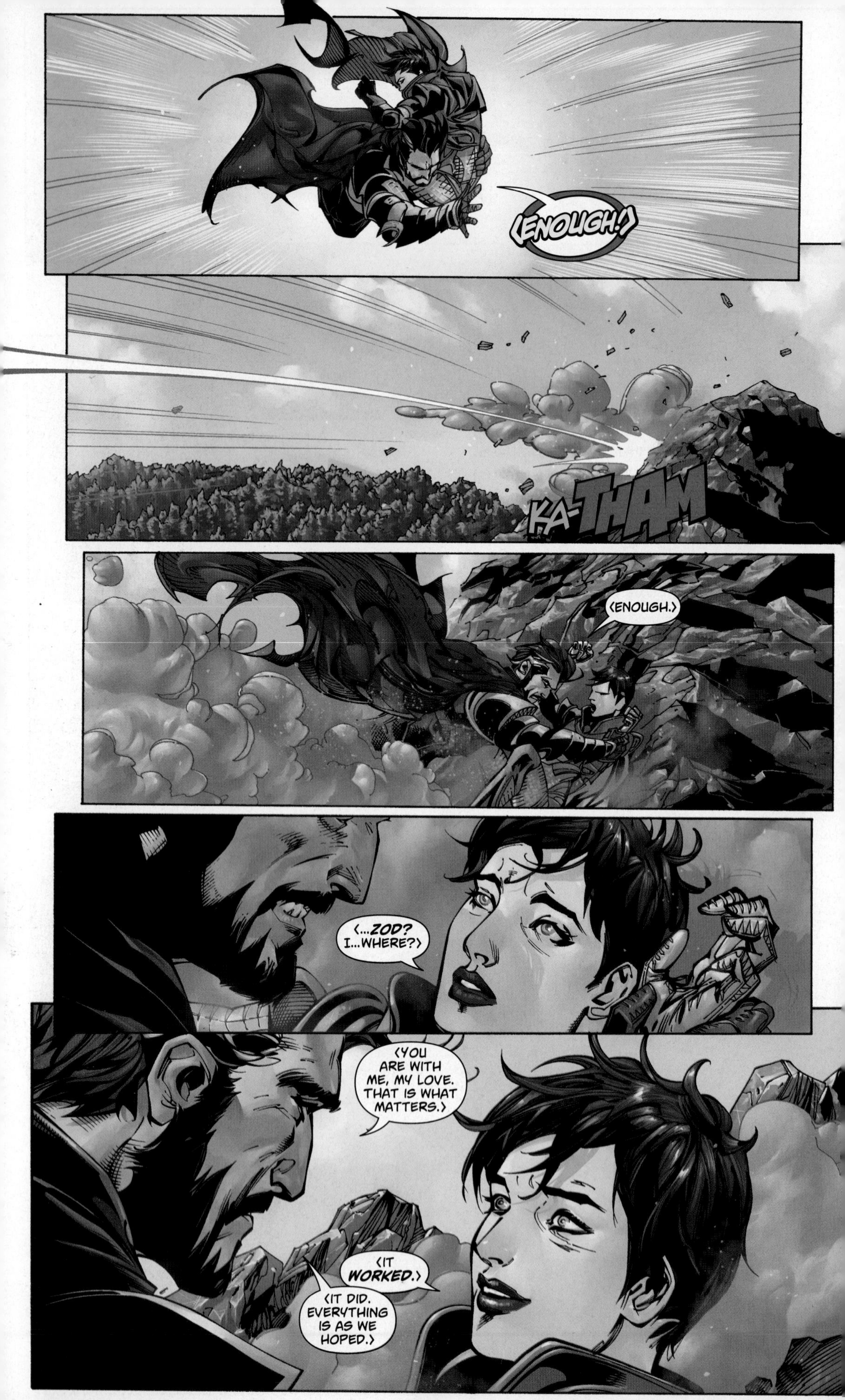

‹ENOUGH!›
KA-THAM
‹ENOUGH.›
‹...ZOD? I...WHERE?›
‹YOU ARE WITH ME, MY LOVE. THAT IS WHAT MATTERS.›
‹IT WORKED.›
‹IT DID. EVERYTHING IS AS WE HOPED.›

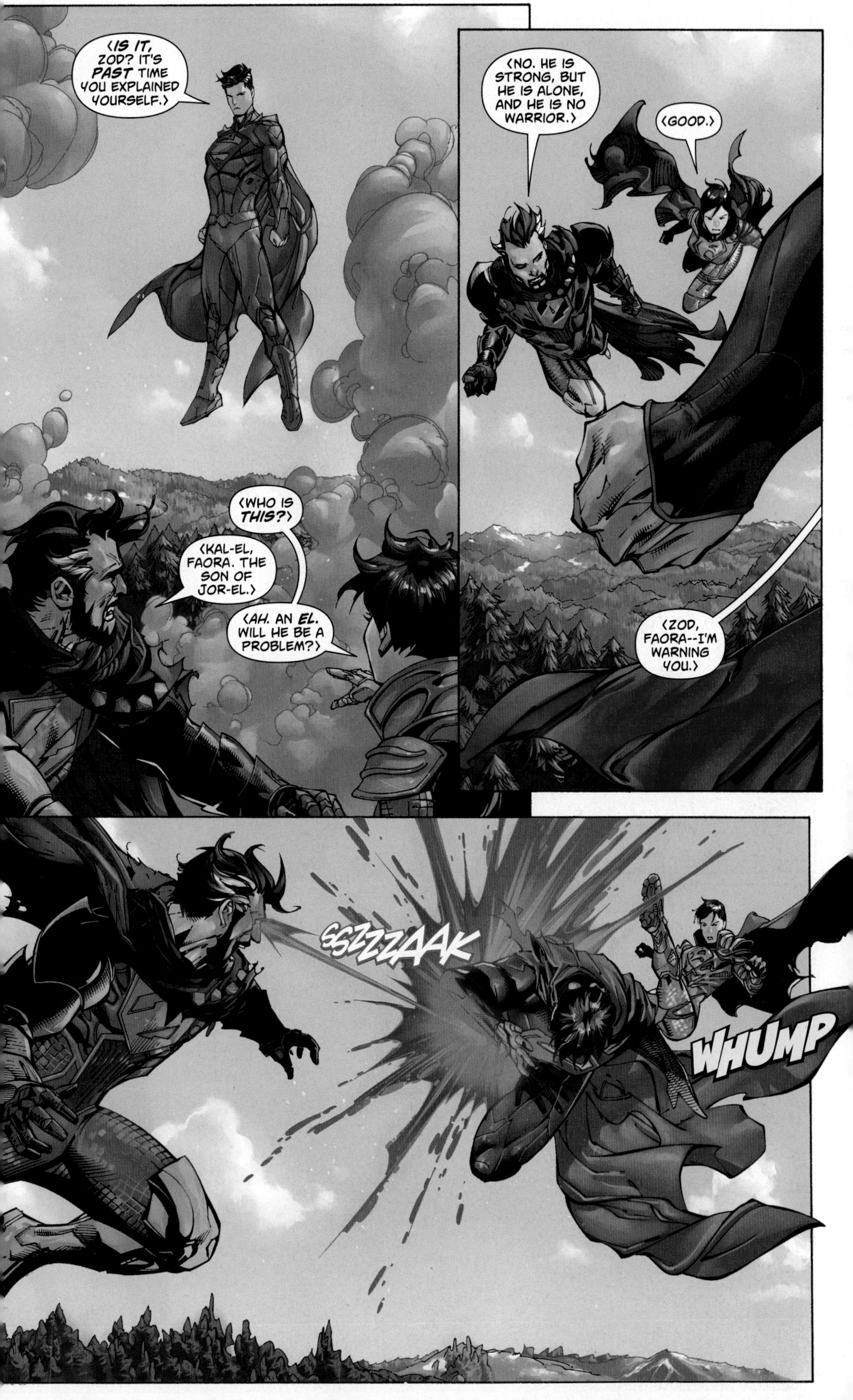

‹IS IT, ZOD? IT'S PAST TIME YOU EXPLAINED YOURSELF.›
‹WHO IS THIS?›
‹KAL-EL, FAORA. THE SON OF JOR-EL.›
‹AH. AN EL. WILL HE BE A PROBLEM?›
‹NO. HE IS STRONG, BUT HE IS ALONE, AND HE IS NO WARRIOR.›
‹GOOD.›
‹ZOD, FAORA--I'M WARNING YOU.›
SSZZZZAAK
WHUMP

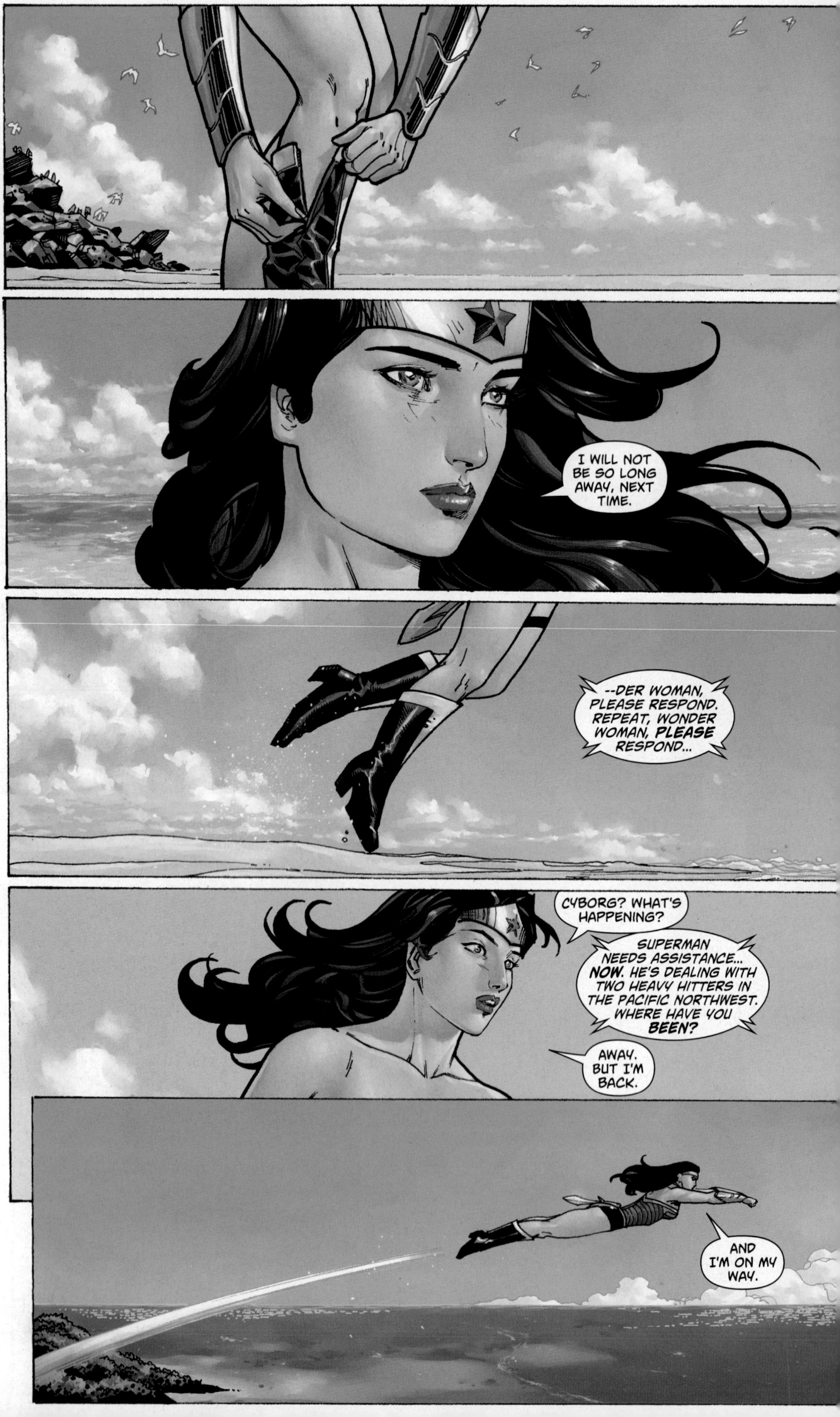
I WILL NOT BE SO LONG AWAY, NEXT TIME.
--DER WOMAN, PLEASE RESPOND. REPEAT, WONDER WOMAN, PLEASE RESPOND...
CYBORG? WHAT'S HAPPENING?
SUPERMAN NEEDS ASSISTANCE... NOW. HE'S DEALING WITH TWO HEAVY HITTERS IN THE PACIFIC NORTHWEST. WHERE HAVE YOU BEEN?
AWAY. BUT I'M BACK.
AND I'M ON MY WAY.

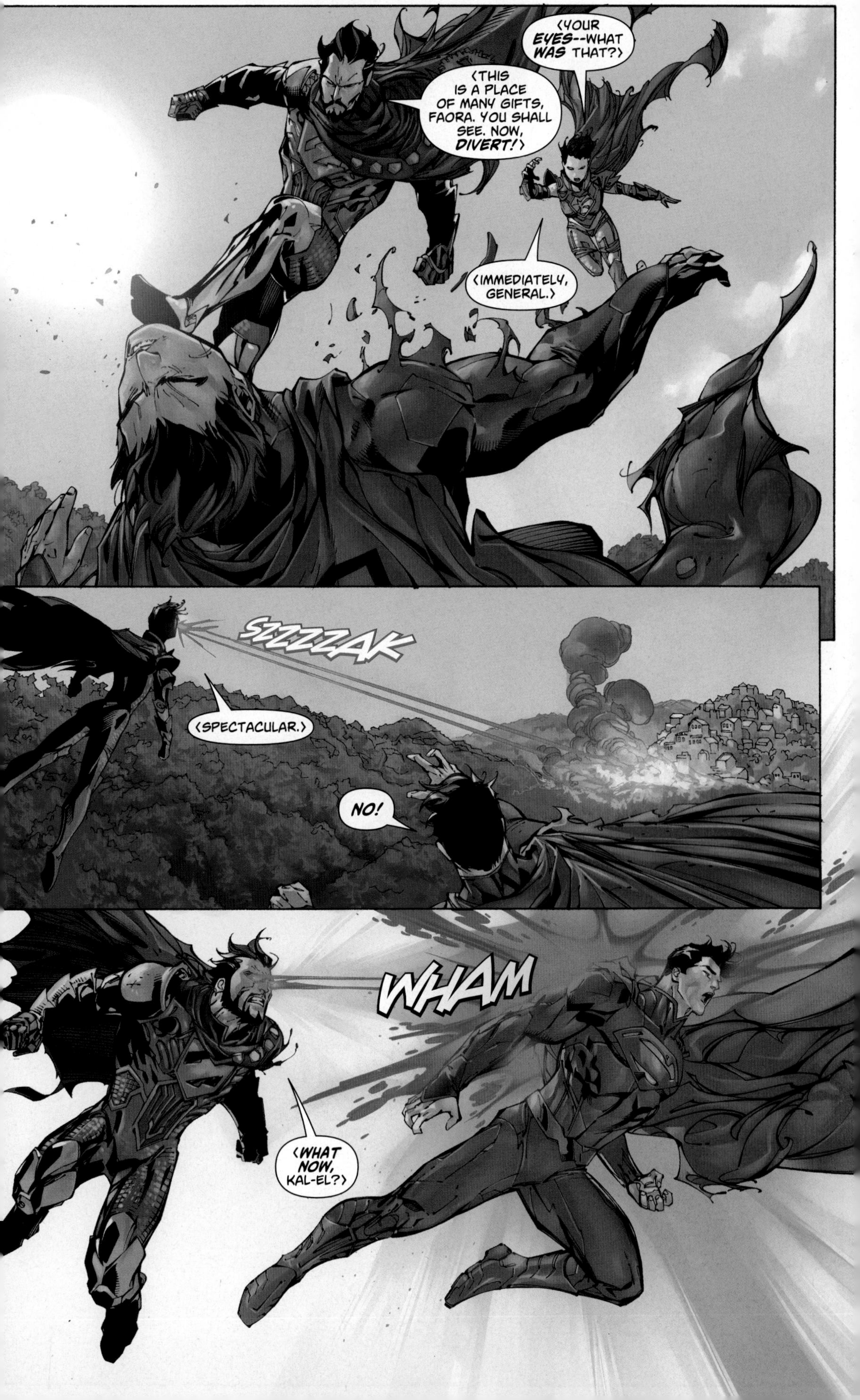

‹YOUR EYES--WHAT WAS THAT?›
‹THIS IS A PLACE OF MANY GIFTS, FAORA. YOU SHALL SEE. NOW, DIVERT!›
‹IMMEDIATELY, GENERAL.›
SZZZZAK
‹SPECTACULAR.›
NO!
WHAM
‹WHAT NOW, KAL-EL?›

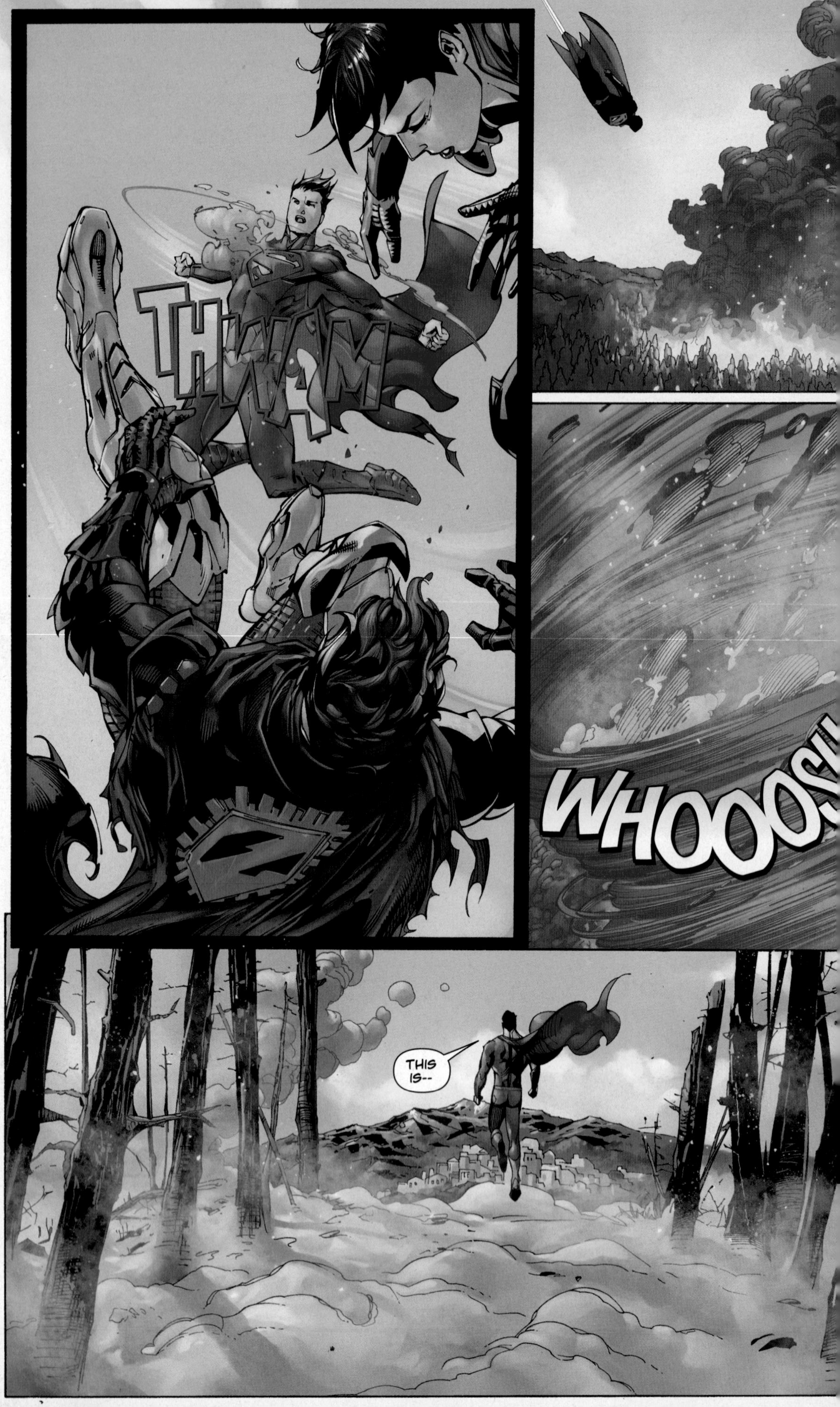
THWAM
WHOOOSH
THIS IS--

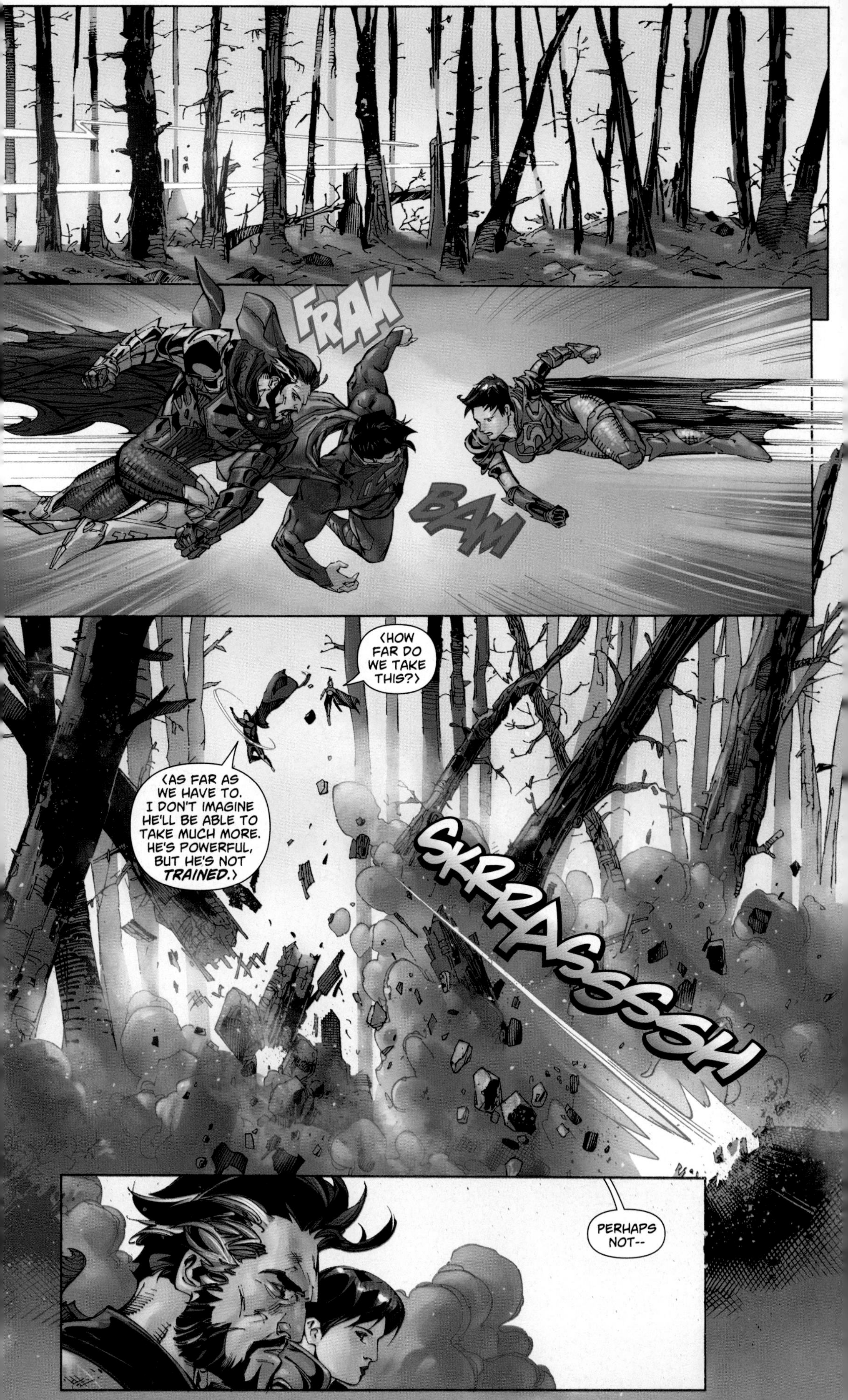
FRAK
BAM
‹HOW FAR DO WE TAKE THIS?›
‹AS FAR AS WE HAVE TO. I DON'T IMAGINE HE'LL BE ABLE TO TAKE MUCH MORE. HE'S POWERFUL, BUT HE'S NOT *TRAINED*.›
SKRASSSSH
PERHAPS NOT--

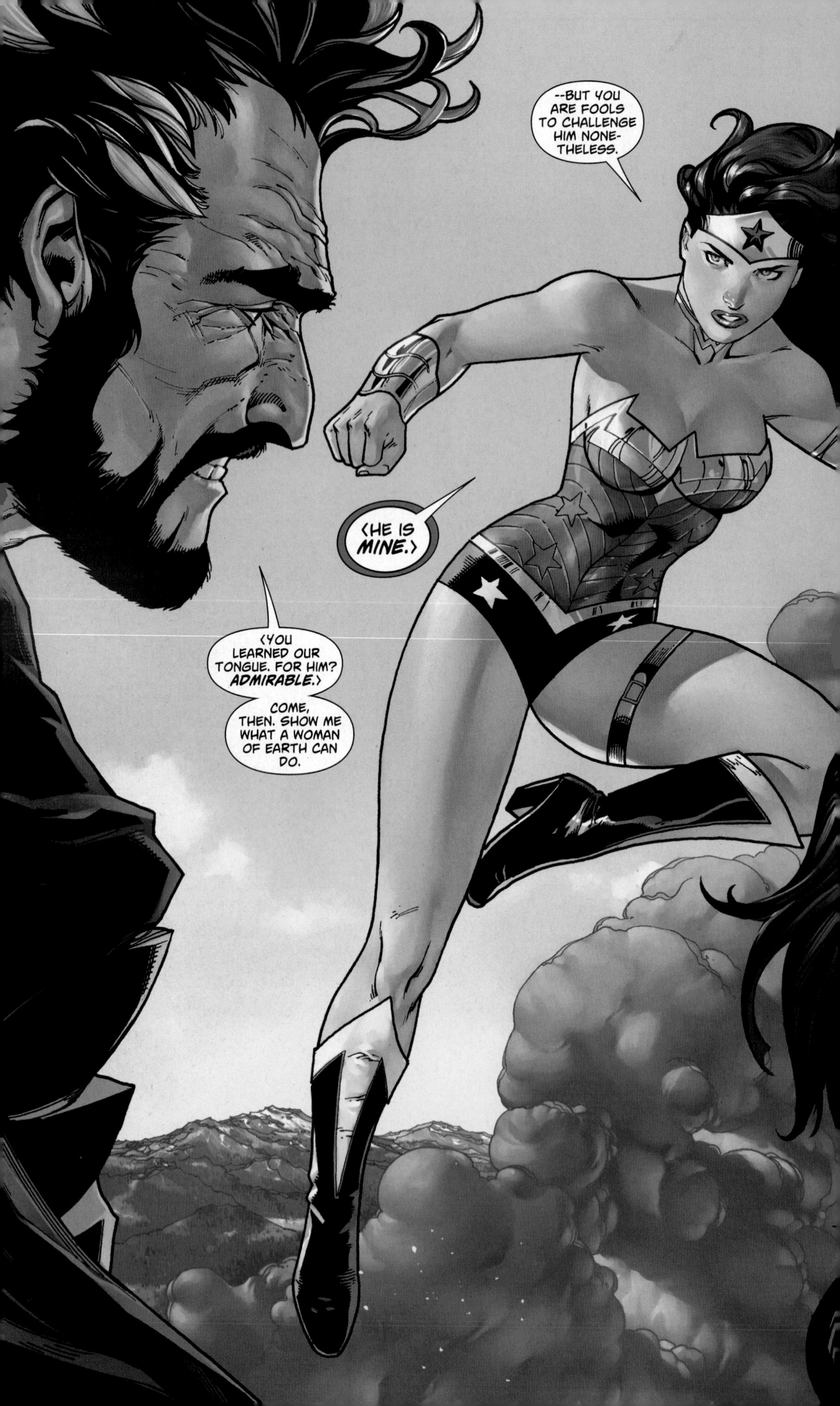
--BUT YOU ARE FOOLS TO CHALLENGE HIM NONE-THELESS.
‹HE IS *MINE.*›
‹YOU LEARNED OUR TONGUE. FOR HIM? *ADMIRABLE.*›
COME, THEN. SHOW ME WHAT A WOMAN OF EARTH CAN DO.

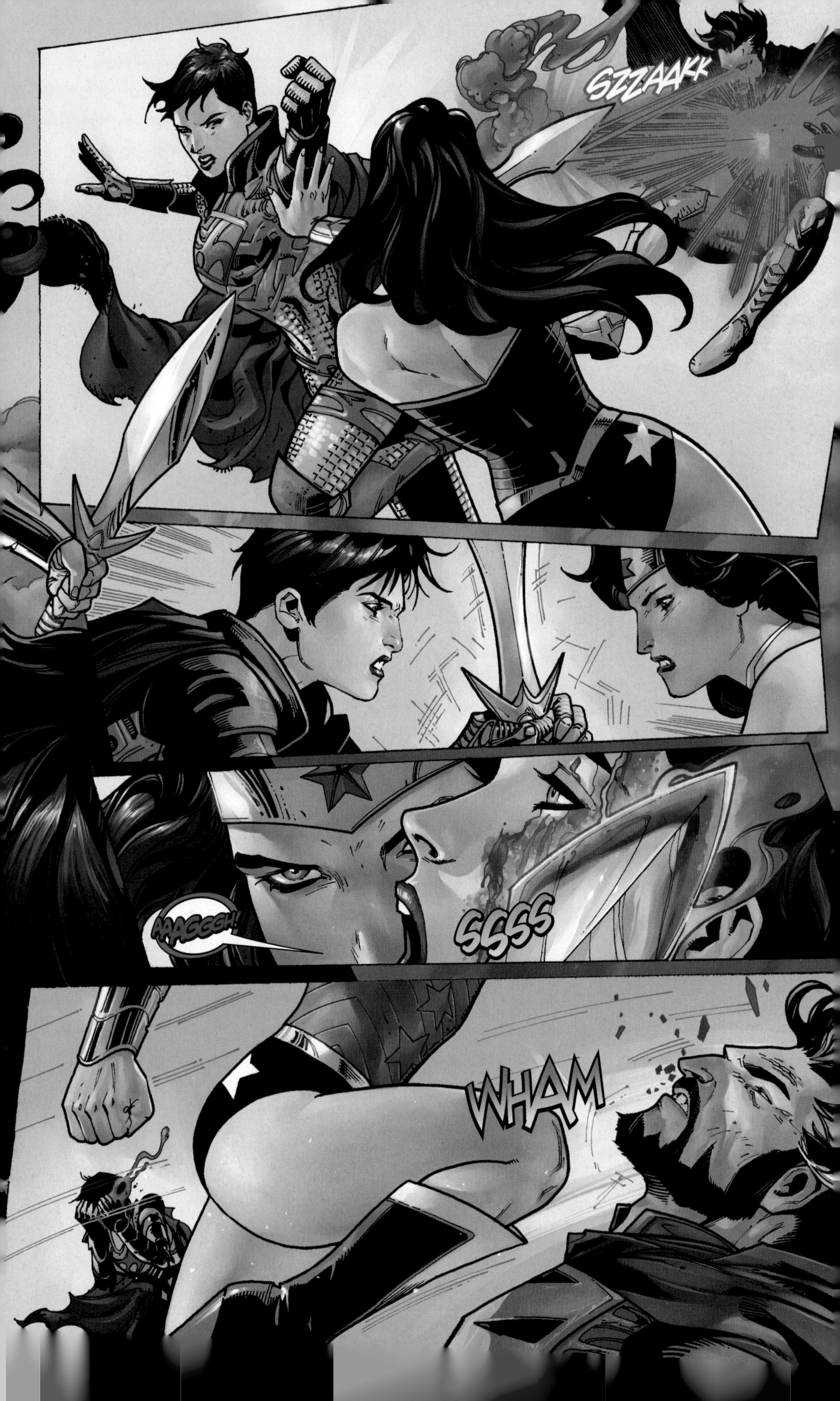

SZZAAKK
AAAGGGH!
SSSS
WHAM

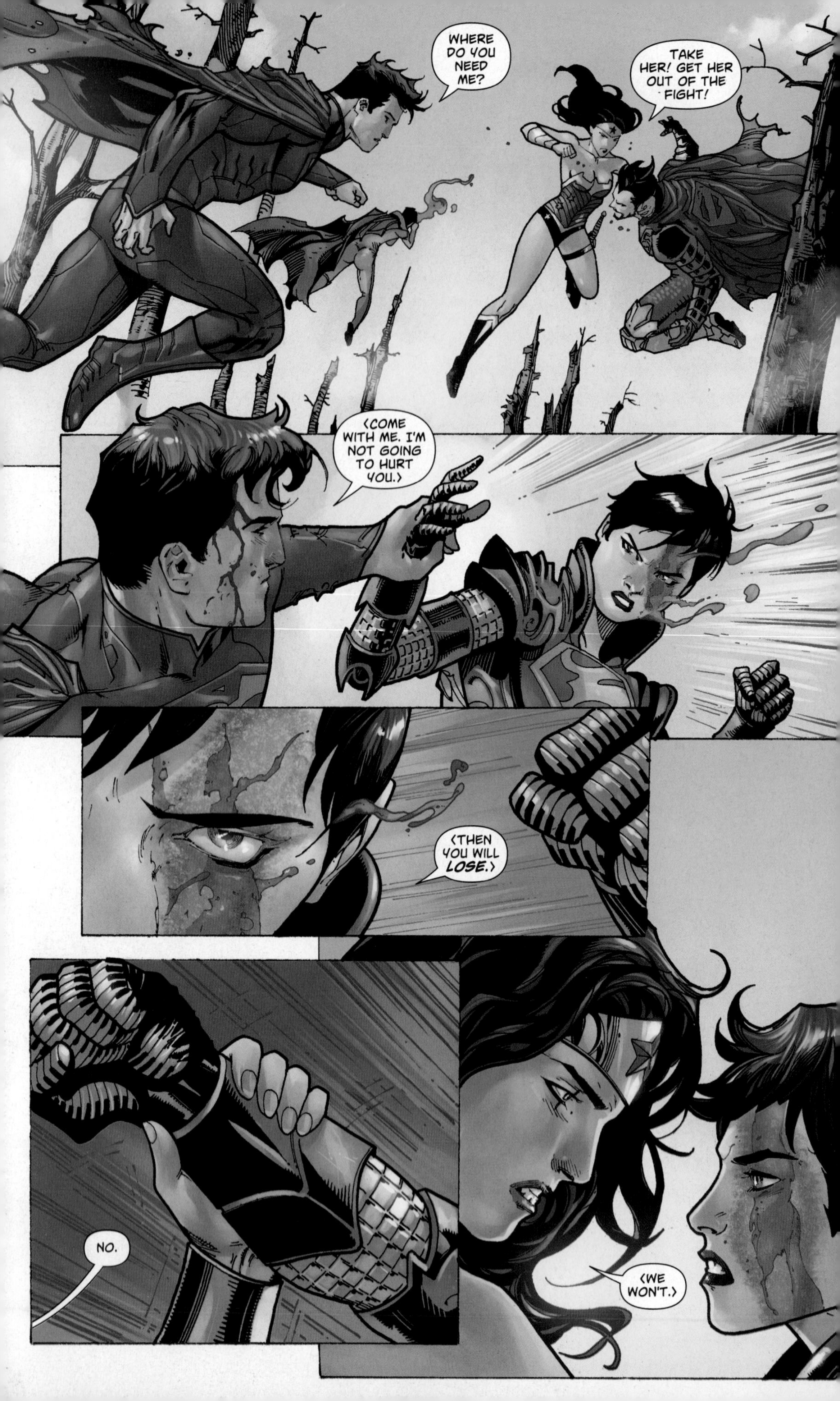
WHERE DO YOU NEED ME?
TAKE HER! GET HER OUT OF THE FIGHT!
‹COME WITH ME. I'M NOT GOING TO HURT YOU.›
‹THEN YOU WILL **LOSE**.›
NO.
‹WE WON'T.›

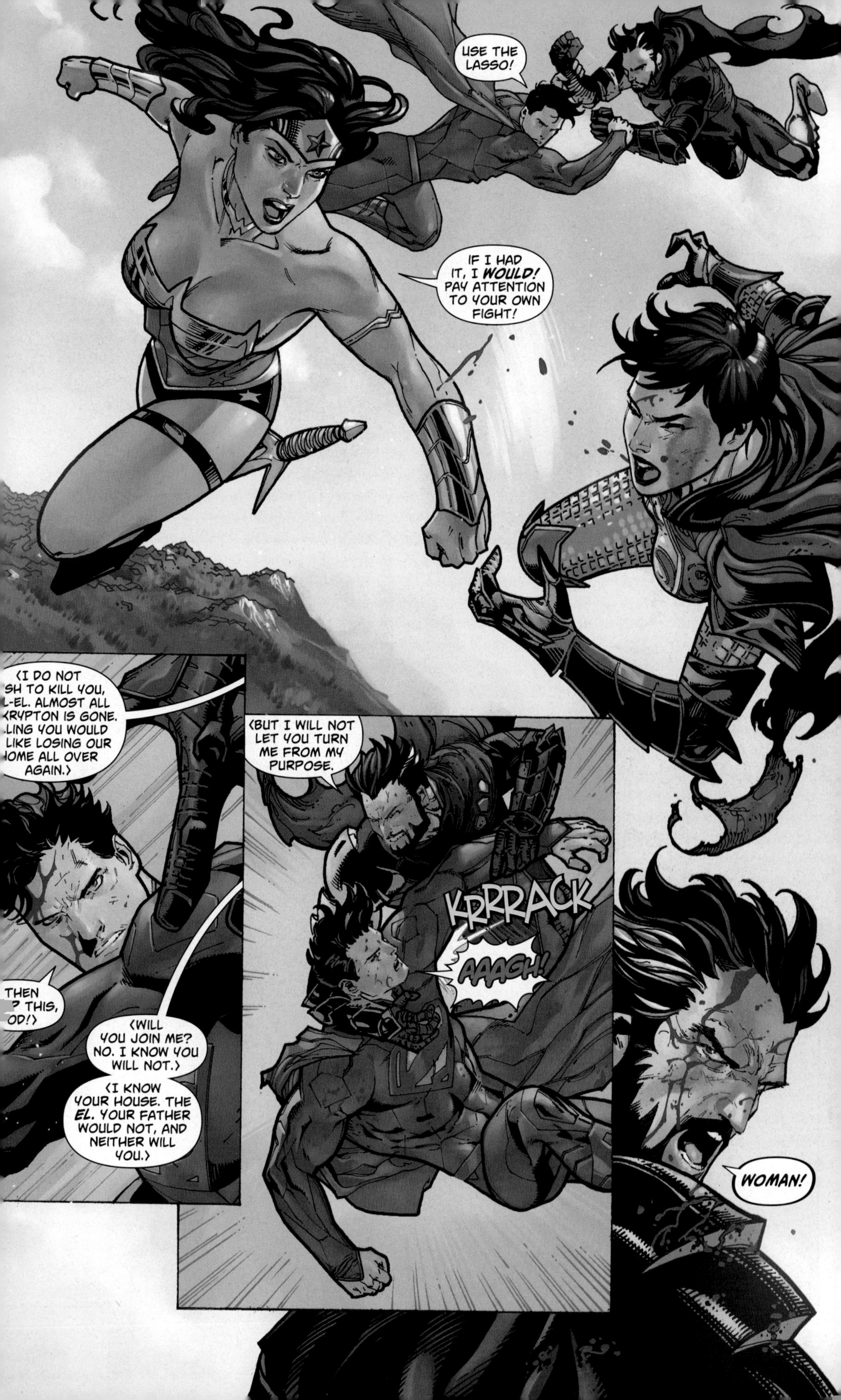
USE THE LASSO!
IF I HAD IT, I WOULD! PAY ATTENTION TO YOUR OWN FIGHT!
<I DO NOT SH TO KILL YOU, L-EL. ALMOST ALL KRYPTON IS GONE. LING YOU WOULD LIKE LOSING OUR HOME ALL OVER AGAIN.>
THEN THIS, OD!>
<WILL YOU JOIN ME? NO. I KNOW YOU WILL NOT.>
<I KNOW YOUR HOUSE. THE EL. YOUR FATHER WOULD NOT, AND NEITHER WILL YOU.>
<BUT I WILL NOT LET YOU TURN ME FROM MY PURPOSE.>
KRRRACK
AAAGH!
WOMAN!

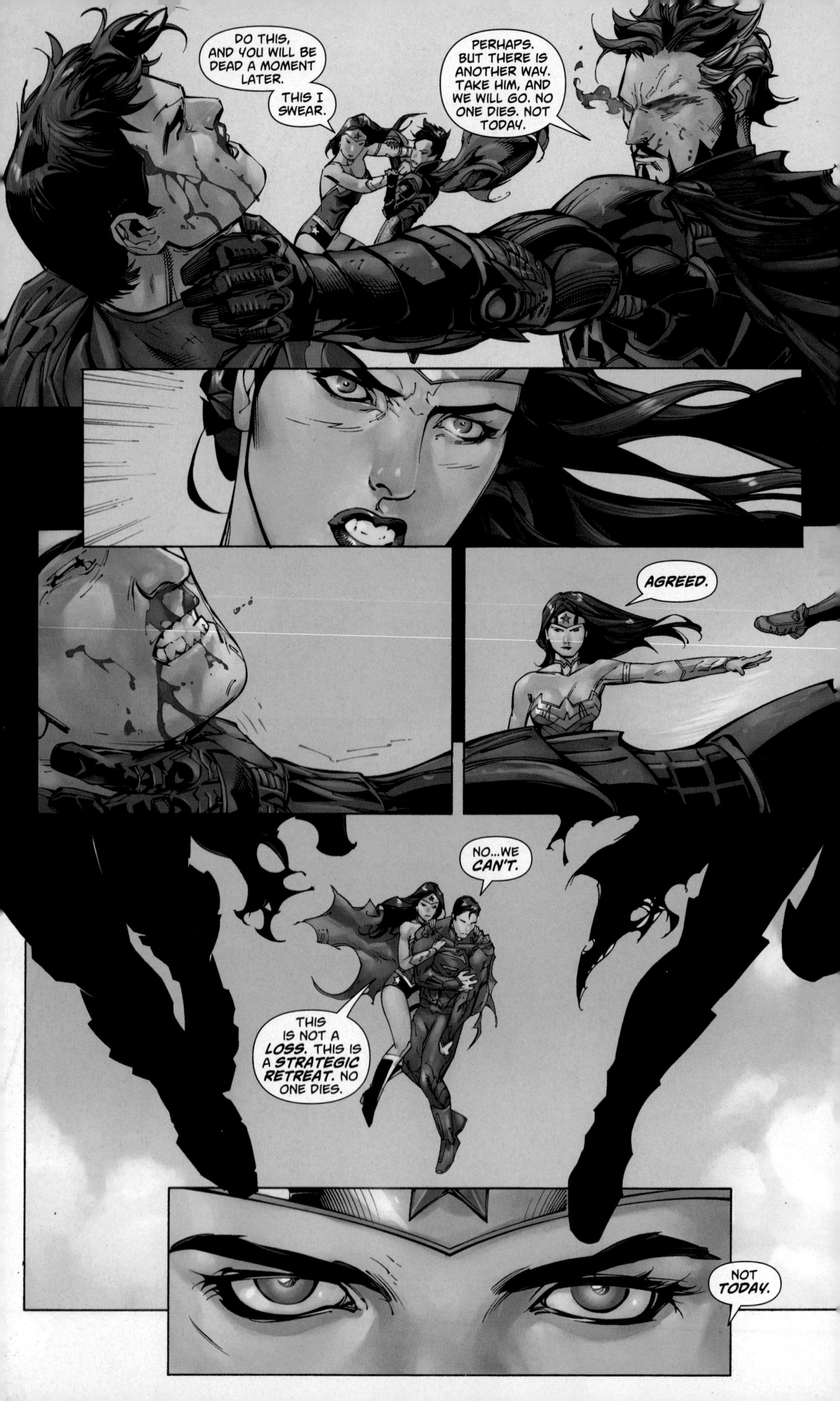
DO THIS, AND YOU WILL BE DEAD A MOMENT LATER.
THIS I SWEAR.
PERHAPS. BUT THERE IS ANOTHER WAY. TAKE HIM, AND WE WILL GO. NO ONE DIES. NOT TODAY.
AGREED.
NO...WE CAN'T.
THIS IS NOT A LOSS. THIS IS A STRATEGIC RETREAT. NO ONE DIES.
NOT TODAY.

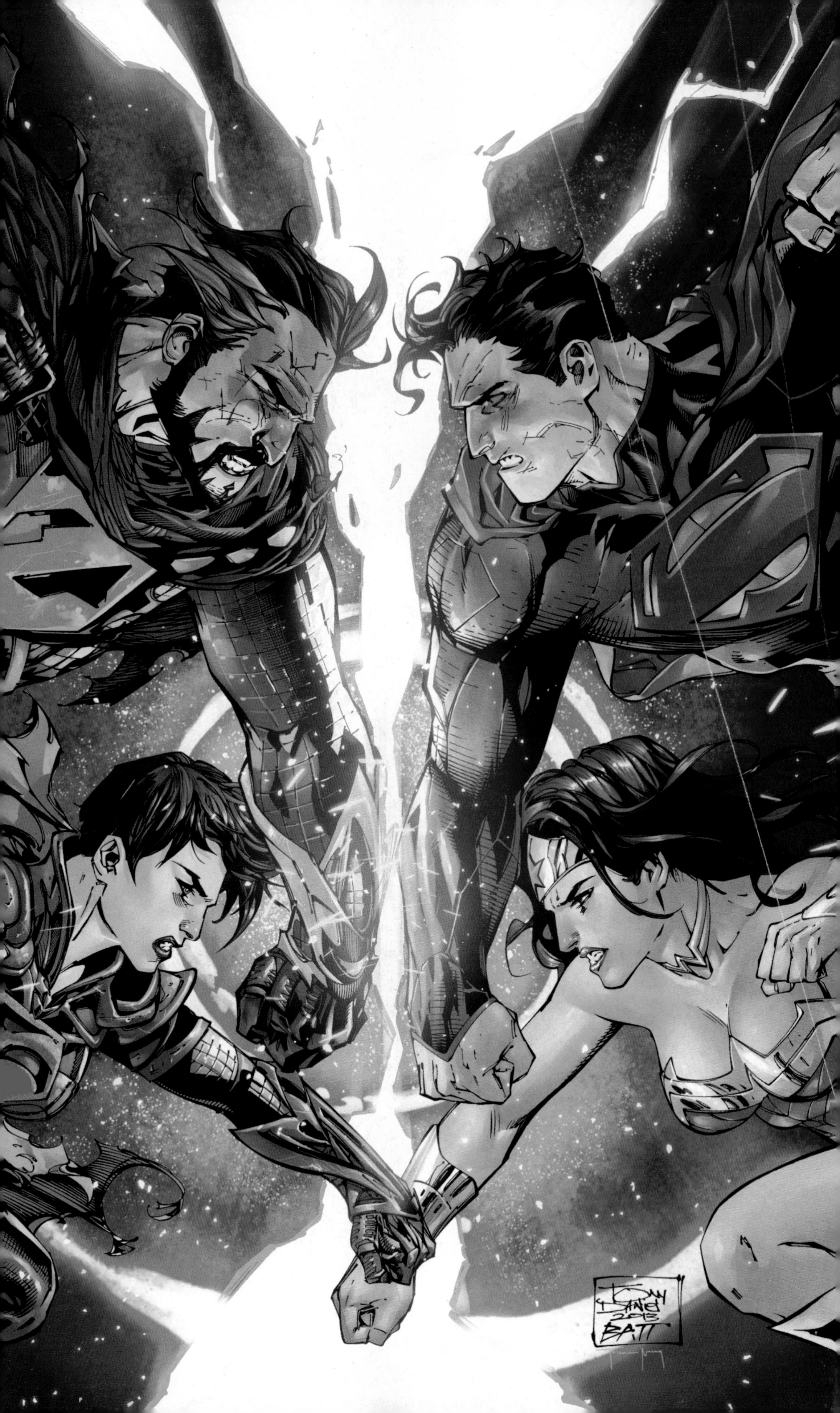

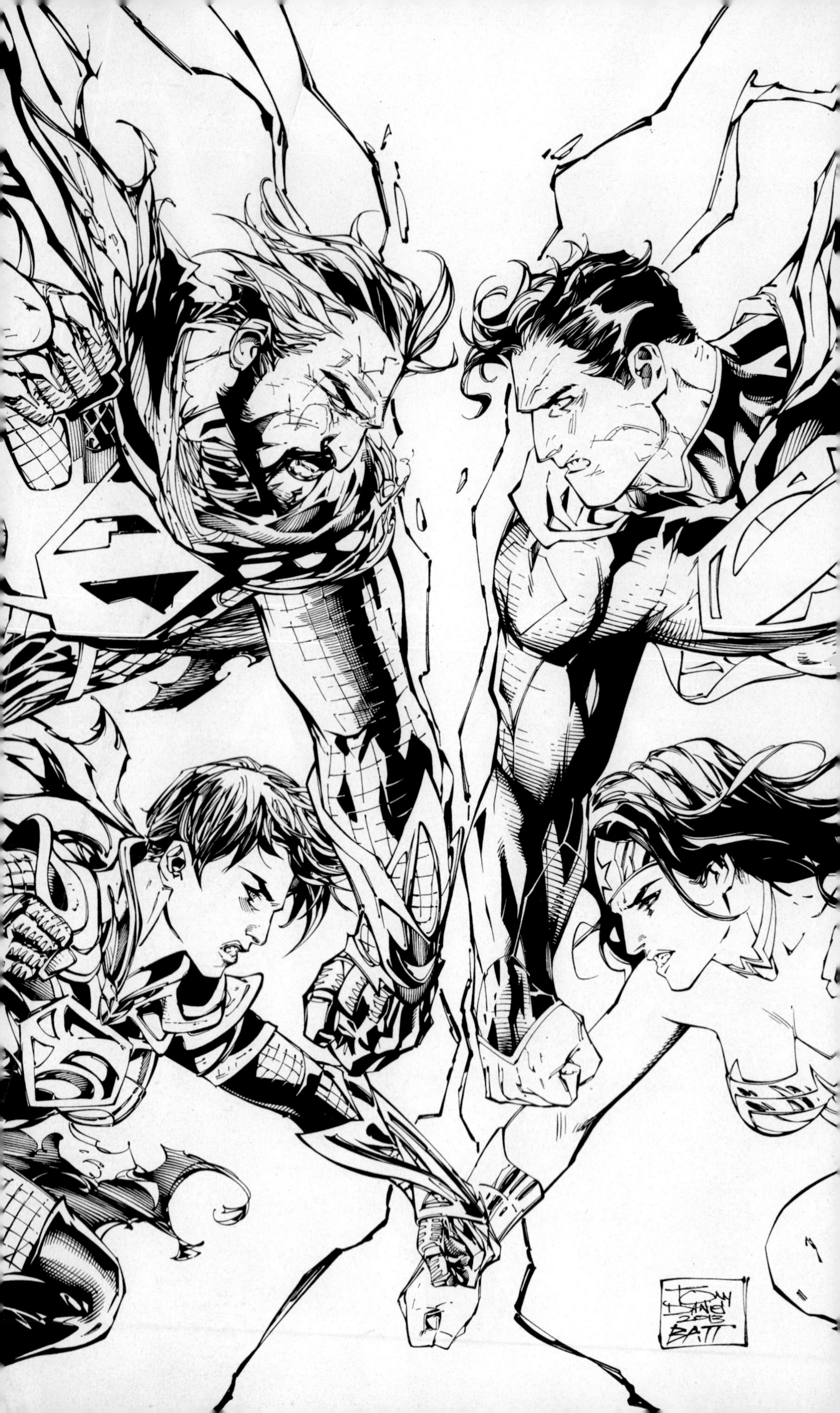

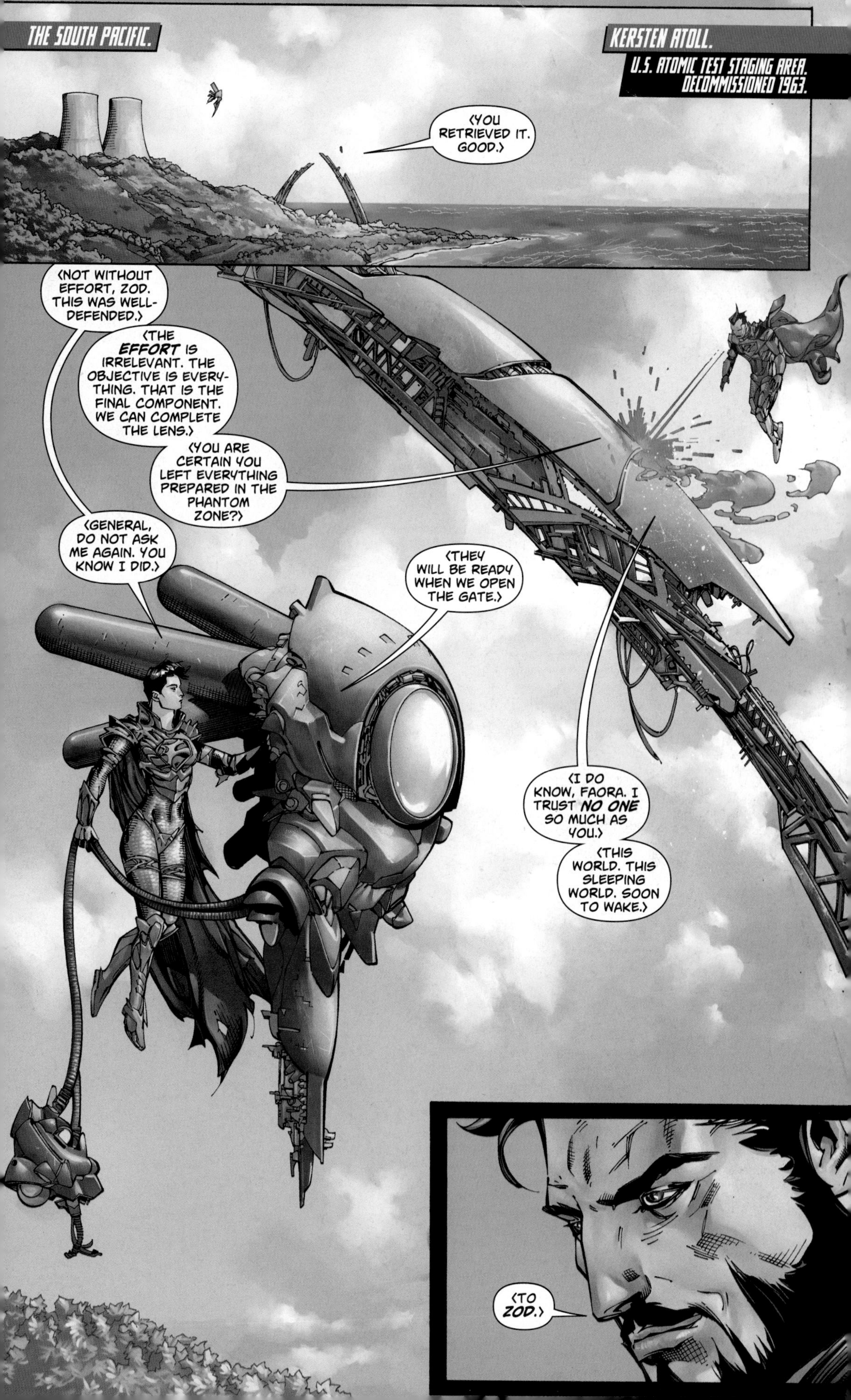
THE SOUTH PACIFIC.
KERSTEN ATOLL.
U.S. ATOMIC TEST STAGING AREA. DECOMMISSIONED 1963.
‹YOU RETRIEVED IT. GOOD.›
‹NOT WITHOUT EFFORT, ZOD. THIS WAS WELL-DEFENDED.›
‹THE EFFORT IS IRRELEVANT. THE OBJECTIVE IS EVERYTHING. THAT IS THE FINAL COMPONENT. WE CAN COMPLETE THE LENS.›
‹YOU ARE CERTAIN YOU LEFT EVERYTHING PREPARED IN THE PHANTOM ZONE?›
‹GENERAL, DO NOT ASK ME AGAIN. YOU KNOW I DID.›
‹THEY WILL BE READY WHEN WE OPEN THE GATE.›
‹I DO KNOW, FAORA. I TRUST NO ONE SO MUCH AS YOU.›
‹THIS WORLD. THIS SLEEPING WORLD. SOON TO WAKE.›
‹TO ZOD.›

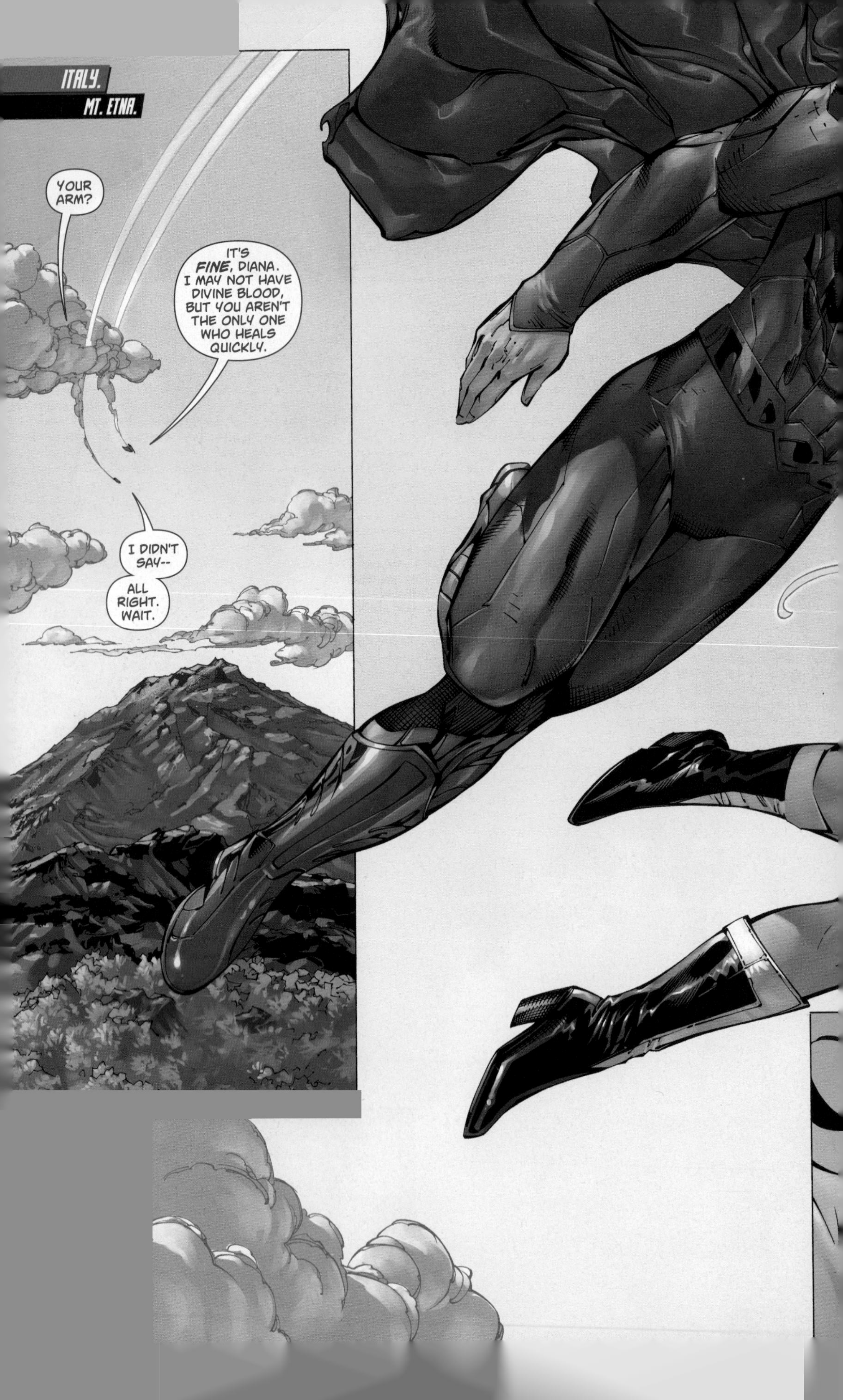
ITALY.
MT. ETNA.
YOUR ARM?
IT'S FINE, DIANA. I MAY NOT HAVE DIVINE BLOOD, BUT YOU AREN'T THE ONLY ONE WHO HEALS QUICKLY.
I DIDN'T SAY--
ALL RIGHT. WAIT.

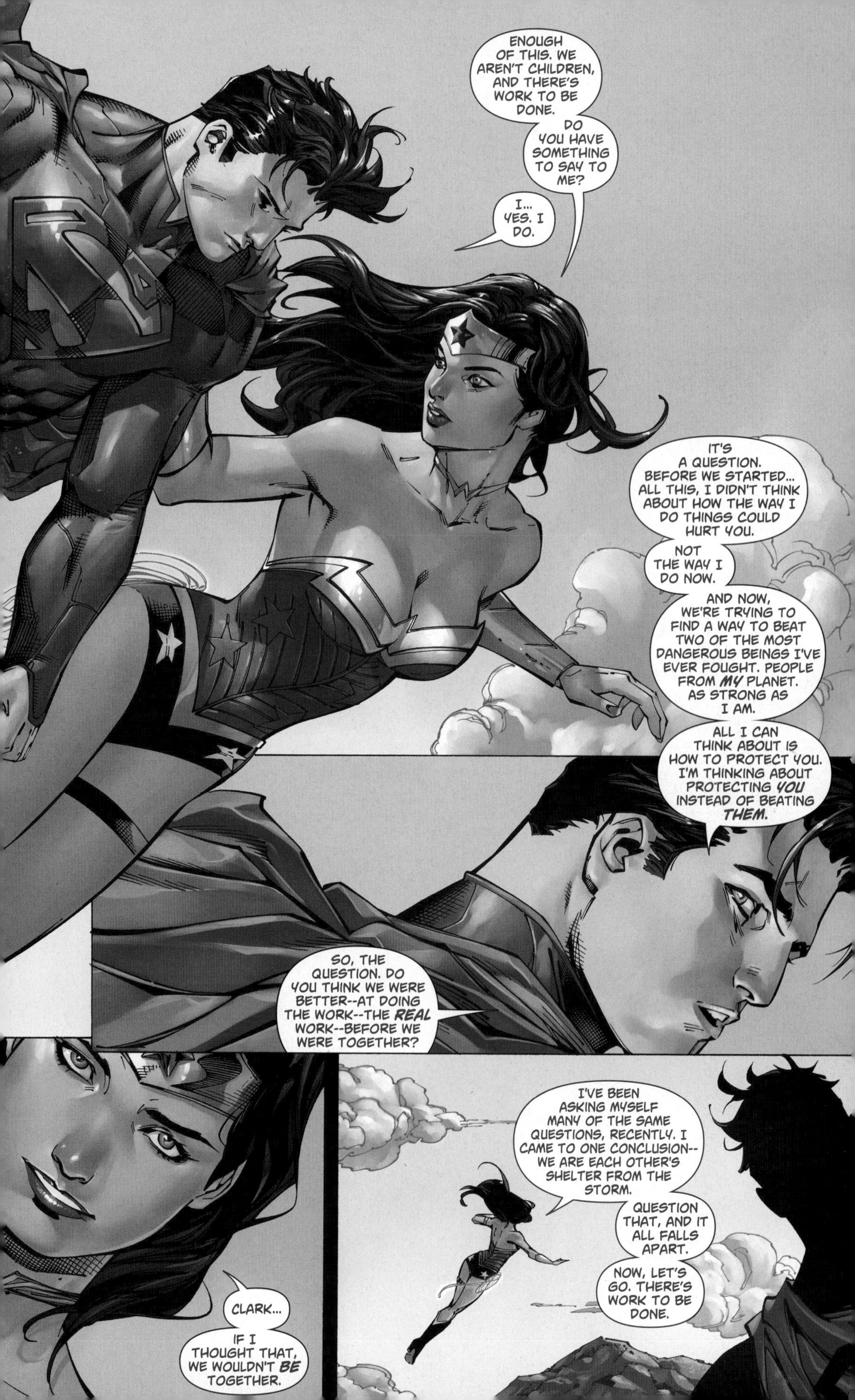
ENOUGH OF THIS. WE AREN'T CHILDREN, AND THERE'S WORK TO BE DONE.
DO YOU HAVE SOMETHING TO SAY TO ME?
I... YES. I DO.
IT'S A QUESTION. BEFORE WE STARTED... ALL THIS, I DIDN'T THINK ABOUT HOW THE WAY I DO THINGS COULD HURT YOU.
NOT THE WAY I DO NOW.
AND NOW, WE'RE TRYING TO FIND A WAY TO BEAT TWO OF THE MOST DANGEROUS BEINGS I'VE EVER FOUGHT. PEOPLE FROM *MY* PLANET. AS STRONG AS I AM.
ALL I CAN THINK ABOUT IS HOW TO PROTECT YOU. I'M THINKING ABOUT PROTECTING *YOU* INSTEAD OF BEATING *THEM*.
SO, THE QUESTION. DO YOU THINK WE WERE BETTER--AT DOING THE WORK--THE *REAL* WORK--BEFORE WE WERE TOGETHER?
CLARK...
IF I THOUGHT THAT, WE WOULDN'T *BE* TOGETHER.
I'VE BEEN ASKING MYSELF MANY OF THE SAME QUESTIONS, RECENTLY. I CAME TO ONE CONCLUSION-- WE ARE EACH OTHER'S SHELTER FROM THE STORM.
QUESTION THAT, AND IT ALL FALLS APART.
NOW, LET'S GO. THERE'S WORK TO BE DONE.

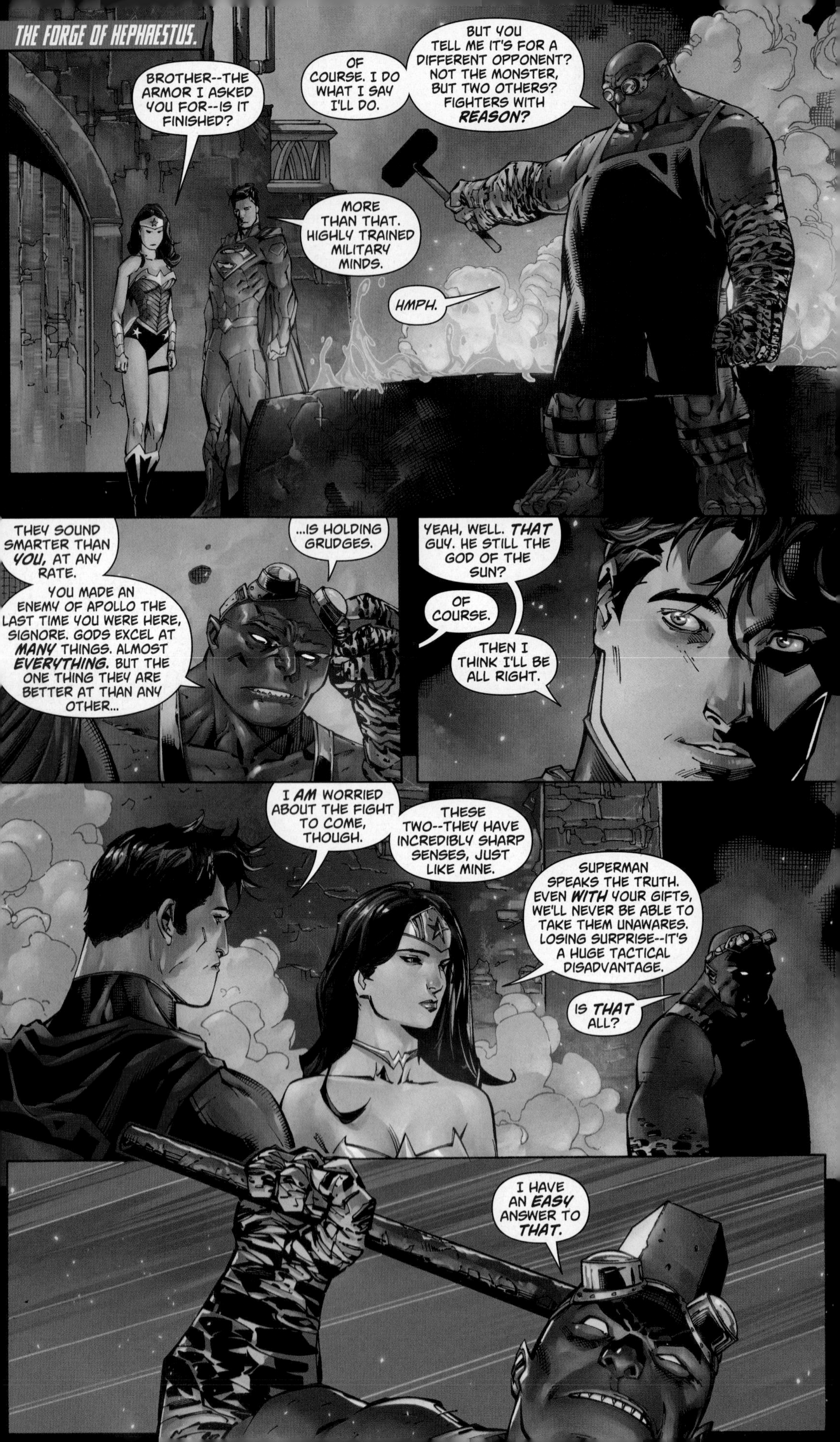
THE FORGE OF HEPHAESTUS.
BROTHER--THE ARMOR I ASKED YOU FOR--IS IT FINISHED?
OF COURSE. I DO WHAT I SAY I'LL DO.
BUT YOU TELL ME IT'S FOR A DIFFERENT OPPONENT? NOT THE MONSTER, BUT TWO OTHERS? FIGHTERS WITH REASON?
MORE THAN THAT. HIGHLY TRAINED MILITARY MINDS.
HMPH.
THEY SOUND SMARTER THAN YOU, AT ANY RATE.
YOU MADE AN ENEMY OF APOLLO THE LAST TIME YOU WERE HERE, SIGNORE. GODS EXCEL AT MANY THINGS. ALMOST EVERYTHING. BUT THE ONE THING THEY ARE BETTER AT THAN ANY OTHER...
...IS HOLDING GRUDGES.
YEAH, WELL. THAT GUY. HE STILL THE GOD OF THE SUN?
OF COURSE.
THEN I THINK I'LL BE ALL RIGHT.
I AM WORRIED ABOUT THE FIGHT TO COME, THOUGH.
THESE TWO--THEY HAVE INCREDIBLY SHARP SENSES, JUST LIKE MINE.
SUPERMAN SPEAKS THE TRUTH. EVEN WITH YOUR GIFTS, WE'LL NEVER BE ABLE TO TAKE THEM UNAWARES. LOSING SURPRISE--IT'S A HUGE TACTICAL DISADVANTAGE.
IS THAT ALL?
I HAVE AN EASY ANSWER TO THAT.

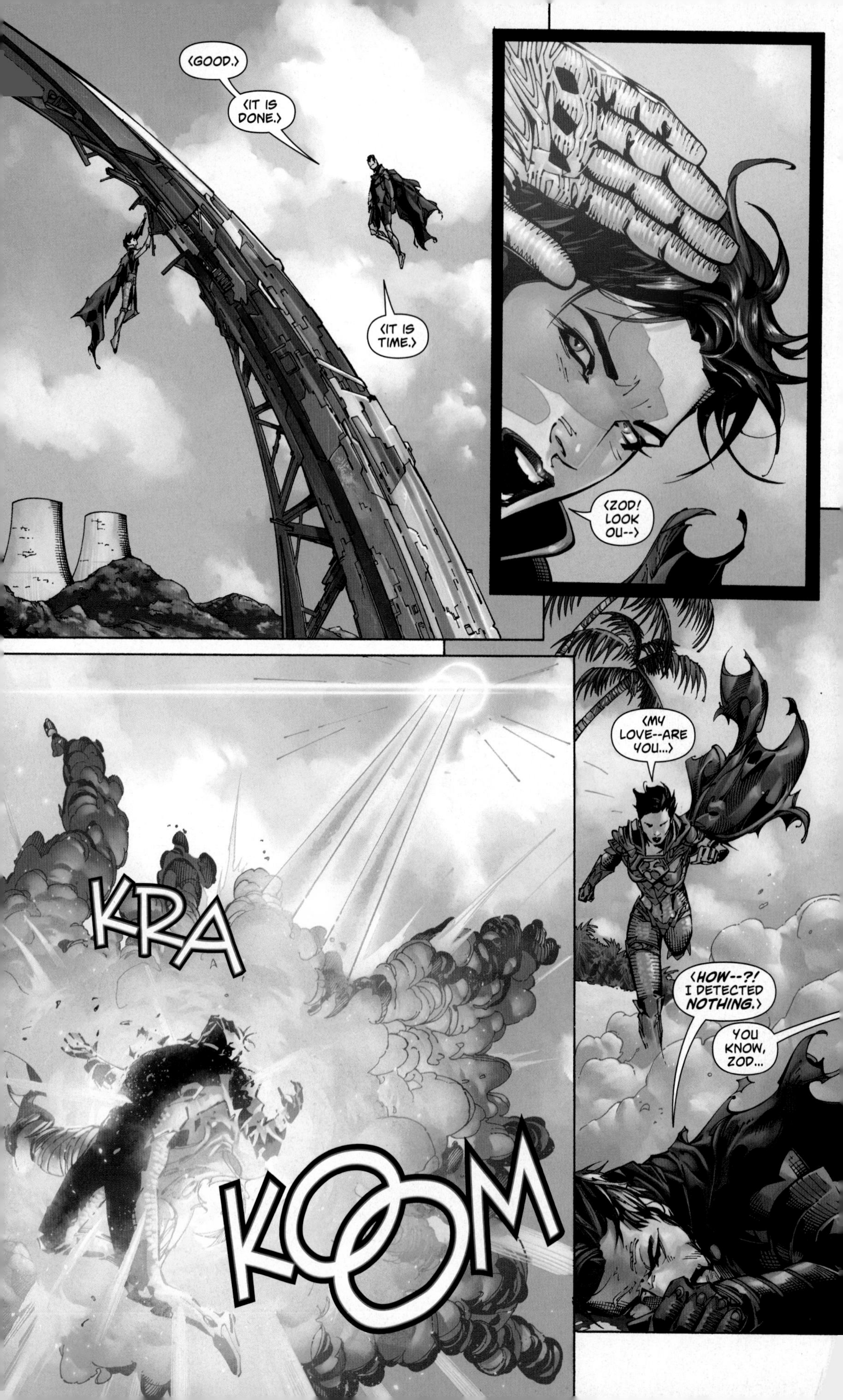

‹GOOD.›
‹IT IS DONE.›
‹IT IS TIME.›
‹ZOD! LOOK OU--›
KRA
KOOM
‹MY LOVE--ARE YOU...›
‹HOW--?! I DETECTED NOTHING.›
YOU KNOW, ZOD...

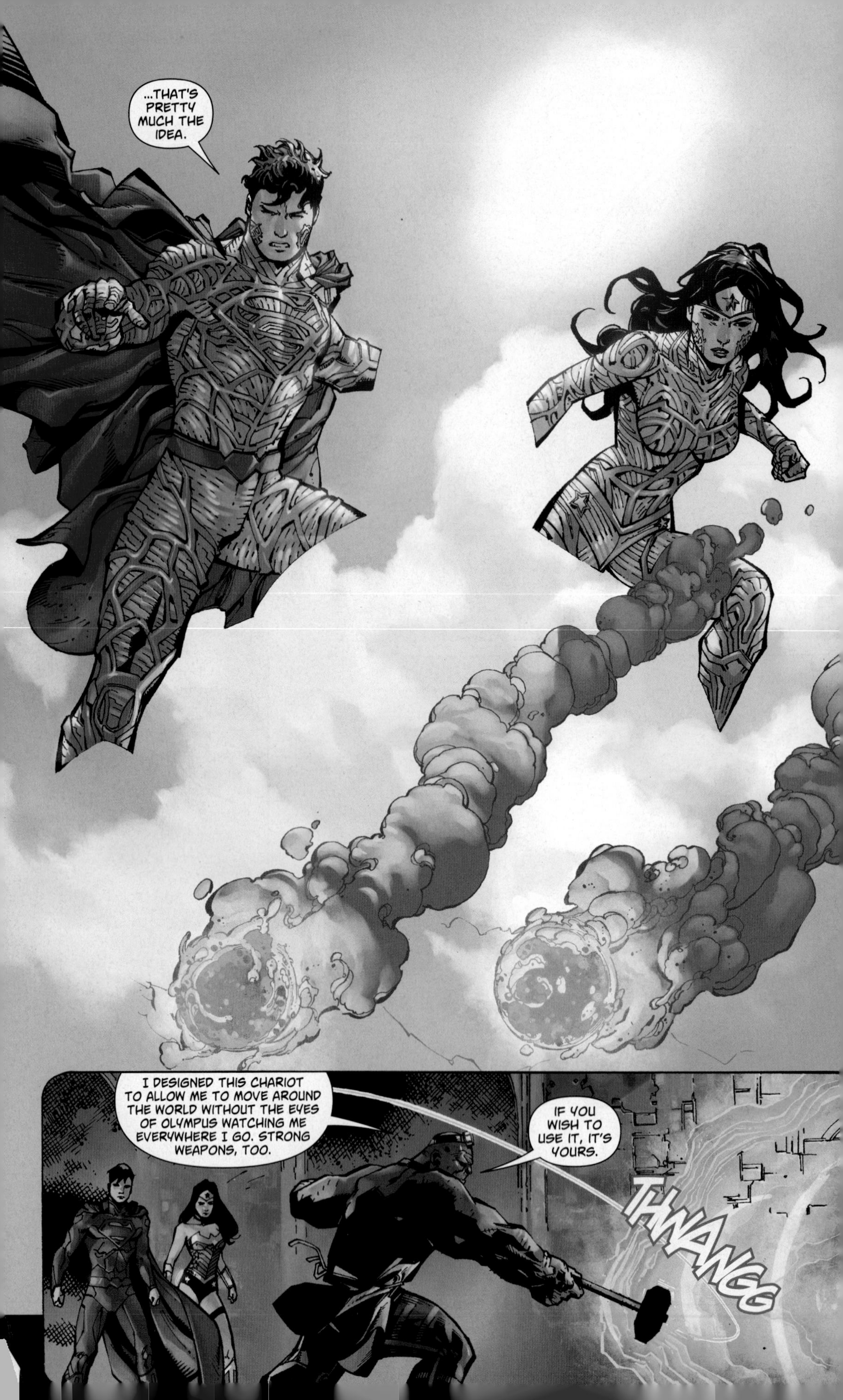
...THAT'S PRETTY MUCH THE IDEA.
I DESIGNED THIS CHARIOT TO ALLOW ME TO MOVE AROUND THE WORLD WITHOUT THE EYES OF OLYMPUS WATCHING ME EVERYWHERE I GO. STRONG WEAPONS, TOO.
IF YOU WISH TO USE IT, IT'S YOURS.
THWANGG

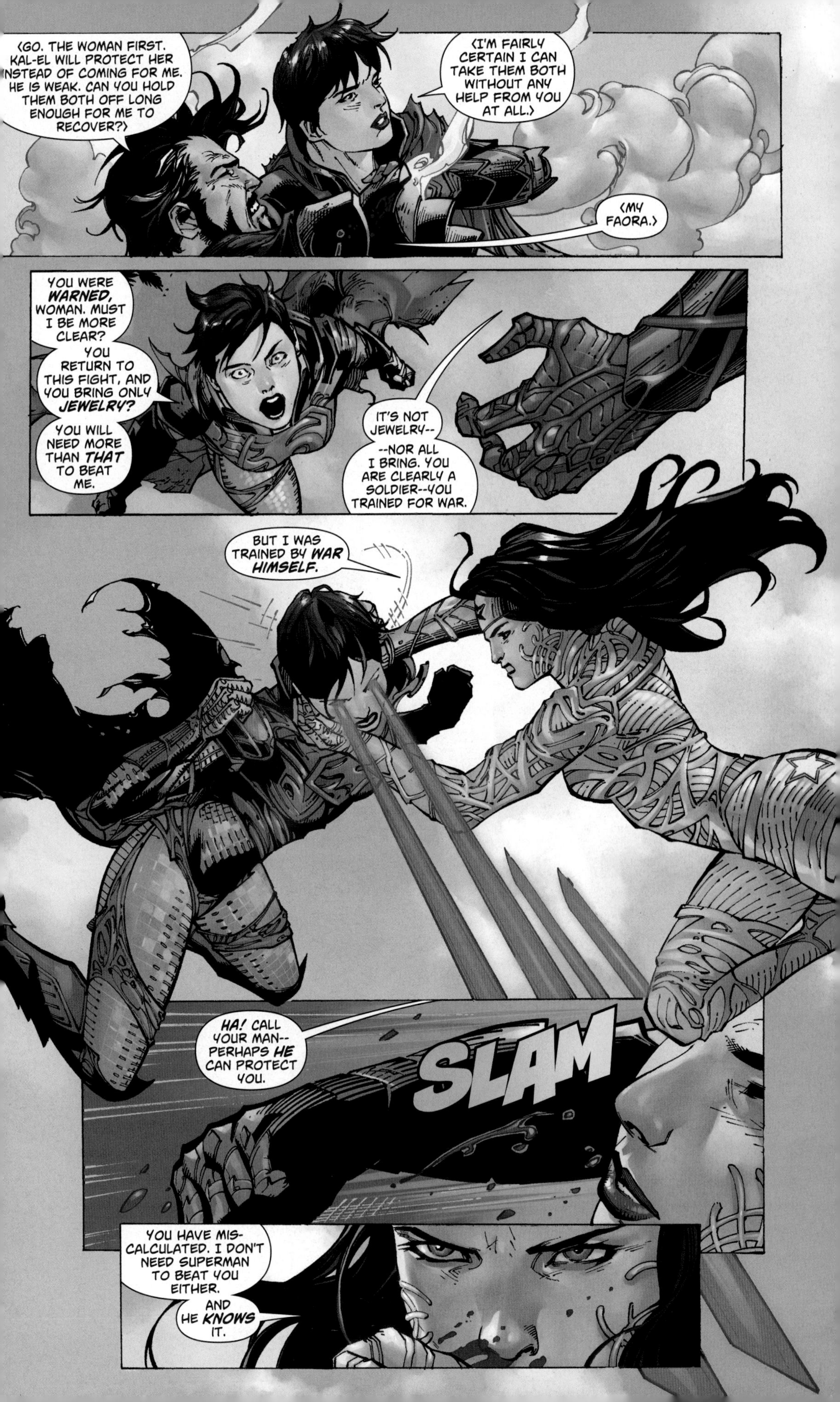

‹GO. THE WOMAN FIRST. KAL-EL WILL PROTECT HER INSTEAD OF COMING FOR ME. HE IS WEAK. CAN YOU HOLD THEM BOTH OFF LONG ENOUGH FOR ME TO RECOVER?›
‹I'M FAIRLY CERTAIN I CAN TAKE THEM BOTH WITHOUT ANY HELP FROM YOU AT ALL.›
‹MY FAORA.›
YOU WERE WARNED, WOMAN. MUST I BE MORE CLEAR?
YOU RETURN TO THIS FIGHT, AND YOU BRING ONLY JEWELRY?
YOU WILL NEED MORE THAN THAT TO BEAT ME.
IT'S NOT JEWELRY--
--NOR ALL I BRING. YOU ARE CLEARLY A SOLDIER--YOU TRAINED FOR WAR.
BUT I WAS TRAINED BY WAR HIMSELF.
HA! CALL YOUR MAN--PERHAPS HE CAN PROTECT YOU.
SLAM
YOU HAVE MIS-CALCULATED. I DON'T NEED SUPERMAN TO BEAT YOU EITHER.
AND HE KNOWS IT.

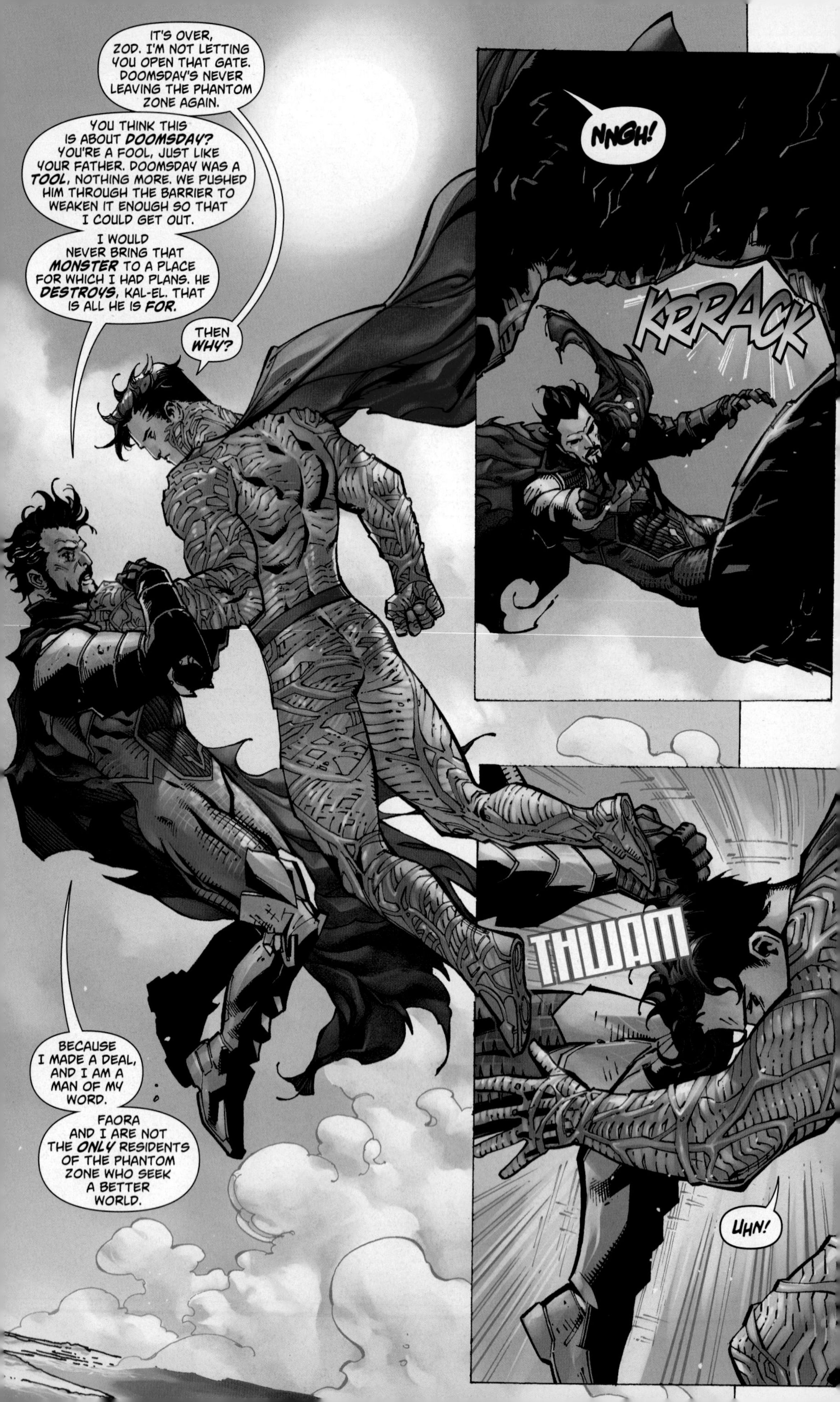
IT'S OVER, ZOD. I'M NOT LETTING YOU OPEN THAT GATE. DOOMSDAY'S NEVER LEAVING THE PHANTOM ZONE AGAIN.
YOU THINK THIS IS ABOUT DOOMSDAY? YOU'RE A FOOL, JUST LIKE YOUR FATHER. DOOMSDAY WAS A TOOL, NOTHING MORE. WE PUSHED HIM THROUGH THE BARRIER TO WEAKEN IT ENOUGH SO THAT I COULD GET OUT.
I WOULD NEVER BRING THAT MONSTER TO A PLACE FOR WHICH I HAD PLANS. HE DESTROYS, KAL-EL. THAT IS ALL HE IS FOR.
THEN WHY?
BECAUSE I MADE A DEAL, AND I AM A MAN OF MY WORD.
FAORA AND I ARE NOT THE ONLY RESIDENTS OF THE PHANTOM ZONE WHO SEEK A BETTER WORLD.
NNGH!
KRRACK
THWAM
UHN!

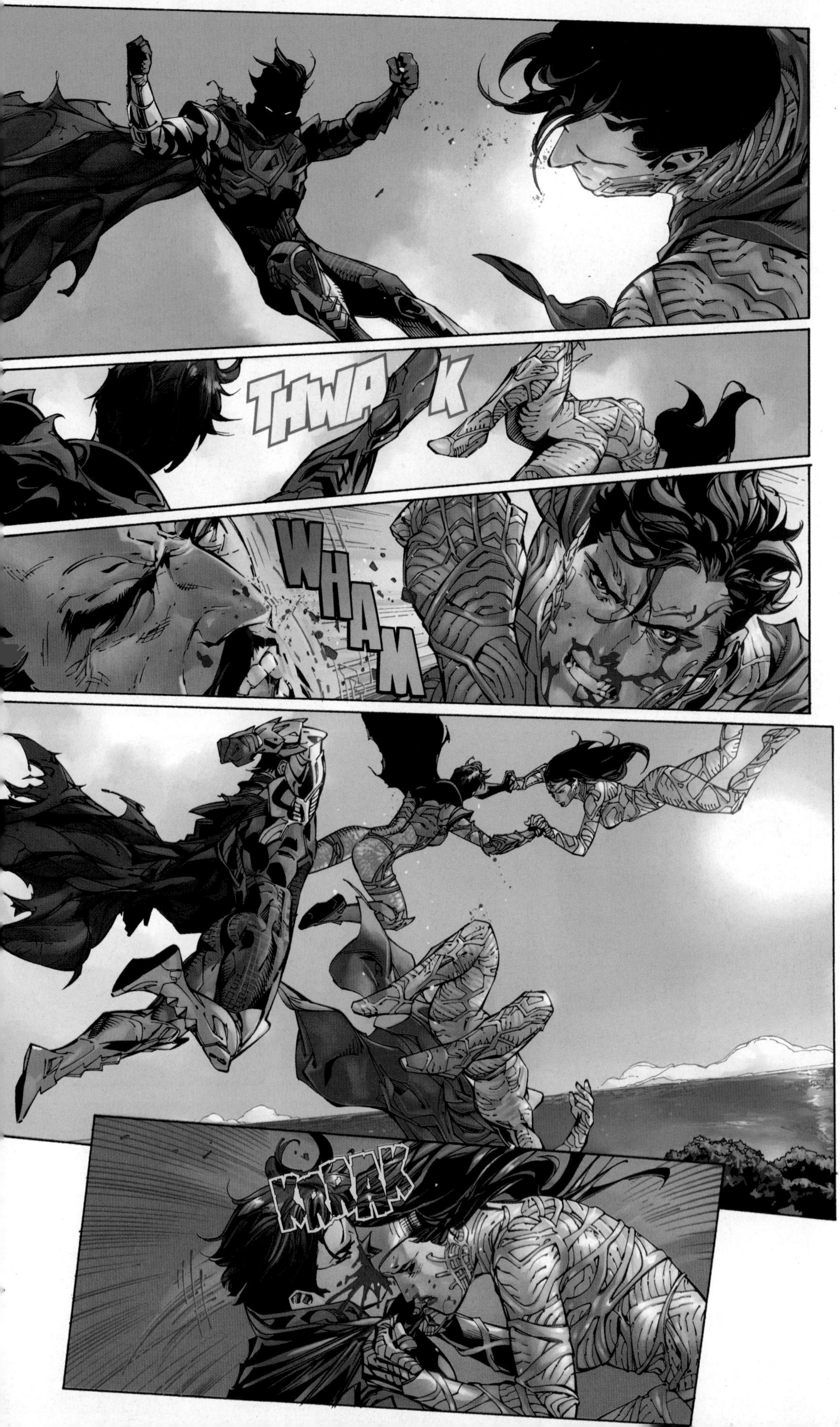
THWA K
WHAM
KRAK

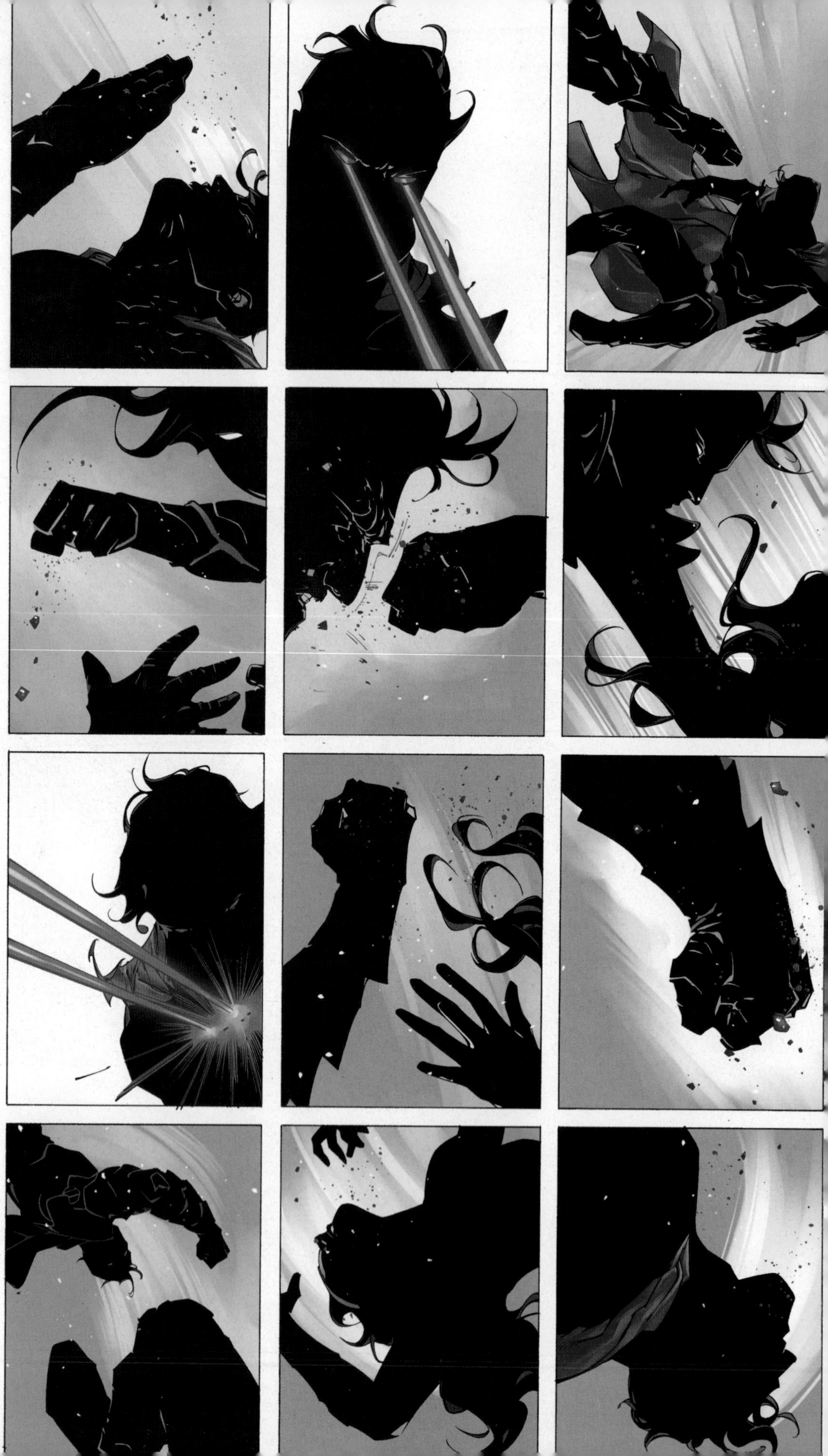

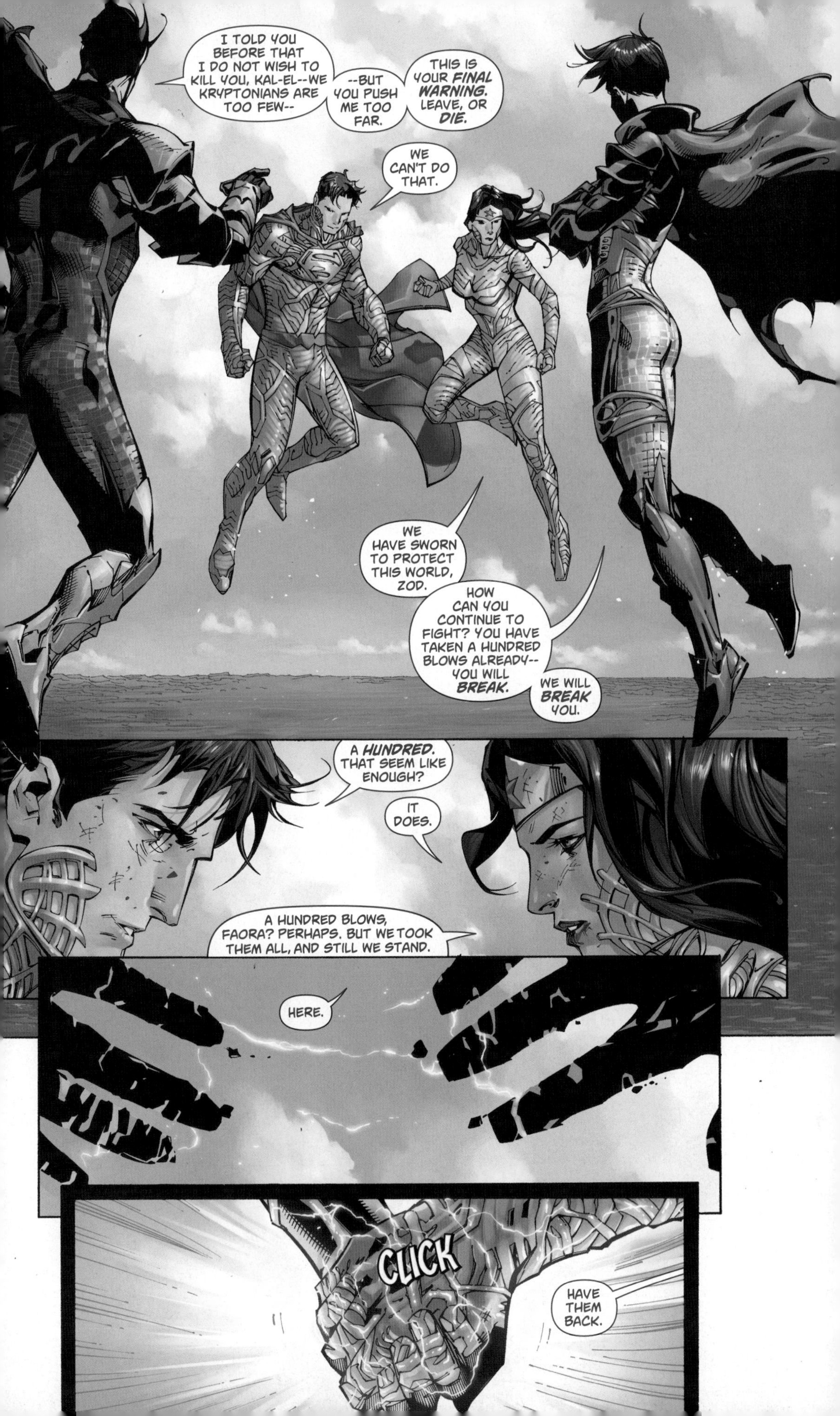
I TOLD YOU BEFORE THAT I DO NOT WISH TO KILL YOU, KAL-EL--WE KRYPTONIANS ARE TOO FEW--
--BUT YOU PUSH ME TOO FAR.
THIS IS YOUR *FINAL WARNING.* LEAVE, OR *DIE.*
WE CAN'T DO THAT.
WE HAVE SWORN TO PROTECT THIS WORLD, ZOD.
HOW CAN YOU CONTINUE TO FIGHT? YOU HAVE TAKEN A HUNDRED BLOWS ALREADY--YOU WILL *BREAK.*
WE WILL *BREAK* YOU.
A *HUNDRED.* THAT SEEM LIKE ENOUGH?
IT DOES.
A HUNDRED BLOWS, FAORA? PERHAPS. BUT WE TOOK THEM ALL, AND STILL WE STAND.
HERE.
CLICK
HAVE THEM BACK.

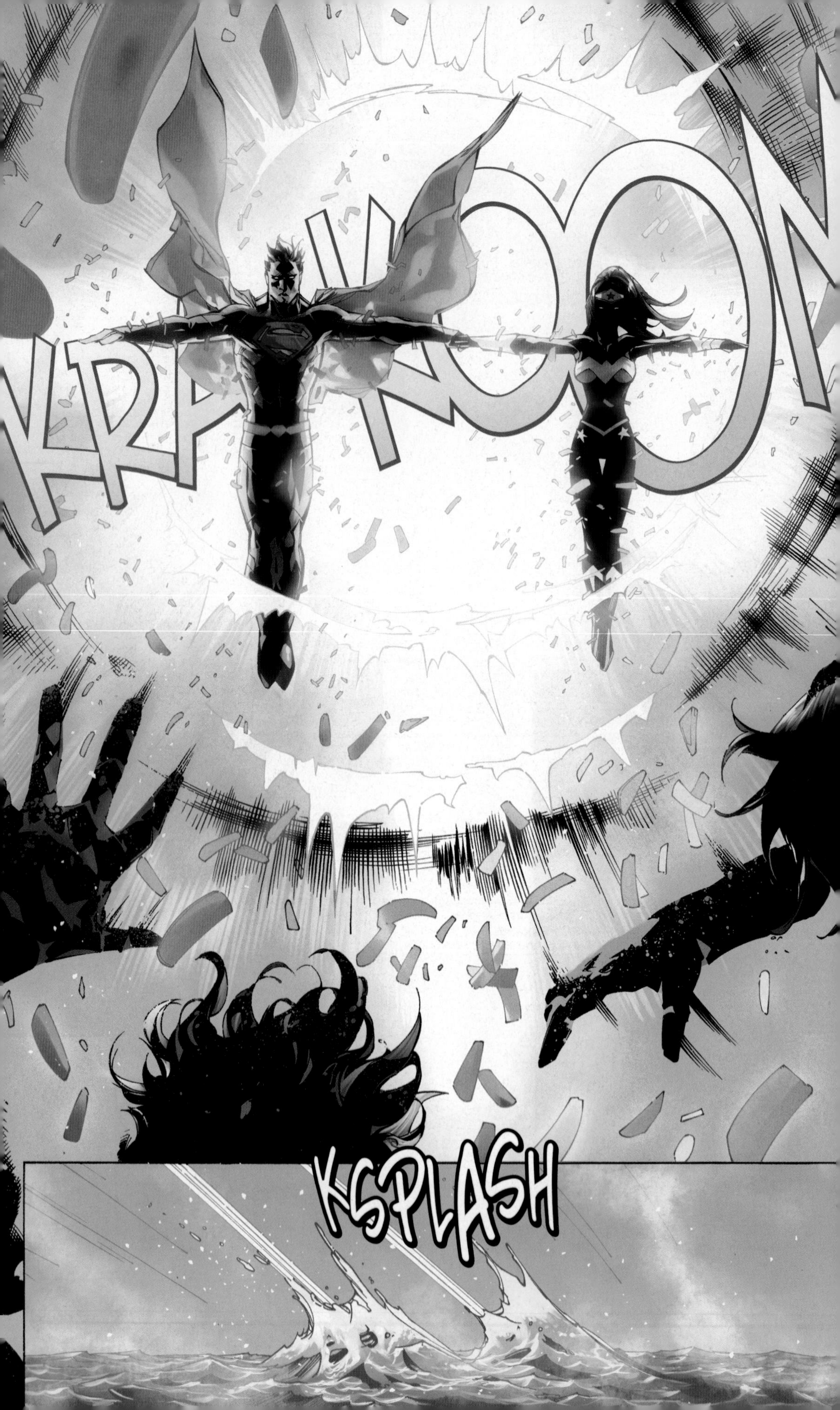
KSPLASH

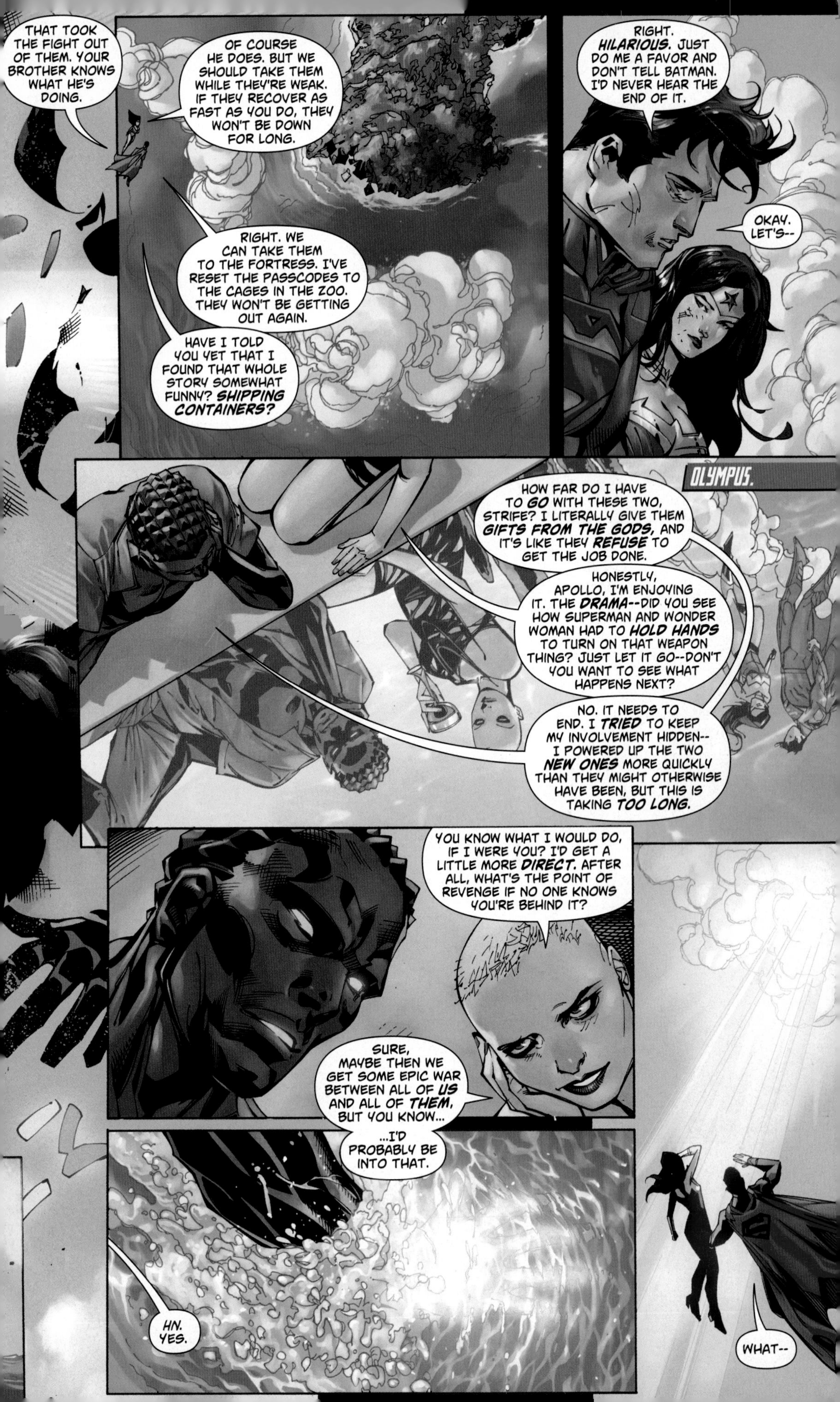
THAT TOOK THE FIGHT OUT OF THEM. YOUR BROTHER KNOWS WHAT HE'S DOING.
OF COURSE HE DOES. BUT WE SHOULD TAKE THEM WHILE THEY'RE WEAK. IF THEY RECOVER AS FAST AS YOU DO, THEY WON'T BE DOWN FOR LONG.
RIGHT. WE CAN TAKE THEM TO THE FORTRESS. I'VE RESET THE PASSCODES TO THE CAGES IN THE ZOO. THEY WON'T BE GETTING OUT AGAIN.
HAVE I TOLD YOU YET THAT I FOUND THAT WHOLE STORY SOMEWHAT FUNNY? SHIPPING CONTAINERS?
RIGHT. HILARIOUS. JUST DO ME A FAVOR AND DON'T TELL BATMAN. I'D NEVER HEAR THE END OF IT.
OKAY. LET'S--
OLYMPUS.
HOW FAR DO I HAVE TO GO WITH THESE TWO, STRIFE? I LITERALLY GIVE THEM GIFTS FROM THE GODS, AND IT'S LIKE THEY REFUSE TO GET THE JOB DONE.
HONESTLY, APOLLO, I'M ENJOYING IT. THE DRAMA--DID YOU SEE HOW SUPERMAN AND WONDER WOMAN HAD TO HOLD HANDS TO TURN ON THAT WEAPON THING? JUST LET IT GO--DON'T YOU WANT TO SEE WHAT HAPPENS NEXT?
NO. IT NEEDS TO END. I TRIED TO KEEP MY INVOLVEMENT HIDDEN--I POWERED UP THE TWO NEW ONES MORE QUICKLY THAN THEY MIGHT OTHERWISE HAVE BEEN, BUT THIS IS TAKING TOO LONG.
YOU KNOW WHAT I WOULD DO, IF I WERE YOU? I'D GET A LITTLE MORE DIRECT. AFTER ALL, WHAT'S THE POINT OF REVENGE IF NO ONE KNOWS YOU'RE BEHIND IT?
SURE, MAYBE THEN WE GET SOME EPIC WAR BETWEEN ALL OF US AND ALL OF THEM, BUT YOU KNOW...
...I'D PROBABLY BE INTO THAT.
HN. YES.
WHAT--

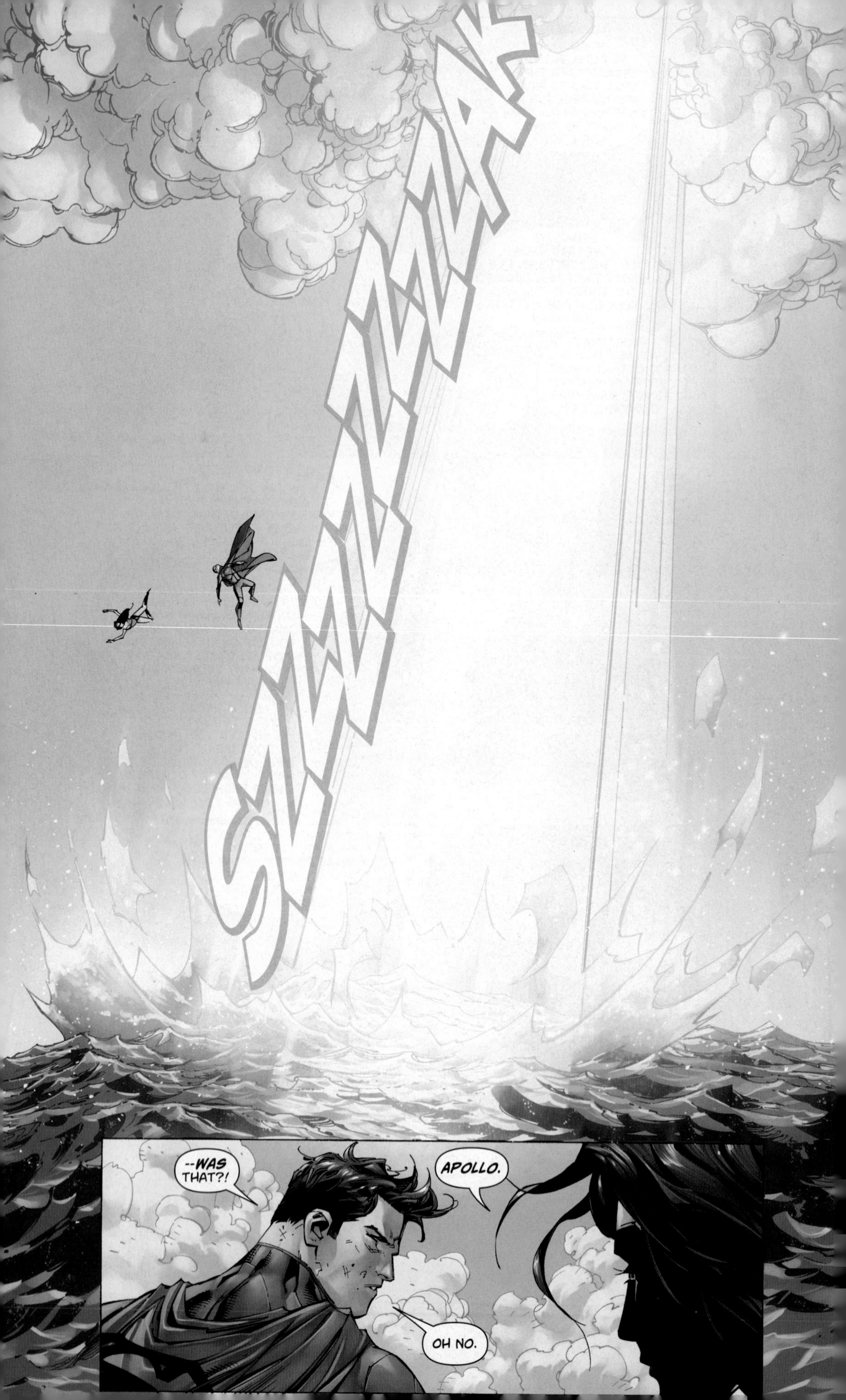
SZZZZZAK
--WAS THAT?!
APOLLO.
OH NO.

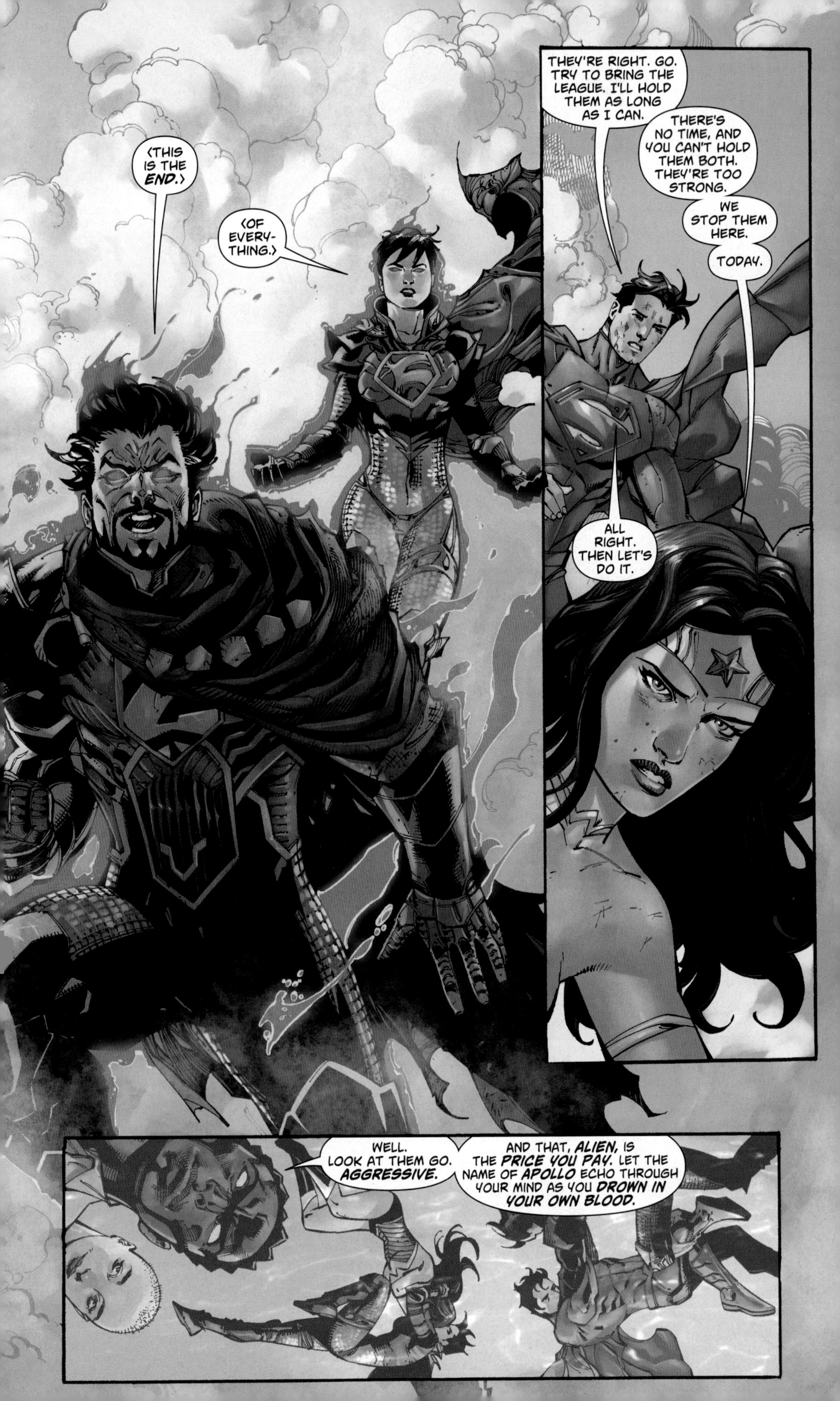

‹THIS IS THE **END.**›
‹OF EVERY-THING.›
THEY'RE RIGHT. GO. TRY TO BRING THE LEAGUE. I'LL HOLD THEM AS LONG AS I CAN.
THERE'S NO TIME, AND YOU CAN'T HOLD THEM BOTH. THEY'RE TOO STRONG.
WE STOP THEM HERE.
TODAY.
ALL RIGHT. THEN LET'S DO IT.
WELL. LOOK AT THEM GO. ***AGGRESSIVE.***
AND THAT, ***ALIEN,*** IS THE ***PRICE YOU PAY.*** LET THE NAME OF ***APOLLO*** ECHO THROUGH YOUR MIND AS YOU ***DROWN IN YOUR OWN BLOOD.***

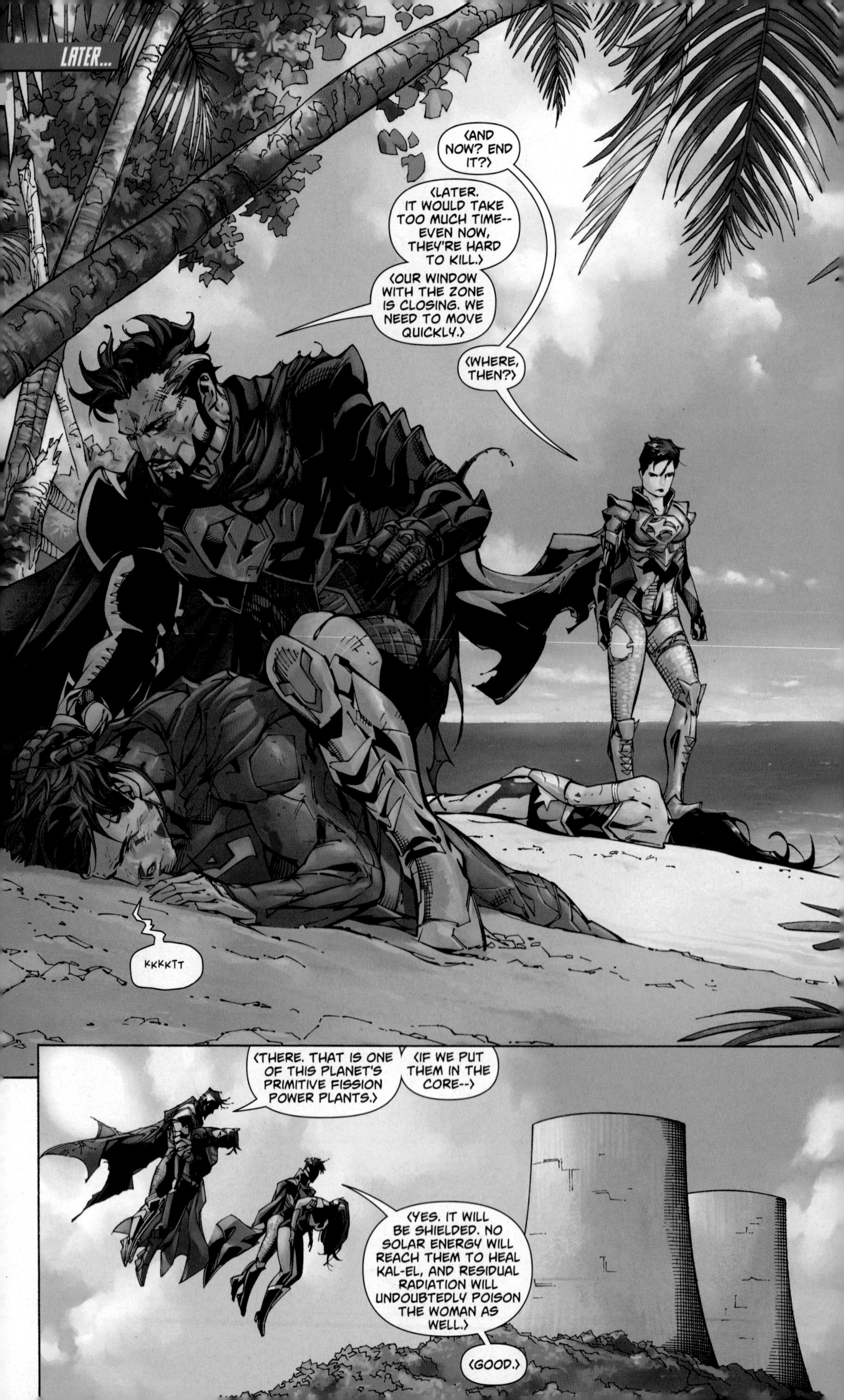
LATER...
<AND NOW? END IT?>
<LATER. IT WOULD TAKE TOO MUCH TIME-- EVEN NOW, THEY'RE HARD TO KILL.>
<OUR WINDOW WITH THE ZONE IS CLOSING. WE NEED TO MOVE QUICKLY.>
<WHERE, THEN?>
KKKKTT
<THERE. THAT IS ONE OF THIS PLANET'S PRIMITIVE FISSION POWER PLANTS.>
<IF WE PUT THEM IN THE CORE-->
<YES. IT WILL BE SHIELDED. NO SOLAR ENERGY WILL REACH THEM TO HEAL KAL-EL, AND RESIDUAL RADIATION WILL UNDOUBTEDLY POISON THE WOMAN AS WELL.>
<GOOD.>

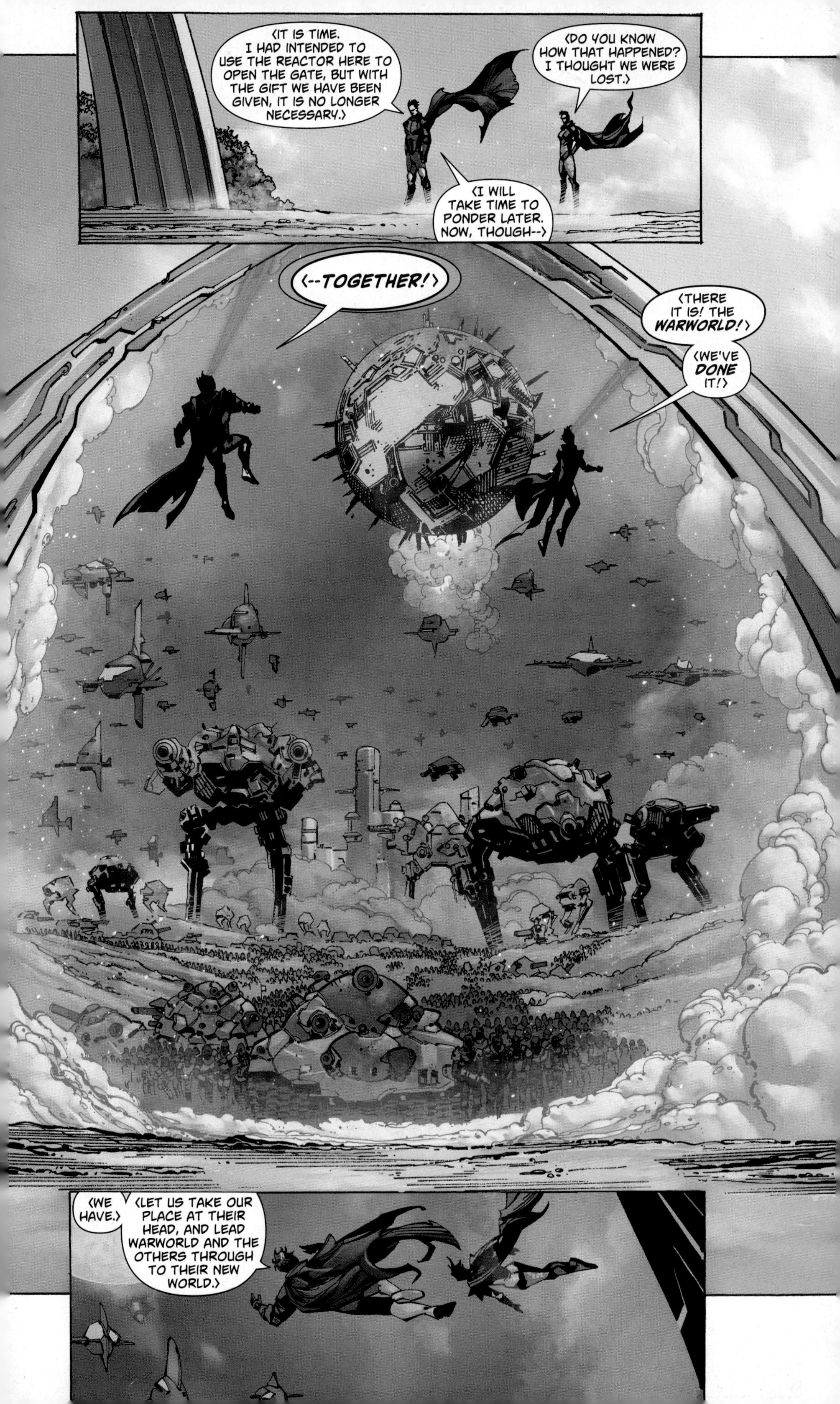
‹IT IS TIME. I HAD INTENDED TO USE THE REACTOR HERE TO OPEN THE GATE, BUT WITH THE GIFT WE HAVE BEEN GIVEN, IT IS NO LONGER NECESSARY.›
‹DO YOU KNOW HOW THAT HAPPENED? I THOUGHT WE WERE LOST.›
‹I WILL TAKE TIME TO PONDER LATER. NOW, THOUGH--›
‹--TOGETHER!›
‹THERE IT IS! THE WARWORLD!›
‹WE'VE DONE IT!›
‹WE HAVE.›
‹LET US TAKE OUR PLACE AT THEIR HEAD, AND LEAD WARWORLD AND THE OTHERS THROUGH TO THEIR NEW WORLD.›

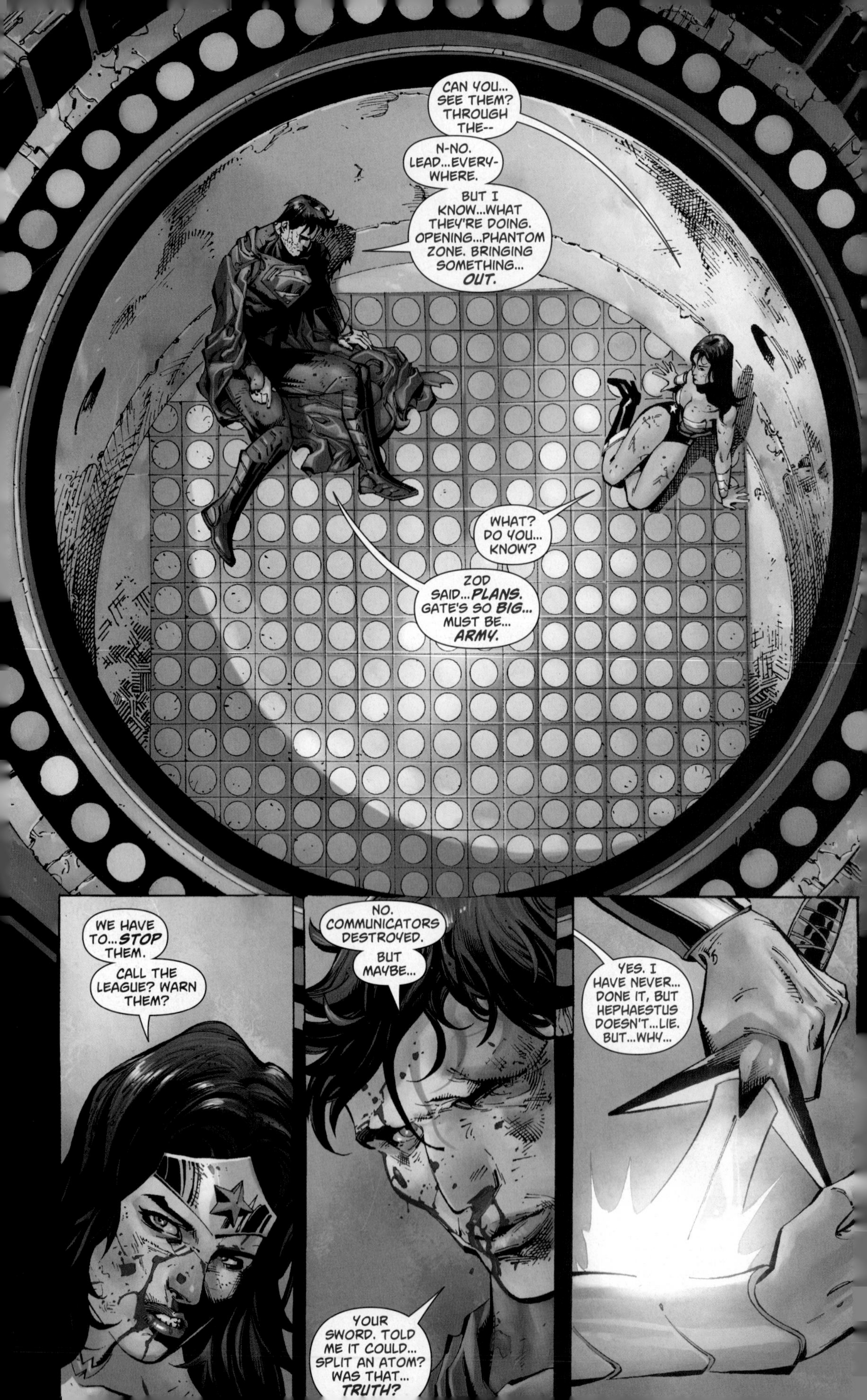
CAN YOU... SEE THEM? THROUGH THE--
N-NO. LEAD...EVERY-WHERE.
BUT I KNOW...WHAT THEY'RE DOING. OPENING...PHANTOM ZONE. BRINGING SOMETHING... OUT.
WHAT? DO YOU... KNOW?
ZOD SAID...PLANS. GATE'S SO BIG... MUST BE... ARMY.
WE HAVE TO...STOP THEM.
CALL THE LEAGUE? WARN THEM?
NO. COMMUNICATORS DESTROYED.
BUT MAYBE...
YOUR SWORD. TOLD ME IT COULD... SPLIT AN ATOM? WAS THAT... TRUTH?
YES. I HAVE NEVER... DONE IT, BUT HEPHAESTUS DOESN'T...LIE. BUT...WHY...

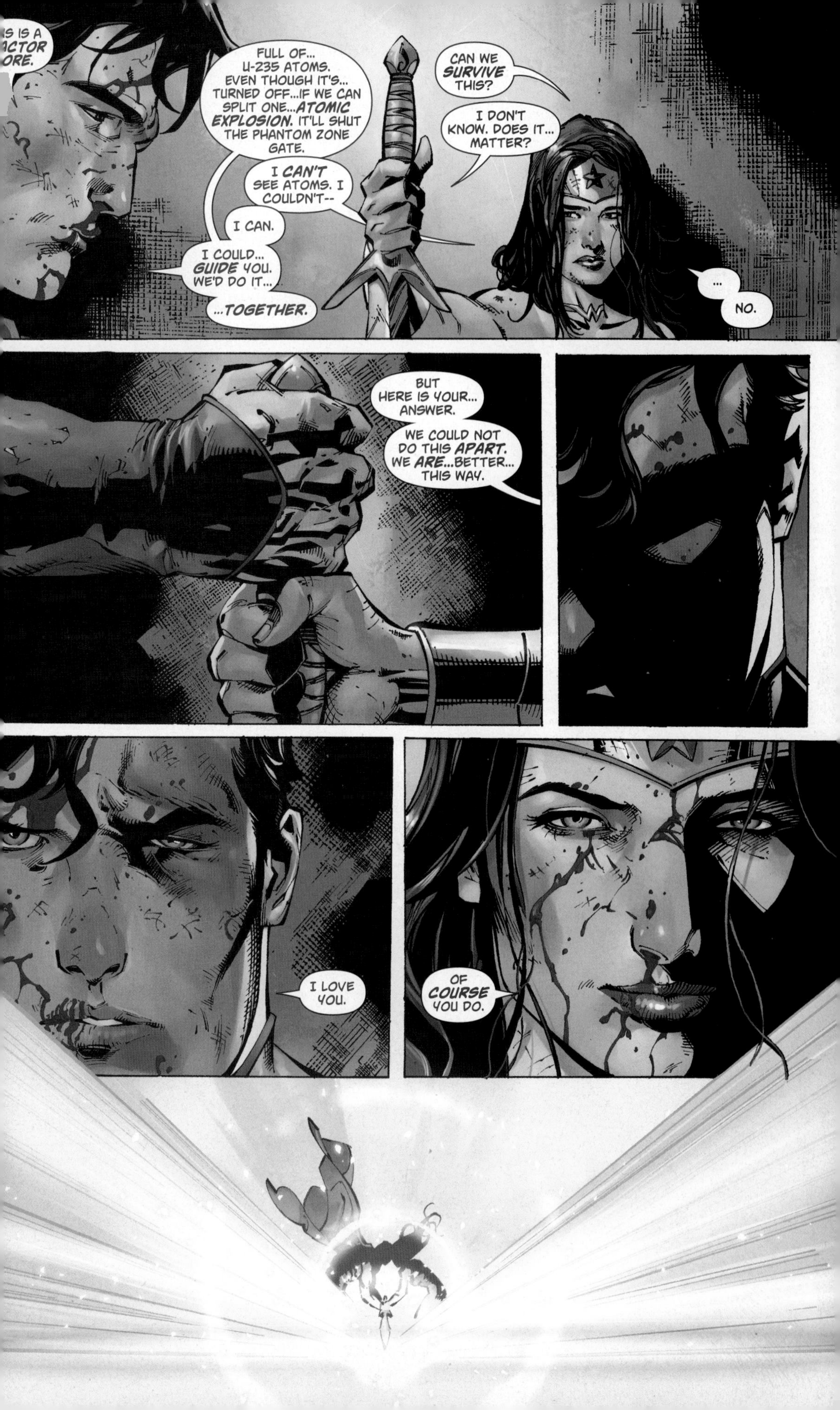

IS IS A
ACTOR
ORE.
FULL OF... U-235 ATOMS. EVEN THOUGH IT'S... TURNED OFF...IF WE CAN SPLIT ONE...ATOMIC EXPLOSION. IT'LL SHUT THE PHANTOM ZONE GATE.
CAN WE SURVIVE THIS?
I DON'T KNOW. DOES IT... MATTER?
I CAN'T SEE ATOMS. I COULDN'T--
I CAN.
I COULD... GUIDE YOU. WE'D DO IT...
...TOGETHER.
...
NO.
BUT HERE IS YOUR... ANSWER.
WE COULD NOT DO THIS APART. WE ARE...BETTER... THIS WAY.
I LOVE YOU.
OF COURSE YOU DO.

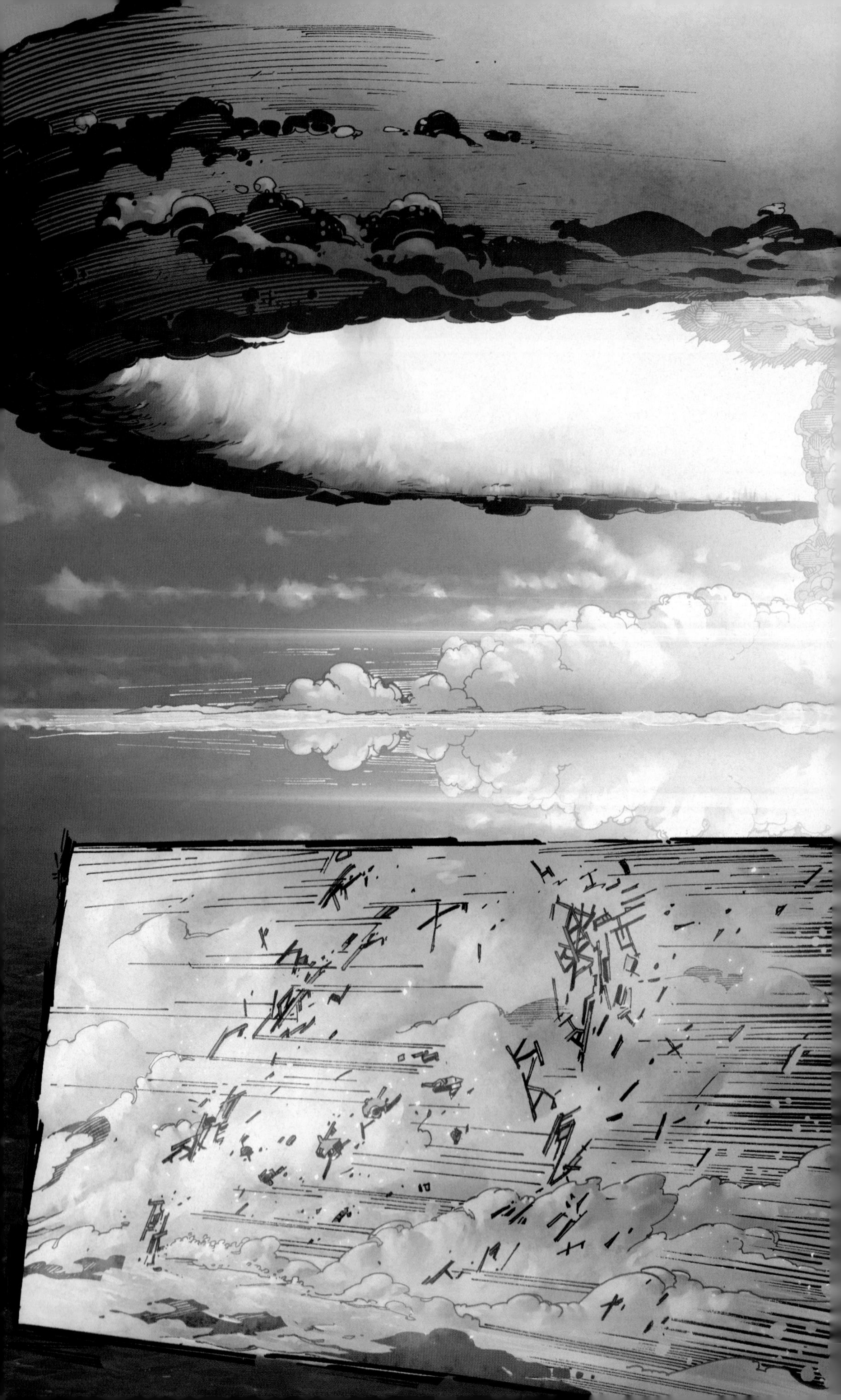

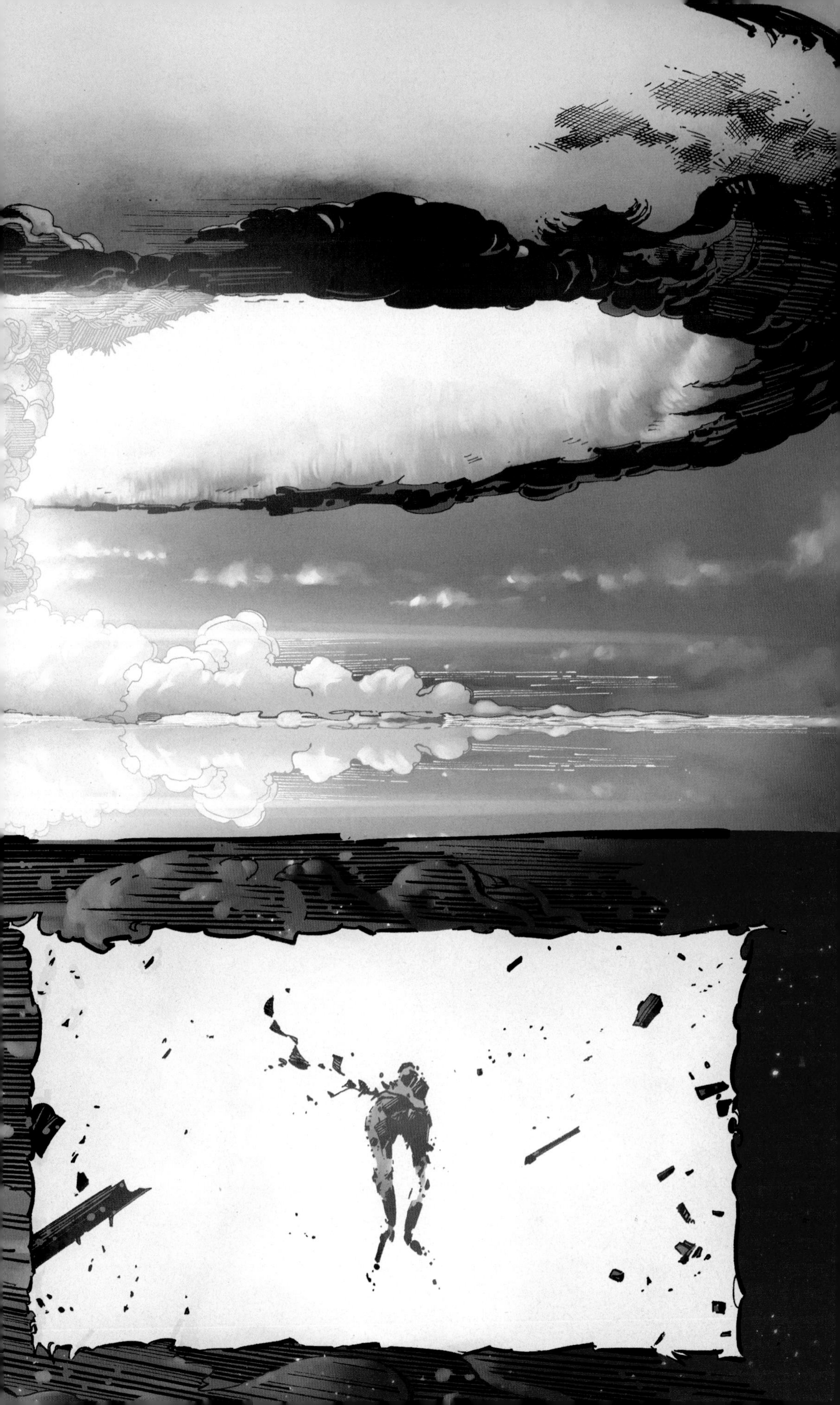

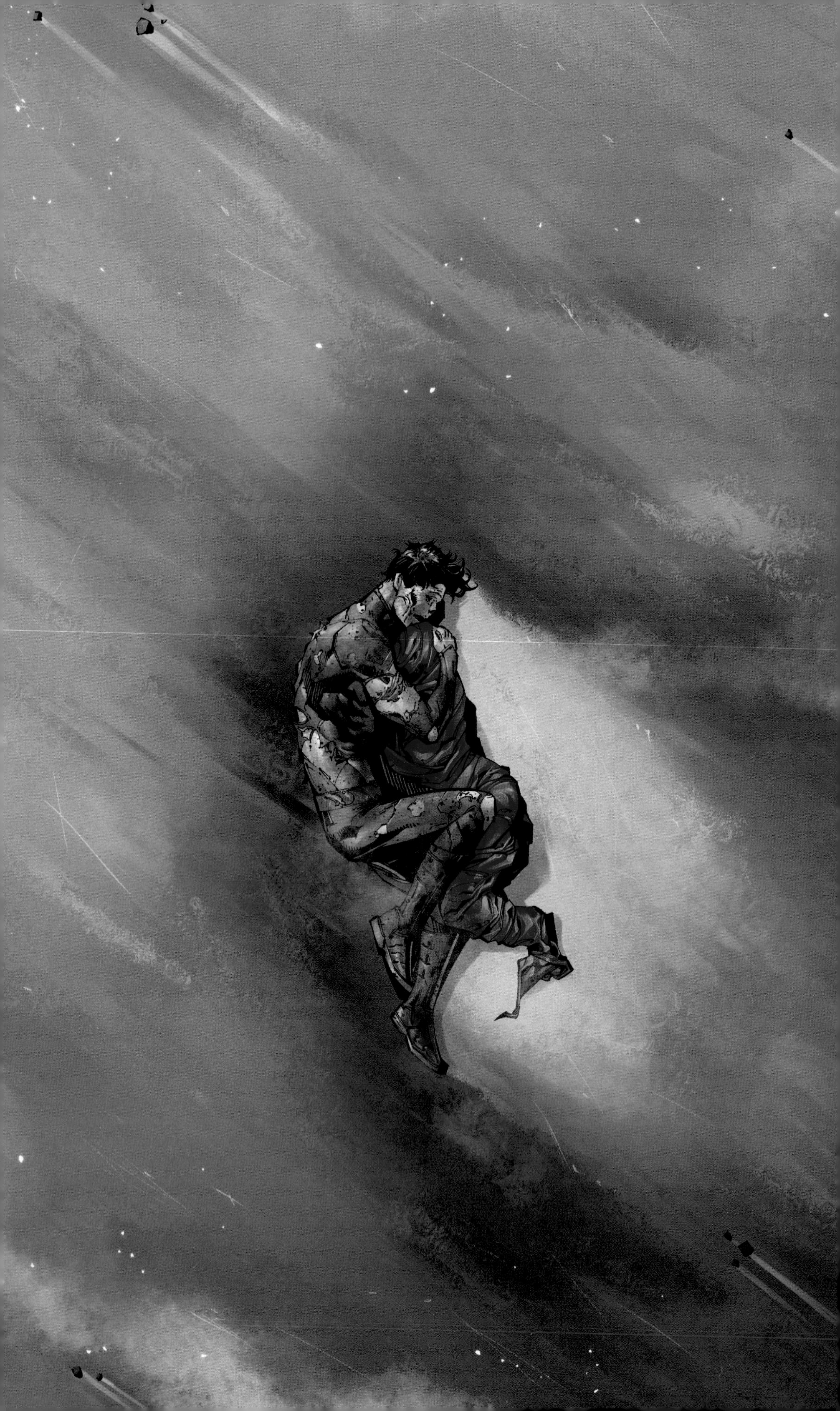

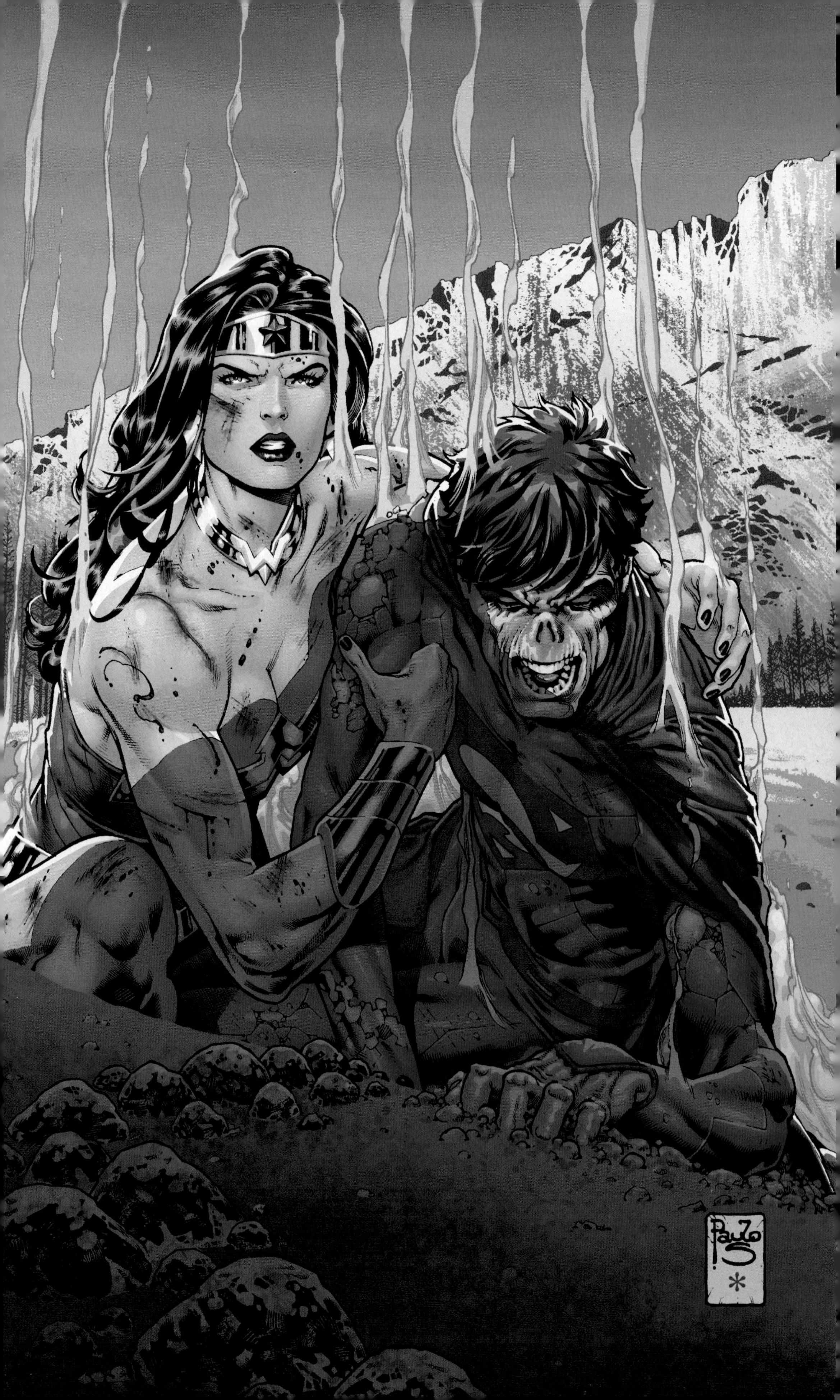

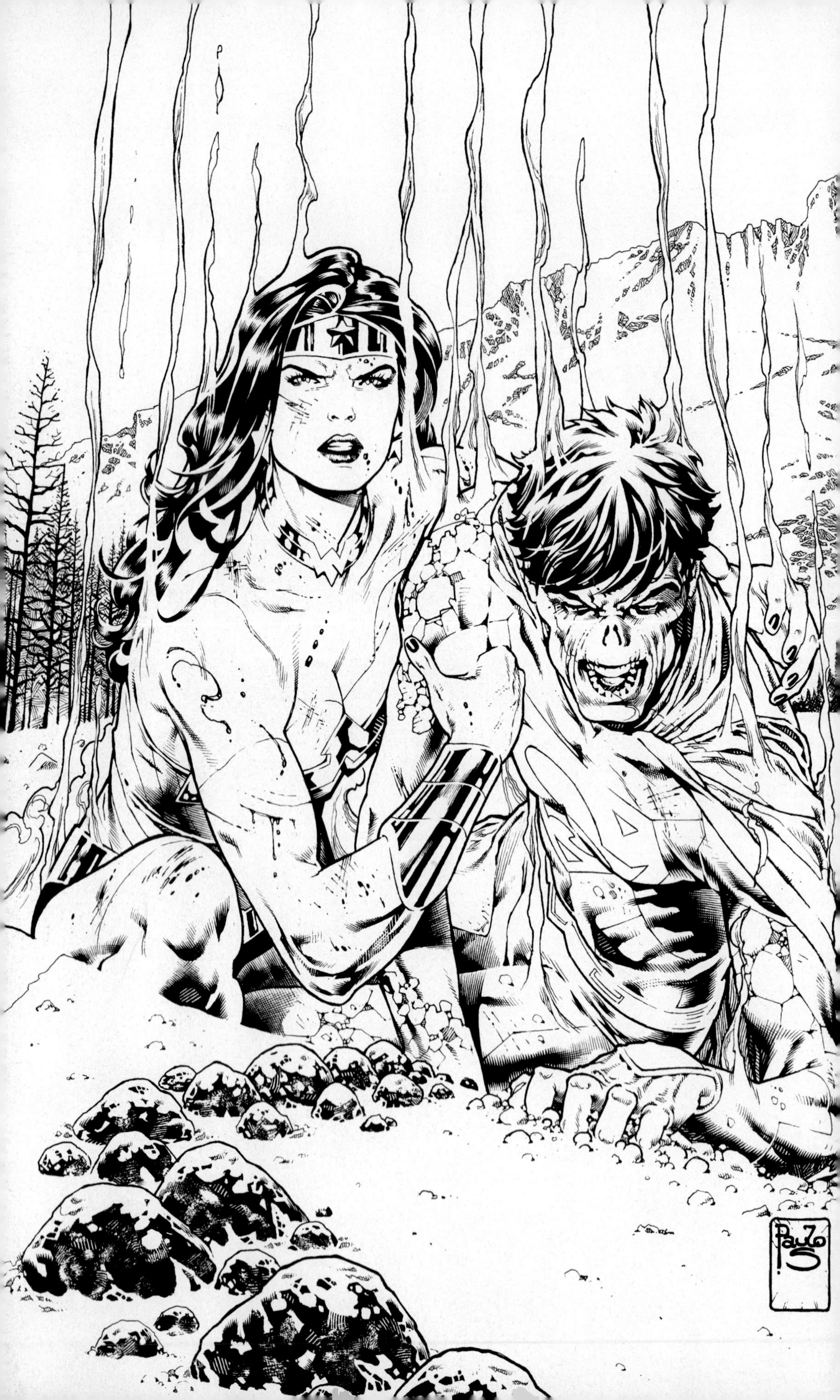

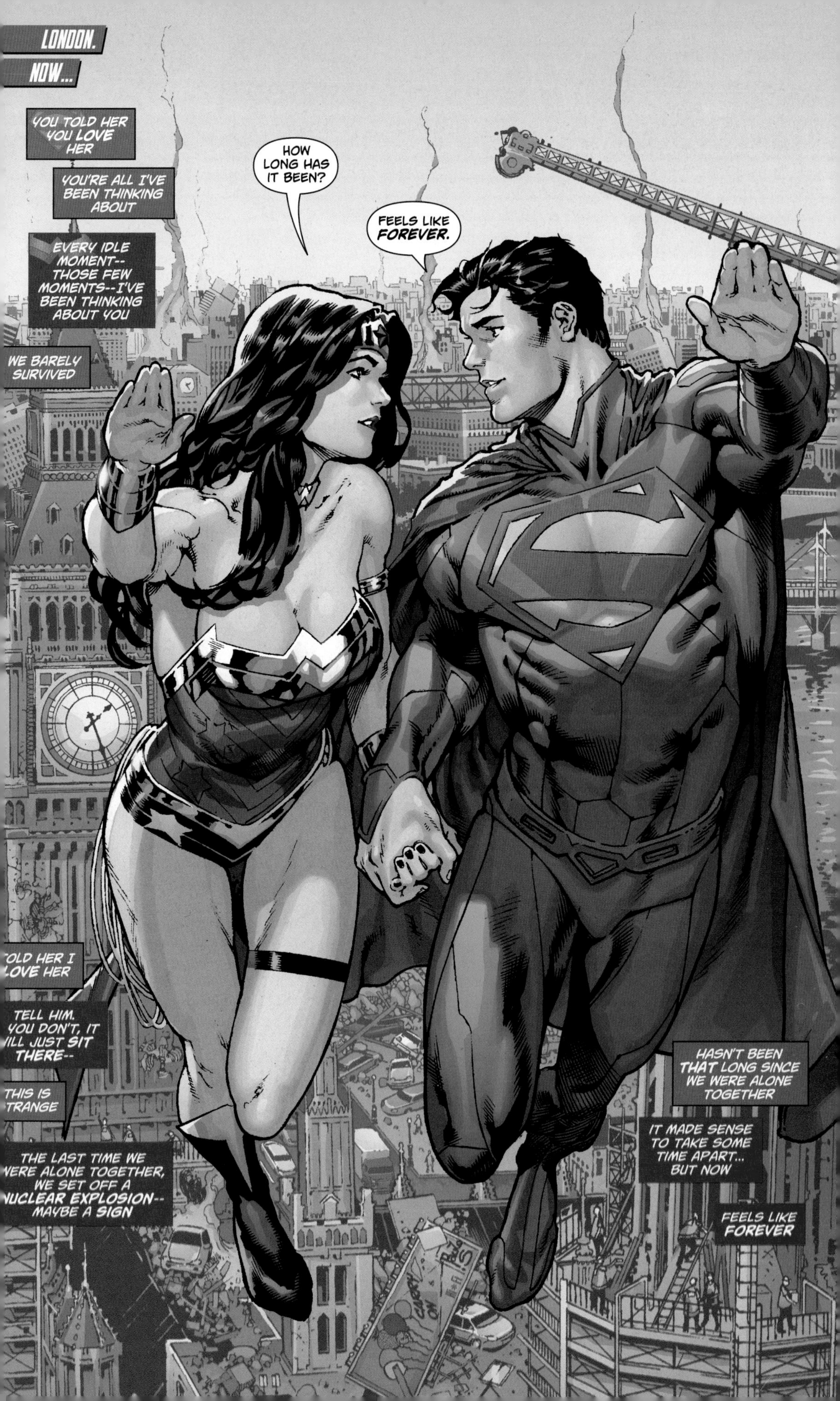
LONDON.
NOW...
YOU TOLD HER YOU LOVE HER
YOU'RE ALL I'VE BEEN THINKING ABOUT
EVERY IDLE MOMENT-- THOSE FEW MOMENTS--I'VE BEEN THINKING ABOUT YOU
WE BARELY SURVIVED
HOW LONG HAS IT BEEN?
FEELS LIKE FOREVER.
OLD HER I OVE HER
TELL HIM. YOU DON'T, IT ILL JUST SIT THERE--
THIS IS TRANGE
THE LAST TIME WE ERE ALONE TOGETHER, WE SET OFF A UCLEAR EXPLOSION-- MAYBE A SIGN
HASN'T BEEN THAT LONG SINCE WE WERE ALONE TOGETHER
IT MADE SENSE TO TAKE SOME TIME APART... BUT NOW
FEELS LIKE FOREVER

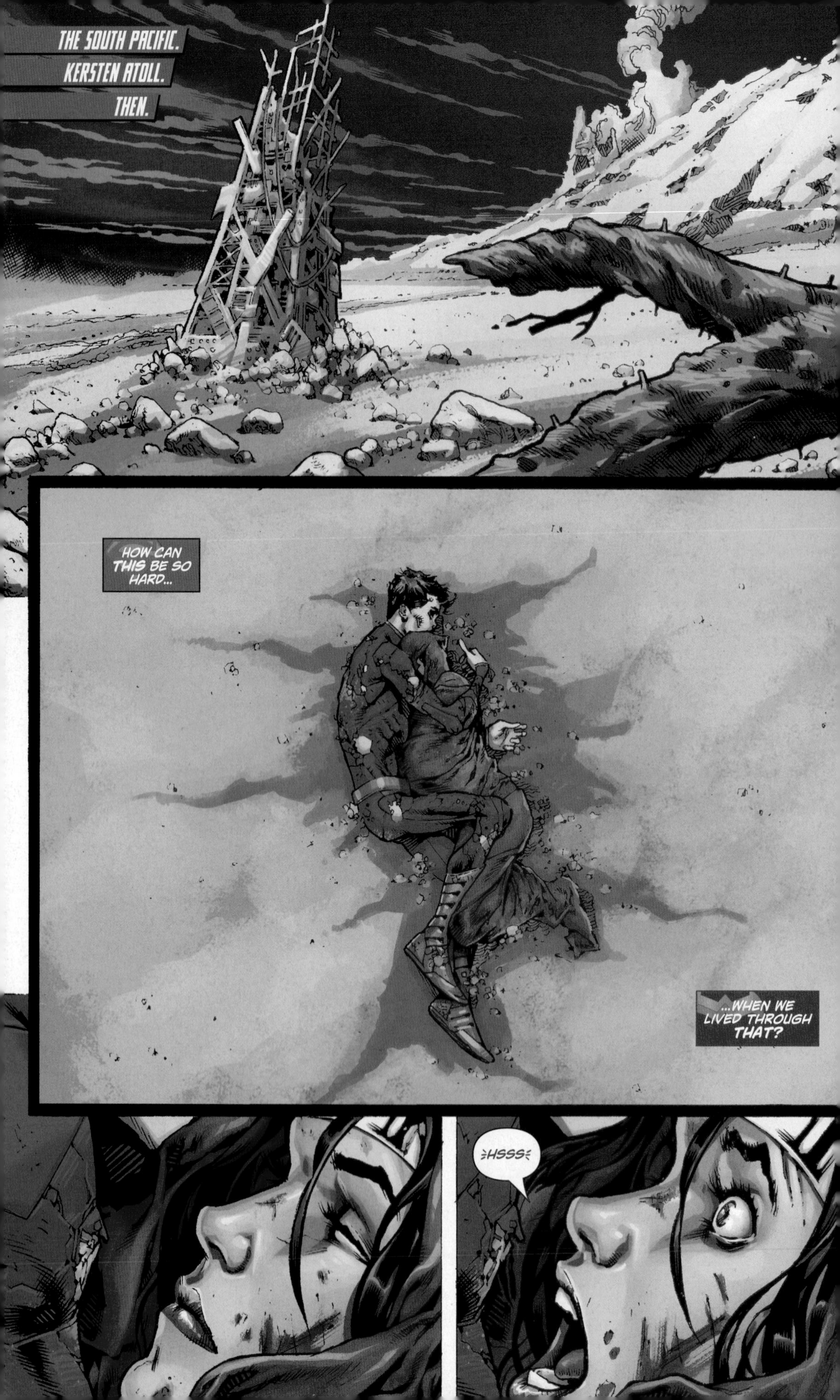
THE SOUTH PACIFIC.
KERSTEN ATOLL.
THEN.
HOW CAN THIS BE SO HARD...
...WHEN WE LIVED THROUGH THAT?
HSSS

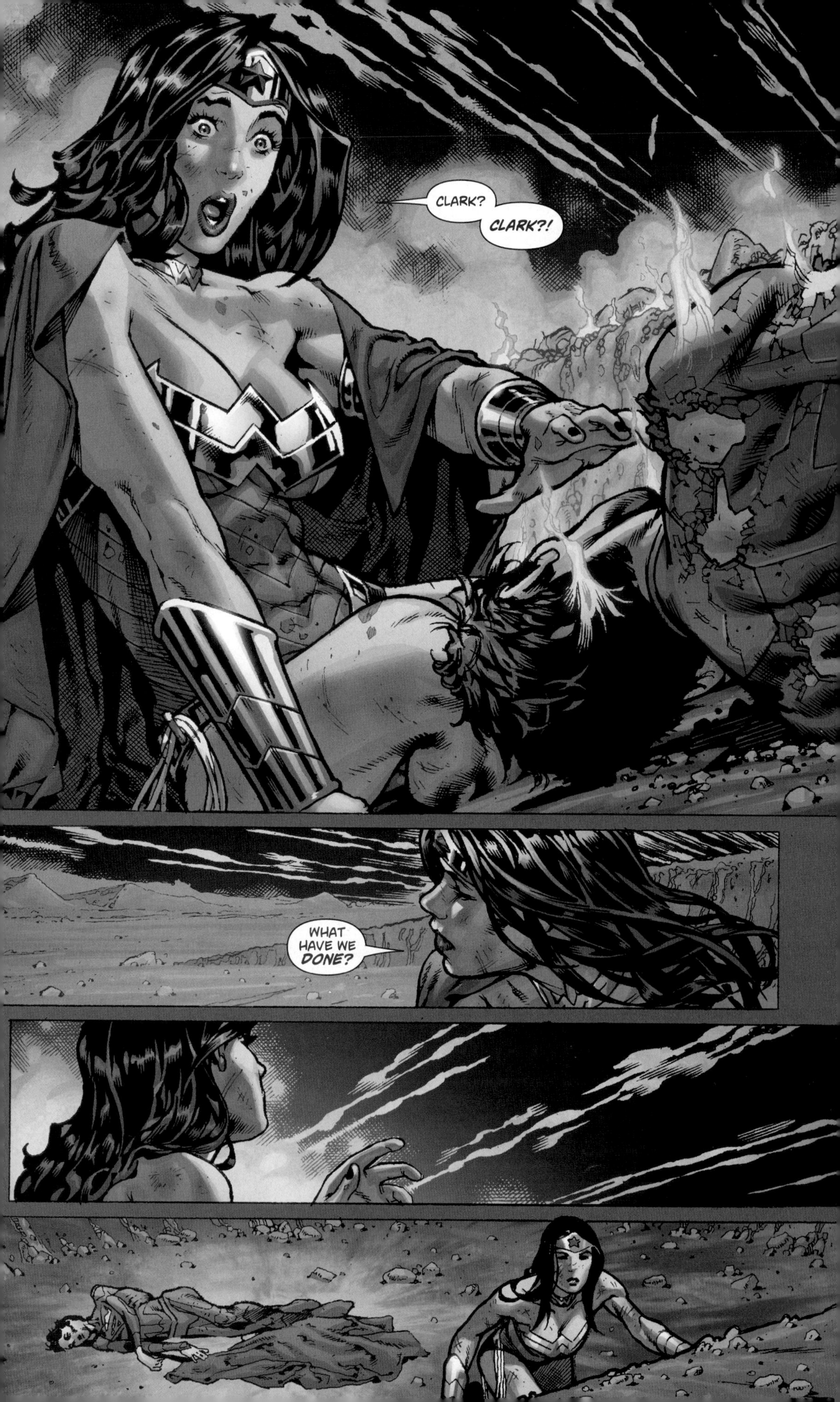
CLARK?
CLARK?!
WHAT HAVE WE DONE?

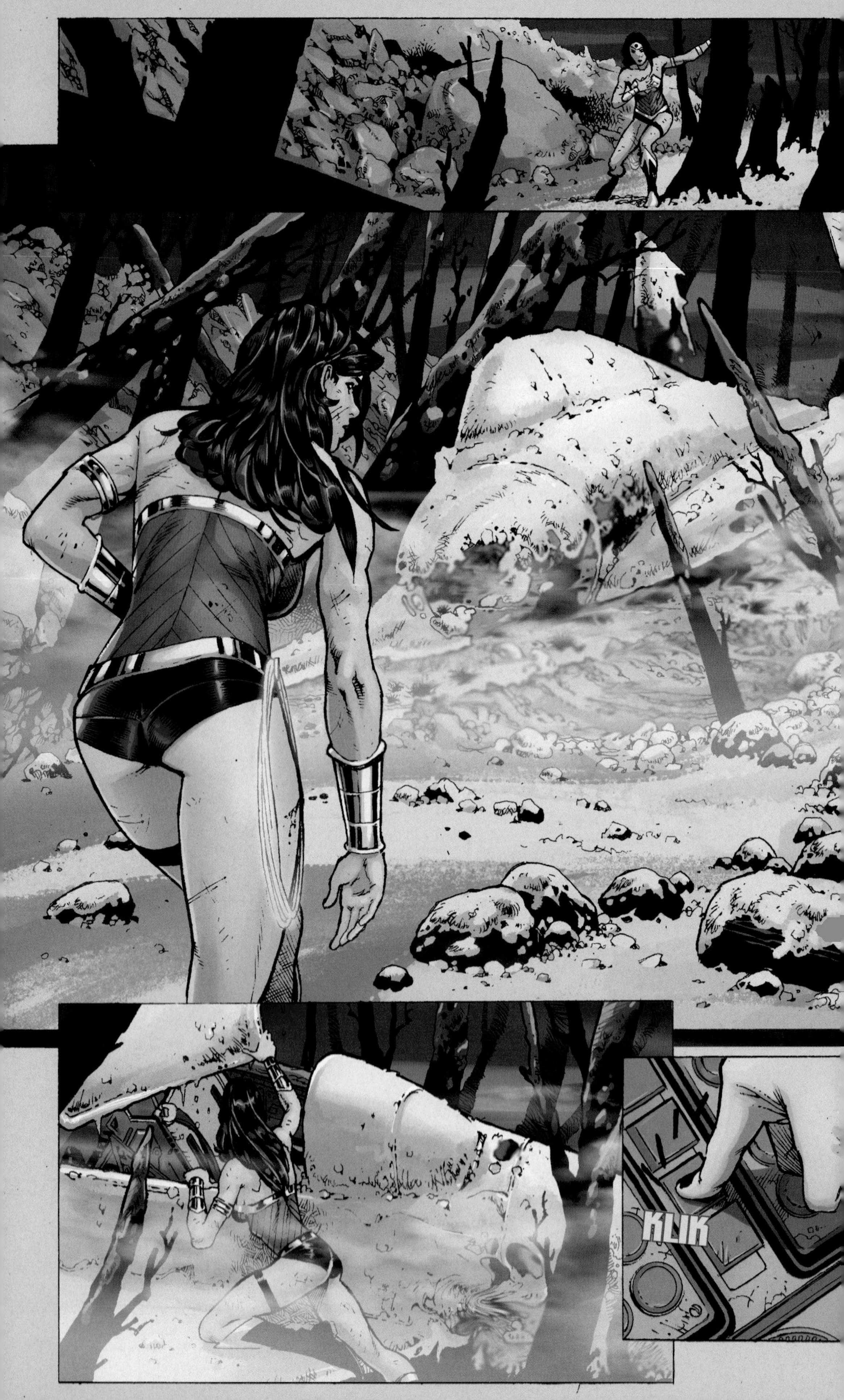
KLIK

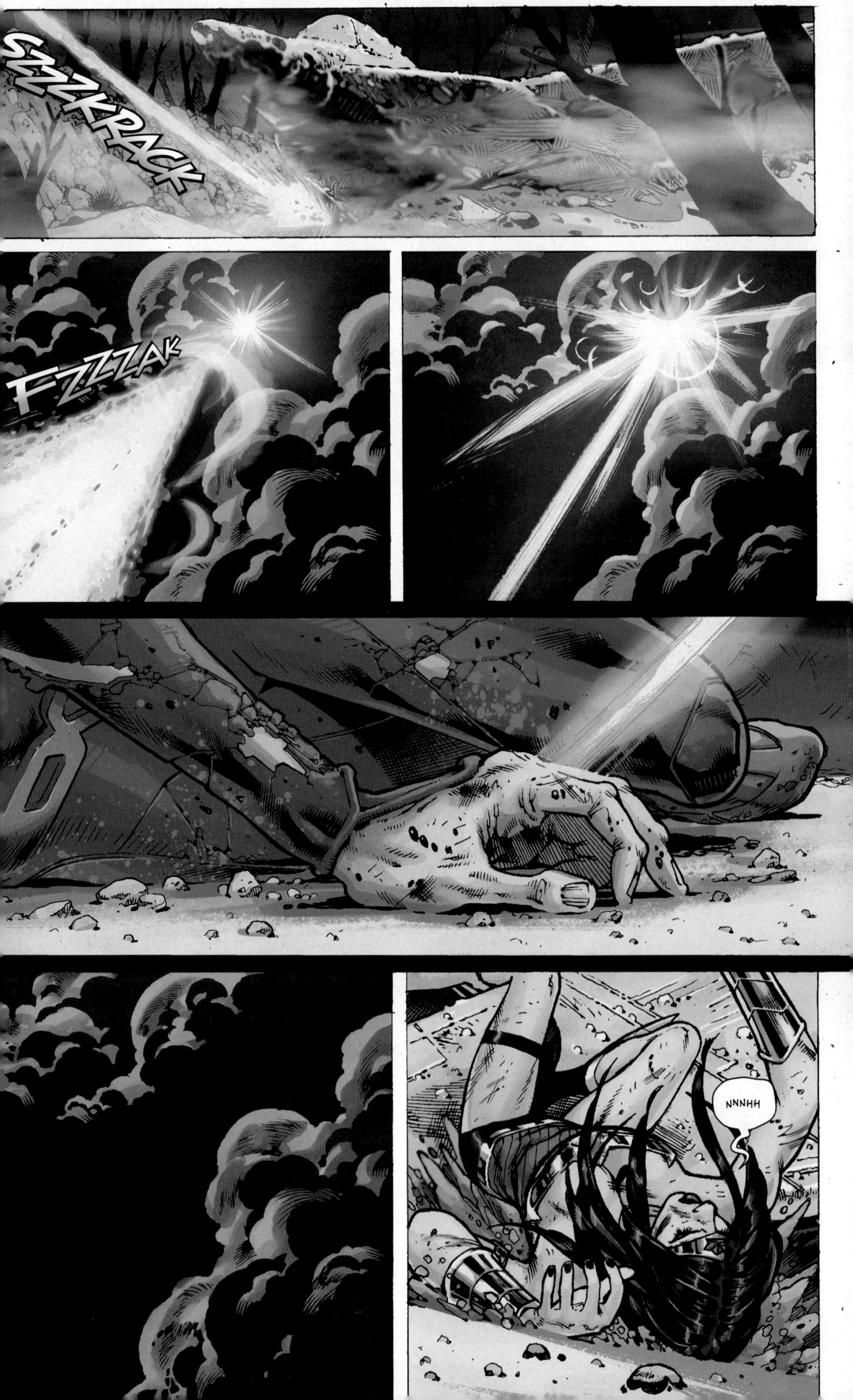
SIZZKRACK
FZZZAK
NNNHH

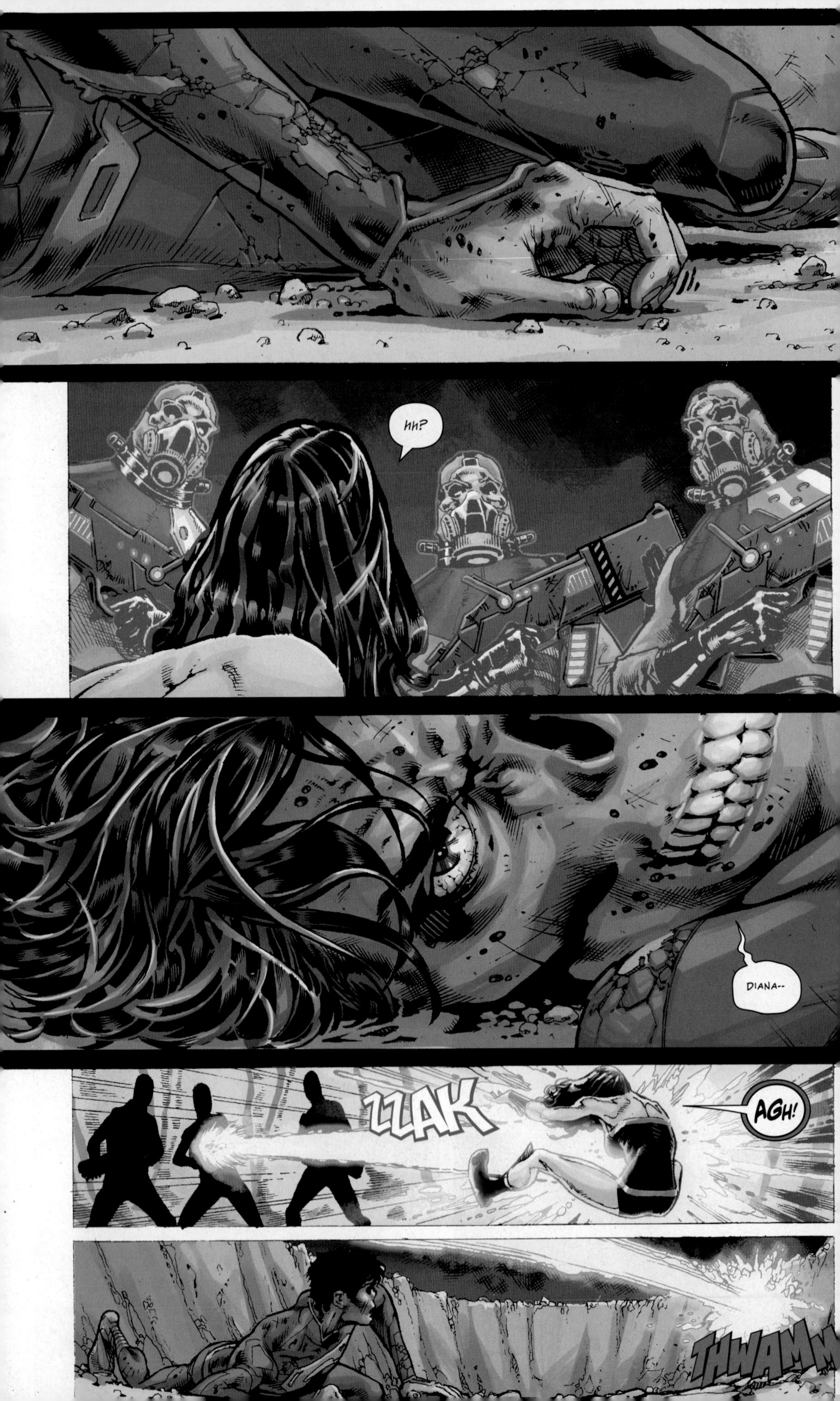
hh?
DIANA--
ZZAK
AGH!
THWAMM

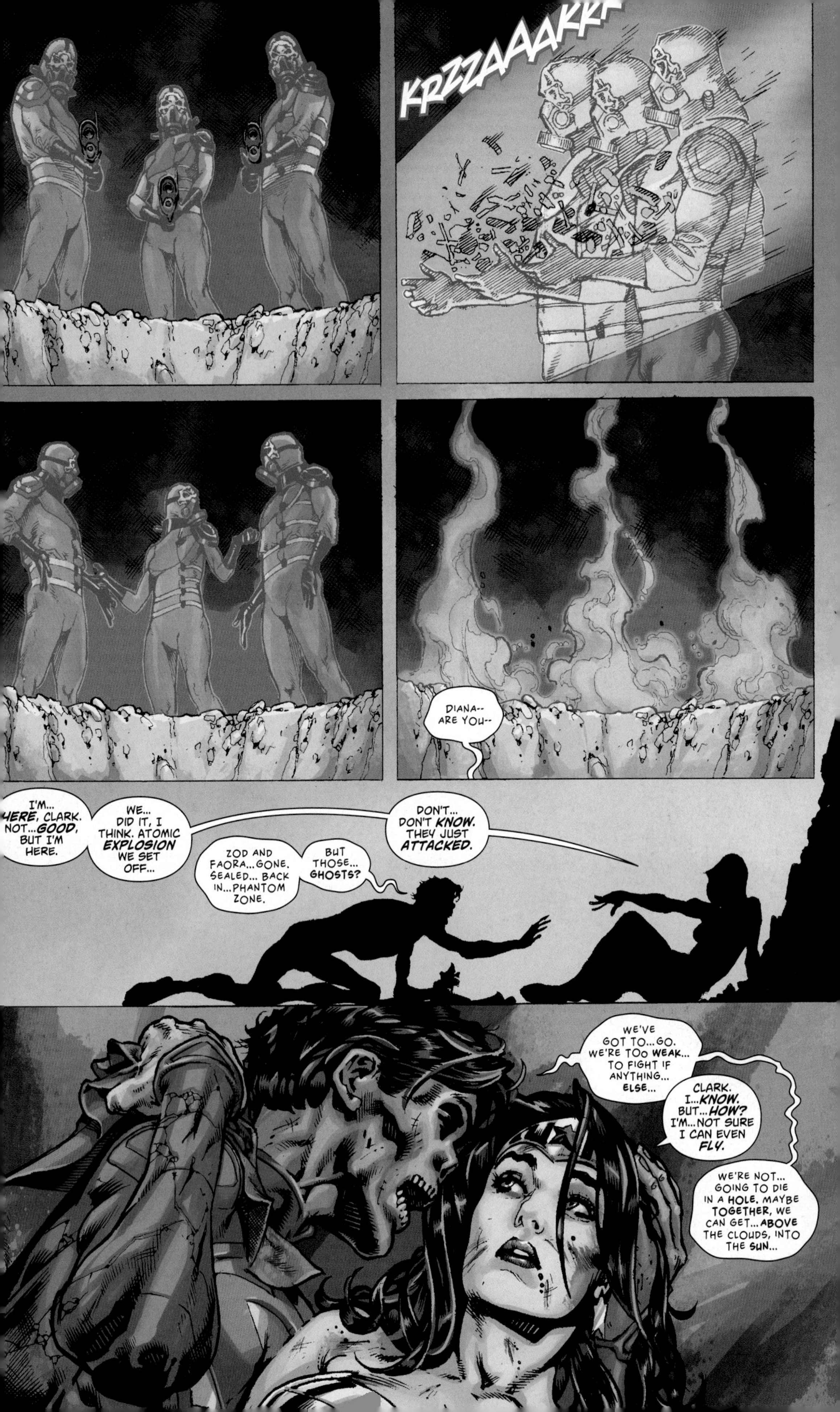
KRZZAAAKK!
DIANA--
ARE YOU--
I'M...
HERE, CLARK.
NOT...GOOD,
BUT I'M
HERE.
WE...
DID IT, I
THINK. ATOMIC
EXPLOSION
WE SET
OFF...
ZOD AND
FAORA...GONE.
SEALED... BACK
IN...PHANTOM
ZONE.
BUT
THOSE...
GHOSTS?
DON'T...
DON'T KNOW.
THEY JUST
ATTACKED.
WE'VE
GOT TO...GO.
WE'RE TOO WEAK...
TO FIGHT IF
ANYTHING...
ELSE...
CLARK.
I...KNOW.
BUT...HOW?
I'M...NOT SURE
I CAN EVEN
FLY.
WE'RE NOT...
GOING TO DIE
IN A HOLE. MAYBE
TOGETHER, WE
CAN GET...ABOVE
THE CLOUDS, INTO
THE SUN...

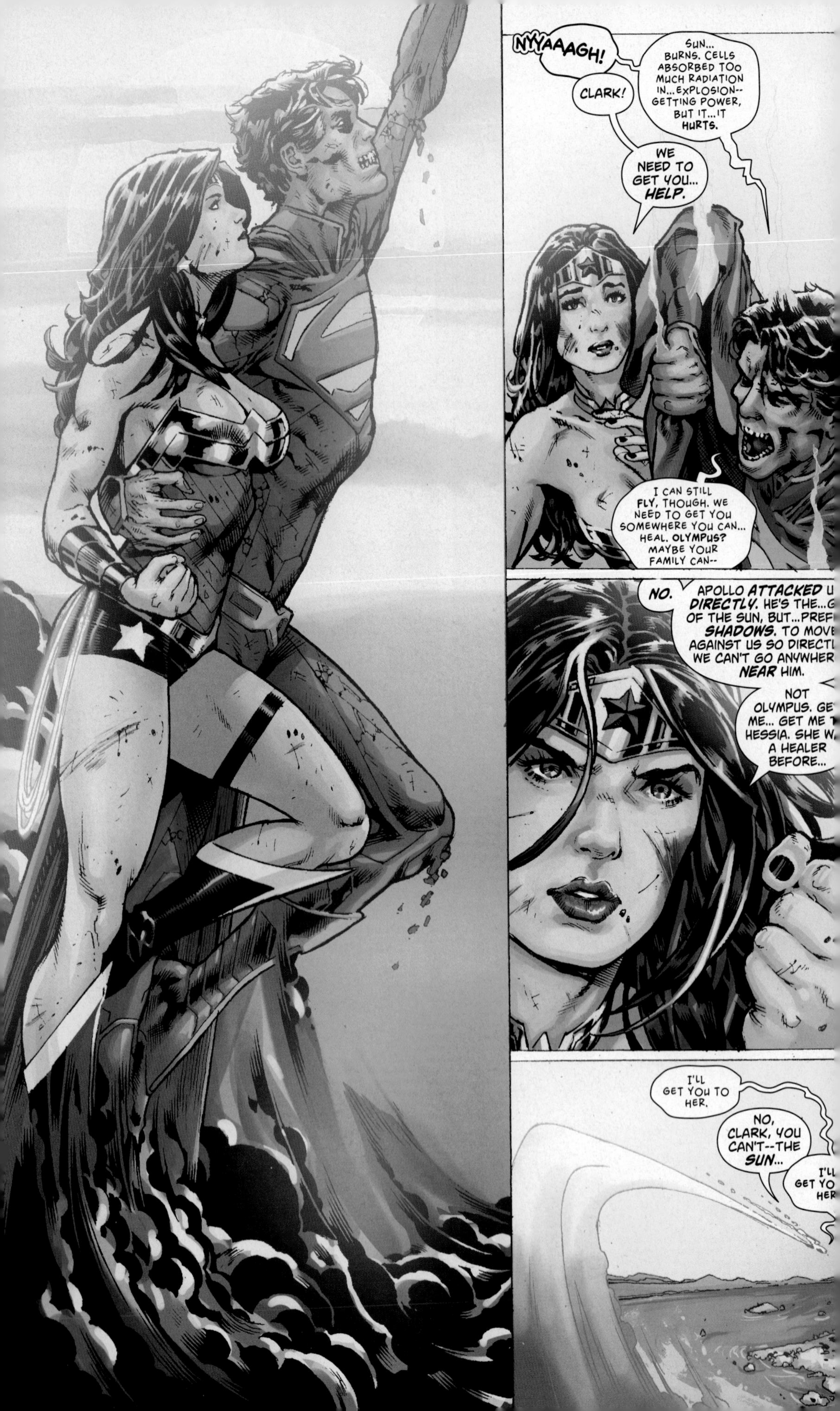
NYYAAAGH!
CLARK!
SUN... BURNS. CELLS ABSORBED TOO MUCH RADIATION IN...EXPLOSION--GETTING POWER, BUT IT...IT HURTS.
WE NEED TO GET YOU... HELP.
I CAN STILL FLY, THOUGH. WE NEED TO GET YOU SOMEWHERE YOU CAN... HEAL. OLYMPUS? MAYBE YOUR FAMILY CAN--
NO.
APOLLO ATTACKED U DIRECTLY. HE'S THE...G OF THE SUN, BUT...PREF SHADOWS. TO MOVE AGAINST US SO DIRECTL WE CAN'T GO ANYWHER NEAR HIM.
NOT OLYMPUS. GE ME... GET ME T HESSIA. SHE W A HEALER BEFORE...
I'LL GET YOU TO HER.
NO, CLARK, YOU CAN'T--THE SUN...
I'LL GET YO HER

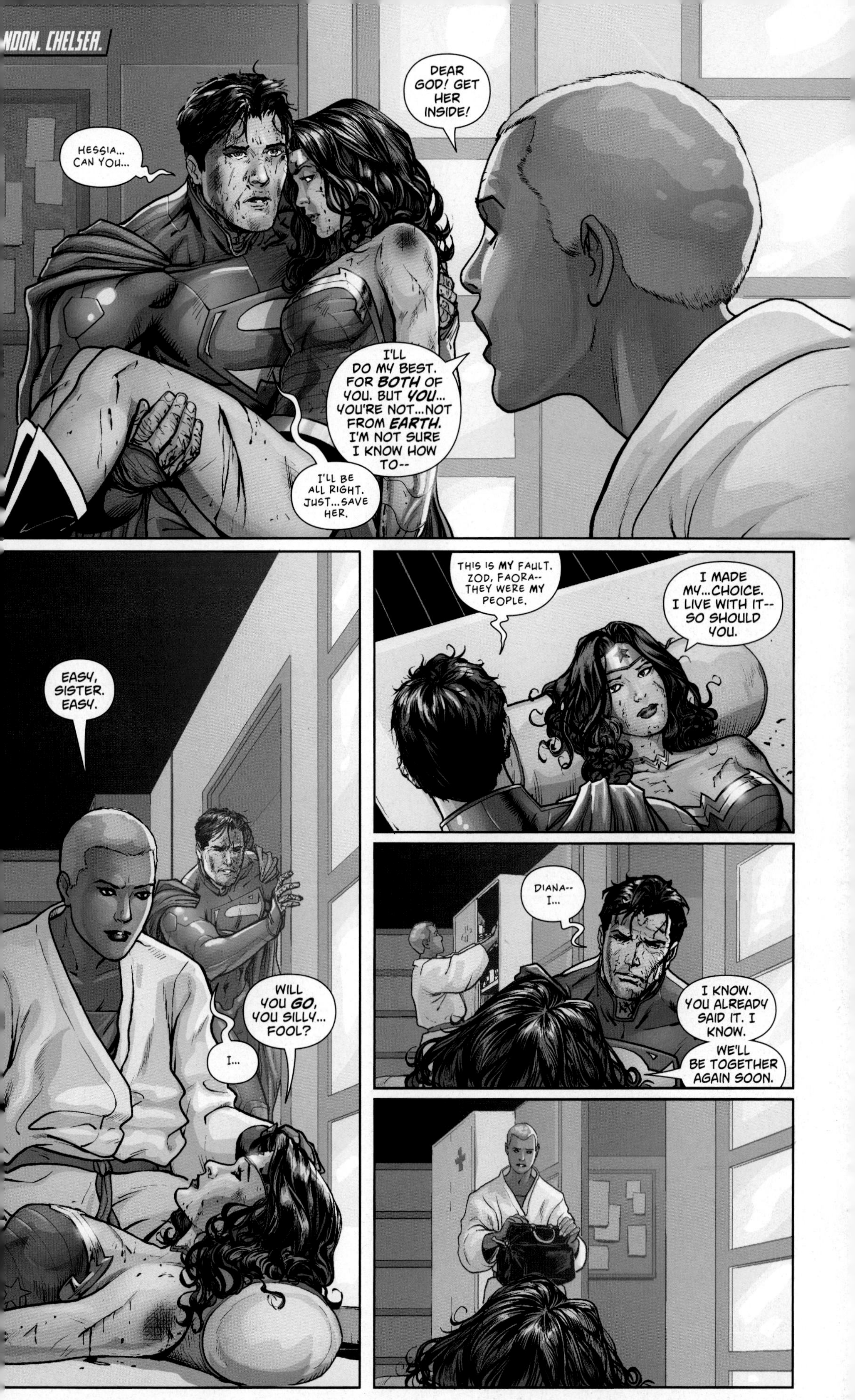
NDON. CHELSEA.
HESSIA... CAN YOU...
DEAR GOD! GET HER INSIDE!
I'LL DO MY BEST. FOR BOTH OF YOU. BUT YOU... YOU'RE NOT...NOT FROM EARTH. I'M NOT SURE I KNOW HOW TO--
I'LL BE ALL RIGHT. JUST...SAVE HER.
EASY, SISTER. EASY.
WILL YOU GO, YOU SILLY... FOOL?
I...
THIS IS MY FAULT. ZOD, FAORA-- THEY WERE MY PEOPLE.
I MADE MY...CHOICE. I LIVE WITH IT-- SO SHOULD YOU.
DIANA-- I...
I KNOW. YOU ALREADY SAID IT. I KNOW.
WE'LL BE TOGETHER AGAIN SOON.

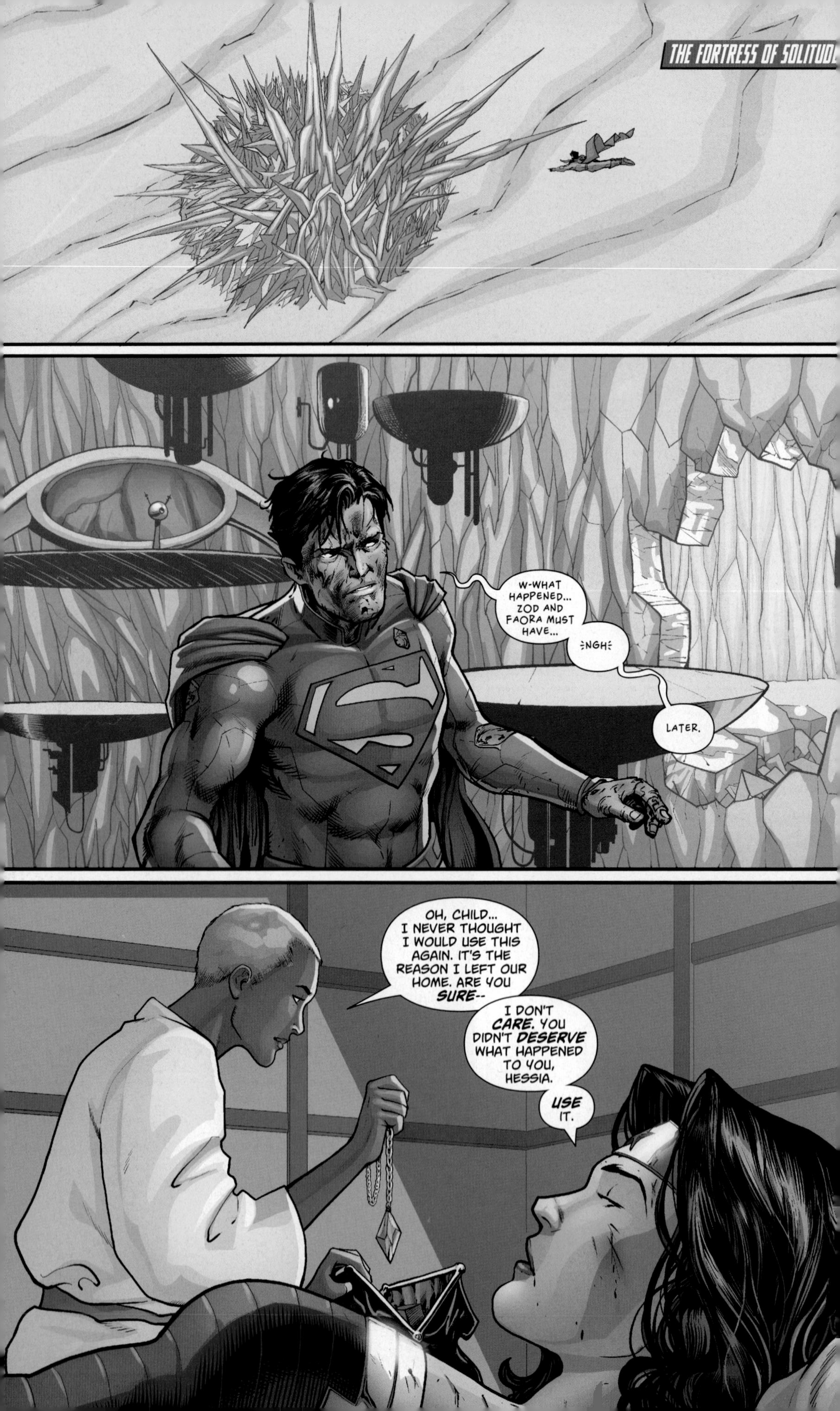
THE FORTRESS OF SOLITUDE
W-WHAT HAPPENED... ZOD AND FAORA MUST HAVE...
NGH
LATER.
OH, CHILD... I NEVER THOUGHT I WOULD USE THIS AGAIN. IT'S THE REASON I LEFT OUR HOME. ARE YOU SURE--
I DON'T CARE. YOU DIDN'T DESERVE WHAT HAPPENED TO YOU, HESSIA.
USE IT.

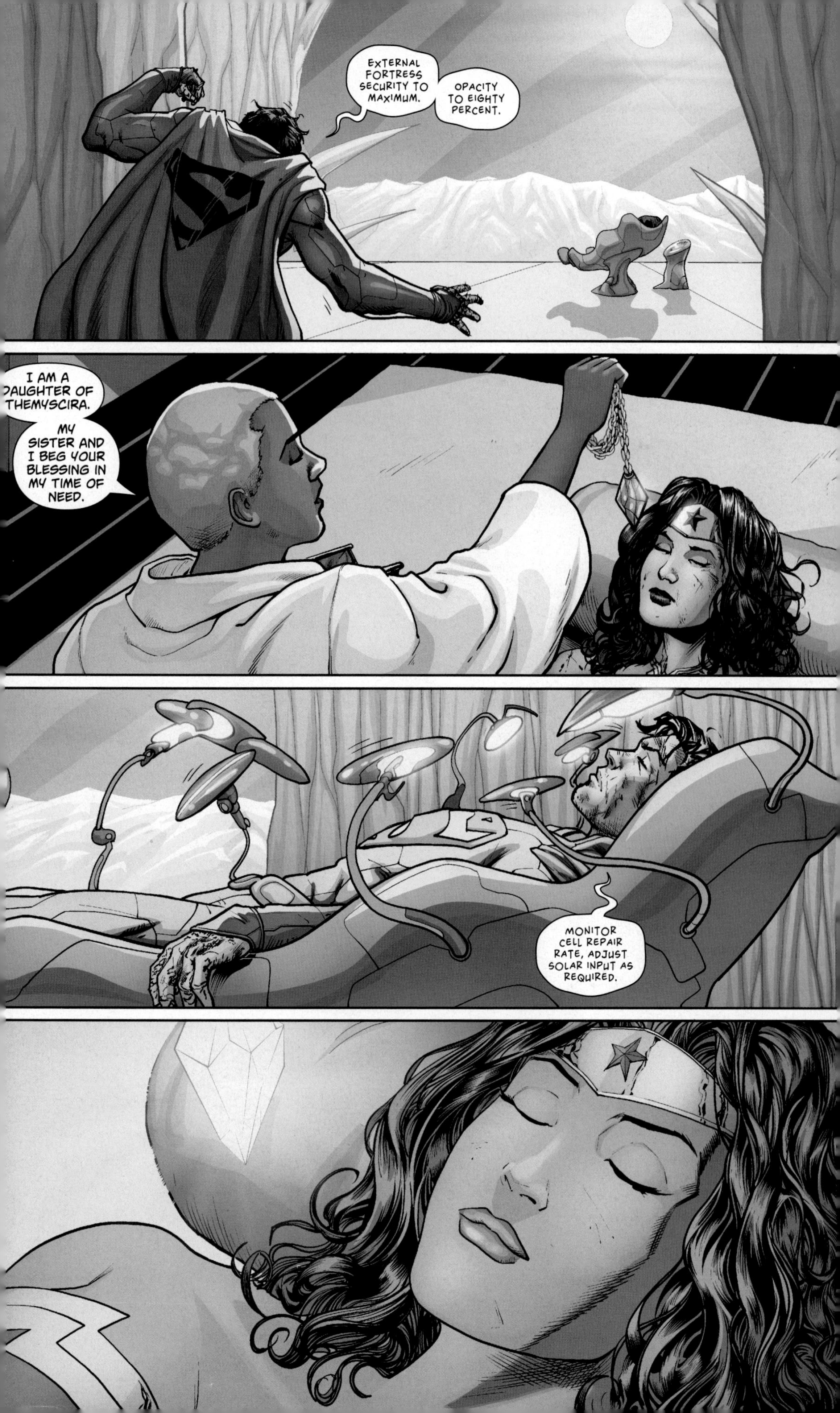
EXTERNAL FORTRESS SECURITY TO MAXIMUM.
OPACITY TO EIGHTY PERCENT.
I AM A DAUGHTER OF THEMYSCIRA.
MY SISTER AND I BEG YOUR BLESSING IN MY TIME OF NEED.
MONITOR CELL REPAIR RATE, ADJUST SOLAR INPUT AS REQUIRED.

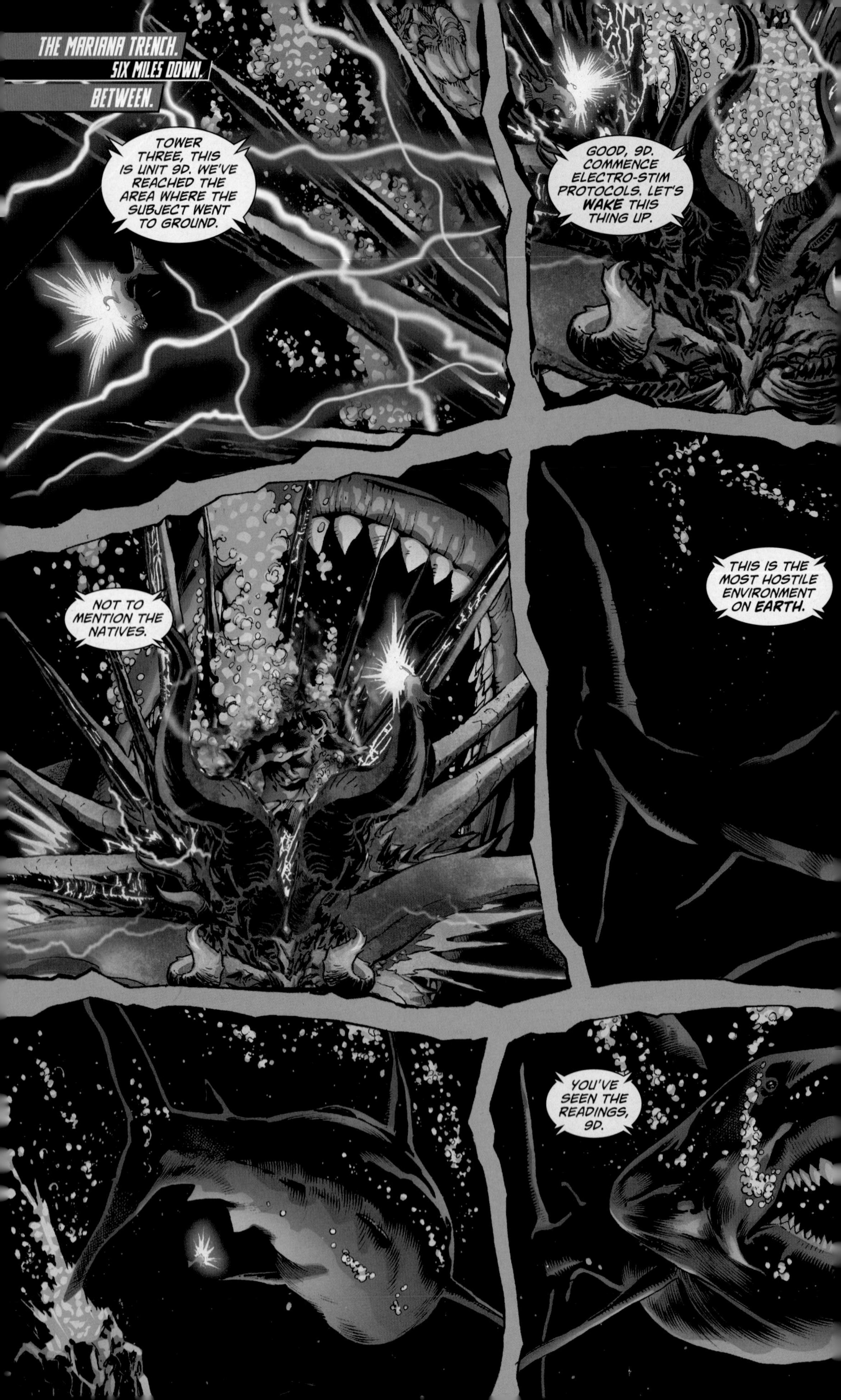
THE MARIANA TRENCH.
SIX MILES DOWN.
BETWEEN.
TOWER THREE, THIS IS UNIT 9D. WE'VE REACHED THE AREA WHERE THE SUBJECT WENT TO GROUND.
GOOD, 9D. COMMENCE ELECTRO-STIM PROTOCOLS. LET'S WAKE THIS THING UP.
NOT TO MENTION THE NATIVES.
THIS IS THE MOST HOSTILE ENVIRONMENT ON EARTH.
YOU'VE SEEN THE READINGS, 9D.

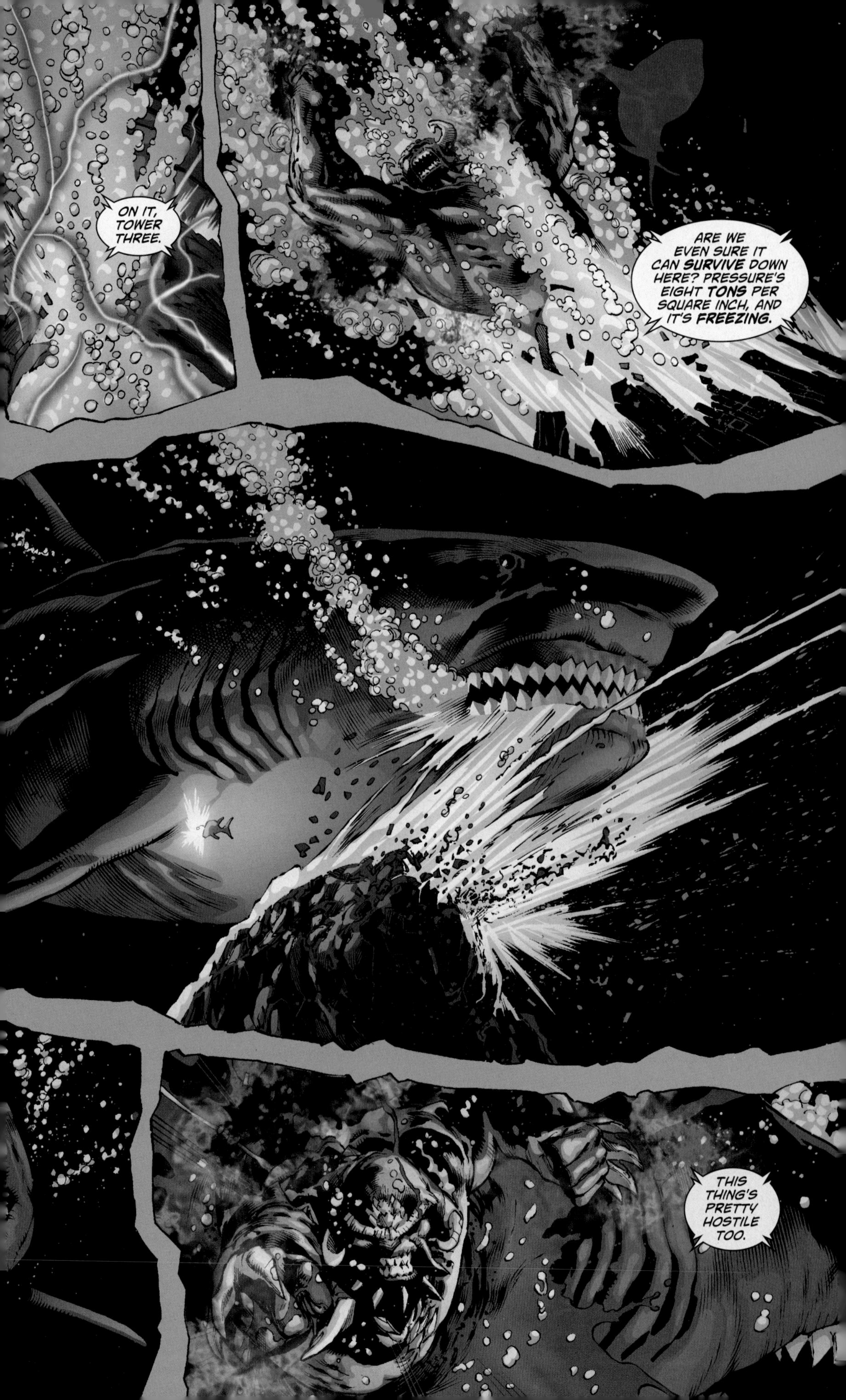
ON IT, TOWER THREE.
ARE WE EVEN SURE IT CAN SURVIVE DOWN HERE? PRESSURE'S EIGHT TONS PER SQUARE INCH, AND IT'S FREEZING.
THIS THING'S PRETTY HOSTILE TOO.

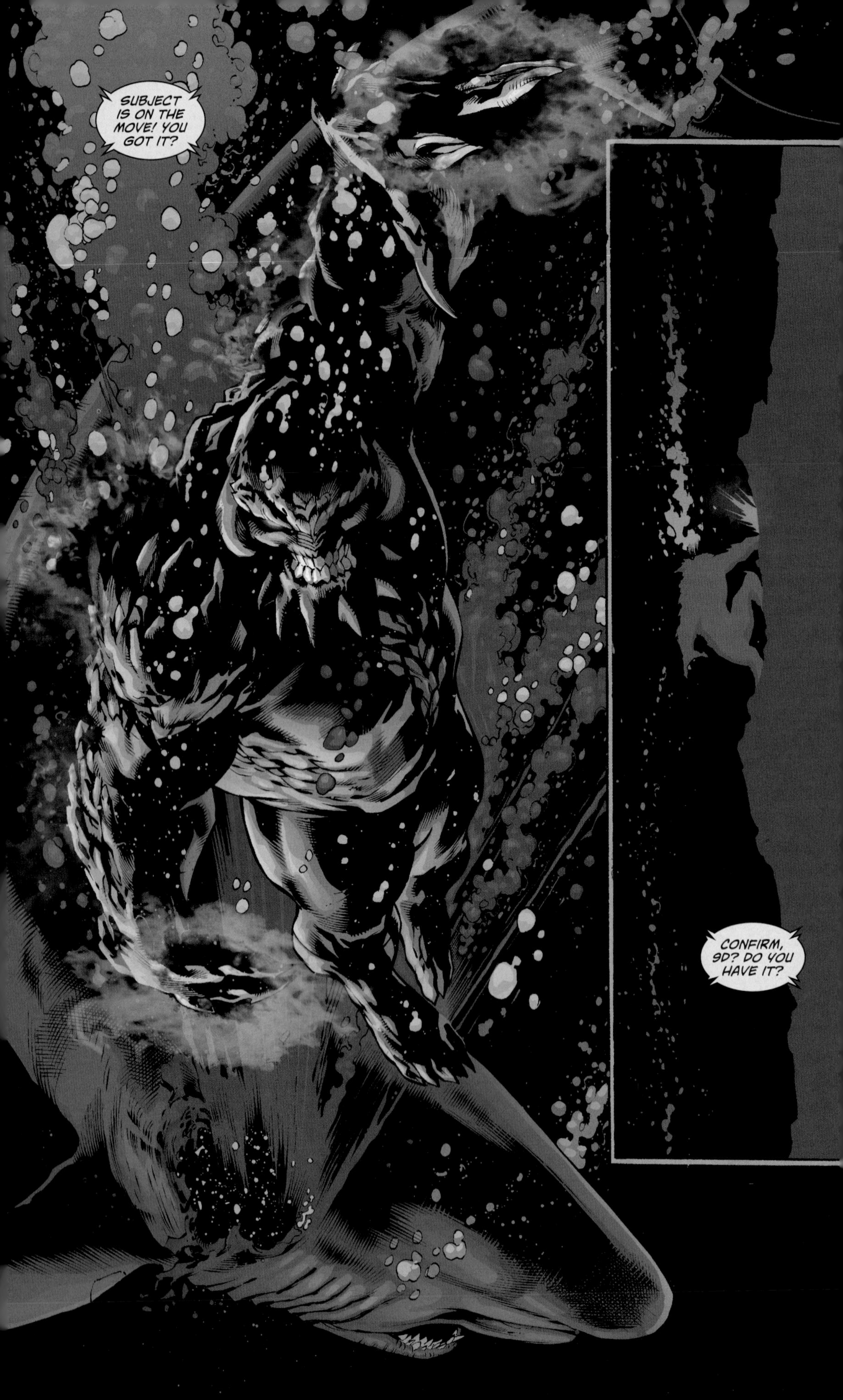
SUBJECT IS ON THE MOVE! YOU GOT IT?
CONFIRM, 9D? DO YOU HAVE IT?

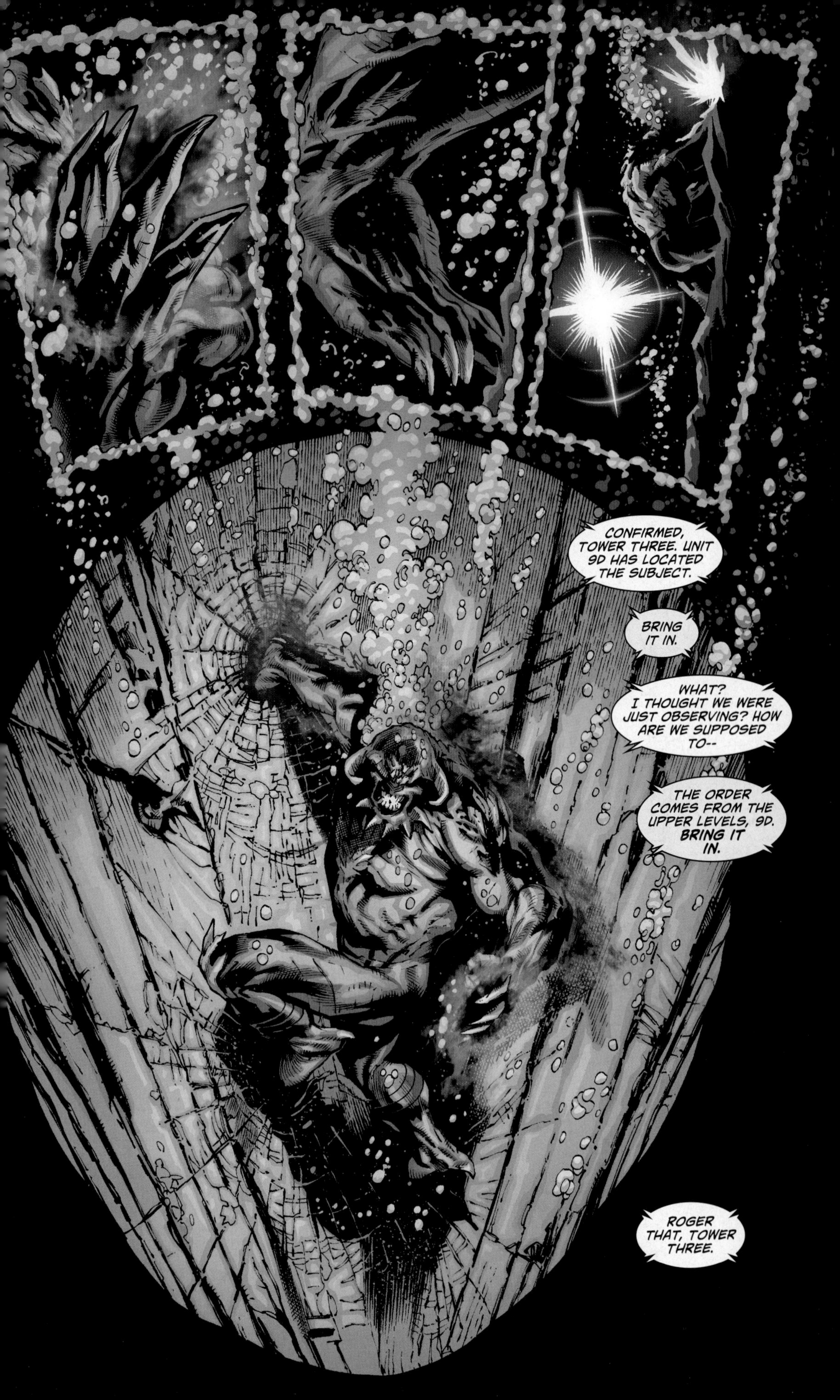
CONFIRMED, TOWER THREE. UNIT 9D HAS LOCATED THE SUBJECT.
BRING IT IN.
WHAT? I THOUGHT WE WERE JUST OBSERVING? HOW ARE WE SUPPOSED TO--
THE ORDER COMES FROM THE UPPER LEVELS, 9D. BRING IT IN.
ROGER THAT, TOWER THREE.

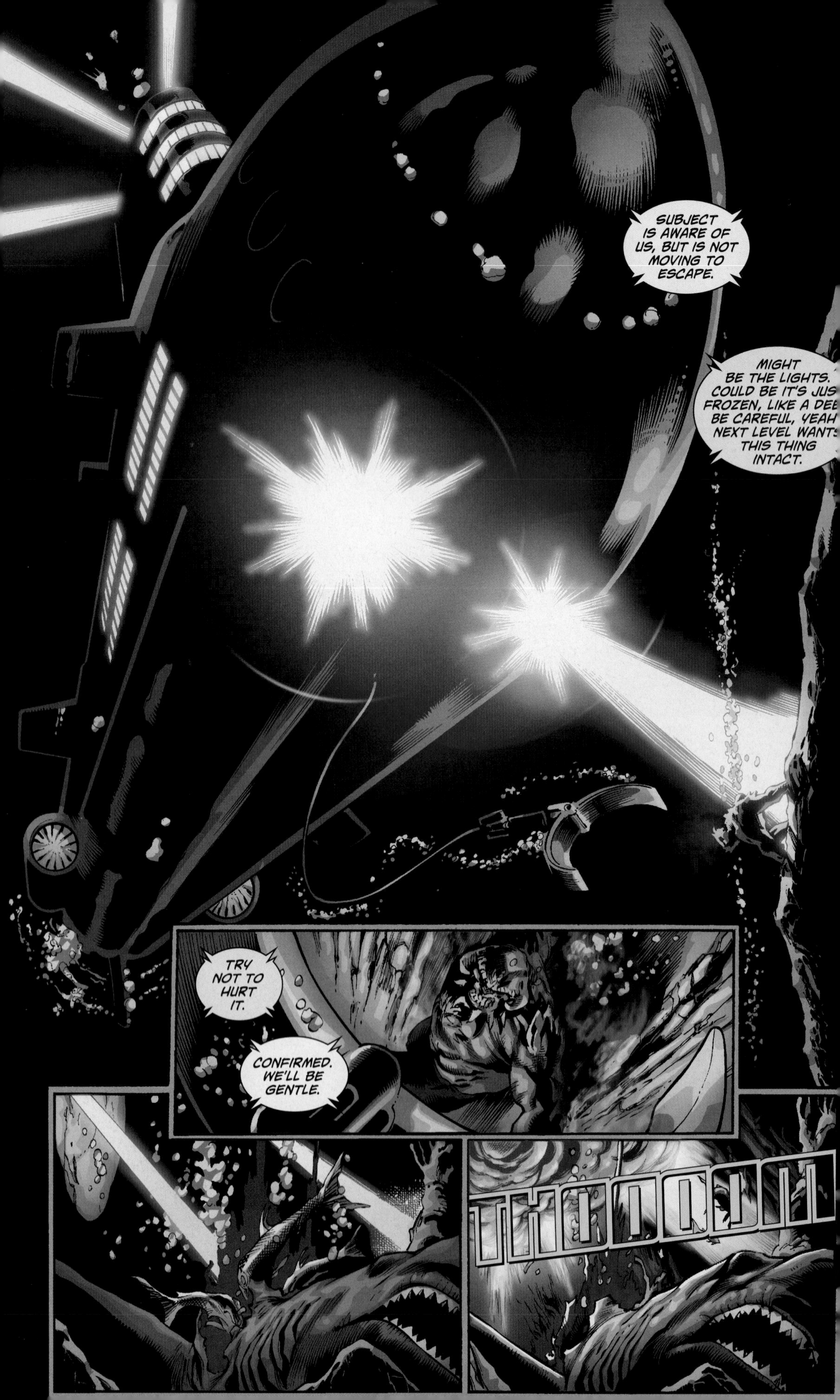
SUBJECT IS AWARE OF US, BUT IS NOT MOVING TO ESCAPE.
MIGHT BE THE LIGHTS. COULD BE IT'S JUS FROZEN, LIKE A DEE BE CAREFUL, YEAH NEXT LEVEL WANTS THIS THING INTACT.
TRY NOT TO HURT IT.
CONFIRMED. WE'LL BE GENTLE.
THOOOOM

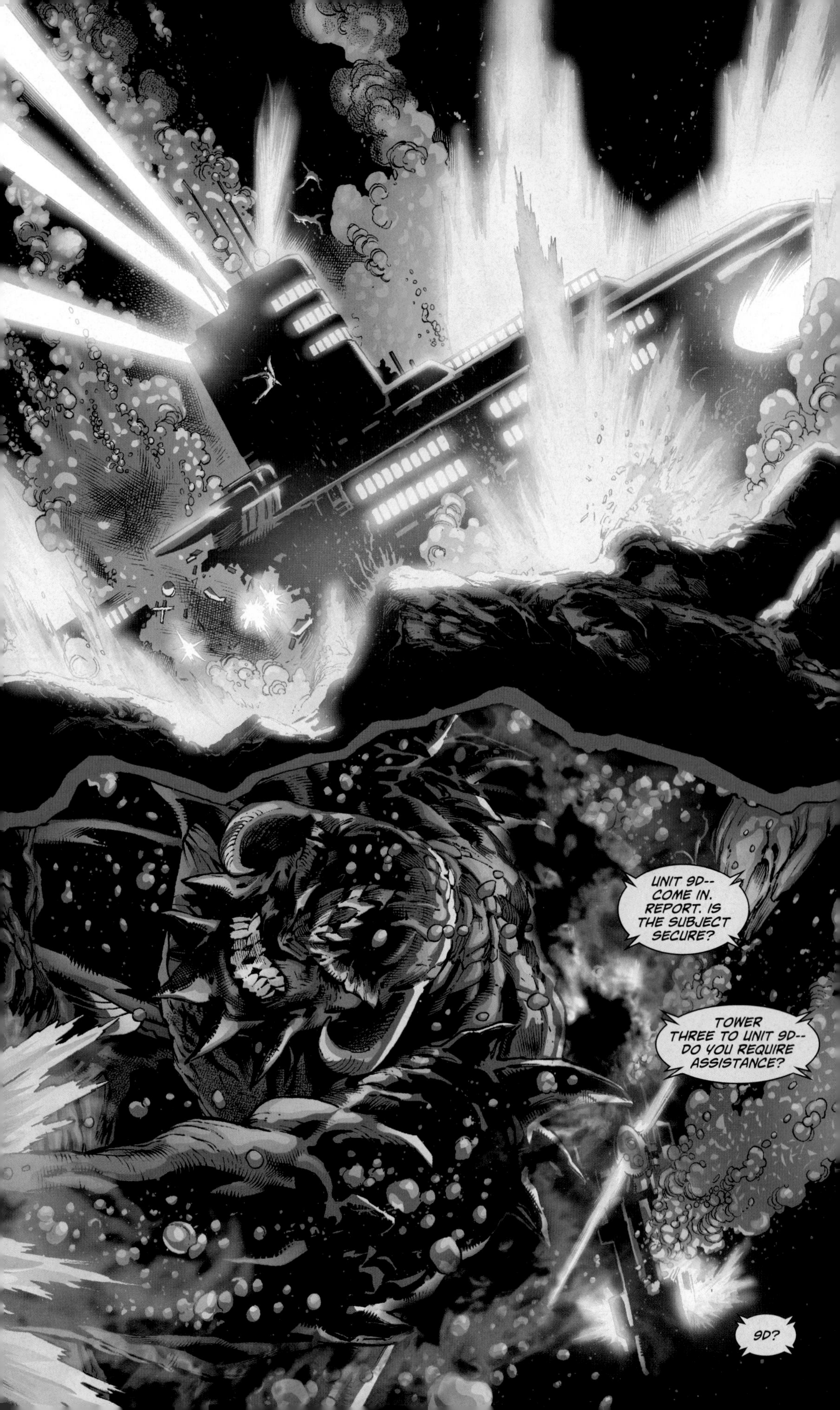
UNIT 9D-- COME IN. REPORT. IS THE SUBJECT SECURE?
TOWER THREE TO UNIT 9D-- DO YOU REQUIRE ASSISTANCE?
9D?

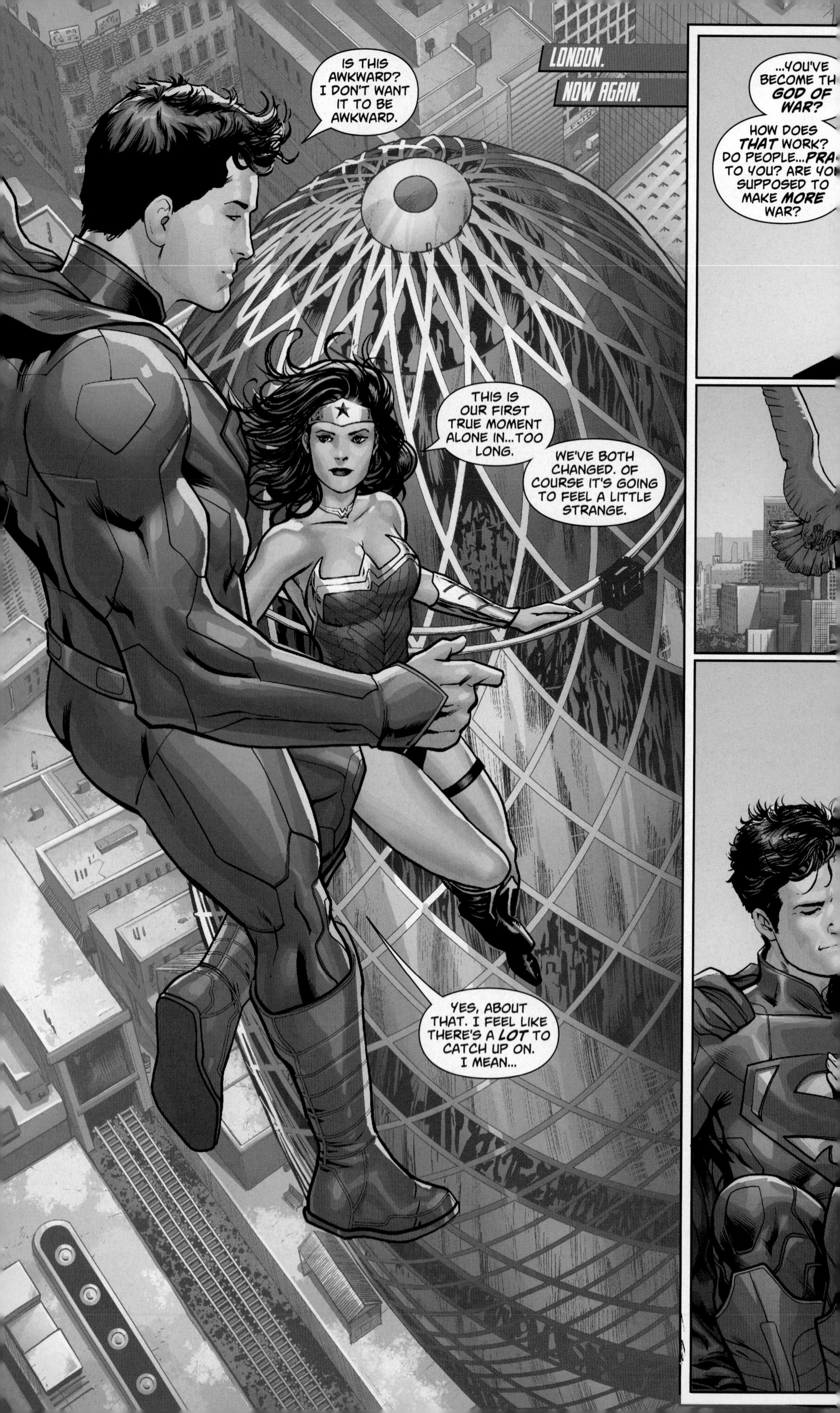
LONDON.
NOW AGAIN.
IS THIS AWKWARD? I DON'T WANT IT TO BE AWKWARD.
THIS IS OUR FIRST TRUE MOMENT ALONE IN...TOO LONG.
WE'VE BOTH CHANGED. OF COURSE IT'S GOING TO FEEL A LITTLE STRANGE.
YES, ABOUT THAT. I FEEL LIKE THERE'S A LOT TO CATCH UP ON. I MEAN...
...YOU'VE BECOME TH GOD OF WAR?
HOW DOES THAT WORK? DO PEOPLE...PRA TO YOU? ARE YO SUPPOSED TO MAKE MORE WAR?

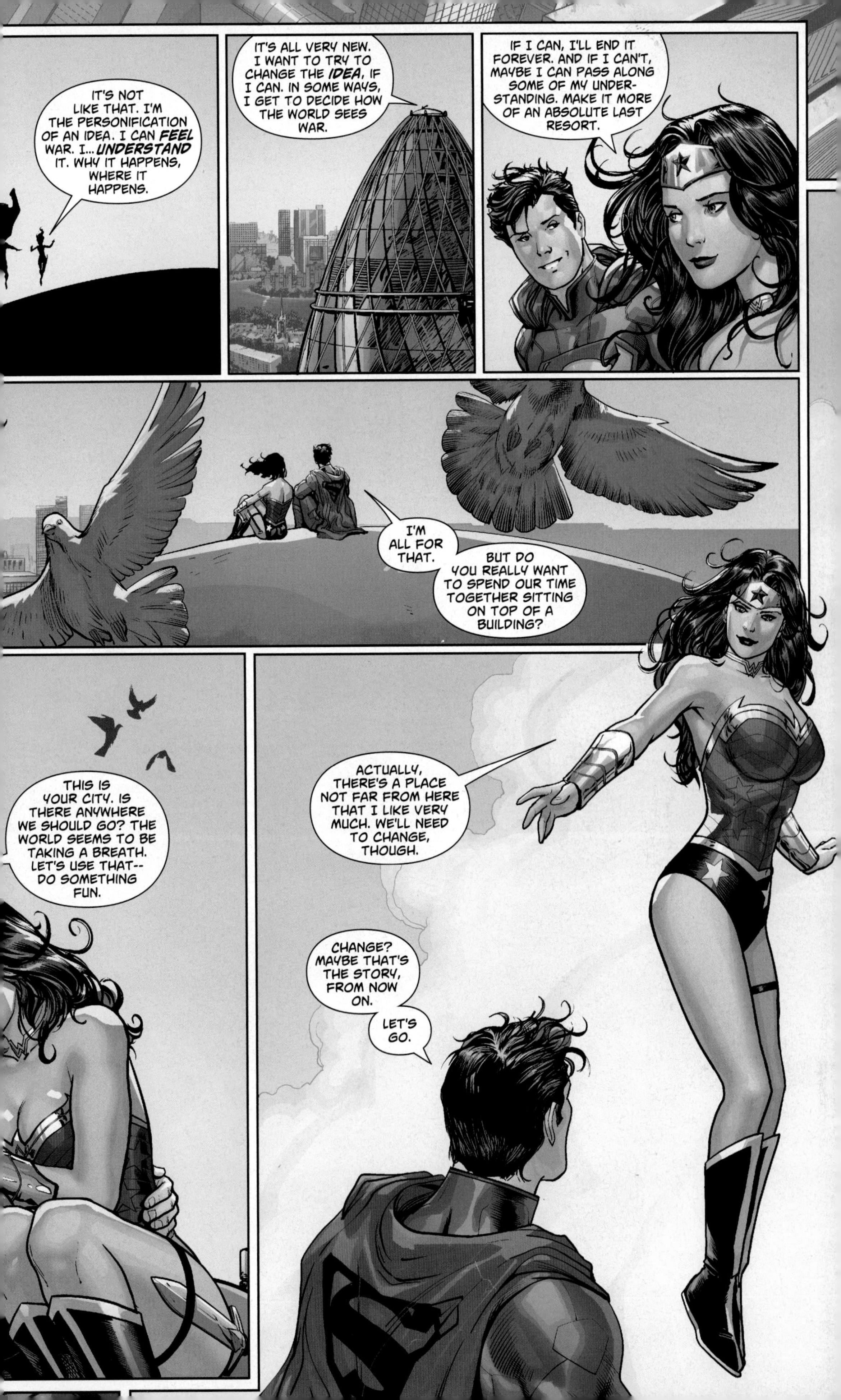
IT'S NOT LIKE THAT. I'M THE PERSONIFICATION OF AN IDEA. I CAN *FEEL* WAR. I...*UNDERSTAND* IT. WHY IT HAPPENS, WHERE IT HAPPENS.
IT'S ALL VERY NEW. I WANT TO TRY TO CHANGE THE *IDEA*, IF I CAN. IN SOME WAYS, I GET TO DECIDE HOW THE WORLD SEES WAR.
IF I CAN, I'LL END IT FOREVER. AND IF I CAN'T, MAYBE I CAN PASS ALONG SOME OF MY UNDER-STANDING. MAKE IT MORE OF AN ABSOLUTE LAST RESORT.
I'M ALL FOR THAT.
BUT DO YOU REALLY WANT TO SPEND OUR TIME TOGETHER SITTING ON TOP OF A BUILDING?
THIS IS YOUR CITY. IS THERE ANYWHERE WE SHOULD GO? THE WORLD SEEMS TO BE TAKING A BREATH. LET'S USE THAT--DO SOMETHING FUN.
ACTUALLY, THERE'S A PLACE NOT FAR FROM HERE THAT I LIKE VERY MUCH. WE'LL NEED TO CHANGE, THOUGH.
CHANGE? MAYBE THAT'S THE STORY, FROM NOW ON.
LET'S GO.

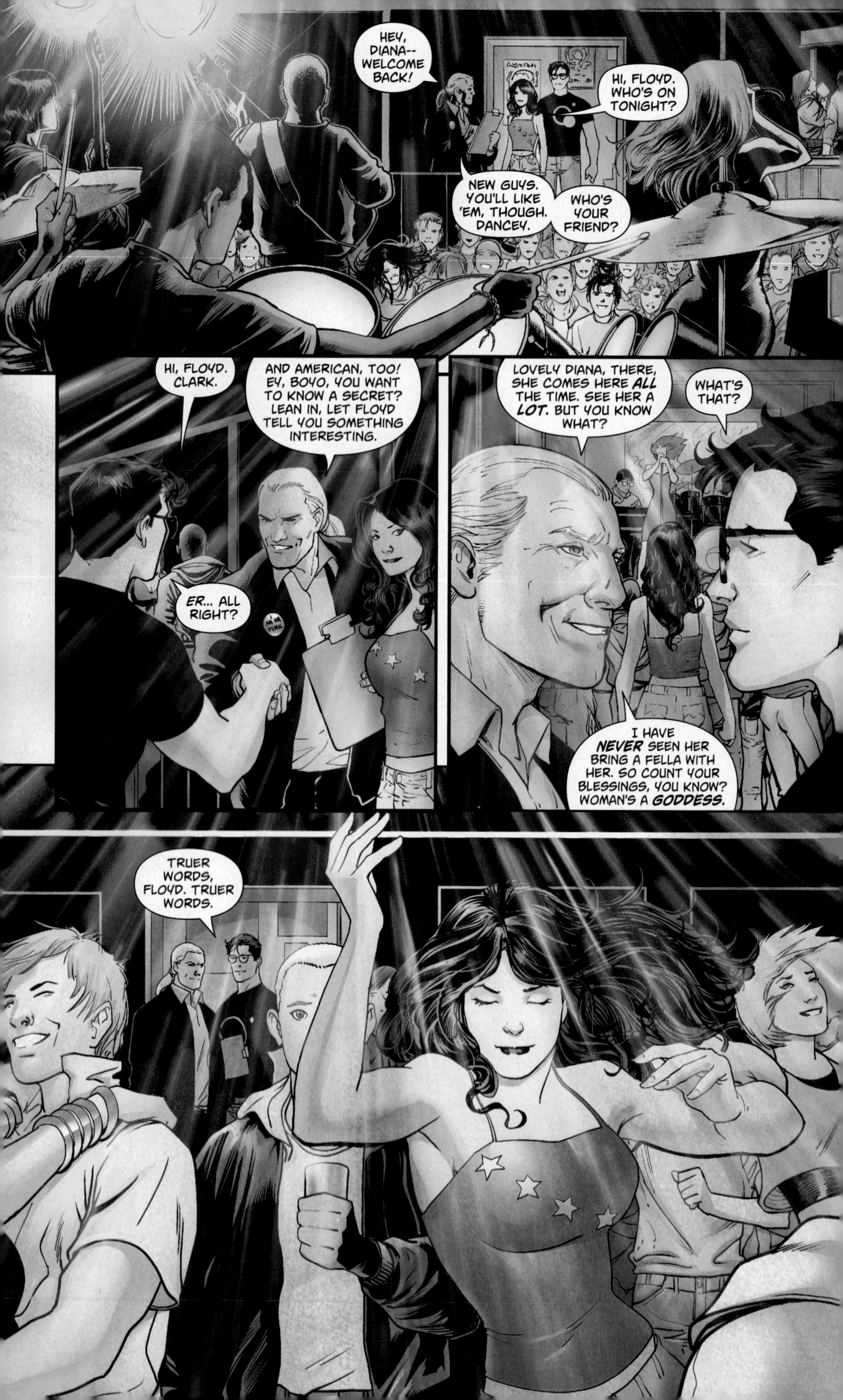
HEY, DIANA-- WELCOME BACK!
HI, FLOYD. WHO'S ON TONIGHT?
NEW GUYS. YOU'LL LIKE 'EM, THOUGH. DANCEY.
WHO'S YOUR FRIEND?
HI, FLOYD. CLARK.
AND AMERICAN, TOO! EY, BOYO, YOU WANT TO KNOW A SECRET? LEAN IN, LET FLOYD TELL YOU SOMETHING INTERESTING.
ER... ALL RIGHT?
LOVELY DIANA, THERE, SHE COMES HERE ALL THE TIME. SEE HER A LOT. BUT YOU KNOW WHAT?
WHAT'S THAT?
I HAVE NEVER SEEN HER BRING A FELLA WITH HER. SO COUNT YOUR BLESSINGS, YOU KNOW? WOMAN'S A GODDESS.
TRUER WORDS, FLOYD. TRUER WORDS.

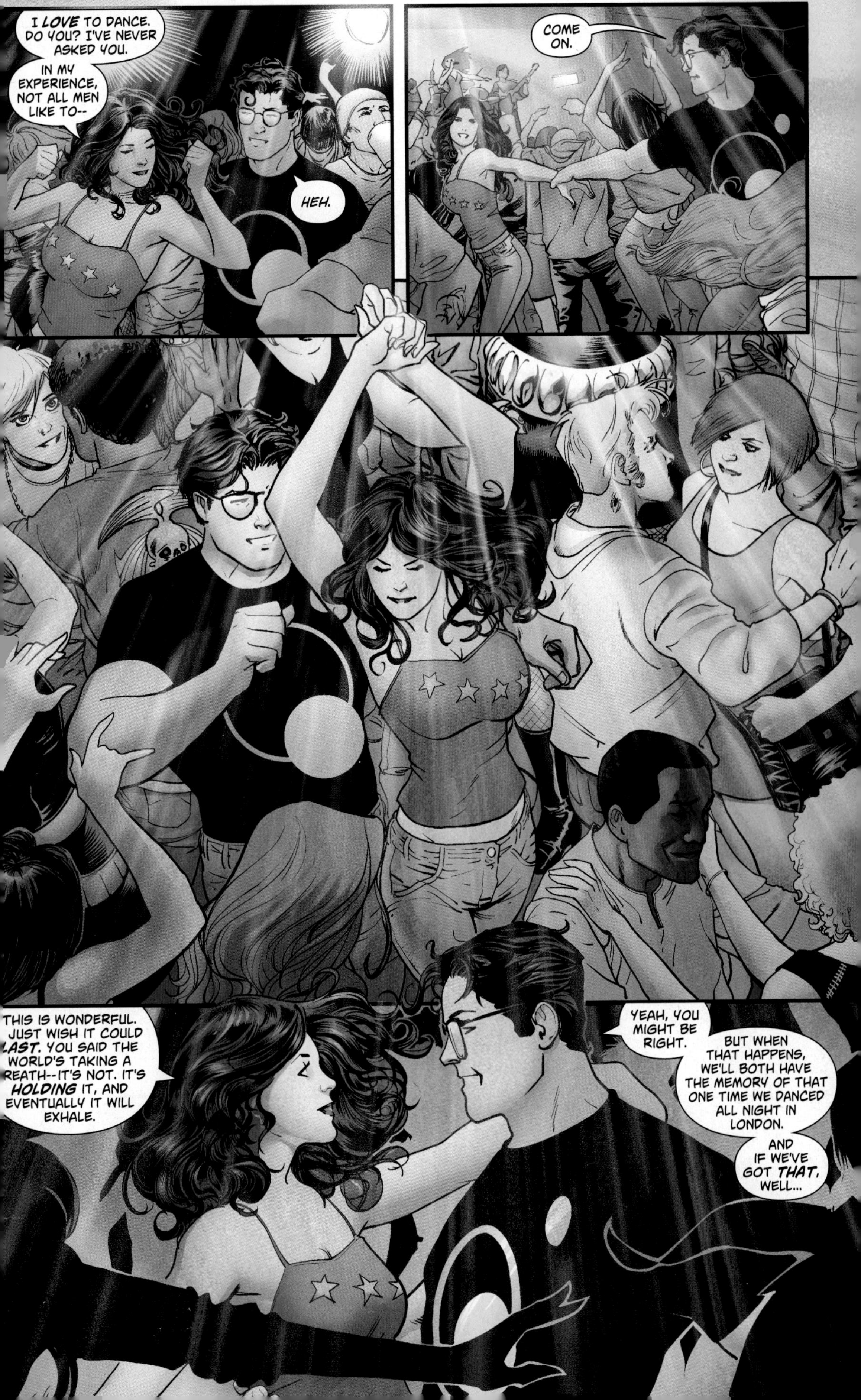
I *LOVE* TO DANCE. DO YOU? I'VE NEVER ASKED YOU.
IN MY EXPERIENCE, NOT ALL MEN LIKE TO--
HEH.
COME ON.
THIS IS WONDERFUL. JUST WISH IT COULD LAST. YOU SAID THE WORLD'S TAKING A REATH--IT'S NOT. IT'S *HOLDING* IT, AND EVENTUALLY IT WILL EXHALE.
YEAH, YOU MIGHT BE RIGHT.
BUT WHEN THAT HAPPENS, WE'LL BOTH HAVE THE MEMORY OF THAT ONE TIME WE DANCED ALL NIGHT IN LONDON.
AND IF WE'VE GOT *THAT*, WELL...

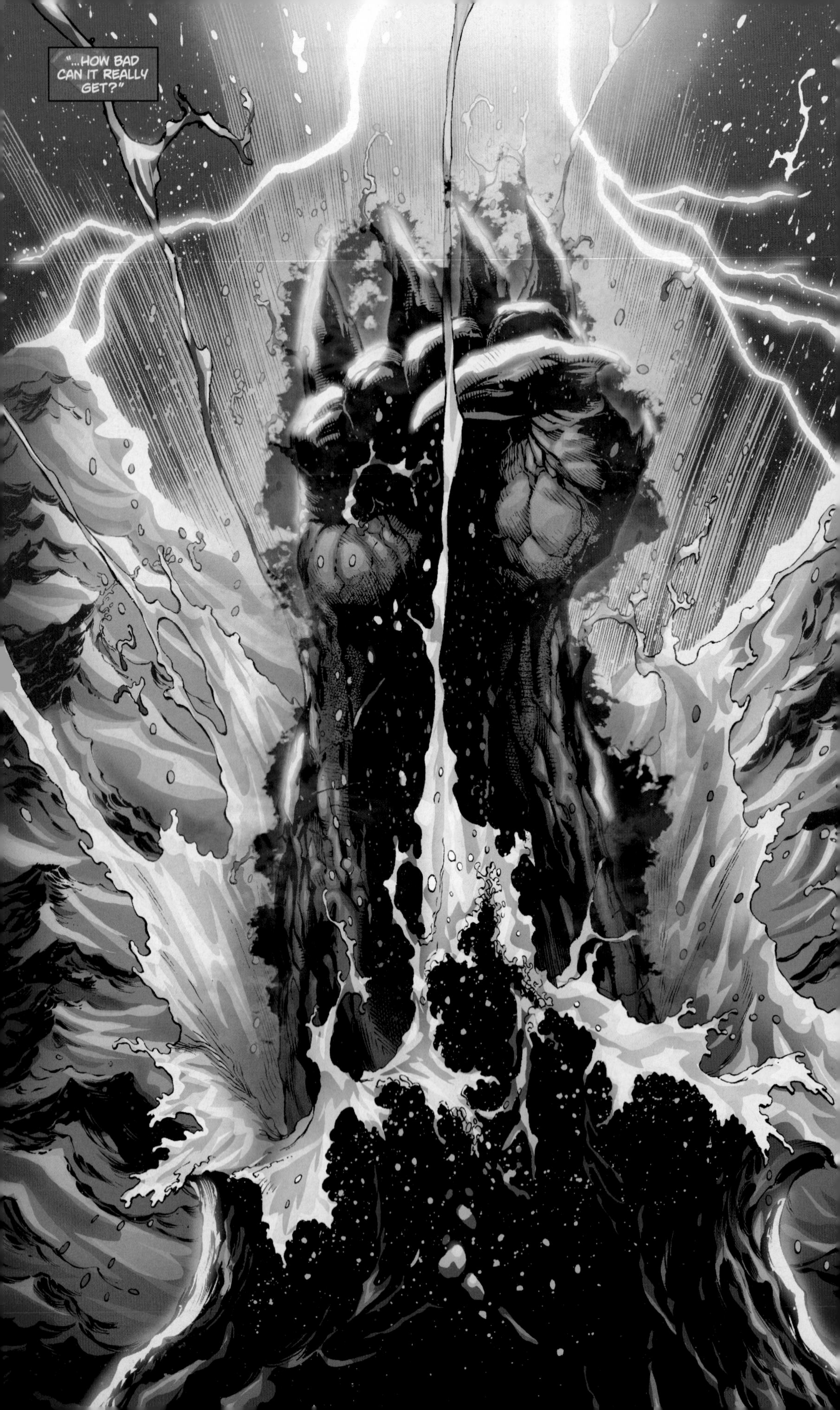
"...HOW BAD CAN IT REALLY GET?"

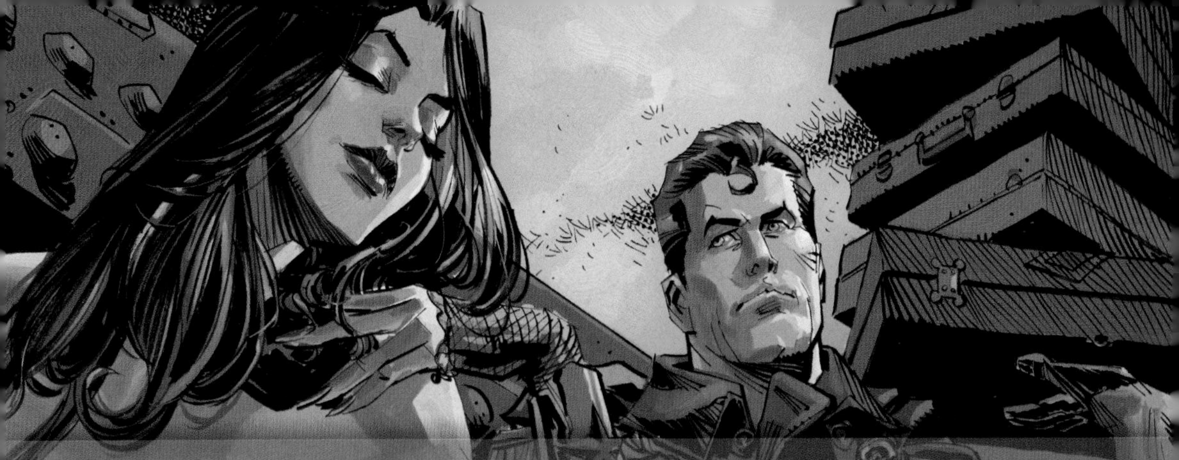

VARIANT COVER GALLERY

SUPERMAN/WONDER WOMAN 1
Variant cover by Cliff Chiang

SUPERMAN/WONDER WOMAN 1
Variant cover by Aaron Kuder & Eva de la Cruz

SUPERMAN/WONDER WOMAN 2
Variant cover by Shane Davis, Michelle Delecki & Barbara Ciardo

SUPERMAN/WONDER WOMAN 3
Variant cover by Guillem March

SUPERMAN/WONDER WOMAN 4
Scribblenauts variant cover by Jon Katz, after Jim Lee

SUPERMAN/WONDER WOMAN 5
Variant by Dan Panosian

SUPERMAN/WONDER WOMAN 6
Robot Chicken variant by RC Stoodios

SUPERMAN/WONDER WOMAN 7
MAD variant cover by Tom Bunk

SUPERMAN/WONDER WOMAN 1
Full wrap-around cover by Tony S. Daniel, Batt & Tomeu Morey

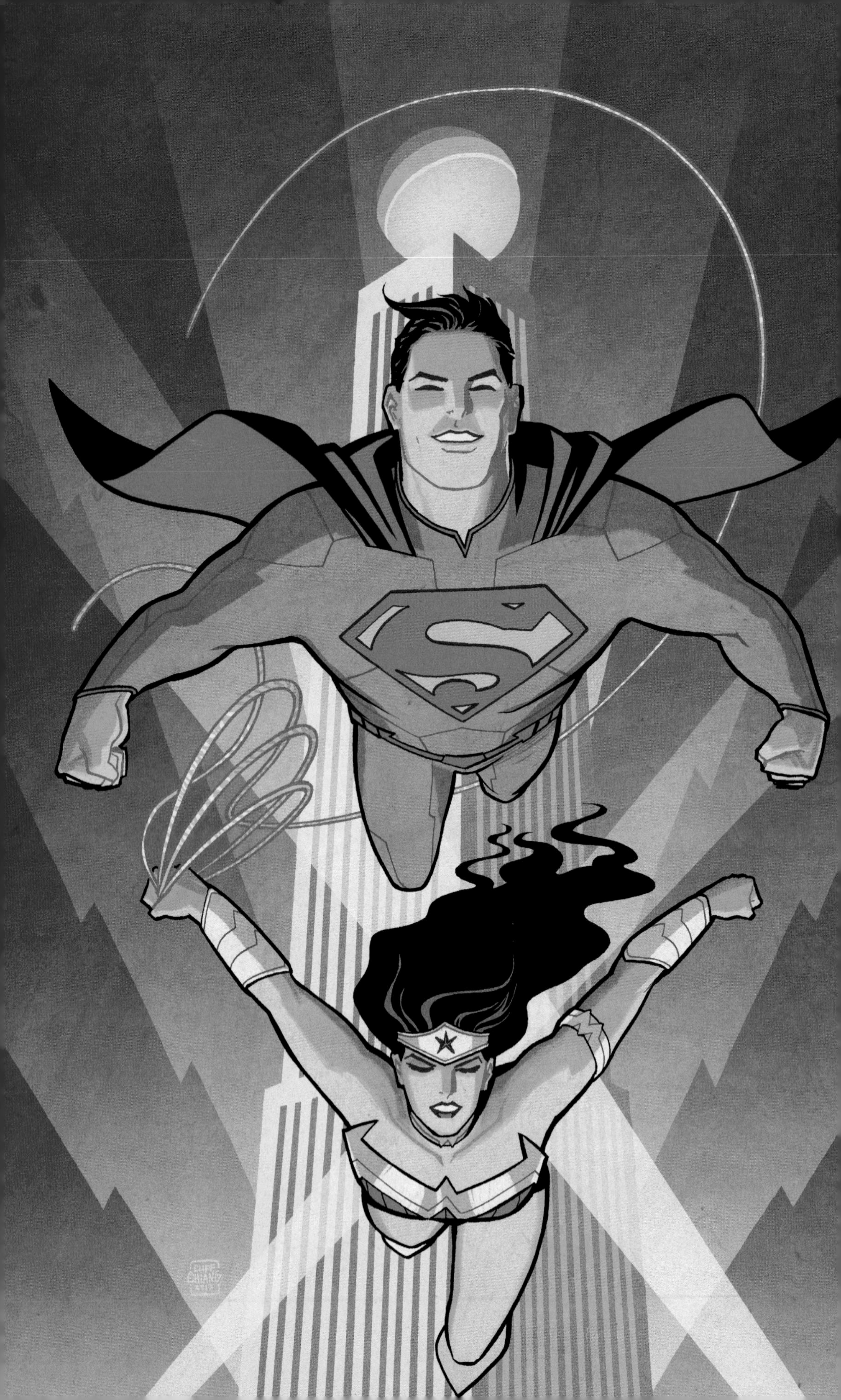
CLIFF CHIANG

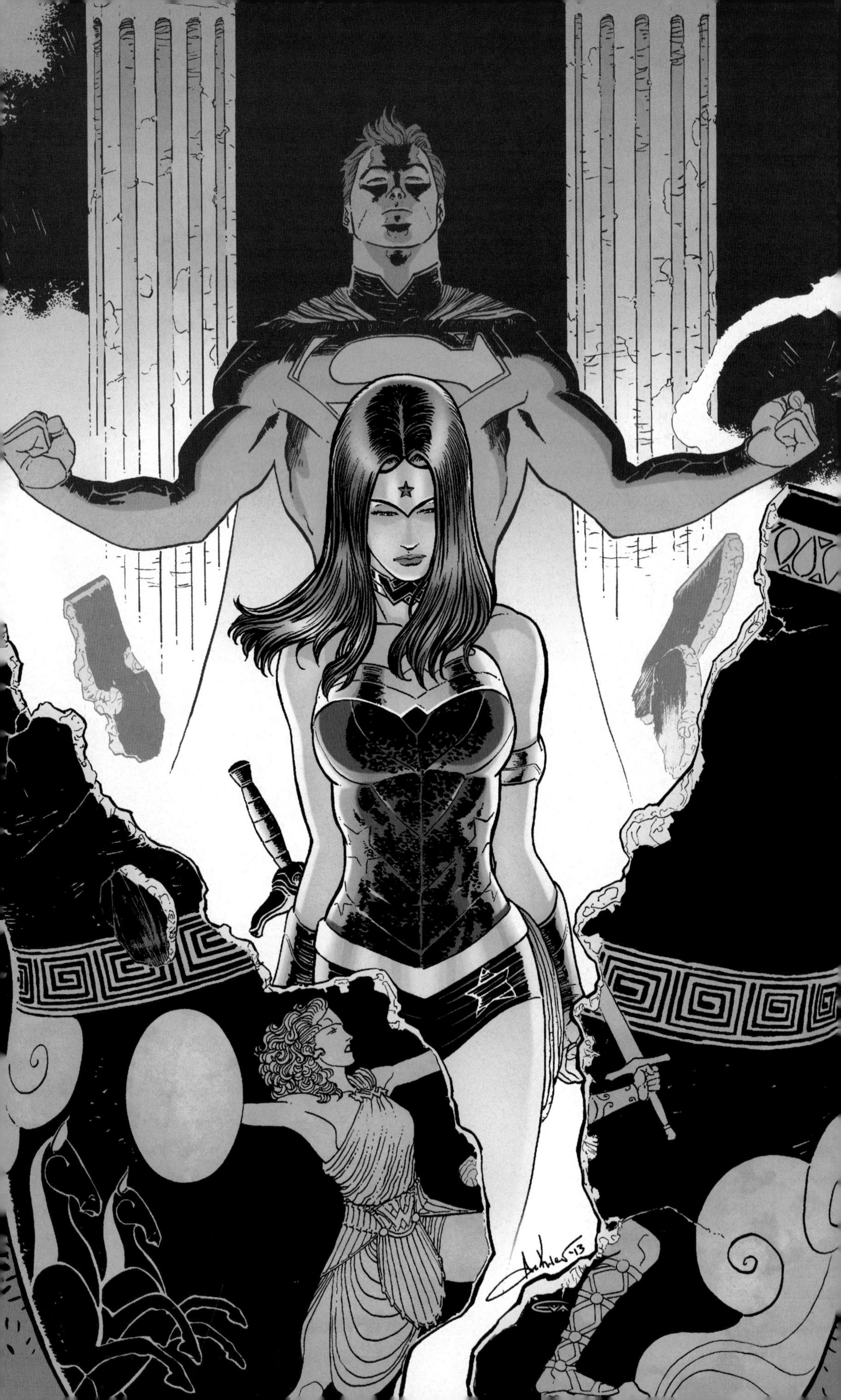

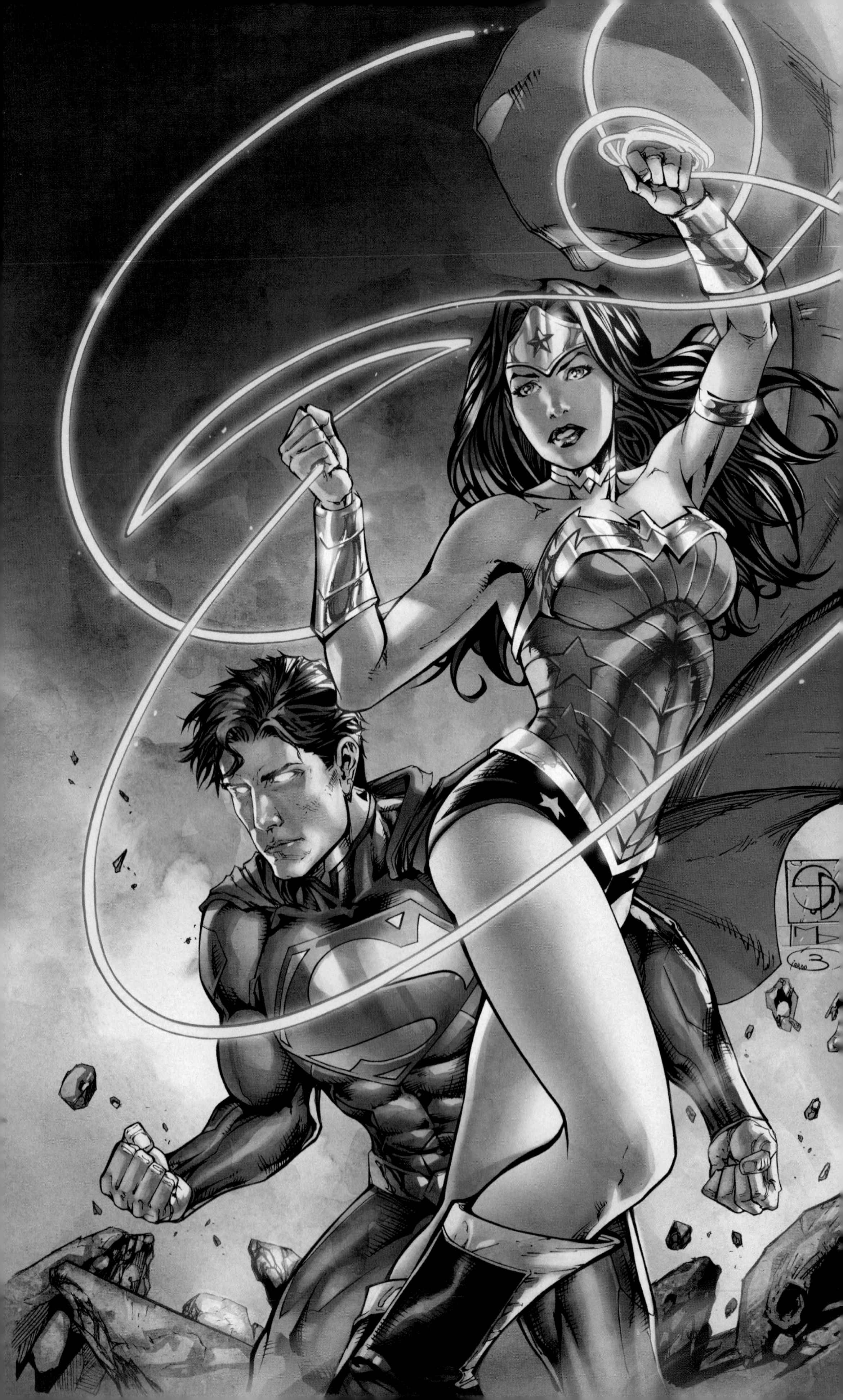

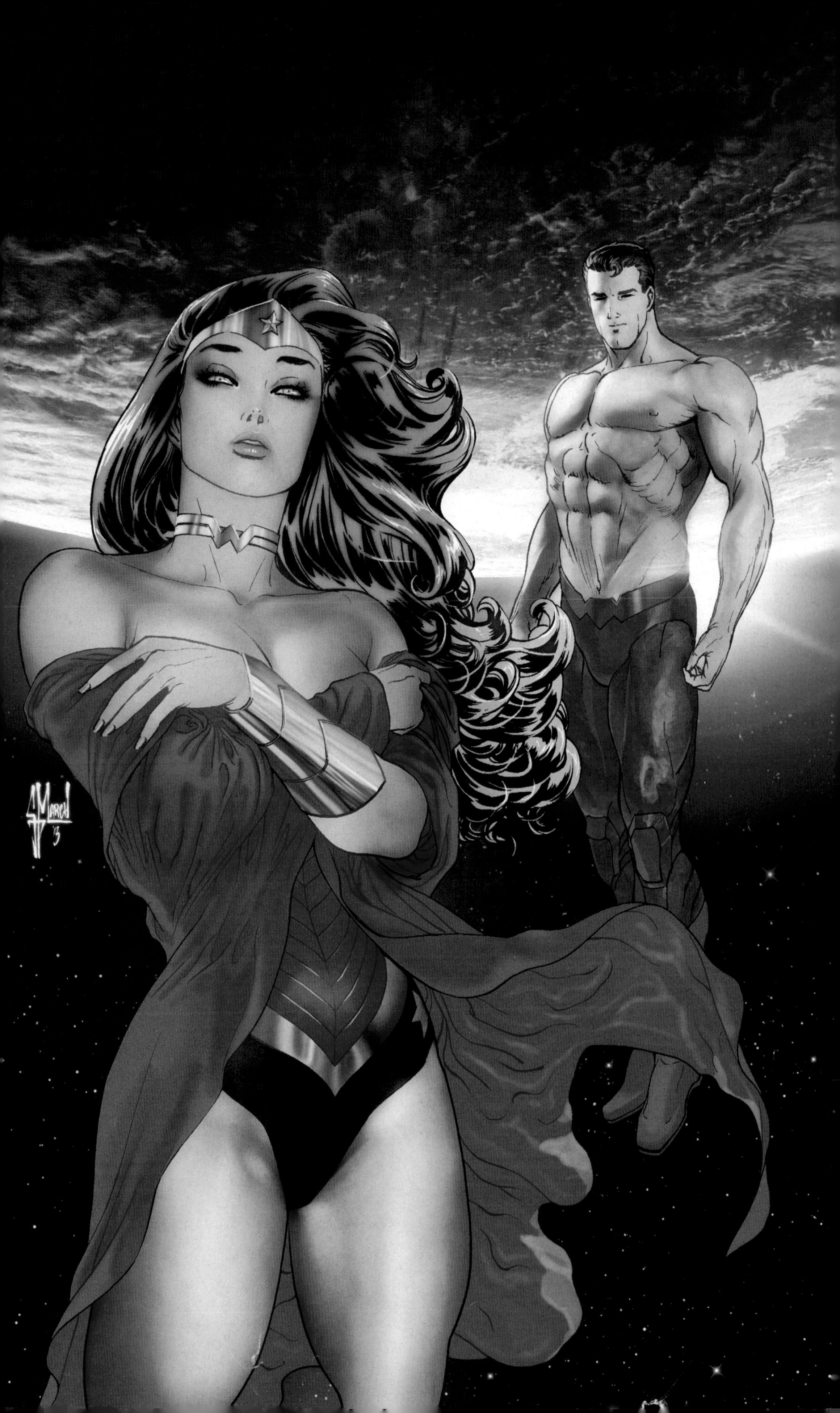

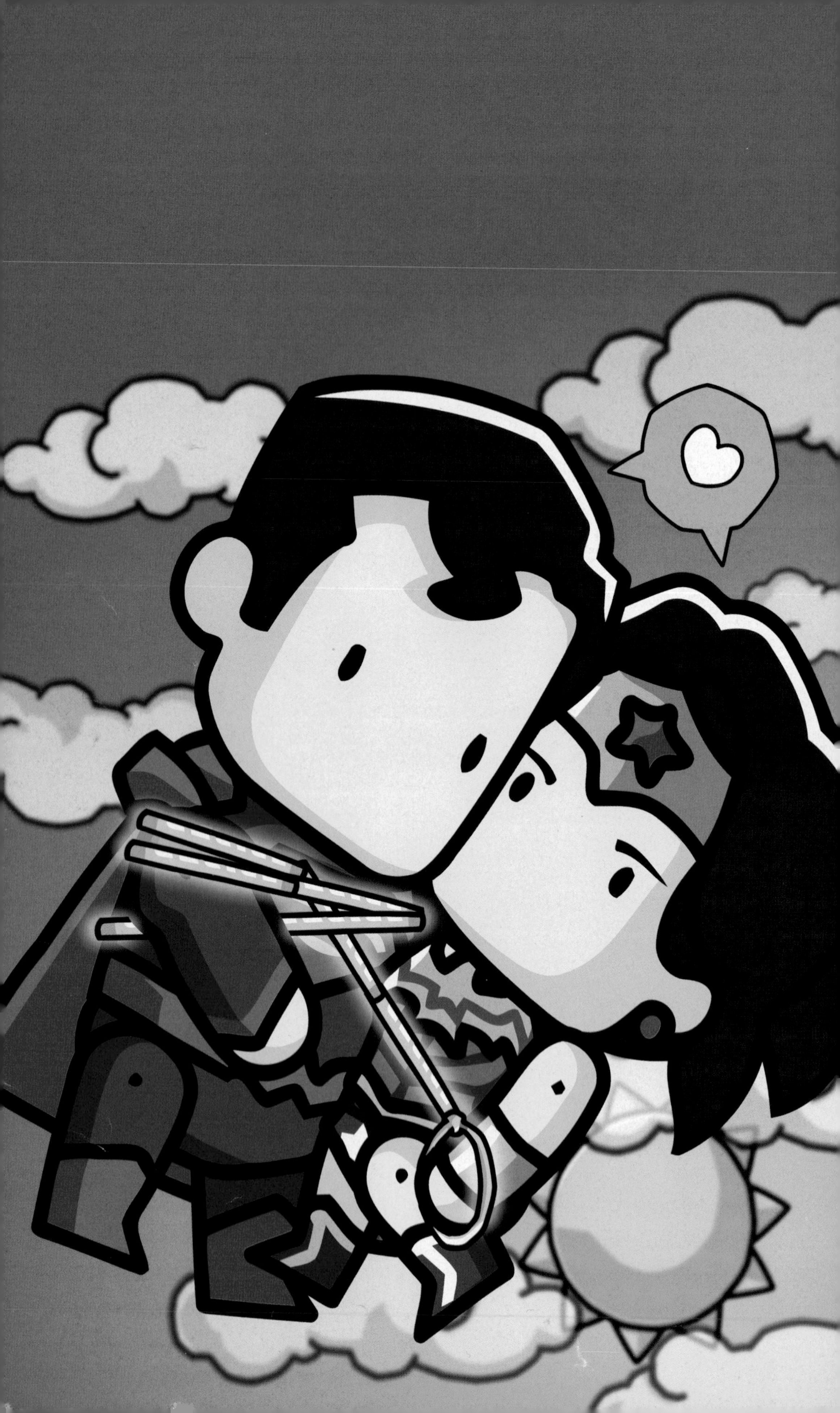

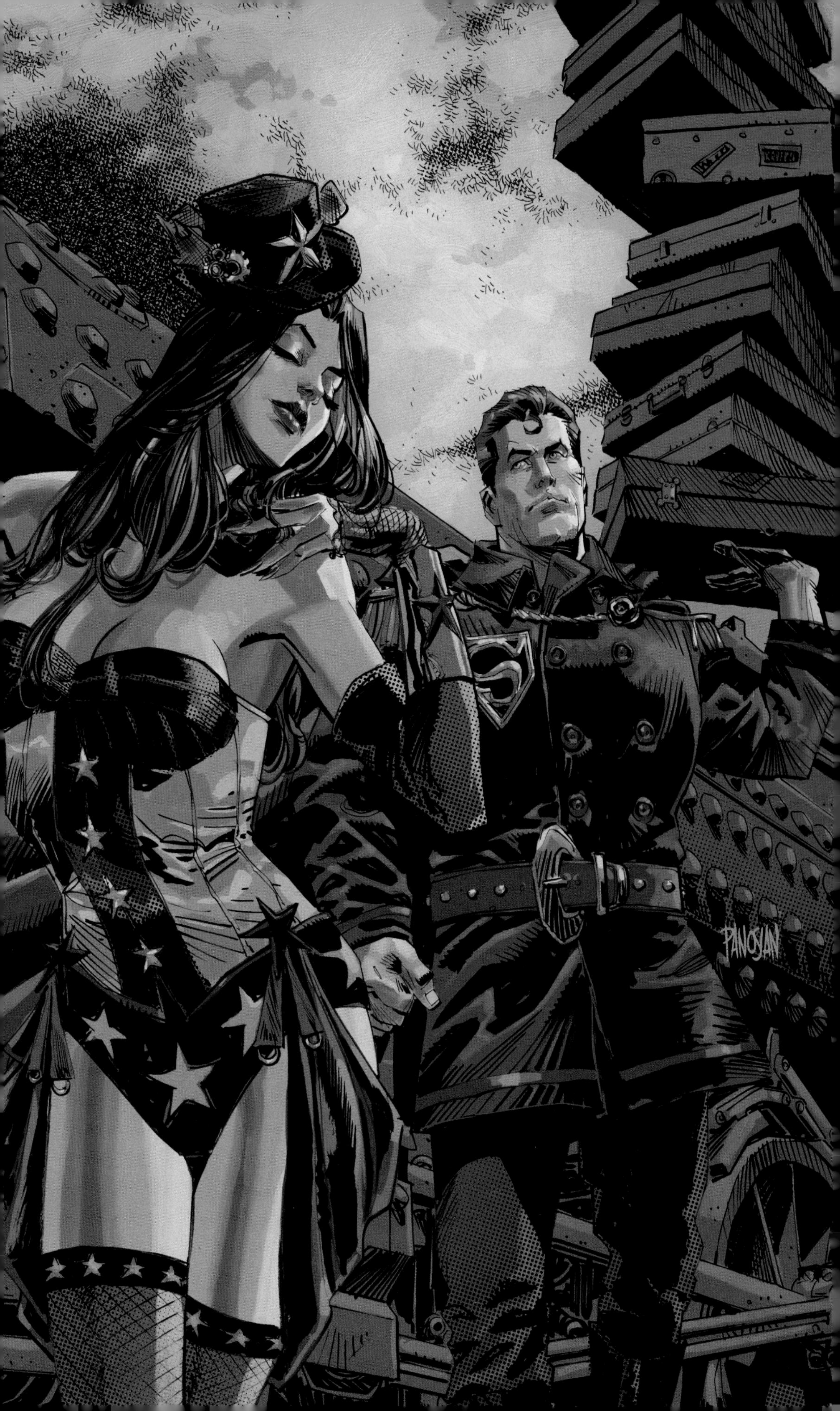
PANOSIAN

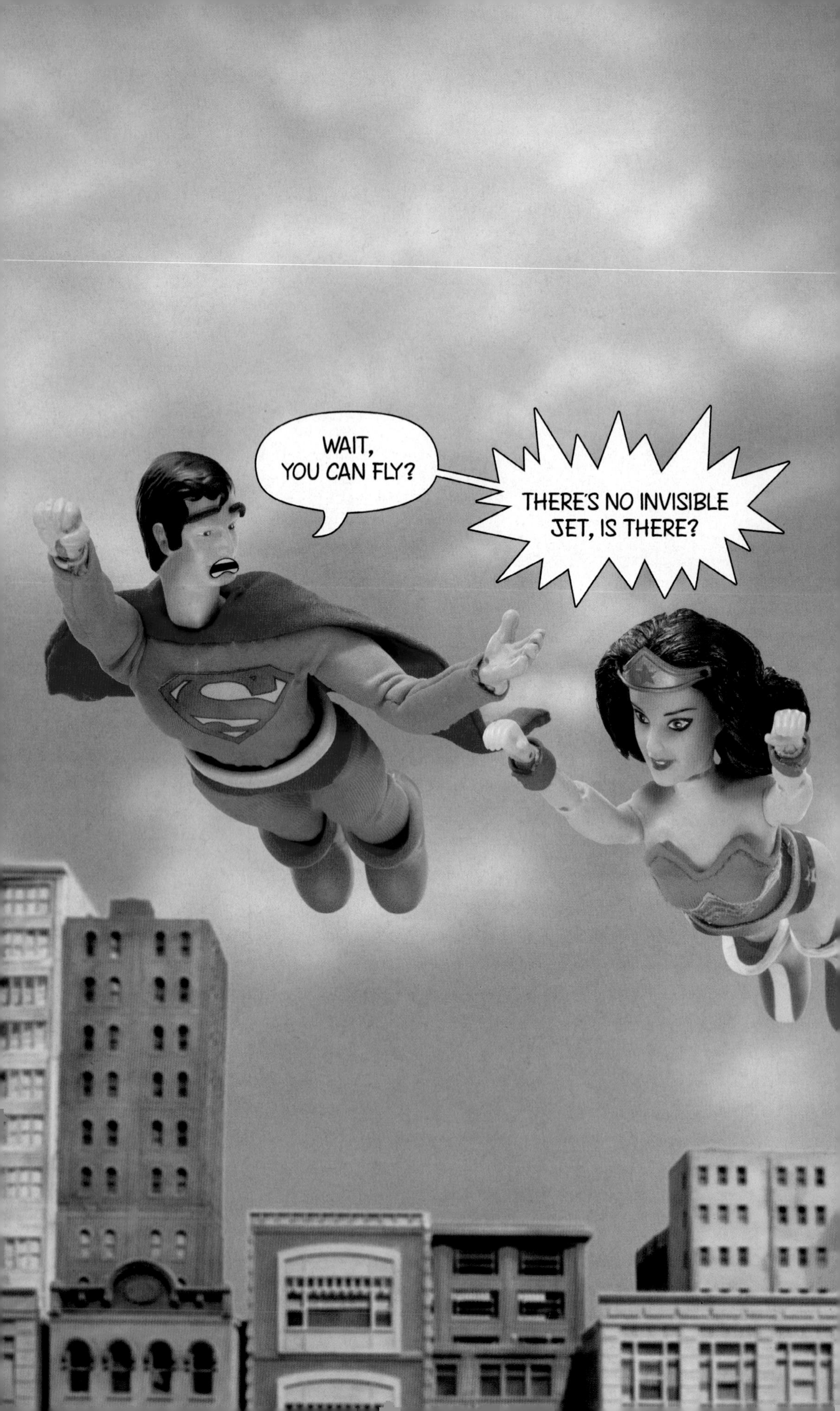
WAIT, YOU CAN FLY?
THERE'S NO INVISIBLE JET, IS THERE?

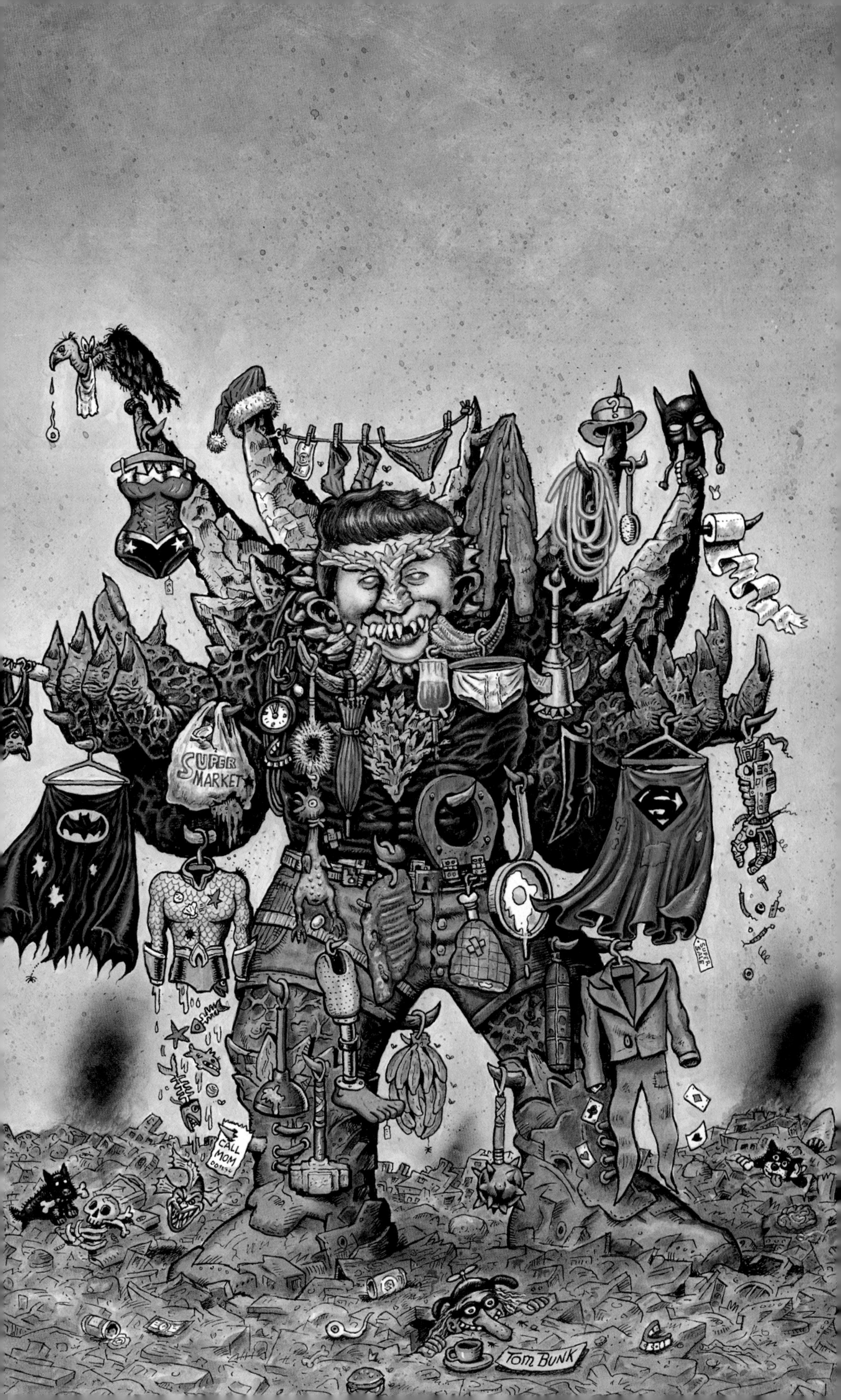
SUPER MARKET
CALL MOM
SUPER SALE
TOM BUNK

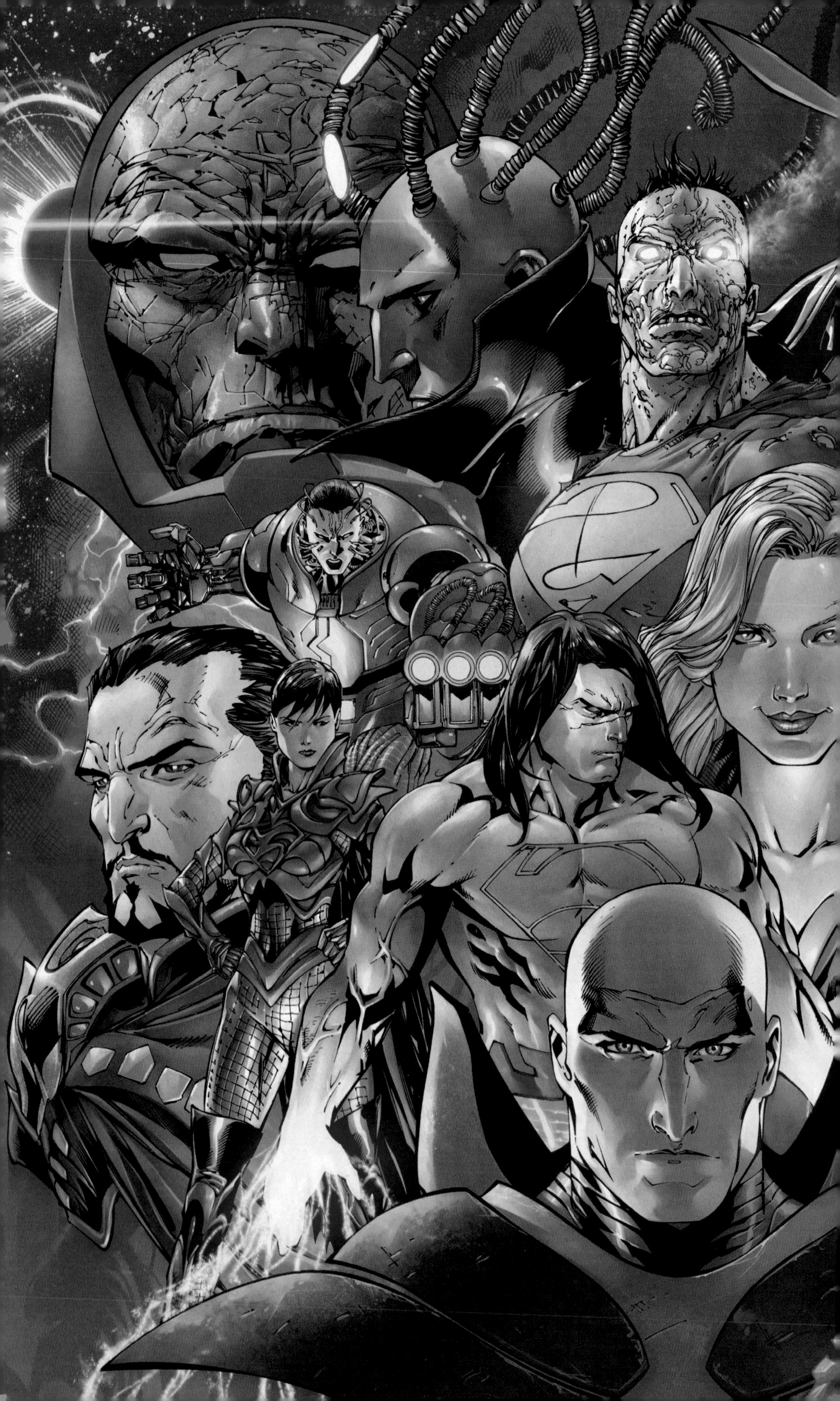

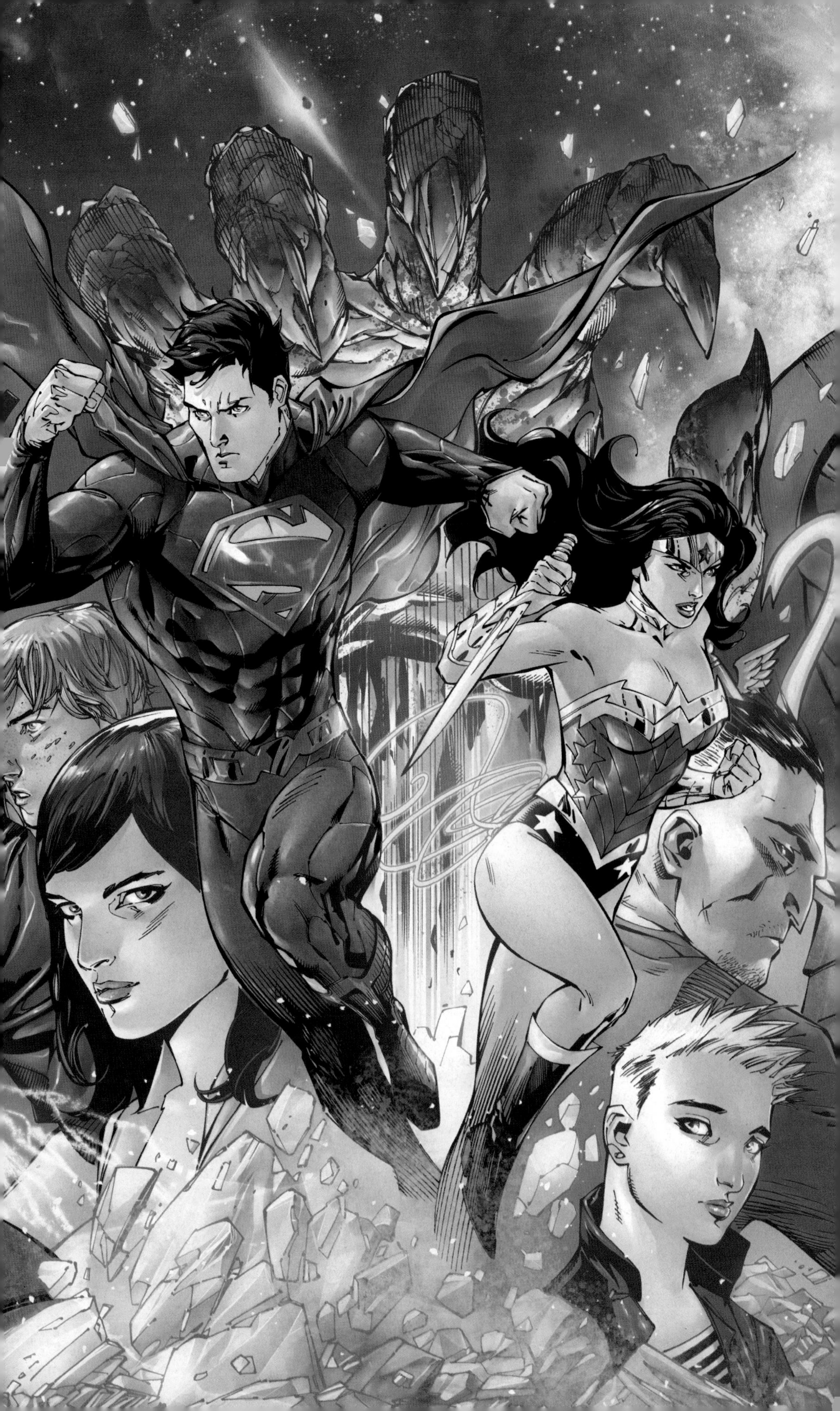

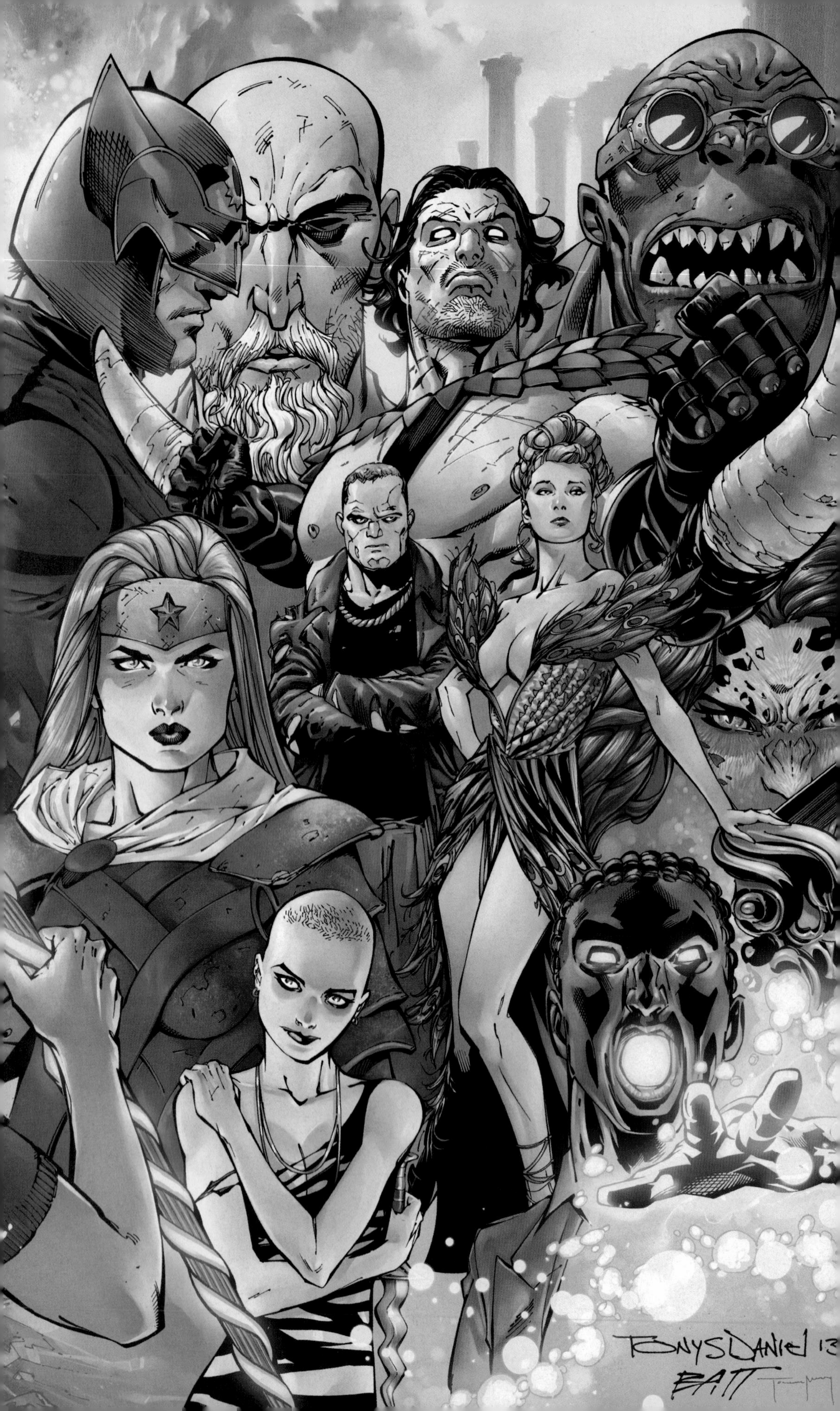
TONYSDANIEL 13
BATT

"Superman is still super."
—WALL STREET JOURNAL

"The SUPERMAN world is also one now where fans new and old, young and not-so-young, can come to a common ground to talk about the superhero that started it all."
—CRAVE ONLINE

START AT THE BEGINNING!

SUPERMAN VOLUME 1: WHAT PRICE TOMORROW?

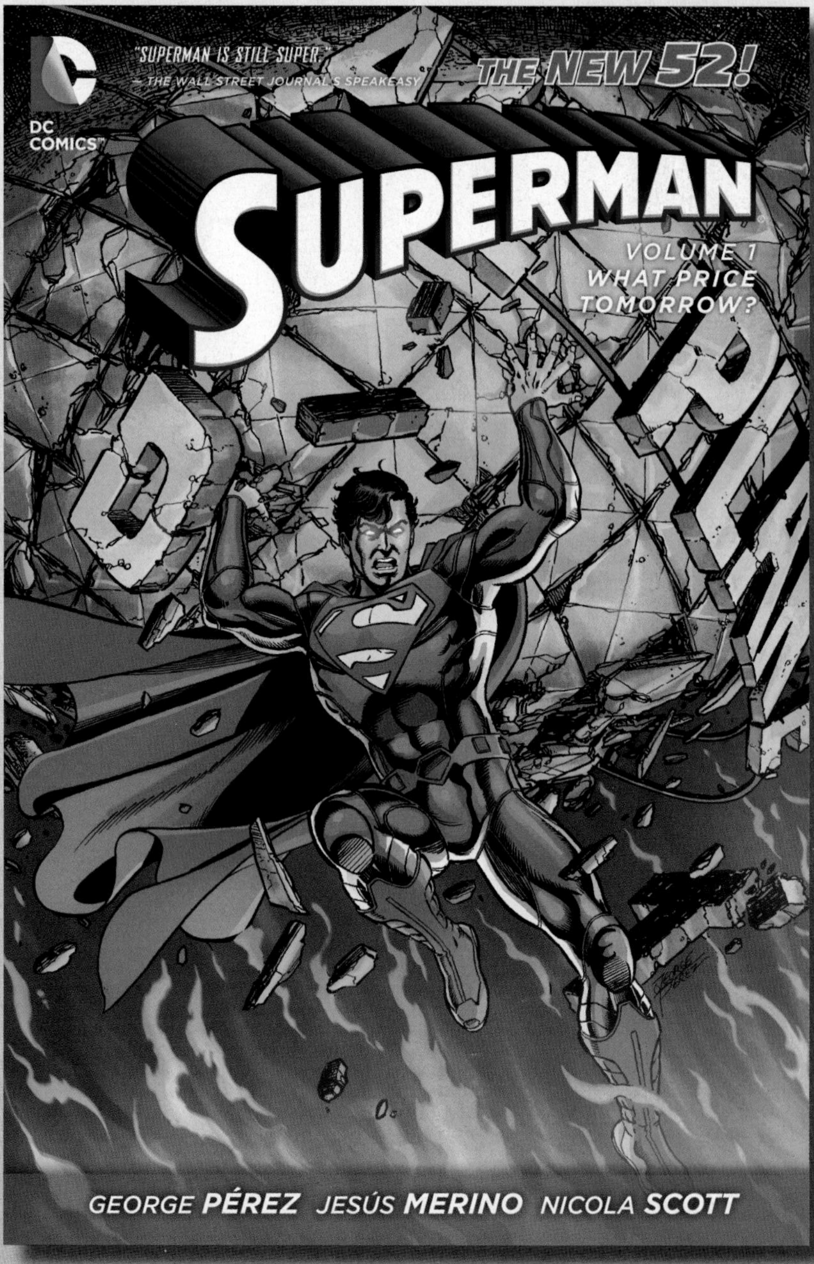

DC COMICS
"SUPERMAN IS STILL SUPER."
— THE WALL STREET JOURNAL'S SPEAKEASY
THE NEW 52!
SUPERMAN
VOLUME 1
WHAT PRICE
TOMORROW?
GEORGE PÉREZ JESÚS MERINO NICOLA SCOTT

SUPERMAN VOL. 2:
SECRETS & LIES

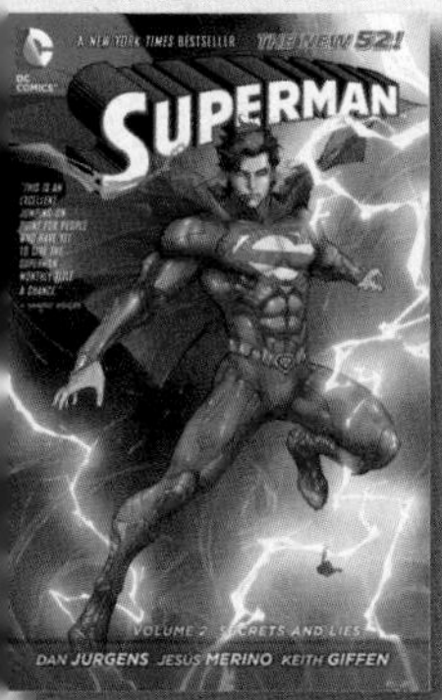

THE NEW 52!
SUPERMAN
DAN JURGENS JESÚS MERINO KEITH GIFFEN

SUPERMAN VOL. 3:
FURY AT WORLD'S END

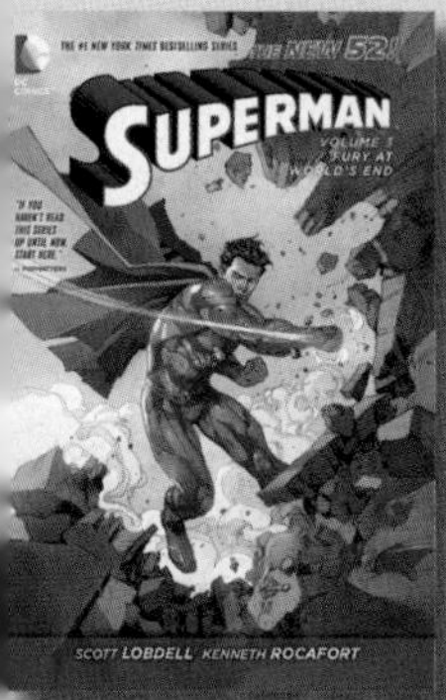

THE NEW 52!
SUPERMAN
SCOTT LOBDELL KENNETH ROCAFORT

SUPERMAN:
H'EL ON EARTH

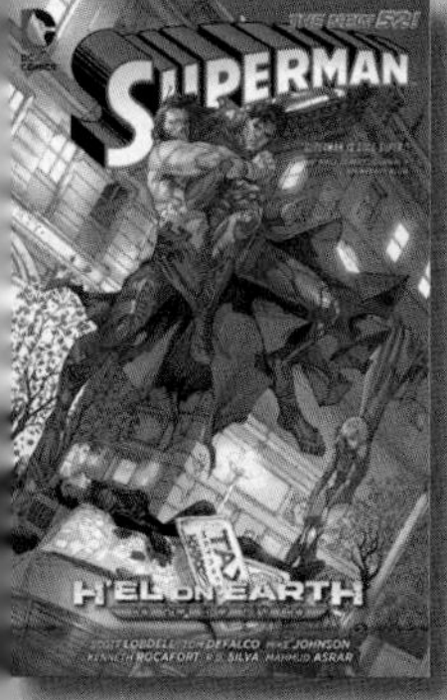

THE NEW 52!
SUPERMAN
H'EL ON EARTH

START AT THE BEGINNING!

WONDER WOMAN VOLUME 1: BLOOD

MR. TERRIFIC
VOLUME 1:
MIND GAMES

BLUE BEETLE
VOLUME 1:
METAMORPHOSIS

THE FURY OF FIRESTORM:
THE NUCLEAR MEN
VOLUME 1:
GOD PARTICLE

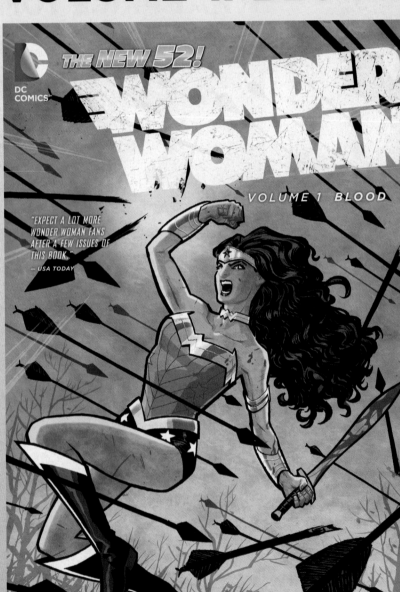

START AT THE BEGINNING!
JUSTICE LEAGUE VOLUME 1: ORIGIN

AQUAMAN
VOLUME 1:
THE TRENCH

THE SAVAGE
HAWKMAN VOLUME 1:
DARKNESS RISING

GREEN ARROW
VOLUME 1:
THE MIDAS TOUCH

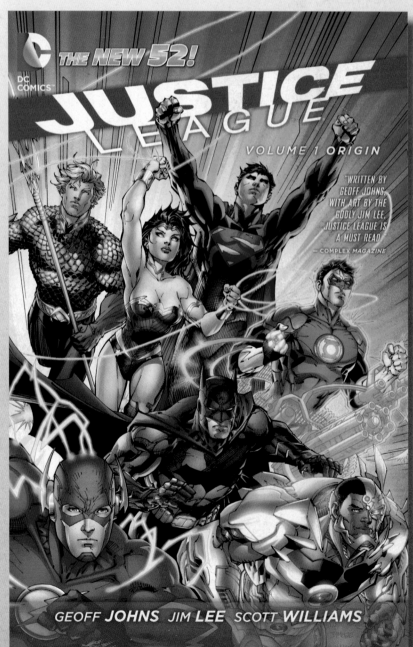

DC COMICS™

START AT THE BEGINNING

SWAMP THING VOLUME 1: RAISE THEM BONES

I, VAMPIRE
VOLUME 1:
TAINTED LOVE

DEMON KNIGHTS
VOLUME 1: SEVEN
AGAINST THE DARK

DC UNIVERSE PRESENTS
VOLUME 1: FEATURING
DEADMAN & CHALLENGERS
OF THE UNKNOWN

SCOTT SNYDER   YANICK PAQUETTE   MARCO RUDY